WOLFGANG LEONHARD

THE KREMLIN
SINCE STALIN

Translated from the German by

ELIZABETH WISKEMANN

and

MARIAN JACKSON

FREDERICK A. PRAEGER, *Publisher*

New York

BOOKS THAT MATTER

Published in the United States of America in 1962
by Frederick A. Praeger, Inc., Publisher
64 University Place, New York 3, N.Y.

All rights reserved

THE KREMLIN SINCE STALIN (*Kreml ohne Stalin*) was first published by
Verlag für Politik und Wirtschaft, Cologne, 1959. The text was revised and
brought up to date by the author for this translation which was published
in 1962.

German edition © Verlag für Politik und Wirtschaft, Cologne, 1959

English translation © Oxford University Press, London, 1962

Printed in the United States of America

Library of Congress Catalog Card Number: 62-14888

CONTENTS

FOREWORD

WHEN I began this book I intended to express my opinions about the evolution of Russia since Stalin's death. But it soon became clear to me that the public increasingly wishes to know in what that evolution consists. I have written, not for Soviet experts, but for the general public which wants to be able to understand the news from the USSR. Since domestic policy always takes precedence in Russia it has been necessary, in order to make sense of Soviet foreign policy, to examine developments within the USSR in detail. I have covered the ground from the Nineteenth Party Congress in the autumn of 1952 to the international Communist Congress in Moscow in November 1960.

I did the preparatory work and wrote a large part of the book during the two years I spent in Oxford at St. Antony's College: the conditions there were ideal. I am greatly indebted, therefore, to the Warden, Mr. F. W. Deakin. I am particularly grateful also to the late R. N. Carew Hunt who at that time directed the seminar on international Communism, as also to Mr. David Footman, director of the seminar on Soviet questions at St. Antony's: Mr. Footman read my manuscript and made comments which were of the greatest value to me. I am no less grateful to Ilse Spittmann, Herbert Ritvo, Boris Levitsky, and the staff of *Ostprobleme* for their understanding help when going through the manuscript. I have asked Professor Elizabeth Wiskemann to be responsible for deciding how far my text shall be abridged and the language adapted for English readers.

1961   WOLFGANG LEONHARD

FOREWORD

WHEN I began to write "book I avoided all scientific opinions about the evolution of ... Stalin ... this. But it soon became clear to me that many simply wishes to know the facts, and that experts have written not for the lay expert, but for the general public. I really wish to be able to understand the news about the USSR. So the domestic policy doesn't lay so particular in foreign policy necessary in order to make sense of Soviet domestic policy to examine developments within the USSR itself. I have covered the ground from the Kingisepp Party Congress in autumn of 1934 to the International Communist Congress in Moscow in October 1961.

I did the preparatory work and wrote ... during the two years I spent in Ireland in St. Antony College. The conditions there were ideal. I am greatly indebted ... the Warden, Mr. F. W. Deakin, and in some measure ... helpful also to the late R. R. Carew Hunt, whose ... I have ... aroused my interest in international Communism. At the Institute for the Study Soviet affairs ... London at St. Antony's, Mr. Leonard Scham ... and most ... many contacts which were of the greatest value to me. I ...

... to the staff ... contacting me for their understanding ... ... which ... through this magazine. I have taken this ... opportunity. With regard to the responsible for ... this ... I am extremely grateful and the Leonhard who has helped the lay reader.

WOLFGANG LEONHARD

THE KREMLIN SINCE STALIN

CHAPTER I

THE RUSSIAN RIDDLE— DOES IT STILL EXIST?

Is it possible to say anything of importance about the evolution of the Soviet Union today? Can somebody who does not live in Russia judge conditions there? Many who are anxious to learn have good reason to doubt this. There are no independent Soviet news organs. The freedom of movement of foreign journalists is limited, their reports are censored,[1] and there is little possibility of private travel. One has to rely mainly on official statements which are intended for propaganda purposes.

In spite of this the Soviet Union is no longer a riddle; there is enough material today for an analysis of topical events there. Two things are important, however, if this is to be done. The first is to discover the general line or policy of the Soviet régime and to recognize what questions are at the centre of attention at a given moment, what changes are planned, what means are employed to carry them out, and what difficulties have to be overcome. The second problem is to analyse any changes in the membership of the most important ruling groups, the party, the state, the army, the economy, and the state security service, in order to decide what groups these measures favour, and what effects the dismissals and appointments of individual persons may have upon further developments.

Different problems occupy the centre of attention at different times—at one time agriculture, at another questions of planning, the role of the trade unions, changes in the control of the economy, disputes with writers, or problems of ideology. As a question moves into the foreground the influence of the officials who are concerned with it increases. Changes in the balance of forces may result in important changes in policy; a new policy, on the other hand, may affect the balance of forces. Thus analysis of Soviet policy must take into account the interplay of both factors.

[1] This censorship was abolished on 23 March 1961.

WHO DECIDES SOVIET POLICY?

The fact that domestic is always given greater weight than foreign policy in the Soviet Union must be constantly borne in mind. The priority of domestic policy was laid down as a constituent part of Soviet ideology in the theory of the 'two functions of the state'. According to this doctrine, which reappears in the textbook *The Foundations of Marxist Philosophy* published in 1958, every state, including the Soviet Union, exercises two functions, an internal one which is described as 'principal' and 'decisive', and an external one which depends upon and reflects the other function. Thus, a leading Soviet periodical, *International Life*,[1] says that it is the principal aim of Soviet foreign policy to 'create international conditions favourable to the development of communism in the Soviet Union', and the Party journal *Kommunist*[2] states that 'foreign policy is the continuation of domestic policy'.

The pre-eminence of domestic policy is given clear expression in Soviet practice. Of the twenty-one full sessions of the Central Committee between Stalin's death and the Twenty-first Party Congress, only three had questions of foreign policy and international communism as main items on their agenda.[3] In the four-year Party schools at which higher Party officials are trained, of a total of 3,200 hours of instruction only 180 are devoted to the international labour and the international liberation movements, and fifty to the economic geography of other countries. In fact the Soviet press gives much less space than the press of non-communist countries to questions of foreign policy.

The Soviet Union has 208 million inhabitants. Political power in Russia is centred in the Communist Party. At the beginning of 1959 it had 7,622,356 full members and 616,775 candidate members. The deciding voices are, however, not those of the members, but of the officials, the paid members of the Party organization which, according to an official announcement of November 1955, then numbered 214,000 persons. In reality, the figure is probably higher. The Party machine is the backbone of the system, but it, too, has only an executive function.

According to the Party statutes the highest organ of the

[1] No. 4, 1957.   [2] No. 11, 1958.
[3] July 1955, Dec. 1957, and May 1958.

Party leadership is the Central Committee, which, between Party Congresses, directs the whole work of the Party. During the last two decades of the Stalin period the Central Committee consisted of 71 full members and 68 candidate members. At the Nineteenth Party Congress in October 1952 the Central Committee was increased to 125 full members and 111 candidate members, and at the Twentieth Party Congress in February 1956 to 133 full members and 122 candidate members. According to the statutes, the Central Committee meets every six months.

Important decisions, however, are not taken by the Central Committee but by two smaller bodies within it, its Praesidium or inner Cabinet[1] and its Secretariat. According to Article 34 of the statutes, the Praesidium directs the work of the Central Committee only between its plenary sessions. In theory the Central Committee Secretariat has the task of watching over the implementation of Party resolutions and of supervising the appointment of officials. But in actual fact these bodies are not auxiliary organs of the Central Committee but centres of power at which decisions are taken.

Although the members of these two highest ruling bodies of the USSR take all important decisions, they are naturally not in a position to elaborate all resolutions in detail. This task is performed by the 'apparatus' of the Central Committee, the brains trust of the leadership. This so-called 'apparatus' is not identical with the main body of the Central Committee. The majority of the 133 full members and 122 candidate members of the Central Committee are Party or state officials who carry out their specific work, as regional Party secretaries or as Ministers, or as generals of the Soviet army. They only come to Moscow from time to time to take part in plenary sessions. The 'apparatus' of the Central Committee, on the other hand, resides at headquarters in Moscow and consists of paid officials. It deals not only with Party work, but also translates the instructions of the leading bodies into directives covering all spheres of public life and supervises their implementation. Party headquarters in Moscow also direct the Institute for 'Marxism-Leninism', the ideological centre of the Soviet Union.

Hardly anything has been published up to now in the Soviet press about the way in which resolutions are passed in the

[1] Formerly the Politburo.

Party Praesidium, or about the collaboration between the Party Praesidium and the Government or Council of Ministers. But certain clues are to be found in the reports of refugees who formerly occupied important positions in the Soviet Zone of Germany. Although conditions in East Berlin are not identical they do not differ fundamentally from those in Moscow.

In East Berlin, according to emigré reports, the Politburo or Party Praesidium used to meet regularly once a week. The meetings began at 10 a.m. and continued, with a longish midday break and a shortish one in the afternoon, until late in the evening. As a rule, there were between thirty and forty items on the agenda; on occasion more than fifty resolutions were passed at a single meeting. Individual Politburo members introduced the subjects in which they specialized and the relevant draft resolutions; sometimes two or three versions of these were discussed. Once a resolution had been passed by the Politburo there were five possible procedures:

1. If the resolution concerned a field which came within the competence of the government it was referred to the Council of Ministers. The Council of Ministers also met once a week in order to put the resolutions of the Politburo into effect.

2. Resolutions which concerned purely Party questions (Party organizations, ideology, &c.), were referred to the Central Committee Secretariat for implementation.

3. Resolutions which concerned both the government and the People's Chamber, for example budgetary questions or drafts of laws, were referred to the Council of Ministers and to the steering committee of the People's Chamber.[1]

4. Particularly important questions, in connexion with which the Party machinery had to be mobilized and a campaign started, were referred to the Central Committee. After a discussion at a plenary session the relevant directives of the Party Praesidium were then published as decisions of the Central Committee.

5. Finally, there were decisions of the Party Praesidium on particularly delicate or confidential questions concerning, for example, the army or the sentencing of a prominent 'enemy of the people'. In that case the Party Praesidium disregarded the

[1] The Russian equivalent of the steering committee is the Praesidium of the Supreme Soviet.

Council of Nationalities, which represents
ities.[1] In the Council of the Union there is
~ ₀₀₀ electors. There is a special
The USSR
lics.[2]

course of action just described and referred the decision directly to the responsible authority (e.g. the Minister for State Security, the Minister of Defence, the Chief of the General Staff).

In extraordinary situations, for instance during the rising of 16–19 June 1953, the Politburo of the Soviet Zone of Germany was in permanent session. It can be assumed that the same happened in similar circumstances in the Soviet Union (for example, on the occasions of Beria's fall, the Hungarian revolt, and the quarrels with the 'anti-Party Group' in June 1957). According to emigrés' reports, the meetings of the Politburo of Eastern Germany have sometimes been very stormy.

The Council of Ministers, that is, the government of the USSR, is in practice an executive organ of the party leadership. It can only take measures which have been elaborated at the headquarters of the Central Committee and decided by the highest Party leaders.

Though ministers must work in accordance with the instructions of the Central Committee they are held fully responsible for their sphere of activity. They are publicly blamed for mistakes, whereas the corresponding departments of the Central Committee are rarely reprimanded in the press. There are two reasons for this: first, criticism of the Central Committee means criticism of the policy of the Party, which, according to Communist doctrine, is infallible. Criticism of ministers, on the other hand, refers only to the faulty execution of fundamentally correct decisions. Second, the formal responsibility of ministers protects the official legend of the democratic mechanism of government within the Soviet order.

THE CONSTITUTION—LEGEND AND REALITY
According to the constitution Soviet policy is not decided by the Party but by the representatives of the people and the bodies they elect. The constitution decrees that the Supreme Soviet of the USSR is the highest organ of state power. It alone has the right to make laws, to choose the Council of Ministers, to elect the Supreme Court, to supervise the organs of state power, to conclude important treaties with foreign states, and, given a two-thirds majority, to change the constitution.

The Supreme Soviet consists of two chambers, the so-called Council of the Union, whose members represent the whole

ACCORDING TO THE CONSTITUTION

Credentials
Commission

Economic
Commission

Commission for
Foreign Affairs

Budget
Commission

Supreme Soviet of the USSR

Meets twice a year

According to the Constitution
the highest political authority
in the USSR

All-Union
Soviet

738
members

Credentials
Commission

Economic Commission

Commission for
Foreign Affairs

Nationalities
Soviet

Budget Commission

640
members

Legislative Commission

Praesidium of the
Committee of [

Praesidium of
the Supreme Soviet

Supreme
Court of
the USSR

1 Chairman, 15 Deputy Chairmen
15 members, 1 Secretary

Chief Public
Prosecutor of
the USSR

Council of Ministers of the USSR
According to the Constitution
responsible to the Supreme Soviet

On 1 August 1959

Praesidium of the Council of
Ministers

Praesidium: 1 Chairman, 2 senior deputies, 3 deputies

17 Ministers for

Foreign affairs
Building of electro-power
  stations
Finance
Geology and mineral
  resources
Health
Higher and medium
  specialized training
Maritime shipping
Interior
Education and the Arts
Agriculture
Medium machine
  building
Posts and telegraph
Transport building
Communications
Defence

State Planning
Commission
(Gosplan)

9 members with
ministerial rank

Director of
the
State Bank

12 Chairmen of Political
Committees on

Work and wages
Automation and
  machine construction
Building
Vocational training

Aircraft construction
Cereal products
Radio electronics
Ship building
Defence
Foreign trade
Science and technology

Director of
the Central
Statistical
Administration

Chairman, Committee
for State Security

Chairman, Commission
for Soviet Control

Chairman, Economic Commission

Prime Ministers of the 15 Union Republics

	...ıc Central ...e of tne Communist Party	Central Committee Bureau for the RSFSR and party leaders of the 14 non-Russian Union Republics
Supreme Court	14 full members (9 are also members of the Central Committee Secretariat) and 10 candidate members	
		Mass organizations (trade unions, Komsomol, etc.)
	Meets at least once a week	
Chief Public Prosecutor	Supreme centre of power in the USSR	
	Takes all important decisions in the USSR	
Praesidium of the Supreme Soviet (32 members)	Council of Ministers Chairman, 2 First and 3 Ordinary Deputy Chairmen; 17 ministries 12 political committees, etc., carry out the decisions of the Party Praesidium at state level	Central Committee Secretariat ('Secretariat of the Central Committee') 10 members (9 of whom are also in the Party Praesidium)
		Prepares decisions of the Party Praesidium and directs their execution
	Central Committee 133 full members 122 candidate members Meets every six months Considers and approves decisions of the Party Praesidium	Central Committee apparatus Departments for the various spheres of domestic, foreign and economic policy, transport, ideology and party work. Carries out decisions of Party Praesidium at party level
	Commission for Party Control	
Supreme Soviet, two chambers: All-Union Soviet and Nationalities Soviet. 'Elected' every four years on single party list. Meets twice a year. Issues laws based on party resolutions	Party Congress Meets every four years according to the Party Statutes	Central Revision Commission

8

population, and
the separate nationali
one deputy for every 300,0
electoral procedure for the Council of Nationalities. The
consists of 15 Union Republics, 18 Autonomous Republic,
10 Autonomous Regions, and 10 National Areas. Each Union
Republic, regardless of its size, sends 24 deputies, each Autonomous Republic 11, each Autonomous Region 5, and each
National Area 1 deputy.

The Supreme Soviet is elected every four years. Up to now
five such elections have taken place: In 1937, 1946, 1950, 1954,
and 1958. Elections are made on single lists of the 'People's
bloc of Communists and non-party candidates'. Only one
candidate stands in each constituency. The elector has the right
to cross out the name of the candidate on the ballot paper and
to insert that of another candidate who will, of course, have no
chance of being elected. In every polling station there is a
polling booth, but voting is usually public; the Soviet citizen
takes the voting paper, folds it before the eyes of the returning
officers and puts it into the box. In this way electoral results with
over 99 per cent. of votes in favour of the candidate are achieved.

According to Article 46 of the Constitution, the Supreme
Soviet meets twice a year. For day-to-day work it elects the
Praesidium of the Supreme Soviet, which has the right to call
meetings of the Supreme Soviet, to issue writs for new elections,
to publish decrees between meetings of the Supreme Soviet, to
appoint members of the government, to declare a state of war—
that is, general or partial mobilization—and to ratify international treaties. The Praesidium of the Supreme Soviet,
which, according to the Constitution, is the highest governing
body of the USSR between meetings of the Supreme Soviet,
has 32 members: A chairman who is the normal Head of the
State,[3] 15 deputies (one from each Union Republic), a Secretary, and 15 other members. According to the constitution the
Supreme Soviet elects the Council of Ministers of the USSR,
who are responsible to the Supreme Soviet. The bodies which

[1] Comparable respectively with the House of Representatives and the Senate
in the U.S.A.
[2] Of these, 14 are in the Russian Republic, 2 in Georgia, and one each in
Azerbaidjan and Uzbekistan.
[3] Leonid Brezhnev since 4 May 1960.

in fact make decisions—the Central Committee, its 'Apparatus', the Party Praesidium, and the Central Committee Secretariat—are not even mentioned in the constitution.

According to the constitution, which all Russian school children in the seventh class learn by heart and also, by the way, the school children in all the other Communist countries—Soviet policy is determined by the Supreme Soviet and carried out by the Council of Ministers. In reality all decisions are drafted by the appropriate department of the Central Committee, agreed by the Party Praesidium and the Central Committee Secretariat, and then passed on to the Supreme Soviet, its Praesidium or the Council of Ministers, which formally raise them to the status of decrees or laws. An analysis of the changes since Stalin must, therefore, in the first place be based on official announcements and changes in the membership of the leading party committees.

In spite of its dominating role the Party leadership cannot rule in a completely arbitrary way. Particularly since the termination of the reign of terror upon Stalin's death it must pay greater attention to the needs and wishes of the population, of which it is informed by reports from the lower ranks of the Party. This applies first and foremost to social and material considerations. The influence of the population on political decisions, however, is exceedingly small because all organs of public opinion are controlled by the Party. The new hierarchy, that is members of the administrative machine, whether economic or governmental, of the army or the police—which has consistently gained in power and importance in recent decades —has incomparably greater possibilities of exerting influence.

THE NEW RULING CLASS IN RUSSIA

The beginnings of the development of a new ruling class in the USSR were already visible in the days of Lenin. In the first years after the October revolution Lenin himself repeatedly uttered warnings against excessive bureaucracy. By this he meant not only bad work and delay on the part of the administration. He defined bureaucrats as 'privileged persons estranged from the masses'. In 1920 Lenin said that Soviet Russia was 'a workers' state with bureaucratic excrescences; in March 1921 he spoke of the 'bureaucratic cancer' and complained that the bureaucratic apparatus was gigantic; in the summer of 1921 Lenin even spoke of the revival of bureaucracy within the Soviet order, and said that 'this evil had become still clearer and more threatening'.

After Lenin's death and the struggles within the Party which led to the victory of Stalin's faction, and particularly during the period of industrialization, the new bureaucratic class rapidly increased. While industrial directors received even greater powers, the rights of the workers were cut down, and the sharp differentiation between wages and salaries increased social contrast. The establishment of new concerns was not accompanied by an increase in the influence of factory and office workers: on the contrary, they were deprived of their rights and excluded from all economic control The growth of the economic potential of the Soviet Union, therefore, brought a manifold increase in the power of the new bureaucracy.

By the middle thirties, a new privileged class had developed, which, on the basis of public ownership in industry and agriculture, directed the whole administrative and economic life of the country and arbitrarily annexed the greater part of the country's wealth. It dominated every sphere of public life, administration, domestic and foreign policy, the army, ideology, learning, and art. The constant increase of the power of the state and of the machinery of oppression was indirect evidence of the growing social divergence between the working people and this new establishment.

The Stalinist leaders naturally wished to conceal the existence of this. Officially, it was always stressed that in the Soviet Union there were two friendly ruling classes; the workers and peasants, and also the intellectuals who constituted not a separate class but a 'stratum' exercising its functions on behalf of the workers and peasants. Indirectly, however, Stalin several times admitted the existence of a ruling class. At a conference of economists on 23 June 1931, for example, he said: 'Do not forget that we ourselves today expect certain things from the worker. We demand from him discipline, intensive work, and overtime. . . .' 'We' meant the official class which had the right to make demands on the others who only worked. In March 1937 Stalin himself publicly referred to the 'ruling stratum' of the Party and in his speech after the victory in 1945 he compared the Soviet Union with a gigantic machine, the population with small cogs, and the ruling or official class with those who used the machine.

In discussions within the Soviet Union as in non-Communist society, the question is often raised whether this is a new ruling class, in the Marxist sense of the word, or what the Communists call a 'ruling stratum'. It can hardly be denied that the new élite in the Soviet Union shows some characteristics of a class in the full Marxist sense. It possesses power over the means of production, it determines the direction and the course of economic events, and distributes the national wealth. For Lenin these were the characteristics of a class when he wrote: 'Classes are to be defined as large groups of people, groups which differ according to their position in an historically given system of social production, their relation to the means of production, their role in the social organization of labour, and, as a consequence, according to the methods of accumulation, and according to the size, of their share in the wealth of society.' Nevertheless, it should not be overlooked that the ruling class of the USSR lacks important characteristics of a Marxist class. The privileges of a member of this élite depend not on his private ownership of the means of production but on the functions he performs in the hierarchy of the system. The composition of the new upper stratum in the USSR is not stable; it has been, and is, constantly transformed by violent change.

THE FIVE PILLARS OF SOVIET SOCIETY

Members of the Soviet hierarchy have a common interest in maintaining and extending their own power. This common interest does not, however, prevent serious conflicts of interest within the ruling class. These are of a structural or functional kind; in part they result also from differences in political attitude.

The new ruling class may be divided into five groups or social 'pillars'.

1. The Party machine composed of the officials of the Soviet state party. These were said by Stalin, in March 1937, to number 192,000 out of a total Party membership of almost one and a half million full members and over half a million candidate members. In November 1955 there were, according to official statements, 214,000 party officials out of a total of 6 million

full members and more than 860,000 candidate members.

The party machine was and is the essential 'pillar' of Soviet society; its importance has increased since Stalin's death. It directs not only the Communist Party of the Soviet Union, but also the most important mass organizations, in particular the Communist Youth Organization (*Komsomol*) with 18 million members, the Soviet Trade Unions with about 50 million members, the 'Voluntary Society for the promotion of the army, air force and navy' (DOSAAF), which deals with the military training of the Soviet population, and the 'Association for the dissemination of political and economic knowledge'; the latter is an organization with a vast network of branch offices and lecturers which, together with scientific knowledge, disseminates the political principles of the party in popular form. All the mass organizations have party groups whose task it is 'to intensify the Party's influence in every way, to carry out its policy among non-Party members, to strengthen Party and State discipline, to lead the battle against bureaucracy, and to control the execution of Party and Soviet directives'. (Article 67 of the Party Statutes.)

The Communist Party machine exerts a controlling influence over all spheres of national life through Party as well as mass organizations. The Party organizations in the factories, collective and state farms, and trading enterprises, are responsible for the management of all these undertakings. Party organizations with comparable responsibilities are active in all educational institutions. In the Ministries it is, according to Article 58 of the Statutes, the duty of the Party organizations 'to signalize defects in the establishments, to report deficiencies in the work of any Ministry, and to transmit their findings and opinions to the Central Committee and the heads of that Ministry'.

Party organizations also exist in the army and navy which, according to Article 64 of the Statutes, work on the basis of special instructions confirmed by the Central Committee, and are subordinate to the main political administration of the Soviet army and navy. The Party organs in the army and navy must maintain close relations with the local Party committees and accept the reports of the political organs of the army on political work in the army units.

The Party's functionaries have been and are the political

shock troops of the régime, the driving force in political campaigns and in the continuation of the revolution from above.
In the era of Stalin, particularly during the period of the
great purge from 1936 to 1938, even they were terrorized by
the state security service. With the suppression of the latter
after Stalin's death, the power of the Party machine has grown
again. Since the beginning of 1957, at the latest, it is again the
absolutely dominant force in the Soviet state.

2. The economic machine consists of the directors of undertakings, industrial managers, senior engineers, technicians, and
members of the central planning staffs. For a long time, owing
to lack of Soviet data, it was difficult to determine the strength
of this group. The only figures were given in a report by
Molotov in 1938, according to which there were in the Soviet
Union at that time 350,000 directors of undertakings, 582,000
chairmen of collective farms, and 19,000 directors of machine
and tractor stations. The statistical yearbook which was published again in 1956 makes it possible to estimate the approxi-
mate size of the economic bureaucracy at about the time of
Stalin's death. According to this source, there were in 1953–4
212,000 industrial enterprises, 4,857 state farms (*soukhozy*),
8,985 machine and tractor stations, and 93,300 collective
farms (*kolkhozy*). If we follow Molotov's example and include
vice-chairmen in the figures, we arrive at 638,284 leading
economic officials. To the economic bureaucracy must also be
added 585,900 engineers, 413,100 agricultural specialists, and
299,900 economists and statisticians. Thus the economic
'pillar' consists of almost 2 million people.

The majority of this group aims at independence. It wants to
be freed from the constant supervision of the secret police,
from Party campaigns, and from the interference of Party
organizations. The qualified economic officials have nothing
to fear from a change in the political system, provided that
public ownership and economic planning are retained. Leanings towards reform are particularly marked in this group.

3. The state or governmental apparatus includes those who
form part of the central state machinery and of that of the
Republics and the Soviets in the regions and districts. No
statistical data are available for them. We must help ourselves
out with a survey of the appropriate authorities. Apart from the

central state administration in Moscow, all the Republics of the Union have their own Councils of Ministers and Supreme Soviet; further, there are 16 Autonomous Republics, with their own government machinery, 137 Territories and Regions (*oblasti*), of which 9 are called Autonomous regions, and 4,817 districts (*rayony*), of which 489 are urban.

The state officials are more closely linked with the political system than are the industrial managers; they show, however, a stronger inclination to let things be than the Party officials, who can justify their existence only by continuing the revolution from above through perpetual activity. The state bureaucracy links the managers with the Party apparatus. It performs both political and economic tasks; it is influenced by the two other 'pillars' and in turn influences them by means of its regulations. This reciprocal relationship is by no means always harmonious.

4. The army. Although according to official statements 86 per cent. of all officers are members of the Party or the *komsomol*, quarrels constantly occur between army and Party. After 1934 Stalin granted the army leaders a number of concessions in order to create a materially and socially privileged officer corps. These included the reintroduction of the old military ranks (September 1935) and of the title of Marshal (November 1935), the readmission of the Cossacks to service with the colours (April 1936), the introduction of the title 'Hero of the Soviet Union' (July 1936), a new oath of loyalty with special emphasis on military discipline (February 1939) and a new disciplinary code (autumn 1940), the substitution of the name Soviet Armed Forces for 'Red Army of Workers and Peasants' (February 1947), and many other measures intended to strengthen the authority of the officers both within the army and in society. Simultaneously, political control over the army was tightened. The political commissars who had been introduced in 1918 were given supreme authority in August 1937, a few weeks after Tukhachevsky and other military leaders had been shot. In August 1940, however, they were replaced by 'deputy commanders for political affairs', called *Sampolit* for short, whose activities were restricted to political agitation among army units. Three weeks after the beginning of the German-Russian war, on 16 July 1941, the political commissars were reintroduced and officially designated 'representatives of

the Party and government'. After the battle of Stalingrad and the stabilization of the front; they were once more abolished and again replaced by the *Sampolits*. After Stalin's death, the independence and influence of the army leaders increased, but since November 1957 the control of the Party over the army has again been strengthened.

The army has much in common with the economic bureaucracy, particularly in its resistance to the constant interference of the Party and state security service. It has closer ties with the Soviet state, but these are rooted in pride in the power of the country, not in party ideology.

5. The state police. Of all the five 'pillars' the state police is most closely linked with the Stalinist régime of coercion and, therefore, most strongly resists any changes in the system. Descended from the Cheka of revolutionary days, the state police in the twenties was the most important factor in the battle against opposition in the Party; it was the instrument both of collectivization and industrialization. In that period the state police, then called the OGPU, developed from an executive organ of the Party into an independent power. It rose above the Party, interfered in the Party's political appointments, and exercised an ever greater influence within Russia through a gigantic network of informers; at the same time it extended its connexions with foreign countries. Members of the state police soon felt themselves to be the true élite of the country and the Party. In the middle thirties the state police, meanwhile renamed the NKVD, acquired far-reaching powers which enabled it to summon even the highest Party and state officials and army leaders before special courts. During the great purge from 1936 to 1938, the state police not only removed Lenin's collaborators, the Bolshevik old guard, but also many of those who had brought Stalin to power. Only after Stalin's death did the new official class feel strong enough to subordinate the state police to the Party machine.

THE SELF-INTEREST OF THE FIVE GROUPS

These 'pillars' or groups are by no means a sociological abstraction; they also have outward manifestations, visible to every Soviet citizen, particularly in the capitals of the Union Republics and the regions and districts. Let us demonstrate this by taking the example of Karaganda, the capital of the Karaganda Region in the Kazakh Union Republic where the author spent nearly a year. The biggest building there, situated in the centre of the 'new town', was that of the *obkom*, the regional Party committee. Nearly opposite, almost as high and even more lavishly appointed, was the regional centre of the NKVD. A third, somewhat smaller building housed the regional soviet, i.e. the state group, and a fourth the *oblastnoy voyenkomat*, the army office for this region. Only the economic bureaucracy had no building or organization of its own.

Most of the officials of all the groups are members of the Communist Party of the Soviet Union. But that in no way implies that they represent the interests of the Party machine. The contradictions within the official class result precisely from the fact that each of its members is involved with his own special group. Within it he has certain tasks to perform, to which he completely devotes himself.

A Soviet economic official is primarily interested in discovering whether 'his' branch of industry or 'his' enterprise can fulfil the plan. He is, therefore, not very enthusiastic if, as a result of a Party campaign to intensify ideological training, his own time and energy and that of his colleagues are diverted from economic tasks in favour of training courses. On the other hand, the Party official is personally responsible for arranging the maximum attendance of workers at such courses. Conflicts arise between members owing different allegiances, particularly when several big campaigns are conducted simultaneously; this happened in 1954, when the consumer goods programme and the development of virgin lands were to be simultaneously put into effect. The officials responsible for the latter—mostly from the Party machine—did everything they could to carry out their assignment as quickly as possible, while the economic officials, on the other hand, demanded labour and material to fulfil the consumer goods programme.

Many high officials belong at one and the same time to two or even three of the groups. A number of Soviet marshals are members of the Central Committee of the Party; more frequently still one finds a combination of Party and state posts. But even in such cases the official knows which is the important one for him.

It is not only a conflict of interest which causes tension between army officers, Party officials, and industrial managers: There is also conflict within each group, for example, between officials in heavy industry and in agriculture. The feeling of being personally involved with an organization is also of importance. During the four years that I belonged to the ideological sector of the central Party machine of the Soviet Zone of Germany, I was—during my free time as well—almost exclusively in the company of my colleagues. At social evenings and private meetings we often made fun of the 'practical men' in the state or economic organization and even more of the people's police. We were convinced that the ideological Party officials were the dominant force. If, on the other hand, I happened to spend an evening with economic or state officials, I would hear that ideological officials only wrote articles or formulated theories while the practical men did the work. Nor are political tendencies within any one group always uniform: Not all Party officials are stubborn Stalinist 'apparachiks', nor all industrial managers reformers.

IS THERE ENOUGH MATERIAL RELATING TO THE SOVIET UNION?

In reviewing domestic events in the Soviet Union, we mainly depend on official information which in the past has been sparse and incomplete. Since Stalin's death, however, much has changed in this respect. The Soviet leaders express themselves more frequently and more openly on topical questions. Considerably more information is published on economic and political events, and foreign contacts are more numerous than before.

In reviewing Soviet policy the congresses of the Communist Party and the full sessions of the Central Committee are of first-rate importance. Although, according to the Party Statutes, a Congress has to be convened every four years, after the Seventeenth Party Congress in January 1934, the Eighteenth Party Congress only took place in March 1939, and the Nineteenth Party Congress more than thirteen years later in October 1952. According to the Statutes, plenary sessions of the Central Committee should be convened every four months. But instead of forty plenary sessions between March 1939 and October 1952, there were, according to official statements, only five—in March 1939, March and July 1940, January 1944, and February 1947.

After Stalin's death, however, there was a striking change. The Twentieth Party Congress was convened at the prescribed time and the Twenty-first Party Congress even before it was due. Full sessions of the Central Committee were again held more frequently. Between Stalin's death and the middle of 1959, there were twenty-one, i.e. in six years four times as many as in the last fourteen years of the Stalin era.

Many crucial questions are still not mentioned in the official reports of the Party Congress and the resolutions of the Central Committee, and yet much more can be learnt from them about real problems than in Stalin's day. At the Twentieth Party Congress in February 1956 and at the Twenty-first Party Congress in January 1959, divergent views were expressed, even if only over one or two points.

The leaders since Stalin, by contrast with him, are not hermetically sealed off from the people and the world; they travel frequently, speak at conferences, visit foreign embassies, receive foreign correspondents, and make political pronouncements on the most varied questions. Dismissals and appointments are as a rule announced quickly and the reasons for them are given. The 'disappearance' of well-known leaders is today already exceptional. The true facts are often concealed, but light is thrown on the political situation by the reasons given.

The Stalinist method of reporting on economic development only in percentages may not yet have been completely abandoned, but it is used much less frequently. As early as 1953 the Soviet leader began to publish absolute figures relating to the economic and cultural development of the country. In the summer of 1956 the first statistical abstract, 'The economy of the USSR' was published; since then five further volumes have appeared, covering the arts and education, trade, industry, certain aspects of agriculture, and a new volume on the economy as a whole in 1956. Further volumes have been announced.

The exchange of delegations with other countries increased by leaps and bounds after Stalin's death. It is not unusual today for Soviet citizens to meet foreigners, whether at home or abroad. Travel regulations have been eased and the exchange of periodicals and books, considerably increased. There are many accounts by former political prisoners who were arrested in the Stalin era and released after Stalin's death, particularly in the years 1954–6. It can be said without exaggeration that during the last six years more has been learnt about events in the Soviet Union than during the twenty-five years of Stalin's rule. The difficulty in informing oneself about Soviet events today lies less in a lack of material than in the evaluation of Soviet publications.

Of course all Russian publications are controlled by the government. They are not intended to provide factual information but to serve certain political purposes, and they therefore give an incomplete and distorted picture. In Moscow in the thirties the *mot* was circulated, '*Pravda* tells so many lies that not even the contrary is true.' These tendentious publications can nevertheless form the basis of a serious analysis. They are intended to popularize the political ideas and aims of the Party leaders. A continuous study of Soviet publications, therefore, provides important clues to the political and economic situation. The analysis of one Soviet Note or one Party resolution will tell even the most perspicacious connoisseur of the Soviet system only little about the trends of development. On the other hand, a comparison of all Soviet Notes on the German question, or all Soviet Party documents and official articles since Stalin's death on the management of enterprises, provides interesting evidence; one can observe all kinds of changes in formulation.

WHAT IS 'THE OFFICIAL PARTY LINE'?

Up to now we have spoken in a general way about 'Soviet publications'. But which publications speak with authority about the general policy of the Soviet leadership? The answer might well be all of them because, in fact, all publications in the Soviet Union are officially censored. This does not mean, however, that all publications are equally important in judging the general line of policy. Following George Orwell, one could say that all Soviet publications are official, but some are more official than others.

For an analysis of current Soviet policy the following material deserves particular attention:

1. The reports of the Party Congresses, particularly the resolutions and the speech of the First Party Secretary. These are the most important documents in the long run.

2. The resolutions of the full sessions of the Central Committee. Between one Party Congress and the next these are the most important official Party documents. Between Stalin's death and the Twenty-first Congress, twenty-one plenary sessions of the Central Committee took place.

3. Joint resolutions of the Central Committee and the Council of Ministers on particular questions between full sessions. These resolutions concern matters which fall within the competence of both Party and state: Thus they are mainly economic questions. The publication of these joint resolutions is one of the methods employed by the Party in order to exercise its political leadership. A state decree is thereby given the authority which the leading organ of the Party enjoys.[1]

4. Resolutions which are taken in the name of the Central Committee alone. As a rule these concern questions of ideology, propaganda, and party organization, e.g. the publication of new periodicals, directives for Party training, political work in the army and navy, the publication of Lenin's writings. Sometimes such resolutions are published at once in the press, sometimes later in collected volumes (e.g. in the 'Party Official's Handbook'). It may be assumed that there are Central Committee resolutions which are not published at all but are sent only to certain members of the party hierarchy.

5. Resolutions which are signed only by the Council of Ministers of the USSR. These are relatively rare. They are mostly concerned with questions of detail arising out of Party resolutions which have already been passed. The precedence of Party resolutions over government decrees is officially established.

6. Decrees of the Praesidium of the Supreme Soviet of the USSR. They are usually worded very briefly and publish on individual questions what has already been dealt with extensively in Party resolutions. Subsequently the decrees become laws at the six monthly sessions of the Supreme Soviet. In addition, the Supreme Soviet can pass its own laws, but as a

[1] See *Theory of the State and Law*, published by the Institute for Legal Questions of the Academy of Sciences of the USSR, 1955.

rule these merely confirm Party resolutions which have already been passed, and often published as well.

7. Slogans of the Central Committee of the Party for May Day and 7 November. Two or three weeks before the most important official holidays of the USSR the Central Committee publishes a number of slogans[1] summarizing the most important tasks in foreign and military policy, industry, national education, ideology, and so on. A comparison of the slogans for several years throws light on political developments over the period.

Apart from official documents important clues are to be found in the speeches of Soviet leaders. Generally speeches at Party congresses and plenary sessions of the Central Committee are of greater importance than speeches before the Supreme Soviet or meetings of activists in individual towns or regions. Recently, however, it has happened several times that fundamental political changes have been announced at meetings of the Supreme Soviet or meetings of activists. In his speech to agricultural activists in White Russia on 22 January 1958, for example, Khrushchev announced the dissolution of the machine and tractor stations.

THE SOVIET PRESS AND LEADING ARTICLES IN
PRAVDA

The most comprehensive material for the study of Russian events is provided by the press. But even the most zealous student cannot keep up with the 7,246 newspapers that appear in the Soviet Union. It is, therefore, a question of selecting the most important. In this the system of the Soviet press is helpful. Soviet papers do not represent different views, but special interests: every branch has its own paper so that one can make one's choice. If one disregards the literary and art journals the Soviet press is primarily intended for Soviet officials, i.e. the paid employees of the Party, the state, and the economic administration. Any review of the policy of the Soviet leaders must start with *Pravda*, the central organ of the Party, and the two most important political journals of the Central Committee, *Kommunist* and *Partinaya Zhizn*. The directives put out in their leading articles in fact constitute political orders.

[1] Between fifty and ninety.

The leading articles in *Pravda* are not leaders in the sense of the non-Soviet world. Only in exceptional cases are topical, domestic or international events discussed; if this occurs, it is only so that the Soviet leaders can express their attitude. A leading article announces the general line of the Party at any given time in a certain field of public life. This policy remains valid until it is revised by a new leading article. On an average there are seven leading articles a month on foreign policy, seven on domestic policy, five on industry, five on 'agitation', propaganda and Party organization, five on agriculture, and one on cultural policy. The directives of the leading articles are binding on all officials of the USSR. For Western observers they are the most important material for the analysis of Soviet policy.

THE DETERMINATION OF THE 'GENERAL LINE'

Soviet policy is conducted, in the main, in the form of 'campaigns'. The leadership sets certain tasks, for example to intensify the cultivation of maize or to extend the rights of industrial directors. First of all the Party hierarchy must be informed of this; it must know why this particular measure is necessary, how long it is to take, what methods are to be used, and to which questions particular attention is to be devoted. Tens of thousands of Party officials, belonging to the economic organization, the state administration, and in some cases the officers' corps, must be prepared for action of this kind in good time.

Secret indications are used for this purpose. There has scarcely been any important change in the Soviet Union not announced through these secret indications. Generally they consist of small changes, which are only noted by a careful reader, in the usual formulation of a *Pravda* leader. Occasionally an article is published which has allegedly been sent in to demand a change. In reality the article has been ordered by the Soviet authorities. To give only one example: On 20 May 1955 the director of the Ural machine factory, Glebovsky, complained in *Pravda* about the supervision of factories and mines by the ministries and expressed himself in favour of an increase in the rights of the directors of these concerns. Several weeks later, at the full session of the Central Committee in July, Prime Minister Bulganin took up this demand in almost the same words. On 8 August *Pravda* dealt with it at length in its leading article, and on the following day there appeared the 'Decree concerning the extension of the rights of the directors of enterprises'.

A further clue to general policy is provided by positive and negative definitions. Thus in the USSR phenomena which are to be encouraged or condemned are given ideological labels which have positive or negative values meaning good or bad. Here are a few examples: From October 1952 until Stalin's death in March 1953 the negative definitions of 'slackness' and 'sloth' and the positive definition 'vigilance' were used in the new campaign of purges. From July 1953 until the summer of 1954 'learning by rote' and 'dogmatism' were denounced in order to free party officials from a doctrinaire interpretation of Stalinist regulations. After the Hungarian revolt, but particularly from November 1956 to February 1957, the public was mobilized against 'nihilism', 'demagogy', 'decayed liberalism', and 'revisionism', that is to say against the circles which voiced 'exaggerated' criticism of Stalin and demanded 'exaggerated' measures of de-Stalinization.

Important clues are also to be found in the slogans of the Party leadership. Each campaign has its motto or slogan. When the state security service was stripped of its power after Stalin's death, this was done with the slogan 'socialist legality must be fortified'. From August 1953 to the summer of 1954 the slogan 'to achieve in two to three years a sudden increase in the production of supplies for the population' was much in evidence. In the spring of 1954 it was hardly mentioned, in the summer of 1954 it disappeared completely, and in the winter 1954–5 the consumer goods programme was abandoned.

Finally, quotations from the works of Marx, Engels, Lenin, and Stalin are also important. Since 1953 Stalin has only very rarely been quoted, whereas the number of quotations from Lenin's work has increased. Political changes are based on so-called articles of principle, which try to prove with quotations that the new policy is consistent with the 'classics', i.e. the writings of Marx, Engels, Lenin, and formerly Stalin. At the Twentieth Party Congress, for example, the theory of a peaceful road to socialism was supported by a Marxian quotation

of 28 September 1872 which was not allowed to be published
in Stalin's day. The abandonment of the consumer goods
programme was justified in a *Pravda* article of 25 January 1955
called 'The General Line of the Party and of Marxists who
over-popularize', with some quotations from Lenin. Even the
economic reorganization in the spring of 1957, the fall of
Marshal Zhukov, and the strengthening of the Party organizations in the army were supported by appropriate quotations
from Lenin.

A careful analysis of the quotations used in the Russian press
over a fairly long period, of the point in time at which certain
quotations are used, of the frequency of these quotations, and
of the differences in emphasis which are thus expressed is no
less important in judging Soviet policy than the study
of secret indications, 'positive' or 'negative' definitions, and
topical slogans.

THE ANNOUNCEMENT OF NEW APPOINTMENTS

New appointments or dismissals are published by the Soviet
press in a precisely determined manner. Personal changes in
the government and economic staff, the army command, and
the diplomatic corps are as a rule published in the bottom half
of the last column on the last page of *Pravda*, above the Moscow theatre programmes, under the heading 'Chronicle'.

The form and style of the announcement are always the
same, whether it is of an appointment of a new Soviet ambassador to Cambodia or of the dismissal of Marshal Zhukov as
Minister of Defence. Let us take the announcement of Zhukov's
dismissal of 27 October 1957 as an example:

CHRONICLE

*The Praesidium of the Supreme Soviet of the USSR has appointed
Rodion Yakovlevich Malinovsky, Marshal of the Soviet Union, as
Minister of Defence of the USSR. The Praesidium of the Supreme
Soviet has relieved Georgi Konstantinovich Zhukov, Marshal of
the Soviet Union, of his functions as Minister of Defence of the
USSR.*

Even in the case of such an important change no reference
to it is to be found on the front page. Many readers, therefore,
begin with the last column of the last page of *Pravda*. It is

different with changes among the Party leaders which have been decided at plenary meetings of the Central Committee. They are announced in enormous type on the front page of *Pravda*. The type is three to five times as big as usual. The change in the Party leadership, announced on 19 December 1957, may serve as an example:

ANNOUNCEMENT

Concerning a plenary session of the Central Committee of the Communist Party of the Soviet Union:

On 16 and 17 December 1957 a plenary session of the Central Committee of the Communist Party of the Soviet Union was held. The meeting dealt with the following questions:

1. The results of the consultations of representatives of the Communist and workers' Parties (speaker: Comrade M. A. Suslov).

2. The work of the trade unions of the USSR (speaker: Comrade V. V. Grishin).

The meeting adopted resolutions on the questions under discussion which are published today.

The meeting of the Central Committee elected Comrade N. A. Mukhitdinov a member of the Praesidium of the Central Committee of the CPSU.

The meeting of the Central Committee elected Comrades N. G. Ignatov, A. I. Kirichenko, and N. A. Mukhitdinov secretaries of the CC of the CPSU.

The reason why changes among the leaders of government and army are published in the smallest type on the last page of *Pravda*, whereas changes in the Party leadership are announced in large type on the front page, has never emerged. This difference in presentation is evidently intended to give outward expression to the precedence of the Party hierarchy over the Government and the army chiefs.

INDIRECT INDICATIONS OF THE SITUATION WITHIN THE SOVIET LEADERSHIP

Apart from these forms of announcing changes, there are others which tell the experienced reader about the position of the various leaders at a given time. Criticism or accusation of a minister, particularly in those torch-bearing articles of *Pravda*, usually point to his fall, even if the articles are signed by apparently unimportant persons. Sometimes inspired criticism of a minister comes from the director of some concern or a local Party secretary disguised as a 'voice from below'. The leadership then complies with 'the justified wishes of the workers' and dismisses the minister.

In many cases public self-criticism is the first step towards dismissal. The best known example since Stalin's death is Malenkov's self-criticism in February 1955 or Molotov's in October 1955. Malenkov and Molotov fell from power in July 1957.

The biographies in the large Soviet Encyclopaedia also permit interesting deductions. The length of the article depends on the rank and importance of the person, and a change is, therefore, politically important. Stalin's biography took up $14\frac{1}{2}$ columns before his death and only $5\frac{1}{2}$ columns in the first edition of the encyclopaedia issued in 1954.

The order in which individual leaders are named is also of significance. Two examples will illustrate this. Until the end of October 1952 the Communist leaders were named in the following order: Stalin, Molotov, Malenkov, Beria, Voroshilov, Bulganin. On 6 November the order was suddenly changed: Beria fell back to sixth place and Bulganin and Voroshilov were named before him. In the first few months after Stalin's death—from March to July 1953—the following order held good: Malenkov, Beria, Molotov, Voroshilov, Khrushchev, Voroshilov, Bulganin, Kaganovich, Mikoyan. Wide circles of the population drew their conclusions. Since June 1954 the Soviet leaders have preferred to be named in alphabetical order.

The signatures to Party and government decrees are also informative. As a rule Party resolutions are published over the signature of the 'Central Committee of the CPSU'. The edict on religion of 10 November 1954 and the resolution of 10 January 1955 on the transfer of the Lenin memorial day were, however, signed by Khrushchev alone. This was a clear indication of his growing strength. The government decree of 8 August 1955 on the extension of the rights of managing directors was signed by Bulganin, who was pushing forward at that time.

In this connexion positions on the tribune of the Lenin and

Stalin mausoleum at the annual demonstrations on May Day and 7 November deserve to be noted. The less important figures usually stand on each side, generally squeezed close together, while the eight or ten most powerful leaders of the USSR stand in the middle with more space between them. Stalin always stood in the centre; the two leaders to his right and left were considered to be favoured, even in the figurative sense of being 'closest to Stalin'. The fact that the grouping of the leaders is of political significance is generally known in Party circles. The leadership consciously exploits this. After the Nineteenth Party Congress, Stalin had himself photographed several times, each time with the leader of a different satellite country at his side.

A particularly obvious example of how policy is made with photographs is a picture, published in *Pravda* on 8 March 1953, three days after Stalin's death. It was taken at the time of the Nineteenth Party Congress in October 1952. Malenkov, on the rostrum, looms large at the centre of the picture. At the left in the corner, small and insignificant, Stalin is sitting listening to Malenkov. This picture was, of course, not published in Stalin's lifetime, but was issued immediately after his death in order to emphasize Malenkov's prominence in an unmistakable manner.

Still more important are the rare examples of photographic 'montage' or, more accurately, photographic forgery. The practice of faking pictures started in the first period of the Stalin era when Stalin had pictures of Lenin with Trotsky, Zinoviev, Kamenev or Bukharin withdrawn from circulation, or in some cases inserted his own likeness instead.

The most characteristic example since Stalin's death was a photograph published on 10 March 1953. It showed only Stalin, Malenkov, and Mao Tse-tung, all the same size as though they were standing next to one another. In fact, this was put together from a group photograph which had been taken on the occasion of the signing of the Sino-Soviet treaty in February 1950. In the original photograph fourteen people could be seen. It is true that Stalin was standing next to Mao Tse-tung, but between the latter and Malenkov there were four persons who had simply been cut away. Voroshilov and Molotov on the extreme right and Beria on the left had also been eliminated.

A last indication of the relative positions of the leaders is provided by the nominations before elections to the Supreme Soviet. Politically these elections are of little interest, since there is only one candidate for each constituency. In the elections of 1946, 1950, 1954, and 1958 the candidates chosen from above received more than 99 per cent. of the votes on each occasion. What is of importance is how many times this or that Soviet leader is 'nominated'. For form's sake, meetings take place in each constituency before the election at which, following, of course, the appropriate instructions from above, one of the leaders is proposed as candidate for the constituency.

The chief political figures, according to their importance, are 'nominated' in a fairly large number of constituencies. Only a few weeks before the election is it announced which constituency the head of them all has chosen; the constituencies which consequently become free are then distributed among the others. As the whole procedure is directed from above, it is, in fact, a conscious campaign to make some leaders popular at the expense of others. Before the elections to the Supreme Soviet in 1958, in the week from 2 to 9 February, Khrushchev was nominated 223 times, Kirichenko, Voroshilov, and Mikoyan 50 to 100 times each and Bulganin only 15 times. On 28 March Bulganin had to resign as Prime Minister, in September he was expelled from the Party and in November he was declared its enemy. Thus this game of numbers is not left to chance; it has, in fact, real political significance and is closely followed by the Party hierarchy. The central organ of the Italian Communist Party, *Unità*,[1] has drawn attention to the importance of this phenomenon.

In gauging the relative authority of individual Soviet leaders, attention must also be paid to the way in which their speeches are published. The speeches of members of the Party Praesidium are usually published in full; cuts or textual changes may indicate a weakening of their position. The best known example of this is Khrushchev's speech in Prague. On 25 June 1954 Khrushchev had made a speech at the Congress of the Czechoslovak Communist Party which was broadcast direct by Prague radio. It was, however, shortened in *Pravda*

[1] 8 Feb. 1958.

and Khrushchev's more violent expressions were toned down. Evidently Khrushchev was not then strong enough to prevent this. A similar cut was made in a speech of Marshal Zhukov's in July 1957 in Leningrad because it 'went too far'.

Even speeches at Party Congresses are sometimes censored. The head of the state security service, Alexander Shelepin, for example, made a speech at the Twenty-first Party Congress on 4 February 1959 which contained two sentences with particularly strong attacks on the 'anti-Party group'. The speech was cabled to Rome by the correspondent of *Unità* and was published verbatim. In *Pravda* of 5 February the two sentences were missing.

Open controversies between Party leaders only rarely find expression in speeches while the leaders still hold office. Instances of this since Stalin have had no immediate consequences. On 10 July 1956 Khrushchev criticized a member of the Party Praesidium, Yekaterina Furtseva,[1] who was then still Secretary of the Communist Party in Moscow. According to Khrushchev she had opposed the sending of the necessary number of young people to Siberia and the Soviet Far East because she believed that to do so would endanger the reconstruction of Moscow. Although Khrushchev publicly took up a position against Madame Furtseva this has had no effect—at least until the time of writing—on her further career.

Frol Kozlov, since November 1953 First Secretary of the Party in Leningrad, and since April 1958 a First Deputy Prime Minister of the USSR, also had to accept a severe reprimand while in office. On 23 April 1954, *Pravda* reproached him for insufficient self-criticism and for failing seriously to analyse the defects in the Leningrad Party organization which was then headed by him. This criticism has not so far harmed his career.

Another example was Khrushchev's challenge to Mikoyan at a demonstration in Moscow on 8 November 1956 at which there were over 10,000 young people. Khrushchev said that Mikoyan had had doubts about the virgin lands campaign and invited him in the following, and until then unusual, manner to admit his mistakes to the assembled company:

'Once I spoke from Alma Ata to Anastas Ivanovich Mikoyan.

[1] The criticism was published on 13 July 1956.

We exchanged views on what possibilities there were of assuring the grain supply of the country. When I told him that Kazakhstan was going to deliver a thousand million puds of cereals (16 million tons. W.L.) he did not reply.

' "Why are you silent?" I asked him.

'He replied:

' "I do not want to argue but I cannot believe in a thousand millions. 750 million may be possible instead of the 650 of the Plan, but a thousand?"

'Do you remember this conversation, Anastas Ivanovich; did you say this?' (Laughter.)

Mikoyan: 'Yes, I did.'

Khrushchev: 'And what did Kazakhstan say?'

Mikoyan: 'It kept its word.'

Khrushchev: 'Did it deliver a thousand million puds?'

Mikoyan: 'Yes, a thousand million.'

After this exchange which was published two days later in the whole Soviet press, Khrushchev continued: 'This shows that even some of us leaders who worked for the development of virgin and fallow land did not expect such excellent results, least of all in Kazakhstan.'

As the virgin lands campaign had for a long time been an integral part of Party policy, Mikoyan's doubt was a serious mistake. Even the light-hearted way in which Khrushchev spoke about it cannot hide the fact that Mikoyan was publicly criticized. This may be of importance later on.

Since Stalin's death there has been more than one case of a dispute over practical details bringing about the dismissal of a prominent Party or state official. Generally the public hears nothing about such clashes. Only one case has been officially announced. At the end of January 1955 Khrushchev explained in a speech[1] at the full session of the Central Committee that Yousupov, a member of the Praesidium of the Supreme Soviet of the USSR and Chairman of the Council of Ministers of Uzbekistan, had been dismissed because he was against reducing the distances between rows in the planting of cotton! The power and influence of the Soviet leaders in a given period can thus be judged not only from what is publicly announced but also from many indirect hints.

[1] Published on 4 Feb. 1955.

CHAPTER II

STALIN'S DEATH:
THE TURNING POINT

O N Wednesday, 4 March 1953, shortly after 6 a.m., Radio Moscow stopped its transmission without a closing announcement. At 6.30 a.m. the voice of the announcer returned with an announcement of the Central Committee of the Communist Party and the Council of Ministers of the USSR about Stalin's illness. After this the medical bulletin was read: In the night of 1 to 2 March—that is to say, more than 60 hours earlier—Stalin had had a stroke which had affected vital areas of the brain. Stalin had lost consciousness, paralysis of the right arm and leg had set in, loss of speech had followed, and there were disturbances in the functioning of his heart and breathing.

The official announcement stated twice that Stalin would 'temporarily' give up his activities in Party and state. Party members and the Soviet population were asked to show the greatest solidarity, fortitude of spirit, and vigilance.

From later reports it becomes clear that the first official statement was interpreted as an announcement of Stalin's death by the population. This statement was repeated every half hour. At 3 p.m. Radio Moscow interrupted its programme without giving a reason and did not come on to the air again until 3.18 p.m. and then with serious music. On Thursday, 5 March 1953 at 4.35 a.m. Radio Moscow broadcast the second medical bulletin. During the night Stalin's health had further deteriorated. *Pravda's* leading article of 5 March, headed 'The splendid unity of Party and people', mentioned, apart from Lenin and Stalin, only one Soviet leader, Malenkov. At 6.30 p.m. Moscow broadcast the third medical bulletin which spoke of acute cardiac disturbance and heavy respiratory deficiency; Stalin's condition was said to be extremely serious.

On the morning of Friday, 6 March, Radio Moscow started its transmission with a roll of drums; this was followed by the

Soviet national anthem. After a few seconds' pause the speaker read a long official announcement beginning as follows:

'From the Central Committee of the Communist Party of the Soviet Union, the Council of Ministers of the Soviet Union and the Praesidium of the Supreme Soviet of the Soviet Union.

'To all members of the Party,

'to all workers of the Soviet Union,

'Dear comrades and friends,

'The Central Committee of the Communist Party of the Soviet Union, the Council of Ministers of the USSR and the Praesidium of the Supreme Soviet of the USSR inform the Party and all workers of the Soviet Union with deep sorrow that on 5 March 1953 at 9.30 p.m. the Chairman of the Council of Ministers of the Soviet Union, and Secretary of the Central Committee of the Communist Party of the Soviet, Josef Vissario-novich Stalin, died after a grave illness.

'The life of the wise leader and teacher of the Communist Party and the Soviet people, Lenin's comrade and brilliant disciple, Josef Vissarionovich Stalin, is over.'

Thus, if we are to believe the official statement, Stalin died on 5 March at 9.30 p.m. Both the form of the announcement and the time of its publication leave a number of questions unanswered. Why was Stalin's illness announced so late? He was supposed to have had a stroke in the night of 1 to 2 March, but the public was informed of this only on the morning of 4 March. Even odder is the mistake in the first medical bulletin to which Dr. Felix Heni has drawn attention.[1] The description of the symptoms mentioned the loss of consciousness before the loss of speech; the ability of an unconscious person to speak cannot, however, be tested. According to Dr. Heni it may be assumed that this point was added later, to leave no doubt about the fact that the sick man could no longer establish contact with his surroundings after his stroke. Then, finally, there is the interruption of the broadcast on the afternoon of 4 March. Possibly Stalin died earlier than was officially announced and the others wished to gain time to decide who was to succeed him.

Further measures followed the official announcement of his death with remarkable speed; already one hour later the

[1] *Osteuropa*, No. 4, 1953.

composition of the Committee to organize Stalin's funeral was announced. The Chairman was Nikita Khrushchev. At 2 p.m. the body of Stalin was taken to lie in state in the Trade Union Hall in Moscow; at 9.30 p.m. Radio Moscow announced a joint resolution of the Central Committee, the Council of Ministers, and the Praesidium of the Supreme Soviet on far-reaching changes in the state and Party leadership. The most important task of the Party, and government was to ensure the smooth running of the country, it was explained. This demanded the 'maximum unity of the leadership' and the 'avoidance of all confusion and panic'. The word panic was unexpected. It was the first time since 3 July 1941 that this word had been used in an official Soviet declaration. No cause for it could be discerned. From all reports it emerges that the population took Stalin's death calmly and did not show the slightest signs of panic. The admonition of the leadership was probably intended more for the Party hierarchy than for the population.

In fact, Stalin's death burst upon one of the tensest phases of Soviet development, a period of violent disagreements within the ruling class and of purges and arrests on a gigantic scale, a period which had opened in October 1952.

THE DEVELOPMENT OF STALIN'S SYSTEM

The Stalinist system of tyranny with its vast forced labour camps, its over-centralized economic control, destruction of trade union rights, and regimentation of literature and art, arose at the end of the twenties, and had been developed to its horrible perfection by the end of the thirties. Simultaneously, however, the USSR was transformed into a modern industrial state. The number of manual and office workers rose from 10·8 million in 1928 to 47·9 million in 1955, and the number of university graduates from 233,000 to 2·2 million.

Such rapid industrialization had been possible in a country so backward as the USSR only through a highly centralized economic system. For the further development of the economy, however, over-centralization proved an impediment. The inflated bureaucratic apparatus absorbed useful labour which was needed in production; a confusion of restrictive regulations paralysed the natural enthusiasm of the specialists who had by then been trained. The clumsy machinery of control was no longer able to make rational use of the quickly expanding economic power of the country. The economy needed new stimuli.

The forced development of industry demanded countless new workers who were recruited from the peasantry into the new factories. To keep their demands low the trade unions were deprived of power and the workers of their rights. Gigantic forced labour camps had been created for the purpose both of political oppression and of the development of new terri- tories. But the further industrialization progressed, the less profitable slave labour proved. The effect of coercion on agriculture was fatal. Stalin had pushed through the collecti- vization of farming with brute force. It had enabled him to use modern large-scale agricultural methods, but had undermined the confidence of the peasants. In the end, Stalin's measures increased the unproductive apparatus of inspection and reduced the peasants' productivity.

As in the economic, so in the political and cultural spheres, the centralized bureaucracy stifled every creative initiative. The revolutionary ideology of 1917 increasingly conflicted with what Stalin had actually created and, though revised to fit the new situation, it now aroused little enthusiasm. Science and art, which had been brought to an unexpected flowering by the Revolution, withered in the hands of a leader who misused them as nothing but propaganda with which to penetrate the whole of society. The paralysing fear which the system had spread, particularly in the years of the great purge from 1936 to 1938, guaranteed the security of the dictatorship but could not stimulate the population to greater exertions. The régime needed a substitute for its lost revolutionary drive; since the middle thirties, therefore, it had encouraged Soviet patriotism which then during the forties, changed into Great-Russian chauvinism. But this, too, proved to be a double-edged sword. Much though it helped Stalin during the war, its effects after 1945 were dangerous. Administrative, political, and cultural measures against the non-Russian nationalities magnified national contradictions. In vain did Stalin try to counter them by campaigns against 'bourgeois nationalism'.

During the first period, from about the middle of the

twenties to the middle of the thirties, Stalin was the chief of the whole Soviet bureaucracy. His reign of terror was directed against 'anti-party' opposition, against factions such as the followers of Trotsky, Zinoviev, and Bukharin, against alleged and genuine 'national deviations', against kulaks and peasants described as kulaks, and against such middle-class intellectuals as survived. The new official class, however, had felt relatively little of the terror up to that time.

This changed during the thirties. When the representatives of this new élite met in 1934 for the Seventeenth Party Congress, they little suspected that most of them would a few years later be among the defeated. During this period, Stalin, with the help of the State Security Service, began to replace the dictatorship of the Party by his own personal dictatorship. But even the great purge of 1936–8 could not stop that process of differentiation within the official class which was induced by the very force of industrial development.

Towards the end of collectivization and the first Five-Year Plan the new ruling class had grown in numbers as well as in power and privilege, and with every additional year of industrialization it became stronger but its sections became more distinct. Thus the economic authorities, the Party, state, army, and the state security service had to master different, and in part conflicting, tasks: their interests inevitably diverged and even clashed.

In the ranks of the economic bureaucracy, among managers, technocrats, and state officials collaborating with them, and certainly also in the officer corps of the army, there grew up a desire for normal conditions of life and work, for freedom from political campaigns and police snooping. These tendencies were dangerous for two of the supporting groups of the system; the Party machine and the state security service. The Party machine could justify its existence only by incessant political campaigns, the state security service only by vigilance campaigns and purges.

The contradictory tendencies counterbalanced one another for some time and this enabled Stalin to manœuvre between them and to play the part of a supreme arbiter. But after the second world war the equilibrium was perceptibly disturbed. The officer corps of the army and the economic leaders had strengthened their position at the expense of the Party. The Zhdanov policy, the so-called *Zhdanovshchina* of 1946 to 1948, was Stalin's first attempt to restore the predominance of the Party. The stronger political pressure of these years did not, however, remove the causes of conflict: when Zhdanov died in 1948 they were again in evidence.

At the beginning of the fifties the situation had become so critical that Stalin decided on a new purge, intended at one blow to consolidate the system as a whole, to weaken the position of the managers striving for peace and security, and to strengthen the influence of the Party and the state security service, the so-called activist forces. The last hectic period of the Stalin era was introduced by two events, the publication of a book by Stalin on economic problems and the Nineteenth Party Congress of the CPSU.

STALIN'S LAST BOOK

The Party Congress was to open on 5 October 1952. On 3 and 4 October *Pravda* appeared unexpectedly in a greatly enlarged edition. It contained Stalin's treatise, approximately 25,000 words in length, on 'The Economic Problems of Socialism in the USSR'. The official occasion for this publication was the preparation of a textbook, *Political Economy*, into which fifteen years of work had already gone. Stalin's last book was intended to put an end to the discussions which had been going on for years about this textbook and about the principles of political economy; it was to provide authoritative guidance for the future policy of the USSR.

In his last work Stalin first expressed himself emphatically in favour of recognizing the existence of economic laws. He rejected the views of those officials who believed that in a socialist society laws could be abolished or changed and new laws created. Economic laws, said Stalin, were objective laws reflecting the fact that the processes of life obey certain laws; they operated independently of the human will. Although the field of application of this or that law could be limited and certain effects prevented, the laws themselves could not be suspended or changed. Stalin turned against those officials who imagined that Soviet power 'could do anything' or that 'nothing could affect it.' The practical intention of this highly detailed treatise was obviously to keep the Soviet economic bureaucracy in its place.

Secondly, Stalin's directives for the transition to communism in the USSR were important. According to Soviet ideology, development after the assumption of power by a communist party takes place in two phases. During the first phase, the introduction of socialism, the landlords and capitalists are deprived of their power; the big estates are divided up and industry is nationalized. Then the private peasants' holdings are combined into collective farms; private trade is taken over by the state or controlled co-operation, and the whole economy is placed under the central direction of a planning commission. Two forms of property remain, however, state and co-operative ownership. The differences between town and country and between intellectual and manual workers have not yet been removed. The state, too, continues to exist. Producers are paid according to their productivity. According to the official Soviet interpretation this first phase had come to an end in the USSR at the end of 1936.

Since 1937 the Soviet Union has entered the period of gradual transition to communism, a second, more advanced phase, in which the two surviving forms of property should fuse into one. The contrast between town and country, between intellectual and manual work have yet to be overcome. Though the state continues to exist—it can wither away only after a victory of communism in the whole world—its functions change. The most important characteristic of this phase is the free distribution of consumer goods. Producers are no longer paid according to their ability but according to their needs.

Since 1937 discussions have been going on in the Soviet Union about the steps to be taken for the transition to communism. In his last book Stalin also expressed his views on this subject. The co-existence of the two forms of property was to be overcome by raising collective farm property to 'the level of public or national property'. This, in fact, meant the eradication of the last relics of co-operation and the complete subjugation of the collective farms to over-centralized state control. Trade was to be replaced by a 'system of direct exchange of products'; a central agency—Stalin even spoke of a 'central authority'—was to distribute all agricultural produce. This system, so Stalin demanded, should be resolutely introduced. Stalin further declared—contradicting, by the way, his own definitions in 1927—that under communism *all* differences between town and country, between intellectual and manual labour, would not disappear, but only the *essential* differences. Inessential differences would remain even under communism, because working conditions in town and country and for managers and workers would not be the same.

Stalin did not express himself on the free distribution of produce according to needs. He said that the working day should be shortened to six and later to five hours, that housing conditions should be improved, and that real wages should be at least doubled. With the aim of the all-round development of the physical and mental capacities of man, Stalin stated that it would be necessary to introduce compulsory technical education. In the future the production of producer goods should still have priority over the production of consumer goods. Thus was Stalin's policy—the primacy of heavy industry, the priority of state over collective property and the direction of the whole economy by a gigantic central state machine—to be continued.

This last book of Stalin's proved extraordinarily significant for the development of domestic policy from October 1952 to March 1953. The main part was already completed by 1 February 1952, more than eight months before publication. Later Stalin added three articles: 'A reply to Notkin' on 21 April, 'A reply to Yaroshenko' on 22 May 1952, and 'A reply to Zanina and Venzher' on 28 September 1952. It emerges from these that the Party had commissioned authoritative Party ideologists and economists to write papers on certain subjects for the drafting of the new Party textbooks. These drafts had been sent to Stalin. They were not published but Stalin quoted from them in his replies. Their authors had evidently expressed views which Stalin—rightly from his point of view—was bound to consider extremely dangerous.

In a paper for the Central Committee the Soviet economist, Leonid Yaroshenko, had gone so far as to criticize the 'fundamental economic law' of Socialism which Stalin had proclaimed—the 'maximum satisfaction of the constantly growing material and cultural needs of the entire population through the continuous growth and constant improvement of Socialist production on the basis of the highest technology'. Yaroshenko held the view that the political economy of Socialism should concern itself with the 'rational organization of the forces of production. He even proposed a new definition of the concept of communism: 'The best scientific organization of productive forces in social production.' Yaroshenko obviously represented influential economic circles which were less concerned with propagandist declarations than with a rationalization of the economy.

Other economists who until then had enjoyed the full confidence of the leadership had voiced heretical views. They had suggested, as Stalin's replies show, that the priority of heavy industry should be abandoned. Zanina and Venzher wanted to dissolve the machine and tractor stations—a favourite achievement of Stalin's—and to sell the agricultural machinery to the collective farms.

Stalin sharply condemned these heresies for he had recognized how dangerous they were for him. If officials close to him harboured reforming ideas of this kind, what must things be like in other sections of the Party hierarchy! According to Khrushchev's secret speech at the Twentieth Party Congress, Stalin had said to members of the Politburo at that time: 'You are as blind as kittens. What would you do without me? The country will perish because you cannot recognize your enemies!' Stalin recognized his own enemies in time. He was not satisfied with ideological replies to Notkin, Yaroshenko, Zanina, and Venzher, but decided also to tame the managers and restore the leading role of the Party. For this purpose he called the Nineteenth Party Congress. The timing of the publication of his last book was well chosen by Stalin for he had anticipated the resolutions of the Party Congress. The other Soviet leaders could only repeat Stalin's theses and congratulate him on his 'work of genius'.

THE NINETEENTH PARTY CONGRESS

From 5 to 14 October 1952 the Nineteenth Party Congress, the last one in the Stalin period, met in the Kremlin: since the Eighteenth Party Congress in March 1939 more than thirteen years had passed. The Congress was attended by 1,192 voting delegates and 167 delegates with consultative status only. They represented 6,013,259 full members and 868,886 candidate members.

The Congress was characterized by a general hardening of Party policy. Molotov, in his opening speech, spoke of 'warmongers', and exhorted the Soviet people not to forget 'the necessary vigilance for one minute'. Malenkov delivered the report of the Central Committee. He attacked 'the mood of complacency' and the 'carelessness' which were to be observed in the Party organization. Vigilance had declined and sloth was becoming noticeable, and it even happened that Party and state secrets were betrayed. Officials were carried away by economic successes and they 'began to forget that capitalist encirclement still exists and that the enemies of the Soviet state persistently try to smuggle in their agents and to exploit unstable elements in Soviet society for their own vile purposes'. A determined fight, said Malenkov, must be fought against all weaknesses. The Central Committee should be informed of all harmful happenings without respect of persons. Party control and ideological work must be considerably intensified because 'when attention to ideology declines the growth of hostile attitudes and opinions is favoured'. No less interesting was Malenkov's threat that 'Wise leadership consists in being able to recognize a danger when it is still in embryo and giving it no chance of growing to menacing proportions.'

After Malenkov's report the then head of the State Planning Commission, Maxim Saburov, announced the directives for the Five-Year Plan from 1951 to 1955. Much more important than the figures of the plan was the fact that the whole thing was announced only at the end of 1952, that is, two years after its start. In the course of 1951 it had become clear from many public statements and from criticism of the administration that the Five-Year Plan targets had been set too high. It emerged that the reserves which had existed until then—war materials which could be used for peaceful purposes, pre-war stocks for the production of consumer goods, slightly damaged machinery and plant which could be repaired more quickly than had at first been assumed—were exhausted. It also appeared that future industrial development demanded bigger investments than had originally been calculated. The dismantling of German plant had come to an end and the deliveries (reparations and compulsory exports) from the current production of the occupied countries had to be reduced because the latter found themselves in great difficulties. Prisoners of war and deported persons were gradually being released. China was in urgent need of help which had to be provided, not only by the Soviet Union, but also by the East European countries.

These and a number of other problems confronted the Soviet leaders with the alternative of admitting the plan's faults and revising it or of concealing its weaknesses behind ideological campaigns which demanded new efforts towards the achievement of its over-ambitious aims. The plan which was put before the Nineteenth Party Congress showed that Stalin had decided in favour of the second possibility.

The other Soviet leaders at the Nineteenth Party Congress spoke on various aspects of Soviet policy, Beria on the nationalities policy, Bulganin on the economics of defence, Mikoyan on the consumer goods industry, Suslov on ideological questions, Kosygin on light industry, and Marshal Vasilevsky on the army. Stalin was the last to speak. He who had begun his rise in 1924 with the thesis of 'socialism in one country' now pleaded in this last brief speech of his for collaboration with communist parties abroad. The Soviet Party would always need the support of foreign parties and would always help them in their struggles to be free. Stalin appealed to the communist parties abroad to raise and carry before them 'the banner of bourgeois, democratic freedom' and 'the banner of national independence' so that they might attract the majority of the people.

Apart from Malenkov's report and Stalin's last speech the changes in the Party statutes proposed by Khrushchev were particularly significant. They all tended towards greater centralization and a stricter control of the lower ranks. The plenary sessions of the Central Committee were no longer to take place every four, but only every six, months. The Control Committee, the highest Party tribunal, was given the right to attach allegedly independent representatives to all Party organizations of the USSR. To the four duties of Party members nine were added. Members were directed to inform the leading Party organs of shortcomings in work without respect for persons and to display political vigilance, bearing in mind that vigilance on the part of communists is necessary in every situation. Almost all speakers at the Party Congress, especially Malenkov and Beria, put particular stress on the duty to be vigilant. This was more than a measure of Party organization; it heralded a new campaign of purges.

The Congress further resolved to change the name of the Party. Until then it had officially been called the 'Communist Party of the Soviet Union (Bolsheviks)'. The addition 'Bolsheviks' was dropped—it had become too inconvenient to be reminded of Lenin's party. The Nineteenth Party Congress dissolved the Orgburo or office of organization which had existed since 1919, and handed over its functions to the Secretariat of the Central Committee. The Politburo was renamed 'Party Praesidium', because this description was said to correspond better to its functions.

THE CHANGES IN THE PARTY LEADERSHIP

On 16 October, one day after the end of the Party Congress, a full session of the newly elected Central Committee took place at which far-reaching changes in the leading bodies of the Party were decided.

The Party Praesidium, the renamed Politburo, which until the Nineteenth Party Congress had consisted of eleven members (Stalin, Malenkov, Beria, Molotov, Voroshilov, Kaganovich, Khrushchev, Bulganin, Andreyev, Mikoyan and Kosygin), was transformed into a clumsy organ with twenty-five. The number of its candidate members was increased to eleven. The Central Committee Secretariat, which until the Party Congress had consisted of only Stalin, Malenkov, Khrushchev, and Suslov, was increased to ten members.

All this permitted the deduction that the old élite of the Party was to be purged. Stalin presumably wanted to exclude the older members of the Politburo, Molotov, Voroshilov, and Mikoyan, and perhaps later Beria, Kaganovich, and Bulganin, and to replace them by new officials who were completely devoted to him. He was probably already planning to remove from the Party leadership those who had proved unreliable or who knew too much, and thus to reduce the Party Praesidium and the Central Committee Secretariat to their original numbers. At the time this was only suspected by foreign students of Russia: later it was confirmed by Khrushchev at the Twentieth Party Congress. A proof of the struggle in progress behind the scenes was the appointment after the Congress of a Central Committee candidate member, an event which has so far remained unique in the history of the Bolshevik Party. It was two weeks after the Party Congress, on 30 October 1952, that it was announced 'for the information of all members of the Communist Party of the Soviet Union' that Marshal Govorov, closely associated with Zhdanov during the war, had become a candidate member of the Central Committee. His name was said to have been omitted owing to an 'error of the scrutineers' at the Nineteenth Party Congress.

THE HARDENING OF POLICY

The new purge began immediately after the Nineteenth Party Congress with a campaign to strengthen political consciousness and Party discipline. The formulations of the leading articles in *Pravda* and *Kommunist* became increasingly sharp. Simultaneously there was a campaign against nepotism and over-friendly relations within the economic, state, and Party machines. Thus mutual distrust was systematically created.

Sharp formulations were not all. In November the Slansky trial took place in Czechoslovakia. André Marty was excluded from the French Party leadership. At the beginning of December the first death sentences were passed on economic officials in the Ukraine: some of those sentenced were of Jewish origin. The campaign was now extended to the Party organizations connected with economic officials if these organizations had not adapted themselves quickly enough to the new policy.

Among the leaders, too, uncertainty grew. On 7 November 1952 their order of precedence was changed. Beria, until then always mentioned fourth (after Stalin, Malenkov, and Molotov) fell back to the sixth place, and Voroshilov and Bulganin moved ahead of the Minister of the Interior.

The vigilance campaign also affected family relationships. In the middle of December *Pravda* wrote: 'We are fighting for vigilance which is also necessary in the family. It is the unfailing duty of all relations to prevent members of their family from committing mistakes and serious crimes against society. . . . They are morally responsible for their actions to Soviet society. And in many cases it may also be a question of being responsible to the law. Let no one forget this.'[1]

The Fedoseyev affair in the last week of December 1952 carried the rage for vigilance into leading circles of the Party, particularly among intellectuals. Professor P. M. N. Fedoseyev, until 1949 on the editorial board of the ideological Party journal, *Bolshevik*, had on 12 December 1952 published in *Izvestia* the first part of an article praising Stalin's 'Economic Problems of Socialism in the USSR'. The second part of the article ('The objective character of the economic laws of development') did not appear, strangely enough, until 21 December. Three days later, to everybody's surprise, *Pravda* carried a sharp attack on Fedoseyev.

Its author was Mikhail Suslov, a Central Committee Secretary, who had earlier emerged as a firebrand both in the Soviet Union and in the Cominform. Suslov accused Professor Fedoseyev of having advocated in 1948 and 1949 the views of the then member of the Politburo, Voznesensky. Voznesensky had disappeared in the summer of 1949. Suslov now quoted a resolution of 13 June 1949 of the Party leadership which had been kept secret until then, from which it emerged that Voznesensky had been relieved of all Party and government functions in March 1949. Thus for the first time the Leningrad Affair[2] was mentioned in public. It was to play an important part after Stalin's death.

In 1948 Nikolai Voznesensky was not only a member of the Politburo but a Deputy Prime Minister of the USSR and Chairman of the State Planning Commission. For his book, *The Economy of the Soviet Union during the Great Patriotic War*, which had appeared in 1948, he had received the Stalin Prize. There was hardly a Party, state or economic official who had not disseminated Voznesensky's ideas in 1948–9 when he was held in the highest honour.

After 24 December the vigilance campaign was increased. Leading Soviet economists and industrial directors were

[1] *Pravda*, 15 Dec. 1952.　　[2] See below.

publicly attacked in the press and forced to engage in self-criticism. Fear and suspicion grew from day to day. The situation was set for a new blow.

THE CONSPIRACY OF THE KREMLIN DOCTORS

On 13 January 1953 *Pravda* announced in the last column on the last page under the harmless heading 'Chronicle' that the state security organs had succeeded in discovering a conspiracy on the part of nine doctors of the medical administration of the Kremlin. The doctors were said already to have murdered prominent Soviet leaders—among them the former Politburo members, Andrei Zhdanov, and the former head of the chief political administration of the Red Army, Colonel-General Shcherbakov. Now they were alleged to have been trying, on the orders of the American and British secret services and the Jewish organization 'Joint', to destroy other Soviet leaders, among them Marshals Vasilevsky, Govorov, and Koniev, General Shtemenko and Admiral Levchenko. The Kremlin doctors were accused 'as secret enemies of the people' of having 'deliberately subjected their patients to harmful treatment', of having purposely made false diagnoses and of having killed their patients through wrong treatment. They had tried 'to undermine the health of leading military personalities of the Soviet Union in order to remove them and thus to weaken the defences of the country'. Of the nine Kremlin doctors accused, five (Professors Vovsi, B. B. Kogan, Feldman, Grinstein, and Etinger) were said to have had connexions with the international Jewish organization 'Joint', and with the American secret service. Three Professors (Vinogradov, M. B. Kogan, and Yegorov) were allegedly agents of long standing of the British secret service. Only Mayorov was not accused of foreign connexions. *Pravda* reprimanded the state security organs for not 'unmasking' the pernicious organization sooner. The Ministry of Health of the USSR was also attacked because it had overlooked 'the pernicious terrorist work of these low fiends'.

On the same day commentaries appeared in all papers about this 'conspiracy'. *Pravda* abused the Kremlin doctors as 'sub-human', 'monsters', 'despicable creatures', 'a gang of poisoners', 'contemptible mercenaries', and 'hired murderers'. It demanded that the organs of the Soviet security service should be constantly reinforced.

The accused Kremlin doctors had for many years enjoyed the undisputed confidence of the Soviet leaders. In 1947 Professor Vovsi had received the Order of Lenin for 'heroic acts during the fighting for Leningrad'. Professor Vinogradov had been politically helpful to Stalin: during the trial of the 'Rightists' and Trotskyists in the spring of 1938 he had acted as medical expert of the court at that time against Pletniov, Kasakov, and Levin, Kremlin doctors then in the dock. As late as 27 February 1952, Vinogradov had received the Order of Lenin for 'meritorious services in the field of medicine'. The decision on a big new purge was, therefore, probably taken after that date and before the Nineteenth Party Congress, i.e. at the time when the inner circle of Soviet leaders was discussing the new textbook *Political Economy*, and when Stalin became aware of the heretical views of Yaroshenko, Notkin, Zanina, and Venzher, which made him fear the stabilizing influence of the managers.

Great stress was laid in the non-Soviet world on the anti-semitic aspects of the doctors' case. Of the nine Kremlin doctors, five (according to some reports, four, and according to others as many as six or seven) were of Jewish origin, but there were also Russians and Ukrainians, and both before and after the 'doctors' plot' the campaign was not by any means directed exclusively against Jews, but against considerably wider circles of the Soviet population.

The 'conspiracy of the Kremlin doctors' was obviously a means of increasing the general fear and uncertainty. The *Pravda* commentary of 13 January was in the first place directed against those sections of the population which had remained detached from the general campaign of vigilance. 'There is no doubt', say the final threatening sentences, 'that so long as gullibility exists among us there will also be pernicious activities.'

STALIN'S LAST PURGE

A vast witch hunt directed against an ever-widening circle of people now began throughout the Soviet Union in hundreds of newspapers, periodicals, and broadcasts, at rallies and conferences: in the organizations of the Party and of its youth in the trade unions, at conferences of scientists, economists, and doctors. Time and again 'lack of vigilance' and 'sloth' were denounced.

On 20 January, one week after the 'unmasking' of the Kremlin doctors, the Praesidium of the Supreme Soviet of the USSR decorated Dr. Lydia Timashuk with the Order of Lenin 'for the help she had given the government in unmasking the murderous doctors'. Denunciation was again officially praised as admirable and worthy of emulation.

The analogy with 1937, the climax of the first big purge, was becoming increasingly clear. The methods of the reign of terror employed at that time were copied in detail. Just as then *Pravda* reported the arrests of leading personalities in the sixth column on the last page under the same heading 'Chronicle' and in the same type. Similarly the papers were full of references to 'spies', 'murderers', 'scoundrels', 'poisoners', and 'gangs of animals in human shape', and the population was enjoined 'to cauterize the dangerous disease of carelessness with a red-hot iron'.

Just as then Stalin's theory that the further socialism develops the more dangerous become its enemies was advanced as the reason for the campaign; the struggle must, therefore, not be lessened, but intensified. After 6 February, the Soviet press frequently quoted Stalin's utterances on vigilance in 1937.

The circle of people who were threatened constantly grew, with the help of a method which had also been used in the years 1936 to 1938. The articles on lack of vigilance, which appeared almost daily, mentioned individual persons with their name, address, and place of work. They stood for a whole group of the population which was included in the purge through this 'typical example'.

Up to the middle of 1953 the purge included the following categories:

1. Intellectuals. Those mainly affected were economists, lawyers, Party ideologists, university professors, historians, scientists, doctors, members of the press and radio, museum and library employees. The chief points of accusation were: subjectivism, objectivism, cosmopolitanism, political unreliability, lack of vigilance, sloth, kow-towing to foreign countries, and the smuggling in of hostile ideas.

2. Economic officials. They were accused of not having sufficiently exploited existing economic capacity, of having damaged national property and of having enriched themselves.

3. Persons of Jewish origins. They were accused of 'rootless cosmopolitanism' and often also of spying for foreign countries.

4. Higher and medium ranking state officials accused of loss of secret documents, betrayal of state secrets, lack of vigilance.

5. Officials of the non-Russian Union Republics accused of middle-class nationalism, cosmopolitanism, and espionage for foreign countries.

6. Party Officials accused of a liberal attitude towards wrong conceptions, lack of vigilance, neglect of ideological work, weak criticism, and the colouring of reports.

7. Officials of the Young Communist League accused of shocking frivolity and lack of vigilance.

8. Soviet citizens who had been abroad during the war. They were accused of having worked for the Gestapo during the war and for the American secret service after it.

9. Former Trotskyists and Mensheviks. They were accused of having made false declarations of loyalty during the twenties and of having for decades been agents of foreign secret services.

Stalin's last purge was thus in the first place directed against the élite of the country. Even the highest leaders were not spared. As Khrushchev confirmed at the Twentieth Party Congress, sessions of the Politburo took place only occasionally; Stalin suspected Voroshilov of being a British agent and a special listening-in equipment was installed in his home. Molotov and Mikoyan were also accused by Stalin: according to Khrushchev they were both in danger of their lives.

It is interesting that no important Soviet leader commented on the purge at that time. Only Mikhail Suslov, one of the Party secretaries, and Frol Kozlov, then Second Party Secretary in Leningrad, published articles calling for increased vigilance.

Why were the Soviet leaders silent? Were they no longer allowed to appear in public? Or was their silence a sign of protest? We do not yet know. In any case, they must all have realized by February 1953 at the latest that this was not one of the 'usual' small purges, but a repetition of the great purge

of 1936 to 1938. Would the leaders of the country who had
lived through those years of terror, look on without doing
anything?

THE DEATH OF STALIN

A few weeks before his death, as the purge was moving towards its climax, Stalin received two foreign visitors, the last
to see the *Vozhdy* before his death. They were the Argentinian
Ambassador, Dr. Leopold Bravo, and the Indian Ambassador,
K. P. S. Menon.[1] Harrison Salisbury says in his book *Stalin's
Russia and After* that both ambassadors later agreed that they
noticed no signs in Stalin of any impending illness. He had
been in a good mood and had laughed and joked. Yet Menon
observed a strange thing. During the conversation Stalin
continuously doodled on a piece of paper: this was an old
habit of his. Menon, however, noticed that Stalin this time
repeatedly made drawings with a red pencil, of wolves. Then
he began to talk about wolves. Russian peasants, he said, knew
how to deal with wolves. They had to be exterminated. But the
wolves know this, said Stalin, and act accordingly.

On the same day, 17 February 1953, *Izvestia* contained the
following announcement: 'The administration of the Com-
mandatura of the Kremlin announces with deep sorrow the
premature death of Major-General Piotr Kosynkin on 15
February 1953 and expresses its condolences with the family of
the deceased.' What does the strange wording 'premature
death' signify? Why did the notice appear only in *Izvestia* and
not, as was customary, in *Pravda*? We can only make vague
guesses. The fact, however, deserves to be remembered, for
later—particularly in connexion with Beria's fall—the Com-
mandatura of the Kremlin was again to play a part.

On 23 February 1953 *Pravda* published a flattering article
on Lydia Timashuk, who was described as a symbol of Soviet
patriotism, of great vigilance, and of an implacably heroic
struggle against the enemies of the fatherland. On the same
day *Pravda* demanded in its leading article that the Soviet
press should 'intensify the education of the Soviet people in
the spirit of a high degree of political vigilance'.

Two days later, on 22 February 1953, the whole campaign

[1] They visited Stalin on 7 and 17 Feb. respectively.

was suddenly called off. Only in a few exceptional cases was the
word 'vigilance' used: Soviet newspapers again reported on
the supply of vegetables, on coal production and the fishing
catch. The appeals for heightened political vigilance and the
struggle against slackness almost disappeared from the Soviet
press.

What had happened? Had Stalin fallen unexpectedly ill
and had the other Soviet leaders immediately exerted pressure
or force on Stalin to prevent him from continuing the purge?

A week later, on 2 March, Stalin is said to have had a stroke,
and on the morning of 6 March his death was announced.
A few hours later groups of Moscow citizens gathered in the
Red Square. Soon there were several thousand, waiting on this
cold day for Stalin's coffin to be brought out of the Kremlin.
The militia, or traffic police, watched this quietly, although it
was the first time for many decades that people had gathered
in their thousands in the Red Square without being ordered
to do so.

Only during the night did the steps taken by the new
leaders, or by some of them, become apparent. The whole
town was surrounded by MVD troops, that is, troops of the
Ministry of the Interior. In the course of the next day all the
streets leading to the Red Square and to important buildings in
the centre of the town were closed.

Official Soviet broadcasts were entirely given over to mourning
for Stalin, in which, it was alleged, the whole population
shared. But Western correspondents, among them Harrison
Salisbury and Henry Shapiro, saw a different picture; it
almost looked as if the Kremlin leaders were anxious that
Stalin should be forgotten as quickly as possible. The prevailing
mood was not genuine mourning but tense anxiety. Some
feared that the Americans would use the occasion of Stalin's
death and attack the Soviet Union, others expected struggles
between the new leaders. Some were indignant about the
almost indecent haste with which these leaders tried to dissociate themselves from the dead tyrant. It was generally noticed
that Stalin lay in state for only three days and not for seven as
Lenin had. Few Western observers noticed signs of genuine
mourning. Generally the impression predominated that the
mood of the population could not in any way be compared

with the feeling which was shown at Lenin's death, when the mourning of the people was deep and sincere; by comparison, Stalin's death acted like a paralysing shock. Harrison Salisbury reported that the population reacted like a horse which had pulled a heavy cart for twenty years and which, when the yoke is suddenly removed, is unable to understand what has happened, and remains motionless.

In form the official funeral ceremonies resembled those after Lenin's death though everything seemed to lack genuine feeling. This made clear how the system, and the people's relationship to it, had changed in three decades.

Prisoners who were in Stalin's concentration camps at that time and who were released in the course of de-Stalinization and returned to the West have described how the news of Stalin's death was received. According to Brigitte Gerland (*Die Hölle ist ganz anders*) an elderly Russian woman in the women's huts in Vorkuta put everybody's fear into words: 'If Stalin dies, perhaps somebody worse will take over, a young man, who will kill us all.' Some religious women, who were called *monashki* in the camp, thanked God that he had delivered the world from a false prophet. Younger Soviet women rebelled against this and started to sing the Soviet national anthem, but only a few women quietly and hesitantly joined in.

The prisoners in the men's huts, particularly the political prisoners, reacted differently. According to Bernhard Roeder (*Der Katorgan*) they all left their places soon after the radio announcement of Stalin's death. They rushed off to spread the news. The 'free' prisoners[1] too were nervous. No work was done that day in Vorkuta, for the prisoners simply stood about in groups, talking excitedly. The first alcohol soon began to flow and towards evening the whole of Vorkuta was drunk, prisoners, 'free' prisoners, soldiers, and particularly the *nachalstvo* or camp leaders.

The political prisoners argued all night. Immediately after Stalin's death the rumour went round Vorkuta that the other Party leaders had murdered Stalin, a measure of how great the tension was which only Stalin's death could ease. One of the prisoners expressed this mood in the words: 'Today is a great day. Today an epoch in history has come to an end.'

[1] Prisoners who have been released but must live in a specified area.

The leaders were confronted with the task of overcoming the feeling of insecurity, particularly in the official class; reversing gear, they had to bring the purge to an abrupt end. They had quickly to decide not only about Stalin's succession but also about their own new policy. Already on the evening of 6 March the Party Praesidium, which Stalin had increased to twenty-five members at the Nineteenth Party Congress, was again reduced to ten. Apart from Malenkov as chairman, only Beria, Molotov, Voroshilov, Khrushchev, Bulganin, Kaganovich, Mikoyan, Saburov, and Pervukhin now belonged to this highest body. Six of them were members of the Praesidium of the Council of Ministers: Malenkov took over the chairmanship of the Council of Ministers; the First Deputy Chairman, Beria, took over the Ministry of the Interior, Molotov the Foreign Ministry, and Bulganin the Ministry of Defence; Kaganovich, also a First Deputy Chairman of the Council of Ministers, was not given a portfolio, although he was probably responsible for industry and transport. Mikoyan took over the Ministry of Domestic and Foreign Trade. Of the other leaders Saburov took over machine building and—this incidentally was not officially announced—the armaments industry, Pervukhin the Ministry of Power and Electrical Industry, while Voroshilov was appointed Chairman of the Praesidium of the Supreme Soviet. Khrushchev was to concentrate, as the first announcement after Stalin's death expressed it, 'on work in the Central Committee'.

Particularly remarkable was the appointment of Marshal Zhukov as Deputy Minister of Defence. Grigori Zhukov, who had been a divisional commander in the Soviet Far East during the big purge of 1936 to 1938, became an army general in 1940 and, in January 1941, Chief of the General Staff of the Red Army. In the autumn of 1946 he was recalled. Stalin obviously feared the growing popularity of the army leader who had become a legendary figure throughout Russia; he was also afraid of some of Zhukov's independent ideas. For years his name was seen neither in the Soviet press nor yet in publications about the war.

On 9 March at 12 a.m. the funeral ceremonies for Stalin began. Khrushchev, as chairman of the commission for the arrangement of Stalin's funeral, opened the ceremony. The funeral orations were made by the three senior leaders of the day, Malenkov, Beria, and Molotov. There was a noticeable difference of tone between Malenkov's and Molotov's speeches. Malenkov used phrases which hinted at a détente in foreign policy and great concern for the consumer goods industry; Molotov, in the name of Stalin, demanded vigilance and an increased struggle against enemies within and without.

After the funeral ceremony, Malenkov, Molotov, Beria, Kaganovich, Voroshilov, Mikoyan, Bulganin, and Khrushchev bore Stalin's coffin to the Lenin mausoleum, now called the mausoleum of Lenin and Stalin. The eight bearers were now the most powerful men in the Soviet Union.

STALIN'S HEIRS

Of these eight leaders, Vyacheslav Mikhailovich Molotov personified the union between Party and state: for many years his activity was mainly concentrated on foreign policy. But it is sometimes forgotten that before that Molotov had exercised Party functions for more than ten years; he had been, among other things, Secretary of the Central Committee of the Ukrainian Communist Party (1920) and after that Secretary of the Central Committee of the CPSU and the Moscow Party organization (from 1928 to 1930). Only at the end of 1930 was he given important government posts: in December 1930 he became Chairman of the Council of People's Commissars (Council of Ministers of the USSR) and in May 1939 also People's Commissar (Minister) for Foreign Affairs. In May 1941, after Stalin had officially taken over the chairmanship of the Soviet government, Molotov became his deputy, although he remained Foreign Minister of the USSR until 1949.

Kliment Yefremovich Voroshilov personified for many years the highest link between the Party and the army. After the mysterious death of M. Frunze (1925), the Supreme Commander of the Red Army, Voroshilov became Russian People's Commissar for Defence (1925 to 1941), and in 1940 he was appointed deputy chairman of the Council of People's Commissars. During the war he was a member of the government committee for defence, afterwards he became Chairman of the Allied Control Commission in Hungary.

Lazar Moiseyevich Kaganovich started, like Molotov, by

holding high Party posts for many years before Stalin en-
trusted him with leading positions in the economic sphere,
particularly in industry and transport. From 1925 to 1928
Kaganovich was First Secretary of the Ukrainian Communist
Party, but in 1928 he returned to Moscow as Secretary of the
Central Committee; from 1930 to 1935 he was Secretary of the
Moscow city and regional Committee, as well as being Chairman of the Central Control Commission of the Party. After
Stalin's final victory—from 1935 onwards—he held high economic posts; among other things he was People's Commissar for
Transport (1935 to 1937), for Heavy Industry and for the Oil
Industry (1937 to 1941); in 1944 he was appointed Deputy
chairman of the Council of Ministers. After the end of the
war he was at first Deputy Minister of Foreign Trade; then in
1946 he became Minister of the Building Industry, and in
1947, when the Party regained a dominating position in the
social life of the Soviet Union, he became Party Secretary in
the Ukraine.

Anastas Ivanovich Mikoyan, too, had early held important
positions in the Party. From 1922 to 1926 he was Secretary of
the 'South-East Bureau' of the Central Committee of the Party.
The turning-point for him came in 1926. First he became
People's Commissar for Trade (1926 to 1930), then for Supply
(1930 to 1934), for the Food Industry (1934 to 1938) and for
Foreign Trade (1939 to 1949). In 1937, in addition, he became
Deputy Chairman of the Council of People's Commissars.

Georgi Maximilianovich Malenkov had been active as a
'political worker' during the civil war. While studying at the
polytechnic in Moscow he was Party Secretary there. From
1925 to 1930 he worked in Stalin's secretariat; in official Soviet
publications this was described as 'responsible work in the
Central Committee apparatus'. From 1930 to 1934 Malenkov
was organizing Secretary of the City of Moscow Party committee, from 1934 to 1939, in his capacity- as head of the
Personnel Department of the Central Committee, he supervised the activities of Party officials and local Party organizations. He continued this supervision even after he became
Secretary of the Central Committee in 1939. After the war he
became Deputy Chairman of the Council of Ministers of the
USSR. Apart from Stalin and Khrushchev, he was the only

person who, at the end of the Stalin period, belonged simultaneously to the Politburo, the Central Committee Secretariat, and the 'Orgburo'. He made the main speech at the Nineteenth Party Congress; Stalin had obviously chosen him as his successor.

Nikita Sergeyevich Khrushchev had worked almost exclusively as a Party official. He was born on 16 April 1894 in Kalinovka near Kursk, the son of a miner; in 1918 he joined the Bolshevik Party, in the summer of 1919 he took part in the fighting on the southern front, afterwards he attended the 'rabfak' (the working men's college) in Kiev and in 1929 he was sent to Moscow to study at the *Promakademiya* (Industrial Academy) where he was Secretary of the Party organization.

In 1931 Khrushchev became Secretary of the Baumansky district and afterwards of the Krasnopresnensky district in Moscow; in 1952 he became Second Secretary of the City of Moscow Party Committee. At the beginning of March 1935 he was appointed First Secretary of the Moscow District and City Party Committee. On this occasion *Pravda* described him as an 'outstanding representative of the post-October generation of Party workers who had been trained by Stalin'. On 30 January 1937, the day of the announcement of the verdict in the trial of Trotsky's followers, Khrushchev said in the Red Square in Moscow: 'These infamous nonentities wanted to break up the unity of the Party and of Soviet power. . . . They raised their murderous hands against Comrade Stalin. . . .' He finished with the words: 'Stalin—our hope, Stalin, our expectation, Stalin—the beacon of progressive mankind, Stalin—our banner, Stalin—our will, Stalin—our victory!'[1] In January 1938 Khrushchev became First Secretary of the Ukrainian Party and in the same year he was promoted to candidate membership of the Politburo. At the Eighteenth Party Congress (March 1939) he became a full member of the Politburo.

During the war he was a member of the war council in the special defence district of Kiev, in the south-west sector, on the Stalingrad front, on the southern front, and on the first Ukrainian front. In 1943 he was given the rank of lieutenant-general. Together with Malenkov, Suslov, and Ponomarenko, who was for many years Secretary of the White Russian

[1] *Pravda*, 31 Jan. 1937.

Communist Party, he belonged to the commission for post-war reconstruction. He was the first Soviet party leader to report publicly on anti-Soviet partisan activities in the Ukraine.[1] For a short time, from March to December 1947, Khrushchev was Chairman of the Council of Ministers of the Ukraine. After that he again took over the position of the First Secretary of the Ukrainian Party. In December 1949 Khrushchev was appointed First Moscow Party Secretary and at the same time made a member of the two leading organs, the Politburo and the Central Committee Secretariat. In the Politburo Khrushchev was responsible for agricultural policy. He was particularly prominent in the campaign for merging collective farms into larger units. His rise appeared irresistible—until March 1951.

On 4 March 1951 there appeared a long article by Khrushchev on the 'establishment and organization of collective farms'. In it he expressed himself in favour of reducing the size of the peasants' personal plots. He also expressed himself against single family houses and demanded the building of settlements in which the peasants could live together. These far-reaching demands, however, met with resistance. On 5 March 1951 *Pravda* declared that 'Comrade N. S. Khrushchev's article was intended as a contribution for discussion'.

After this public repudiation of a member of the Politburo the campaign for the extension of collective farm units slackened. But the attack upon Khrushchev had far-reaching consequences for he was given a new field of activity among the highest leaders. Instead of being responsible for agriculture he took over the internal organization of the Party. He thus received an important position in the control of internal Party affairs, a fact which, two years later, after Stalin's death, was to help his advance.

Lavrenti Pavlovich Beria represented the state security service at the highest level. He several times switched from work in the Party to work in the state security service and back again. From 1921 to 1931 he worked in the state security service, first as Deputy Chairman of the Cheka in Azerbaidjan and then in Georgia; after that he became Chairman of the OGPU of Georgia, Deputy Chairman and finally Chairman of

[1] *Pravda*, 16 March 1944.

the OGPU of the whole of the Caucasus. Having been appointed Secretary-General of the Georgian Communist Party in 1931, he was promoted to become Secretary-General of the Party for the whole of Transcausasia in 1932. In 1935 he published his book *On the history of Bolshevik Organization in Transcaucasia*, glorifying Stalin. From 1938 to 1946 he was People's Commissar (Minister) for Internal Affairs and State Security. In 1941 he was appointed Deputy Chairman of the Council of People's Commissars.

Nikolai Alexandrovich Bulganin's political career shows two peculiarities: he alone has never been exclusively a Party official and he has frequently changed his field of activity. From 1927 to 1931 he directed with much success the Moscow enterprise *Elektrosavod*; from 1931 to 1937 he was Chairman of the Moscow Soviet (Lord Mayor) and from 1938 to 1941 Deputy Chairman of the Council of People's Commissars and at the same time director of the State Bank of the USSR. During the war Bulganin was at first a member of the war council on the Western front and then on the second Baltic and the first White Russian fronts. In 1944 he became Deputy Chairman of the Council of Ministers; from 1947 to 1949 he was also Minister of Defence of the USSR. Bulganin is the only one of the higher leaders who over a fairly long period held economic as well as civil and military positions and who also acquired practical economic experience as a managing director and director of the State Bank.

All these eight leaders not only supported Stalin's policy but carried it out. But their activities differed. Malenkov, Kaganovich, and Molotov were particularly involved in the great purge of 1936 to 1938, but Beria, Khrushchev, and Voroshilov also several times expressed themselves publicly in favour of extending it.

Malenkov was a member of the Party commission which dissolved the Association of Old Bolsheviks[1] and during the great purge held a leading position in Stalin's private secretariat.

Molotov signed the notorious decree of 8 April 1935 which declared children over twelve years of age fully responsible under criminal law, and, at the full assembly in March at which Stalin justified the purge ideologically, Molotov made

[1] *Pravda*, 26 May 1935.

the second speech: 'Our duty in the fight against Trotskyists and other vermin, diversionists and spies'—one of the most ferocious speeches made during the purge.[1] In the summer of 1937 Molotov headed a special commission which arrested almost all the Ukrainian party and state leaders.

Kaganovich was one of those who prepared the lists of people who were to be liquidated. The famous telegram signed by Stalin and Zhdanov on the organization of the great purge was sent not only to Molotov but also to Kaganovich.

In January 1937 Khrushchev justified the trial of the Trotskyists before 200,000 people in the Red Square in Moscow. After his appointment as Ukrainian Party Secretary in January 1938 he continued the purge in the Ukraine.

Beria, too, took an active part in the purge, particularly in Georgia. After the Tenth Party Congress of the Georgian Communist Party he wrote in *Pravda* on 5 June 1937: 'Let our enemies know that anybody who even tries to raise a hand against the will of our people, against the will of the Party of Lenin and Stalin, will be crushed and destroyed without mercy'. Even though Beria took over the Ministry of the Interior and the direction of the state security service only towards the end of the great purge, it continued after his appointment.

Voroshilov, whose closest colleagues in the highest ranks of the Red Army were shot on 12 June 1937, on the following day published an order-of-the-day to the Red Army, justifying the executions and praising Stalin.

In contrast to Malenkov, Molotov, Beria, Khrushchev, and Voroshilov, Bulganin and Mikoyan hardly appeared in public in the years 1936 to 1938. Although both were members of the Politburo, they held no leading Party positions; Mikoyan was People's Commissar for the Food Industry and Bulganin Deputy Prime Minister and director of the State Bank.

Although Malenkov, Beria, Khrushchev, and Molotov actively supported Stalin in the great purge it is not improbable that these leaders finally turned against Stalin's despotism, some because they themselves were threatened by him, others because, with leading positions in the state, economic, and military administration, they best realized the contradictions

[1] *Pravda*, 21 April 1937.

of the system and saw that the problems of the country could not be solved by Stalin's methods. Probably none of the senior leaders thought of a change in the system at that time; but they were all in favour of greater personal security and wished to avoid unnecessary friction while seeking for more flexible, modern methods. The first measures taken after Stalin's death provided evidence of this.

THE REORGANIZATION OF THE SOVIET LEADERSHIP

It is surprising how quickly the new leaders set to work both to guarantee their own safety and to cause Stalin to be forgotten. Lenin was given a mausoleum of his own; the Party decided not to build one for Stalin, but to erect a great pantheon outside Moscow for all the founding fathers of the USSR. The fact that not a single Soviet leader published an article in memory of Stalin had an absolutely sensational effect. After all, when Stalin celebrated his sixtieth birthday on 21 December 1939 *Pravda* contained far more pages than usual; all members of the Politburo and many other leading officials praised this or that activity of Stalin's in lengthy articles. On Stalin's seventieth birthday on 21 December 1949 not only did *Pravda* appear in a special edition but also an enormous portrait of Stalin was raised into the sky on captive balloons, illuminated by all the searchlights of the town. A museum to receive the presents of the communist parties of all the world was opened. One and a half years afterwards—in the summer of 1951—*Pravda* was still publishing the names of organizations and institutions which in December 1949 had congratulated Stalin on his seventieth birthday. At Stalin's death *Pravda* restricted itself to the publication of some short commemorative articles by junior officials and some foreign communist leaders, Wilhelm Pieck (East Germany), Enver Hoxha (Albania), Rákosi (Hungary), and Chervenkov (Bulgaria).

One of the most important measures after Stalin's death was the closing down of Stalin's private secretariat headed by General Alexander Poskrebyshev, for it was feared even by the highest officials. The private secretariat had been the centre of Stalin's power; here the Party, the army, and the state had been played off against each other, here purges had been prepared and organized.

The press, of course, said nothing about the end of the private secretariat. Only one fact was noticeable: Alexander Poskrebyshev was never mentioned after Stalin's death. According to an earlier edition of the Soviet Encyclopaedia,[1] Poskrebyshev performed special duties in the Central Committee 'apparatus' as early as 1922; from 1928 onwards he directed the special sector in the Central Committee Secretariat headed by Stalin. In March 1939 he received the Order of Lenin 'for many years of exemplary self-sacrifice in the apparatus of the leading organs of the Central Committee of the CPSU'; in the autumn of 1946 he was appointed major-general. From then until Stalin's death his power was probably second only to Stalin's, although officially he was merely the head of the Legislation Commission in the Supreme Soviet. After Stalin's death he was mentioned only once—in Khrushchev's secret speech, in which he was referred to ironically as Stalin's 'faithful shield-bearer'.

The new Soviet leaders were undoubtedly agreed about discrediting Stalin and closing his private secretariat; but apparently there were serious differences of opinion between 6 and 21 March about the relation between the highest Party and state officials within the leadership and about the highest appointments. There seems to have been a dispute as to whether Malenkov should remain at the head of both Party and state. Of the ten leading figures only Malenkov was mentioned in *Pravda*'s leading article on 6 March; on 7 March it was announced that the changes in the leadership which had taken place immediately after Stalin's death would be considered at a session of the Supreme Soviet on 14 March. On 8 March *Pravda* carried on its second page the photograph of the Nineteenth Party Congress to which reference has already been made.[2] Again in the photograph, published on 9 March on the front page of *Pravda*, of the leaders at Stalin's grave, Malenkov is standing nearest to the coffin.

On 11 March, however, in *Pravda*'s leading article, Malenkov was no longer mentioned by himself but with Beria and Molotov. This happened again on 12 March; on that day Malenkov's double position as Chairman of the Council of Ministers and Secretary of the Central Committee of the Party

---

[1] Vol. 46 published in 1940. [2] See above, p. 27.

was mentioned for the last time. This leads one to suspect that the decision in favour of collective leadership was made between 10 and 12 March.

On 14 March, the day the Supreme Soviet was supposed to meet, it was announced that the meeting had been postponed until the next day. No reason was given, and the cause only later became clear. On 14 March the first full session of the Central Committee since Stalin's death took place, at which Malenkov was relieved of the post of secretary of the Central Committee of the Party ('at his request', said the official announcement). The Central Committee Secretariat was re-organized; apart from Khrushchev—it was certainly no accident that his name appeared first—Mikhail Suslov and the Party theorist, Piotr Pospelov, it consisted of the official in charge of organisations, Nikolai Shatalin, and the then Minister of Security, Semyon Ignatiev.

After a political compromise had thus been reached between the Party leaders and the heads of the government and a personal one between Malenkov and Khrushchev, the session of the Supreme Soviet went off smoothly on 15 March. In the name of the Party and state leaders, as well as of the representatives of Moscow, Leningrad and the Ukraine,[1] Khrushchev proposed Voroshilov as Chairman of the Praesidium of the Supreme Soviet. After that Beria, as expected, proposed Malenkov as Chairman of the Council of Ministers, who in turn announced the composition of the government. Beria, Bulganin, Molotov and Kaganovich were appointed Chief Deputies of the Prime Minister. Beria retained the Ministry of the Interior, Molotov the Foreign Ministry and Bulganin the Ministry of Defence; Kaganovich remained officially without portfolio. Mikoyan, oddly enough, was designated only as an ordinary Deputy Prime Minister, but at the same time continued to be Minister of Domestic and Foreign Trade. Two further members of the Party Praesidium, Saburov and Pervukhin, were appointed respectively to the Ministries for the Machine Building Industry and for Power Stations. Alexei Kosygin became Minister for Light Industry and the production of Consumer Goods. At the same time the number of

[1] This indicated that all these Party organizations were already solidly behind Khrushchev.

ministries was reduced at one stroke from 55 to 25. Malenkov justified this by saying that during Stalin's lifetime a reduction in the number of ministries had been intended, hardly a convincing explanation. The new leaders were clearly disregarding one of Stalin's decisions.

With the session of the Supreme Soviet on 15 March the first differences after Stalin's death came to an end. Malenkov did not become the sole successor of Stalin, and his attempt to place the state above the Party had failed. The post-Stalin leaders had agreed to make the Party at least the equal of the state, not to unite the leadership of both in one person, and, instead of having a successor to Stalin, to set up collective leadership. This did not mean that all members of the Party praesidium had equal rights—the names of Malenkov, Molotov, and Beria were strongly emphasized at first—but for the present no leaders had the power to rule without or against the others. At last, on 21 March, after a week's delay, the resolution of the plenary session of the Central Committee on 14 March, relieving Malenkov of his position as First Party Secretary, was published. The interregnum had come to an end.

CHAPTER III

SILENT DE-STALINIZATION

(March 1953 to February 1956)

In the spring of 1953 the new Soviet leaders faced the task of preserving and modernizing the state that they had inherited from Stalin. His methods of ruling had become unsuitable, and new ways had to be found.

THE REHABILITATION OF THE KREMLIN DOCTORS

During the first fortnight after Stalin's death, the new Soviet leaders, through the changes they had made, had achieved the personal security they required for the unhindered direction of both Party and Government. Further measures, however, were necessary to deprive the state security service of its power and to consolidate the collective leadership.

The first indication of this was given in *Pravda's* leading article on 27 March 1953, which proclaimed collective leadership as a principle of the Party and demanded 'a sense of the modern' from every Party official. The next day an amnesty was declared. This did not indeed extend to persons sentenced for 'counter-revolutionary crimes', the majority of Stalin's prisoners. Nevertheless, all prisoners serving sentences of not more than five years, women with children under ten, pregnant women, and young people under eighteen were to be released, as well as those who had been sentenced for minor military or economic offences. The penal code was to be examined with a view to making it less severe.

On 4 April 1953, scarcely a week after the amnesty and less than four weeks after Stalin's death, it was announced that the Kremlin doctors had been released from detention and rehabilitated. The Ministry of the Interior announced that the Kremlin doctors had been arrested without any legal justification in January. Their confessions had been obtained by members of the investigations department of the former Ministry of

State Security by the use of methods strictly forbidden by Soviet law. Thirteen rehabilitated Kremlin doctors were named, among them six—Professors Vasilenko, Selenin, Preobrazhensky, Popova, Zakurov, and Sherenshevsky—whose arrest had not been reported on 13 January, perhaps because confessions had not at that time been extracted from them.

On the other hand two of the Kremlin doctors who had been arrested in January were missing from the list of 4 April—Professors J. G. Etinger and M. B. Kogan. It remains unclear whether these doctors had died as a result of torture in the meantime or whether they were not rehabilitated in April because in January, that is, before Stalin's death, they had assisted the organs of the state security service in the preparation of the trial and were, therefore, regarded as their accomplices by the new authorities.

It may also be mentioned as curious that Doctor Lydia Timashuk, who in February had still been fêted as the saviour of the fatherland, now had to return her Order of Lenin. On the day of the rehabilitation of the Kremlin doctors the whole Soviet press published a resolution of the Praesidium of the Supreme Soviet revoking the bestowal of the Order of Lenin on Lydia Timashuk 'in view of the state of affairs which had now been discovered'.

The rehabilitation of the Kremlin doctors was a clear sign that the vigilance campaign belonged to the past, and that Stalin's last purge had come to an end: it made plain to responsible officials that they were no longer in danger. It was interesting that the Kremlin doctors were rehabilitated by an announcement of the Ministry of the Interior, an unusual procedure. This suggested that Beria, who had been Minister of the Interior since Stalin's death, had taken a particularly active part in the new policy.

On 6 April *Pravda* published an article with the characteristic title, 'Soviet socialist legality is inviolable'. This attempted to explain the case of the Kremlin doctors. 'How could it happen that a case of provocation was staged in the Ministry of State Security of the USSR, the victims of which were honest Soviet citizens, eminent representatives of Soviet science?' This had happened because the responsible officials of the former Ministry of State Security 'had cut themselves off from the people and the Party and forgotten that they were servants of the people whose duty was to watch over Soviet legality'.

The main responsibility for the wrongful arrest of the Kremlin doctors was put on the then Deputy Minister of State Security (MGB) and Head of the Investigations Department, Mikhail Ryumin, who had been appointed Deputy Minister of Russian State Security in 1952, in preparation for the forthcoming trials as it was supposed.

Apart from Ryumin, whose case, according to *Pravda*, had already been handed over to the courts, the Minister of State Security at the time, Semyon Ignatiev, was also attacked. Ignatiev had been First Secretary of the Party District Committee in Bashkiria during the war. In the autumn of 1946 he was appointed deputy head of a department of the Central Committee Secretariat and in the winter of 1951-2 he was appointed Minister of State Security, as Viktor Abakumov's successor. Ignatiev was now accused of 'political blindness'; he was said to have been 'duped by criminal adventurers'. The form of the removal of Ryumin and Ignatiev suggested that it was not by any means a question of these two people only, but that the investigations department of the State Security Service was to be publicly discredited. Ignatiev, incidentally, turned up again in March 1954 as Party Secretary in Bashkiria; Ryumin was not sentenced until June 1954.

'LEGALITY' AND 'COLLECTIVE LEADERSHIP'

The criticism of the state security service, sacrosanct until then, was supplemented by a great campaign to fortify Soviet legality. *Pravda* announced on 6 April 1953 that the Soviet leadership was 'courageously exposing governmental shortcomings, among them arbitrary and illegal acts, which had been committed by individual officials'. Such things would now be uncompromisingly eradicated. The protection of the constitutional rights of Soviet citizens was the basis 'for the further development and consolidation of the Soviet state'. None would be allowed 'to offend against Soviet legality' and the citizens of the USSR could 'work in tranquillity and security, in the knowledge that their rights as citizens were under the firm protection of Soviet socialist legality'.

At the May Day demonstration of 1953 the unusual slogan

was to be seen: 'The rights of the Soviet citizens, guaranteed by the constitution, are unalterable; they are protected by the Soviet government.'

Simultaneously the Soviet leaders began to suppress the cult of Stalin and to spread the principle of collective leadership. Stalin's name, which during the last few years had appeared on an average forty to sixty times on a single page of *Pravda*, was only rarely mentioned after the beginning of April 1953. On 16 April 1953 *Pravda* carried an article by Slepov, demonstrating that the collective solution of all vital questions was one of the main principles of the Party. 'Conclusions reached by individuals are always, or almost always, partisan.'

In the first weeks after Stalin's death Malenkov tried to extend the powers of ministers and to restrict Party control over the state machine, that is to strengthen the state at the expense of the Party. *Pravda* announced on 26 April that ministers had been granted the right 'in conformity with the decisions of the Soviet Government to determine the use of materials and funds within the competence of their ministry and to decide without reference to others all important questions relating to the activity of the enterprises and institutions under their control'. On 20 May *Pravda* demanded 'that a stop should be put to the lack of independence which had characterized the ministries': the rights of ministers and heads of the central administration should be extended.

THE 'PURGE OF THE PURGERS' IN GEORGIA

Shortly after Ryumin had been arrested and Ignatiev dismissed, startling changes were made in the Soviet Republic of Georgia. On 15 April 1953, A. Mgeladze, until then acting First Party Secretary in Georgia, lost his job and the Georgian Minister of State Security, Rukhadze, was arrested. The latter was succeeded by V. Dekanozov, who had been Soviet ambassador in Berlin at the time of the Hitler-Stalin Pact and one of Beria's closest collaborators in the foreign department of the Ministry of State Security. As successor to Mgeladze, T. A. Mirzkhulava became Georgian Party Secretary. V. M. Bakradze, who had already been Chairman of the Council of Ministers of the Georgian Republic before 1937, was given back this post; he had been dismissed during the great purge and degraded to the position of Minister of Food. Mgeladze and Rukhadze were accused of the same crimes as the members of the central Ministry of State Security in connexion with the affair of the Kremlin doctors; they had 'purposely collected slanderous material against active officials of the Georgian Communist Party and the government of the Republic in order to overthrow it'. Rukhadze had tried 'to fan the flames of discontent among the Soviet people and to kindle feelings of national hostility'. Mgeladze did not even possess 'the elementary capacity . . . to subject the provocative material which Rukhadze had invented to a critical analysis, but, on the contrary, had contributed to his foul activities'.[1]

The accusations related to the Georgian purge of November 1951 to which Khrushchev, in his secret speech at the Twentieth Party Congress, referred as the 'Mingrelian affair'. Thousands of Party and government officials had been arrested at that time because of allegedly separatist activities. The most prominent victims, the Deputy Chairman of the Georgian Council of Ministers, I. Sodelava, the Minister of Agricultural Procurement, M. Baramiya, and the Minister of State Control, A. Rapava, were now officially rehabilitated and reinstated in the government, while the purgers of 1951 were purged in their turn.

Shortly after Stalin's death the first signs of a change in policy towards the nationalities began to appear. The russification campaign which had become more rigorous under Stalin was slackened, and more attention was paid to the non-Russian nationalities. In June 1953 the Central Committee of the Ukrainian Communist Party dismissed the first Party Secretary, Leonid Melnikov, on the grounds that he had made mistakes over the problem of the nationalities. He was succeeded by the Ukrainian, Alexei Kirichenko.[2] Shortly afterwards the Central Committee of the Lithuanian Party also censured 'distortions in the nationalities policy'; the leading posts of the Party, state, and economic machine were in future to be filled mainly by Lithuanian officials.[3] The Central

[1] *Sarya Vostoka*, 18 April 1953.
[2] *Pravda Ukraini*, 13 June 1953.
[3] *Sovietska Litva*, 18 June 1953.

Committee of the Latvian Communist Party used similar phrases to criticize the former nationalities policy and demanded that Latvian officials should be given leading positions in the Party, the government, and the economy.[1]

THE FALL OF BERIA

Trotsky's *Communism or Stalinism*, which appeared in the spring of 1939, contained the following prophetic sentences:

'If a socialist society possesses so little inner elasticity that, in order to save it, one has to fall back on an omnipotent, universal, and totalitarian spy service, then things are in a bad way, particularly if the service is headed by a scoundrel like Yagoda who has to be shot, or like Yezhov, who has to be sent away in disgrace. On whom are they to rely? On Beria? The bell will toll for him too.'

Fourteen years later this prophecy came true. On the evening of 9 July 1953 the Party officials of all big towns in the USSR were called to closed meetings, at which they were informed that Beria, who for many years had been Minister of the Interior of the USSR and a member of the Party Praesidium had been relieved of all Party and government positions as an 'enemy of the Party and state' and had been arrested. The next morning the public was also informed.

It has not yet become clear when and why Beria was overthrown. On 10 June 1953 an article defining policy still mentioned Beria together with Malenkov and Molotov as leaders of the USSR. On 18 June the Chief Public Prosecutor, Safonov, published in *Pravda Ukraini* the strongest article until then against the state security service. He openly attacked 'members of the administration who have permitted themselves unlawful or arbitrary acts' against Soviet citizens. Safonov directed the courts and public prosecutors' offices 'to guard the honour of Soviet citizens by energetically resisting all slanderous attempts through anonymous denunciations' to discredit honest Soviet people.

On 25 June 1953 the Soviet leaders attended a performance of the opera *The Decembrists* in the Bolshoi Theatre in Moscow. On 27 June *Pravda* reported on its front page that of the Party and state leaders, Malenkov, Molotov, Voroshilov, Khrushchev,

[1] *Sovietskaya Latvia*, 28 June 1953.

and Bulganin had attended this performance. Beria was no longer one of them. He must thus have been overthrown between 10 and 25 June.

Several weeks later, on 9 August 1953, it appeared from a news item in *Pravda* that the decision about Beria's dismissal and arrest was taken on 26 June. In fact, Beria was probably arrested some days earlier. But this did not end the quarrels among the leaders, for the population was not informed until two weeks later of this momentous change.

On 10 July *Pravda* announced on its front page that Malenkov had reported on Beria's 'criminal and treasonable acts' at a full session of the Central Committee at the end of June. Beria had tried to undermine the Soviet state, 'in the interests of foreign capital', he had attempted to 'put the Soviet Ministry of the Interior above both Party and Government'. The Central Committee of the CPSU had, therefore, decided to relieve Beria of all Party functions 'as an enemy of the Communist Party and the Soviet people'.

In addition there was published the decision of the Praesidium of the Supreme Soviet of the USSR which relieved Beria of his post as Deputy Prime Minister and Minister of the Interior. In view of his crimes, Beria's case had been referred to the Supreme Court of the USSR.

In *Pravda's* long leading article of the same date entitled 'The unshakeable unity of the Party and Government of the Soviet people' Beria was accused of four crimes:

1. He had disregarded 'the directives of the Central Committee of the Party and the Soviet Government about the consolidation of Soviet legality and the liquidation of a number of cases of illegality and arbitrariness', he had 'slowed down' the execution of these directions and 'tried in a number of cases to distort them'.
2. He had 'done everything to hinder decisions on very important and urgent agricultural questions'.
3. He had tried to 'undermine the friendship of the peoples of the USSR' and had been guilty of 'bourgeois-nationalist deviations'.
4. He had tried 'to place the Ministry of the Interior above the Party and government and to misuse the organs of the Ministry of the Interior at the centre and in the country

against the Party and its leadership and against the Government of the USSR'.

Of these four accusations it has been seen that the fourth was repeatedly emphasized, while the second was never explained. But according to Bernhard Roeder (*Der Katorgan*) there were rumours at that time that Beria planned further relaxations in the collective farm system. The third accusation was only explained much later. In a new textbook on the history of the USSR which appeared in 1958 Beria was accused of having encouraged the nationalist elements in the non-Russian Union Republics, particularly in Georgia. Beria and his co-plotters, it was claimed, had tried to inject the Georgian population with a feeling of national exclusiveness and to tear Georgia away from the united family of the peoples of the USSR.

The decisive issue in Beria's fall was probably the relationship between the state security service on the one hand and the Party and Government on the other. It is likely that Beria supported the first measures of the new leadership and welcomed 'de-Stalinization'. It seems to have been a question not of whether certain reforms should be carried out, but rather of who should be responsible.

Questions of foreign policy probably also played an important part in Beria's fall. Several things seem to indicate that Beria in the spring of 1953 had expressed himself emphatically in favour of an international détente, particularly over the German question. On 25 April *Pravda* had for once reported a speech of Eisenhower's at considerable length, adding favourable comment in a full length front page article, and declaring the readiness of the Soviet Union to discuss thorny questions. On 1 May appeared an obviously inspired article by Ehrenburg called 'Hope', which was written in a conciliatory spirit. And on 24 May *Pravda* again expressed itself in favour of a settlement of international differences at a summit conference. Indeed, between April and June the Soviet press showed an unusual reticence over foreign affairs.

People who held responsible positions in Eastern Germany during this period, but who have since fled to the Federal German Republic[1], reported to the writer that this new policy

[1] Fritz Schenk and Heinz Brandt, a member of the Secretariat of the SED in Berlin.

was carefully noted in East Berlin, with delight by the reformers but with the greatest apprehension by the 'apparachiks'. It was confidentially known in May that Beria supported
these views and that he had chosen Rudolf Herrnstadt to
prepare a change in the SED[1] leadership. After the end of
April the SED leadership was pressed from the Soviet side to
accept the new line: In the economic field to increase the production of consumer goods and in the political field to show
willingness to make concessions to middle class and church
circles and to be more restrained in criticism of the German
Federal Republic. At the end of May and the beginning of
June Soviet pressure increased. When the 'New Course' with
its economic and political concessions was finally proclaimed in
Eastern Germany on 9 June 1953 it still lagged behind Russian
wishes. For the Soviet representatives desired the far-reaching
changes which they had proposed to be announced not
only in a Politburo statement but also at a full session of the
SED.

When the rising in East Berlin started on the evening of 16
June 1953 the SED leaders demanded the immediate intervention of Soviet troops. This request was not at once complied
with. The Soviet representatives had always advised moderation, in accordance, it was said, with Beria's directives. Only at
midday on 17 June, when the rising had already spread far
and wide, were Soviet tanks used. It is thus very probable that
Beria's readiness to make concessions in Germany contributed
to his fall. The struggle over the Soviet attitude towards
Eastern Germany continued after 17 June.

It was striking that the newspapers in the USSR at first
published very little on the rising in Eastern Germany and
made no comments. Only on 25 June—i.e. after Beria's fall—
did meetings take place in the big towns of the USSR at which
the rising was described as a 'foreign mercenaries' affair'. But
even then the Soviet press described the New Course as an
important measure which would bring both parts of Germany
closer together. Ulbricht was by no means in Moscow's favour
at that time. The SED leaders had decided to hold great celebrations on Ulbricht's sixtieth birthday on 30 June and had

---

[1] SED = Socialist Unity Party, the Communist Party of the German Democratic
Republic or Eastern Germany.

prepared an Ulbricht biography, an Ulbricht film, and many Ulbricht memoirs. These preparations were stopped after energetic Soviet protests and the glorifications of Ulbricht that had already been printed were pulped. On 30 June the Soviet leaders restricted themselves to a short congratulatory message which, contrary to customary usage, did not mention Ulbricht's posts. He was not described as 'First Secretary', but as 'one of the best-known organizers and leaders of the SED'.

The importance of the German question in precipitating Beria's fall is also shown by the fact that several weeks later at a meeting of the Politburo of the SED an internal letter from the Soviet Party leaders about the fall of Beria is said to have been read. In it Beria was accused of having demanded a policy of compromise which might have led to the abandonment of Eastern Germany. The existence of a document for internal circulation about the fall of Beria in the form of a circular from the Soviet Party leaders to those of the other Communist countries was confirmed by Seweryn Bialer. Bialer was a member of the Propaganda Department of the Central Committee of the Polish Party and fled to the West in January 1956. According to his report[1] this secret circular contained additional accusations, for instance that Beria had used the security service to strengthen his own position in the Politburo and that he had brought the Kremlin guards under his control and had, with their help, listened to conversations of members of the Party Praesidium. Further he was said to have instructed the head of the state security service in Lwow (who informed the other members of the Praesidium) to watch a member of the Party Praesidium who was there on a visit. In the circular Beria was also accused of ideological mistakes in the past, in particular of historical falsifications in his book *The History of Bolshevik Organization in Transcaucasia*, which had appeared in 1935.

It was interesting that this circular referred to the so-called Leningrad Affair, which was later to play an important part. In the spring of 1949 a great purge had taken place in Leningrad, the victims of which had been the supporters of Zhdanov, the Politburo member and former Party secretary who had died on 30 August 1948. Among those arrested were Vozne-

---

[1] *Hinter dem Eisernen Vorhang*, Munich, No. 10, Oct. 1956.

sensky[1] the former Secretary of the Central Committee responsible for security questions, A. Kuznetsov, and the Leningrad
Party Secretary, A. Popkov, together with a great number of
Party officials and intellectuals. The death of Zhdanov, which
remains unexplained to this day, had resulted in a change in
the balance of power in favour of Malenkov and Beria. At the
time the press had reported the Leningrad Purge. In the secret
circular Beria was now held responsible for the whole thing:
he had fabricated the evidence for the secret trials in which the
flower of the political activists of the city had been executed.
In public, however, Beria's responsibility for all this was in no
way suggested. Only in Khrushchev's celebrated speech at the
Twentieth Party Congress and later in the new Soviet textbook
on the history of the Soviet Union was Beria officially accused
of having staged the Leningrad Affair.

THE EFFECTS OF BERIA'S FALL

One of the most harmless consequences of Beria's fall was the
confiscation and revision of all publications which mentioned
Beria with approval. This led to grotesque results. The sub-
scribers to the Large Soviet Encyclopaedia found in the
twenty-first volume, which was being distributed at that time,
a notice telling them to cut out 'with scissors or a razor' in
volume 5 on pages 21, 22, and 23 the biography and photograph of Beria, so 'that a margin remains for a new page to be
glued in'. As substitutes new articles were provided, including one
about F. W. Bergoltz and a page of pictures of the Bering Straits.

On 10 July 1953 a big public campaign against Beria began.
Party and trade union conferences took place as well as meetings in factories, offices, and collective farms at which Beria's
fall was commented on in the usual way. The newspapers
reported on this under such headings as 'The name of this
traitor will be accursed for ever', 'For enemies there is and will
be no mercy', or 'The dirty plans of the enemy unmasked'.
Beria was said to be a 'bourgeois renegade' who had 'recently
become insolent and impudent, showing his true face', a
'hireling of imperialist forces' and 'an accursed spy of international imperialism'.

At a meeting in the Ministry of Defence, reported in *Pravda*

[1] See above, p. 44.

on 16 July, Bulganin spoke about the Beria case. Several Soviet marshals, including Zhukov and Sokolovsky, welcomed Beria's arrest. The members of the Ministry of Defence adopted a resolution saying that the Soviet army welcomed Beria's condemnation and would faithfully support the Central Committee—a Central Committee, be it observed, which restricted the power of the state security service and had its leaders arrested.

The reports and commentaries on the fall of Beria showed that fundamentally it was not Beria's person which was at stake but the omnipotence of the secret police represented by him. About the destruction of this the Soviet élite was unanimous. The state security service was not to be abolished; it was to become an instrument of the leaders instead of an independent power which threatened them. Therefore, the Party organizations were asked in emphatic terms to keep members of the Ministry of the Interior under constant observation.

Shortly after Beria's fall the dreaded special tribunals of the Ministry of the Interior, set up by Stalin in December 1934, which had played such a fateful part during the great purge, were dissolved. Many prisoners were released from the camps and the situation of those who remained was considerably improved. The economic concerns formerly under the direction of the state police were handed over to the relevant ministries. The Ministers of the Interior of the Ukraine, of Azerbaidjan and Georgia, Meshik, Yemelyanov, and Dekanozov respectively who had only been appointed by Beria on 15 April 1953, were dismissed. The special representative of the Ministry of State Security in the Soviet East, Goglidze, and the First Party Secretary in Azerbaidjan, Mir Bagirov, were also dismissed.[1] In Moscow the Commandant of the Kremlin, Lieutenant-General Spiridonov, the Commandant of Moscow City, Lieutenant-General Smirnov, and the Commander-in-Chief of the Moscow military district, Colonel-General Artemiev, lost their posts. At the beginning of August 1953 the order of precedence of the leaders was changed. Until then Malenkov, Beria, and Molotov had been named first, followed by Voroshilov, Khrushchev, Bulganin, Kaganovich, and Mikoyan. Now Khrushchev moved to third place. This resulted in the

[1] See *Pravda*, 19 July 1953.

following order: Malenkov, Molotov, Khrushchev, Voroshilov, Bulganin, Kaganovich, Mikoyan.

In the second half of December 1953 Beria and his most important supporters were tried. Apart from Beria, Meshik, Dekanozov, the former Minister of State Control, Merkulov, the former Deputy Minister of the Interior of the USSR, Kobulov, and the former head of the 'Department for the examination of particularly important questions in the Ministry of the Interior of the USSR', Vlodzimirsky, were sentenced to death and shot.

The case against Beria and his supporters was presented by the new Chief Public Prosecutor of the USSR, Rudenko, who had been appointed immediately after Beria's fall. Marshal Koniev was chairman of the special tribunal. The other members were General Moskalenko, the Deputy Minister of the Interior, Luniev (who came from the Party hierarchy), and Mikhailov who was then Secretary of the Moscow Party. Beria and his closest collaborators were thus tried by two representatives of the army and two of the Party.

Beria's fall had far-reaching consequences outside the Soviet Union as well. In Eastern Germany the Minister of State Security, Wilhelm Zaisser (a member of the SED Politburo), and the editor-in-chief of the main SED newspaper, *Neues Deutschland*, Rudolf Herrnstadt (a candidate member of the Politburo), were dismissed in July 1953 and expelled from the Politburo and the Central Committee, and later also from the Party. The SED leadership accused them of having followed, at Beria's behest, a policy of compromise which had amounted to a surrender of the achievements of Communist Germany. At the beginning of August a great purge of the North Korean Communist Party took place, of which ten leaders became victims, among then Li-sin-ep, Secretary of the Central Committee and Chairman of the Commission for People's Control, Pak-si-won, Deputy Personnel-Chief in the Party leadership, and Pek-han-bok, head of the inspection department of the Ministry of State Security. Shortly afterwards it was announced that the Deputy Minister of North Korea, Hokay, had committed suicide. These events suggest that Beria had been prepared to make considerable concessions in Korea as well as in Eastern Germany.

THE 'THAW' IN LITERATURE

In the Stalin era Soviet writers had been forced into the strait-jacket of 'socialist realism', described as the technique of Soviet literature. The concept was used in the press for the first time in 1932. It bound artists to portray reality in its revolutionary development and to re-educate the working population in the spirit of socialism. This meant that Soviet writers were not allowed to represent reality as it was, but as it should be, or rather as the Party policy in force at the time would like it to be.

The concept of 'party-mindedness' which was linked with socialist realism goes back to an article by Lenin, called 'Party organizations and Party literature'. In this Lenin said that literary activity must 'become a constituent part of organized, planned Party work'. Lenin wrote this paper in 1905 at a time when the Bolshevik Party—except during the few months of the revolution of 1905—was working illegally under the conditions imposed by the tsarist autocracy, and he was referring to Party literature. This, however, did not prevent the leadership under Stalin from applying the term 'party-mindedness' forty years later, in the Soviet state, to the whole of literature. After the war, on Zhdanov's initiative, several resolutions were passed on questions of art and literature, binding all writers and artists to party-mindedness.

After Stalin's death writers and artists hoped that they could free themselves from the strait-jacket of socialist realism, or at least from the methods imposed by Party control. The famous Soviet composer, Aram Khachaturian denounced 'thoughtless tendencies towards adaptation' and said: 'I believe that the time has come to change the existing system of the official supervision of composers. Further, the musical authorities must desist from the harmful practice of interfering in the artistic activities of the composer. Creative problems cannot be solved by bureaucratic methods.'[1]

Shortly afterwards Ilya Ehrenburg attacked the Party regimentation of literature in the periodical *Znamya*.[2] The author was 'not a machine which mechanically registered events. He did not write a book only because he was a member

---

[1] See *Sovietskaya Muzyka*, No. 9, 1953.   [2] No. 10, 1953.

of the Union of Soviet Writers and had to give an account of why he had been silent for so long.' It was much better to criticize authors who had written books without inspiration. 'In art statistics do not play the same part as in industry.' Though the writer received a social order (in the sense of ordering goods) from the people, the concept 'social' had disappeared and the concept 'order', which came from the world of business, had remained.

Ehrenburg implied that he had waited for Stalin's death to write with such frankness: 'Only after mature reflection did I decide to publish this essay on the tasks of the writer. I considered carefully whether this was the right moment to put forward this complex of questions for discussion and finally came to the conclusion that the moment had arrived, because in the Soviet Union the time is ripe for great literature. Our strength until now lay in the description of what had been achieved. Through describing those who achieve Soviet literature must now bear fruit.'

The critic, W. Pomerantsev, writing in the periodical *Novy Mir*, put in the place of party-mindedness and socialist realism another principle—that of sincerity: 'Honesty is what in my opinion is lacking in some of our books and plays. . . . Insincerity is not necessarily the same as lying, for stiltedness is also insincere.' Dialogue in Soviet novels was often 'pure tirading in the style of a gramophone record'. As an example Pomerantsev quoted a mechanic in a machine and tractor station who with the girl he loves dreams of how they can get the stock back into order, and the hero of a play who gives his daughter a watch because the standard of living has gone up. 'One only talks like that at a meeting.' As a precaution Pomerantsev put these words into the mouth of the other party to the discussion, but his own opinion was not very different: 'I do not like the sound of machines in literature, nor monotonous subject matter, nor the pathos of insipid tales. I need more books written with earnestness and warmth.' He, too, had new hope after Stalin's death: 'I often think about genuine works of literature: in a year or two we may have reached the stage when we can present them.' At that time many writers were already at work on such books. The most famous were Ilya Ehrenburg's *The Thaw*, Vera Panova's *The Seasons*, and

Leonid Zorin's play *Guests*. The thing common to all of them is criticism of conditions in the USSR and of its ruling class.

Ilya Ehrenburg contrasts two types: A time-serving painter who adapts himself to the Party line of the moment, gains success and money but feels himself to be without talent, and an unsuccessful but talented artist who has the sympathy of the author. For the first time in Soviet literature the terror of 1936 to 1938 is mentioned: The young Dmitri, whose step-father was arrested, describes how his friends and schoolmates avoided him for that reason. He had never forgotten this.

Vera Panova's *The Seasons* also reveals the evil sides of Soviet life. The director of an enterprise, Bortashevich, lives in undeserved luxury, is exposed as a profiteer and commits suicide; another functionary, Retkovsky, defrauds the state; the chairman of the city soviet or mayor is a weakling who kow-tows before his superiors.

The strongest criticism is expressed by Leonid Zorin in his play *Guests*. The old revolutionary Kirpichev, his daughter Varvara, and the journalist Trubin are the good characters; they live through the transformation of Soviet society with amazement and bitterness. Kirpichev's son, Piotr, the head of a department in the Ministry of Justice is an opportunist greedy for power. 'The state apparatus is like an orchestra,' Zorin makes him say, 'if you want to play in it you must watch the conductor and follow his beat.' In a conversation between Varvara and Trubin, Zorin reveals Soviet society as dominated by a new class.

Criticism of bureaucratic shortcomings was not in itself new. What was new and revolutionary was that these were no longer portrayed as the remains of capitalism but as typical products of Soviet society.

The government at first deliberately supported the critics because it hoped reciprocally for their support in the changes which had been planned. But when it became clear that the writers were not attacking individual faults but the system, the Party tried to harness them again. An organized campaign against rebellious authors began on 25 May 1954 with an article in *Pravda* entitled 'Under the banner of socialist realism': It was written by Alexei Surkov, Secretary of the Soviet Writers' Union, a Party member since 1925 and a member of

the Commission for Foreign Affairs of the Council of Nationalities of the Supreme Soviet. Surkov attacked Pomerantsev in
particular because he offended against the principle of party-
mindedness and the most important postulates of socialist
realism. Apart from *The Thaw*, *The Seasons*, and Zorin's *Guests*,
the plays *When we are Beautiful* by F. Panfiorov and *Decent
People* by Surov were also described as 'ideologically harmful'. A
few days later Vera Panova was accused of having 'paid exaggerated attention' to the darker sides of Soviet reality in *The Seasons*.

Zorin's play was forbidden because it 'libelled Soviet
reality'. The chief editor of the periodical *Octyabr*, Fyodor
Panfiorov, was dismissed at the beginning of June 1954, and
the chief editor of *Novy Mir*, Alexander Tvardovsky, at the
beginning of August. *Kommunist* commented on this with
amazing frankness: 'It is enough if the attention paid to
ideological questions slackens in any one sector, as in the case of
the direction of the Writers' Union. Immediately, new views
and theories which are hostile to us appear.'[1]

The second Soviet Writers' Congress (14 to 25 December
1954) was to establish the new Party position. The official
address of welcome from the Party leaders demanded a confession of socialist realism from writers and reminded them of
their obligations towards the Party, without, however, using
the term 'party-mindedness'. But it turned out that a complete
return to Stalin's regimentation of art was no longer possible.
A strong opposition had formed, whose chief spokesmen at the
congress were Sholokhov and Ovechkin. Although they were
obliged to submit they could no longer be silenced.

THE NEW COURSE IN ECONOMIC POLICY

It was hardly an accident that the advance and retreat of
the thaw in literature more or less coincided with the great
experiment of the new course in economic policy. In his last
book Stalin had described the priority of heavy industry as the
unshakeable foundation for the further development of the
USSR and had demanded that normal trade should be replaced by a centrally controlled exchange of goods. Already on
14 May there was, however, the first indication that the post-
Stalin leaders had no intention of keeping to these directives.

[1] No. 9, 1954.

An article in *Pravda* defining policy on the Party teaching courses passed over Stalin's 'Economic Problems' in silence. On 29 May *Pravda* reprimanded those who underrated trade, and among the formulations published on 26 July 1953 on the occasion of the fiftieth anniversary of the foundation of the Bolshevik Party was one saying: 'The Party is responsible for satisfying to the full the growing requirements of the Soviet people.'

On 8 August 1953, Prime Minister Malenkov officially announced the new consumer goods programme before the Supreme Soviet. 'The Soviet people has the right to demand from us, and particularly from those engaged in producing goods for the masses, durable, well-finished, high-class goods.' Malenkov did not attack the principle of the priority of heavy industry, but he said that modern industry now existed in the Soviet Union and that light industry and the production of consumer goods could therefore be more encouraged. 'The Government and Central Committee consider it necessary . . . to raise the targets for the production of goods for the masses very considerably.' The supply of food and industrial goods to consumers was to be notably improved. A pre-requisite for this was above all the development of agriculture, which supplied food to the population and raw materials to light industry. The material interest of the collective farms and their peasants in production would have to be increased. At Malenkov's suggestion the Supreme Soviet resolved to raise the prices paid for contractual sales and compulsory deliveries, and to remit arrears of agricultural taxes. Trading by collective farms, moreover, was to be developed, and the sale of their surplus produce organized.

Simultaneously, a new attitude towards the individual holdings of peasants on collective farms was announced. The kolkhoz statutes of 17 February 1935 entitled every kolkhoz peasant to a private holding of a quarter to half a hectare for his personal use, as well as one cow, up to two calves, one sow with piglets, up to ten sheep and goats, and up to twenty beehives in addition to poultry and rabbits. Under Stalin even this modest personal property was regarded with suspicion. Malenkov openly admitted that in the last few years the receipts of the collective farm peasants from their individual holdings and the number of cows which they owned had decreased. This, however, was in contradiction to the 'policy of our Party with regard to collective farming'. Deliveries from, and the money tax on, the holding of each collective farm peasant were considerably reduced and arrears of taxes from past years were remitted.

The importance of the new economic course announced by Malenkov on 8 August 1953 went far beyond a few practical economic questions. Fundamentally it was a withdrawal from important Stalinist principles: in place of the predominance of heavy industry was put the demand that heavy and light industry should be developed at the same rate; instead of the gradual replacement of trade by a direct exchange of goods which Stalin had called for, the extension of trade was proclaimed; material stimuli were stressed more than ever; the private property of the peasants on collective farms was not to be reduced.

In his big speech on the new policy Malenkov hardly mentioned the organizations of the Communist Party. This intentional snub presumably induced the Party hierarchy to take a greater interest in the New Course. Three weeks later a full session of the Central Committee was called which must be regarded as one of the most important events since Stalin's death. The Central Committee met from 3 to 7 September; the chief item on the agenda was agricultural policy; Khrushchev made the main speech.

He refrained from the success reports usual in the Stalin era and concentrated instead on shortcomings in agriculture. The area growing potatoes was not even half that existing before the war, while the area growing other vegetables had decreased by more than 250,000 hectares compared with 1940. The decrease in livestock was sensational: The number of horses had fallen from 38·2 million in 1916 to 21 million in 1941, and now amounted to 15·3 million. At the beginning of 1953 there were 3·5 million less cows than in 1941 and 8·9 million less than in 1928.

Khrushchev was particularly severe in his criticism of the administration of Soviet agriculture. Agricultural planning involved too much superfluous calculation of figures and preparation of accounts. Out of 350,000 experts only 5 per cent. worked in collective farms, while most of them 'hang about in various offices'. As a result, there was a serious shortage of specialists in the collective and state farms. Only one-sixth of the heads of collective farms had been to a secondary technical school or college, while scarcely a third of the directors of Soviet state farms had had a secondary technical education. The heads of collective and state farms were constantly dismissed because of unsatisfactory work, but many of them were subsequently forced upon other collective organizations as chairmen.

The September meeting of the Central Committee adopted a number of measures designed to increase agricultural production. The delivery system was simplified by the introduction of 'hectare norms'. Each collective farm had to deliver to the state a fixed quantity of vegetable products per hectare of arable land and a fixed quantity of animal products per hectare of pasture land. The state delivery and contract prices were considerably increased. The arrears of payment from the collective farms to the state were cancelled. A hundred thousand agricultural experts and 50,000 Party officials were to be sent to improve the collective farms from a political as well as an economic point of view.

Concessions were also made to the collective farm peasants. Khrushchev, who in March 1951 had still favoured the restriction of 'the size of personal plots to 10 to 15 hectares' and who had wanted to put the personal holdings of these peasants outside the collective farms, now unexpectedly spoke in favour of personal holdings within them: 'Only people who cannot understand the policy of the Party and the policy of the Soviet state think that the existence of productive cattle owned by individual peasant families on collective farms represents any danger to the socialist order. An end must also be put to the idea that it is disgraceful for a factory or white collar worker to have his own cattle.'[1]

On 28 October 1953 a resolution was adopted, prohibiting the prosecution before the courts of peasants who failed to fulfil their quota of work on the collective farms. This resolution, signed by the Praesidium of the Supreme Soviet of the USSR,

[1] *Izvestia*, 15 Sept. 1953.

was passed on to all local authorities but was not published.[1]

The second important result of the September session was a change in the balance of power in favour of the Party machine. Until then, the New Course had been announced by representatives of the state: now Party officials intervened. The resolution of the full meeting in September contained an important passage about improving Party organization in the countryside.

The third result of the September plenary session was of crucial importance for the future. Nikita Khrushchev was officially appointed First Secretary of the Central Committee. That was an important concession on the part of Malenkov and his followers to Khrushchev and the forces in the Party apparatus behind him. *Pravda* announced the appointment in enormous letters on the front page.[2] Until then, Khrushchev had been only one of the secretaries. The September full session was a landmark in his career.

A few weeks later Khrushchev made use of his new power. The first sign of it was a sensational and decisive change among the Leningrad party leaders. In Khrushchev's presence the Leningrad Party Secretary, Vassili Andryanov, was dismissed on 28 November 1953 without a reason being given. Frol Kozlov, the third Party secretary of the Leningrad Region, became his successor.

Andryanov had been one of Malenkov's closest collaborators since 1939. In 1946 he became deputy head of the new council for collective farm questions of the Council of Ministers of the USSR. At the same time he was chairman of the foreign affairs committee of the Council of the Union of the Supreme Soviet of the USSR.

In 1949 Frol Kozlov was Party secretary at the great Kirov factory in Leningrad. In 1950 he became First Secretary of the City of Leningrad Party Committee. At the Nineteenth Party Congress in October 1952 he was promoted to membership of the Central Committee. To the public he was known above all for his strong article in the second number of *Kommunist* in January 1953 in favour of a purge. Very soon after his appointment Boris Meissner pointed out that Kozlov stood close to

---

[1] Late in Jan. 1955 it was condemned in *Partinaia Zhizn* (No. 2, 1955), a Party periodical, as having impaired labour discipline.

[2] 13 Sep. 1953.

Khrushchev.[1] This was confirmed by Kozlov's meteoric rise during the following years.

Soon after the Leningrad *coup d'état* there was a change in the leadership of the Armenian Communist Party. In the presence of the Central Committee Secretary, Piotr Pospelov, all the three secretaries, at their head Arutinov, were dismissed. Grigori Arutinov, who had been First Secretary of the Armenian Central Committee, had also been a candidate member of the Central Committee of the CPSU since 1939 and a full member since 1952. During the discussions in 1950–1 about agro-towns, a pet project of Khrushchev's, he had opposed the merging of collective farms, i.e. Khrushchev's policy.

The changes in Leningrad and Armenia were little noted at the time, because they were overshadowed by propaganda for the New Course and the consumer goods programme. But they were of decisive importance in strengthening Khrushchev's position and helped to prepare Malenkov's fall. In the middle of September 1953 the Soviet Ministry for Trade was divided into two Ministries, one for Internal and one for External Trade. Mikoyan, who until then had been head of the combined ministry, became Minister for Internal Trade. The fact that a Soviet leader of Mikoyan's stature was given this post shows how much importance the post-Stalin rulers attributed to this field. In the Stalin era trade had had a shadowy existence and Stalin wanted gradually to abolish it altogether: now an expansion of trade was announced.

On 17 October 1953 Mikoyan made a speech formulating policy on 'measures for the further development of actual turnover and the improvement of the organization of state trading in farm produce'. His demands were incorporated in items of the Party and Government resolutions of 23 September, 18 and 30 October 1953 on the development of Soviet trade and of the production of consumer goods and food.

Now at last the full extent of the New Course became visible. These resolutions meant a complete change of the Five-Year Plan (1951–5) adopted while Stalin was still alive. The Plan had envisaged an 80 per cent. increase in the production of clothing, whereas now the increase was to be one of 240 per cent. over the same period. The planned increases in production

[1] *Osteuropa*, Feb. 1954.

were raised from 90 to 230 per cent. for meat, from 70 to 190 per cent. for butter, from 70 to 180 per cent. for textiles. The production of industrial goods for the needs of the population was to be raised during the next three years—i.e. by 1956—by almost 50 per cent. Mikoyan openly said that there was a discrepancy between the production of goods and the actual needs of the population in the Soviet Union: this was to be eliminated by a steep rise in the production of consumer goods.

Particularly interesting was what Mikoyan had to say on the problem of competition and the use of foreign experience. Without beating about the bush he declared that competition 'in capitalist countries had brought about by no means bad examples of the organization and technique of trade and of service particularly for the more prosperous customer'. It was important 'for us to take over what is necessary from the organization of trade and the service of the customer in the best firms in capitalist countries; we should not be afraid of employing this useful experience, but master it in the interest of the masses'.

Astonishingly enough, Mikoyan suggested the import of food and consumer goods for the masses from abroad. The Soviet Union had grown richer, and therefore it should import from abroad the consumer goods which were greatly sought after by the population.

The Ministry of Trade was ordered to carry out exact inquiries into the preferences of the population. The trading organizations were to call together meetings of consumers and to transmit the wishes of Soviet citizens to the relevant industrial ministries. 'The speed with which we shall make up for lost time will no doubt surprise all the sceptics', said Mikoyan hopefully.

THE DIFFICULTIES OF THE NEW POLICY

The thirty-sixth anniversary of the October Revolution, 7 November 1953, was entirely given over to the New Course. Soviet workers were asked to support the new policy 'which was directed towards a quick rise in the standard of living of the working class, of the collective farmers, and indeed the whole people'.

The realization of the new economic course, however,

encountered great difficulties. The consumer goods programme had been, as it were, grafted on to the current Five-Year Plan. As the official economic plans remained unchanged the directors of the various establishments found themselves in a dilemma. If they fulfilled the tasks laid down in the Plan they were unable to produce consumer goods in addition. If, instead, they diverted part of their capacity to the production of consumer goods they were unable to fulfil the Five-Year Plan. Another fact acted as a brake. For almost a quarter of a century the absolute priority of heavy industry had been hammered so firmly into the minds of Party officials and economic authorities that the changeover in favour of the production of consumer goods—in the days of Stalin this was contemptuously called 'the consumer's point of view'—met with opposition in many circles. In addition, the cumbersome machine of the over-centralized economic system was not fit for the new tasks.

The Soviet leaders tried to overcome these difficulties by appointing on 21 December 1953 five senior officials with a great deal of experience in the economic field to advise the Praesidium of the Council of Ministers, which until then had consisted of Malenkov,[1] Molotov,[2] Bulganin,[2] Kaganovich,[2] and Mikoyan.[3] All five had had an academic technical education and had worked for many years as engineers and factory managers before they were entrusted with the direction of certain economic ministries.

The new five were: Maxim Saburov who from 1941 to 1944 and again since 1949 had been chairman of the State Planning Commission of the USSR, Mikhail Pervukhin who had been Minister of Power Stations (1939–42), of the Chemical Industry (1942–50), and of Power Stations and Electric Power after 1953. Ivan Tevosyan who had been Minister of the Shipbuilding Industry and then from 1940 Minister of the Iron and Steel Industry. Vyacheslav Malyshev who had been Minister of Medium Machine Building (1940–2), of the Armoured Car Industry (1942–9), of Heavy and Transport Machine Building (1945–7) of the Shipbuilding Industry (1950–3), and after Stalin's death again of Medium Machine Building, Alexei Kosygin who had for many years been the head of Soviet light industry, first as Minister of the Textile Industry

---

[1] Chairman.   [2] First Deputy Chairman.   [3] Deputy Chairman.

(1939–40), then briefly Minister of Finance and finally after Stalin's death Minister of Light Industry (including foodstuffs) and Mass Commodities.

The fate of the New Course depended mainly on achieving a rapid increase of agricultural production. Soon it became clear that the hopes which had been placed on the September reforms had not been realized. In spite of some relief measures agriculture was in a situation which could only be described as catastrophic. The new leaders had several meetings in the Kremlin with agricultural officials; the most important of these conferences were with the functionaries of the machine and tractor stations (24–28 January) and of the directors of state farms (3–6 February). Both conferences were attended by about 2,000 officials, who reported with astonishing frankness about the situation in the countryside. On both occasions all the members of the Party Praesidium were present from morning to evening (with the exception of Molotov, who was at the Foreign Ministers' conference of the Big Four in Berlin). Probably it became clear to them at these meetings that they would have to use other means to increase agricultural production. At the next full session of the Central Committee at the end of February 1954, Khrushchev announced the great virgin lands programme, according to which 2·3 million hectares in Siberia and Kazakhstan were to be brought under the plough for the first time in 1954, and an additional 10·7 million hectares in 1955. The object of increasing the extent of arable land was, according to Khrushchev, to satisfy the needs of the whole population, to add to the state grain reserves, to raise the production of fodder grains so that the number of cattle could be increased, and to expand grain exports. The newly developed land was to provide a further 18 to 19·5 million tons of grain, of which 10·5 to 11 million tons was to come from the Russian Republic and a little more than 8 million tons from the Union Republic of Kazakhstan.

The joint resolution of the Party and state leaders about the development of new land in 1954 and 1955, published on 28 March, laid down that the greater part of Soviet annual production of agricultural machines, among them 10,000 combine harvesters and 120,000 tractors, should be made available for the virgin lands programme.

Paradoxical though it may sound, it was in fact the virgin lands programme which made the fulfilment of the consumer goods programme more difficult. The economic policy of the Soviet Union was caught in a vicious circle: in order to realize the consumer goods programme food production had to be increased; the virgin lands programme was decided upon with this purpose in view, but in order to carry it out successfully the production of agricultural machines had to be increased; this task could only be accomplished by heavy industry, i.e. the very industrial sector which was to play a decisive part in the consumer goods programme. As it was impossible for a long time to realize both programmes simultaneously, it would have to be decided sooner or later which of them was to have priority.

THE TUG OF WAR IN THE SUMMER OF 1954

The controversy about the consumer goods programme split the Soviet rulers into two groups. To the one belonged Malenkov, Mikoyan, Kosygin, Ivan Benediktov, who was Minister for Agriculture, and the officials at the lower and middle levels of the economic machine who were connected with these circles. They tried to save what was possible of the consumer goods programme. To the second group belonged Khrushchev, Bulganin, then Minister of Defence, his Deputy, Marshal Zhukov, Saburov, and the Party officials associated with them, as well as an important number of the Soviet army leaders. They pleaded more and more frankly for a return to the priority of heavy industry.

Until the middle of July 1954 the Malenkov group appears to have had the upper hand. In the second half of July its influence was still strong enough for it to edit a speech of Khrushchev's at the Party Congress of Czech Communists in Prague according to its own discretion and to publish it in an altered version in *Pravda*. Two paragraphs were completely omitted, among them the statement: 'We were even quicker than the capitalist camp and invented the hydrogen bomb before they had it; and we, the Party of the working class, we know the importance of this bomb.' An alleged quotation from Lenin which Khrushchev produced, 'as long as there is capitalist encirclement any understanding will be very difficult and complicated', had also disappeared. The following remarks of Khrushchev were formulated much more carefully in *Pravda*: 'We know that bourgeois politicians are idle gossips. They gamble on people with weak nerves. They think they can intimidate us. But we cannot be frightened because, if they know what a bomb is, so do we.' These corrections were politically significant. They show that Khrushchev was not yet able to enforce his will without hindrance. This is also supported by the fact that the main speeches at the full session of the Central Committee on 27 June 1954 on agricultural questions were not made by Khrushchev, but by the expert ministers, the Minister of Agriculture, Benediktov, the Minister of State Farms, Kozlov, and the Minister of Agriculture for the RSFSR, Pavel Lobanov.

In June and July 1954 the internal dispute about whether the New Course was to be continued or not became increasingly sharp. As the Party functionaries were wholly in favour of the virgin lands campaign, but large sections of the state and economic officials continued to demand the continuation of the New Course, this controversy had developed into a struggle for power between the groups personified by Khrushchev and Malenkov respectively. During this struggle the trial of Ryumin[1] took place in Moscow from 2 to 7 June 1954 after a delay of one and a half years. The sentence, however, was made public only on 23 July 1954.

On 17 July 1954 the award of 'medals for the development of virgin land' was announced. On 12 August *Pravda* published a sharp criticism by the Soviet Party leaders of certain ministries, because the transport of agricultural machines to the virgin land regions had lagged behind requirements; this was said to have endangered the virgin lands programme. This criticism was directed directly against the Ministry of Agriculture headed by Benediktov. It is interesting that it was signed by the Party leaders alone and not by the Council of Ministers as well.

The 17 August 1954 was probably the day of the victory of Khrushchev's group in the Party 'apparatus', and, from the point of view of economic policy, the date of the beginning of the retreat from the New Course. A declaration by the Central Committee and the Council of Ministers on the further

[1] See above, p. 65.

continuation of the virgin lands programme was published
on that day. This not only laid stress on the virgin lands
programme afresh; at the same time it revealed a highly
important change in the balance of power within the Soviet
Union.

Until the summer of 1954 all joint declarations of the state
and Party leadership appeared as 'resolutions of the Council of
Ministers and the Central Committee'. The state 'apparatus'
was invariably mentioned *before* the Party's 'apparatus'. Since
17 August 1954, however, all joint declarations without exception have been published as 'resolutions of the Central Committee and the Council of Ministers'. On 2 September the Party
organizations were called upon in a leading article in *Pravda* to
intensify their activity in the government departments.

THE RETREAT FROM THE NEW COURSE

In the autumn of 1954 the fiasco of the New Course became
apparent. Less and less was heard of the consumer goods programme announced with such pomp in the autumn of 1953.
On 23 September 1954 Khrushchev said openly in an interview
with Professor Bernal that heavy industry would continue to
have priority in the Soviet economy. But the interview was not
published until three months later, on 24 December 1954; by
the end of September the Khrushchev faction was probably
strong enough to speak openly against the consumer goods
programme, but not yet powerful enough to publish their views.
The decisive phase of the controversy probably occurred between the end of September and the end of December

During these dramatic three months several events took place
which justify this theory. On the occasion of the fifth anniversary of the foundation of the Chinese People's Republic in
October 1954, a Soviet delegation headed by Khrushchev,
Bulganin, and Mikoyan went to Peking. It had discussions
there with the Chinese government and expressed its readiness
to grant China a long-term credit and to further China's
industrialization by the delivery of factory equipment and the
construction of factories. Soviet heavy industry was thus
placed under additional obligations from which the Soviet
leaders could not withdraw. This operated in favour of the
opponents of the New Course. In the slogans for 7 November

1954 the phrases about the consumer goods industry were already considerably toned down, and Saburov, in his ceremonial speech on the occasion of the state holiday, again described heavy industry as the very foundation of the Soviet economy. Three days later Khrushchev demonstrated the increase in his strength by the so-called edict on religion of 10 November which was not, as usual, signed by the Central Committee, but by Khrushchev alone.

The next blow against the Malenkov group was the trial[1] of the former Minister of State Security, Viktor Abakumov, in which the Leningrad Affair was brought into the open. Abakumov had been for many years a collaborator of Beria and Malenkov. He had worked for several years with Malenkov in Stalin's private secretariat, became People's Commissar for Internal Affairs and thus Beria's deputy in February 1941, and in October 1946 Minister of State Security; in 1951 or 1952 his place had been taken by Semyon Ignatiev.[2]

The trial of Abakumov and five of his colleagues discredited the leading members of the state security service. Like Ryumin and Ignatiev in April 1953 and Beria in July and December 1953, Abakumov was now accused of arresting upright Party members and intellectuals from whom he had extorted false confessions by criminal methods of investigation. But whereas the accusations against Ryumin, Ignatiev, and Beria had been couched in general terms, Abakumov was openly held responsible for the arrests in the spring of 1949 in the Leningrad Affair. This must have been a red light for Malenkov, since he had led the political fight against the Zhdanov group in the spring of 1949 and might be considered as the instigator of the Leningrad Affair.[3] Abakumov and three[4] of his collaborators were sentenced to death. Two other officials of the state security service, Chernov and Browermann, were sentenced to fifteen and twenty-five years respectively in a labour camp.

The report on the Abakumov trial appeared in the Soviet

---

[1] 14–19 Dec. in Leningrad.   [2] See above, p. 65.

[3] According to Bialer, a secret circular sponsored by the Party leaders went round in Feb. 1955 in which Malenkov was held responsible for the Leningrad Affair.

[4] The former head of the department in the Ministry for State Security which investigated particularly important cases, Leonov, and the two former deputy heads of this department, Komarov and Likhachov.

press on 24 December 1954, together with the interview of 25 September in which Khrushchev stressed the priority of heavy industry. This sealed the fate of the Malenkov faction. From now on the Khrushchev group determined events. On 10 January 1955 there appeared a second Party resolution, signed by Khrushchev only, which changed the date of the memorial day for Lenin. On 24 January 1955 Dmitri Shepilov justified the return to the priority of heavy industry in *Pravda*. Heavy industry was 'the granite foundation of all branches of the Soviet economy'; it was the general line of the Party to carry on the development of heavy industry at a greater pace. On the same day, Mikoyan, one of the firmest defenders of the New Course, lost his post as Minister for Internal Trade, but remained Deputy Prime Minister. On the next day, 25 January, Khrushchev, at the full session of the Central Committee, accused the supporters of the consumer goods programme—without, however, mentioning the name of Malenkov—of 'right-wing deviations', and compared their views with those of Rykov and Bukharin.

MALENKOV'S RESIGNATION

The form of Malenkov's resignation on 8 February 1955 was unusual for Soviet Russia. In the presence of all the members of the Praesidium of the Party, the Chairman of the Council of the Union, at a meeting of the Supreme Soviet, read Malenkov's request to be allowed to resign. Malenkov asked to be relieved of the functions of Chairman of the Council of Ministers of the USSR and to be replaced by 'another comrade with greater administrative experience'. After this he made the following self-critical statement: 'I recognize clearly that my insufficient experience in local work has an unfavourable effect on the fulfilment of the complicated and responsible duties of the Chairman of the Council of Ministers, as well as the fact that I have not had the opportunity of being directly responsible for individual branches of the economy in another ministry or any other economic body. I also regard it as my duty to state in this declaration that today, when the Communist Party of the Soviet Union and the workers of our country are concentrating their efforts on the rapid development of agriculture, I recognize particularly clearly my responsibility for the unsatisfactory situation which had developed in agriculture, because earlier, for a number of years, I had been entrusted with the task of controlling and directing the activity of the central agricultural organs and the activities of the local Party and Soviet organizations in the field of agriculture.' Thus Malenkov did not admit any political or ideological errors, but only a lack of experience in the running of the economy. His statement ended with a declaration of support for the priority of heavy industry, and the promise to carry out conscientiously, under the direction of the Central Committee of the Party and the Government, all the tasks which he might be given in a new field of work.

At the suggestion of Alexander Pusanov, then Prime Minister of the RSFSR, Malenkov's request for resignation was accepted. The American journalist, Kingsbury Smith, who attended the meeting, reported that most members of the Supreme Soviet were completely taken by surprise; but when the vote was taken they all promptly raised their hands in agreement. Only one woman omitted to do so, in Kingsbury Smith's view because she had not had time to recover from the shock.

Then, on behalf of the Central Committee of the Party, Khrushchev proposed that the new Prime Minister be Nikolai Bulganin, who had until then been First Deputy Prime Minister and Minister of Defence of the USSR. On this occasion, Khrushchev could not praise Bulganin too highly: 'We all know Nikolai Alexandrovich Bulganin as a faithful son of the Communist Party, who puts all his energy into the service of the Soviet people. As a worthy pupil of the great Lenin and one of the closest colleagues of Lenin's heir, J. V. Stalin, Comrade Bulganin is known as an outstanding Party and state official.' In particular, Khrushchev praised Bulganin's 'great experience in the political, state, economic, and military fields'. Marshal Zhukov took Bulganin's place as Minister of Defence while Malenkov was degraded to be Deputy Prime Minister and appointed Minister of Power Stations.

Malenkov's fall had an interesting sequel. One year earlier, in a speech on 12 March 1954, he had justified the rejection of the policy of the Cold War on the grounds that it might lead to a new holocaust which, in view of the technical means offered by modern war, would mean the end of civilization.[1] Six weeks later Malenkov had to withdraw this opinion. In a new speech he said that an atomic war would 'inevitably lead to the end of the capitalist system of society'.[2] In an article on 5 March 1955 commemorating the death of Stalin, the Party leaders made their own position clear; it was claimed that if the imperialists should succeed in unleashing a third world war, not civilization, but the decaying capitalist system would collapse.

A little noticed but important event announced soon after Malenkov's fall, was the removal of Nikolai Shatalin from the Central Committee Secretariat. Shatalin, deputy head of the Personnel Department since 1939, and from 1939 to 1941 a member of the revision commission, had become a member of the Central Committee Secretariat immediately after Stalin's death, thanks clearly to the influence of Malenkov. In the spring of 1954 he was a prominent member of the Supreme Soviet. Now he was sent off to the Far Eastern provinces.

Malenkov's resignation affected the whole Communist world. The New Course was stopped in all the satellite countries. In Hungary the Prime Minister appointed in June 1953, Imre Nagy, had to resign. The accusations against him were on the same lines as those against Malenkov, but were more strongly worded. He was accused of having supported 'right-wing deviations', of having made too many concessions to the peasants, of having belittled heavy industry, and—this point was particularly interesting—of having denied the leading role of the Party.

In China too, Malenkov's fall was followed by an important change in the leadership. At a national conference of the Chinese Communist Party, the Chairman of the State Planning Commission and Mao's representative in Manchuria, Kao Kang, and the Party leader of Shanghai and East China, Jao Shu-shi, were accused of having formed an 'anti-Party group' to seize power in the Party and the state. Kao Kang was also accused of separatist leanings. As in the Soviet Union it was primarily economic policy that was in question, since at the same conference the economic plan was changed.

[1] *Pravda*, 13 March 1954.   [2] *Pravda*, 27 April 1954.

BULGANIN'S REORGANIZATION OF THE GOVERNMENT

It soon became evident that a kind of united front of the economic and army leaders had arisen under the new Prime Minister, Bulganin. On 1 March 1955 the staff of experienced economic leaders in the Praesidium of the Council of Ministers was expanded. Mikoyan, Saburov, and Pervukhin, until then Deputy Prime Ministers, were promoted to be First Deputy Prime Ministers. Four other economic leaders were made Deputy Prime Ministers: the former Minister of the Aircraft Industry, Mikhail Khrunichev, the Minister of Medium Machine Building, Colonel-General Avram Savenyagin, the deputy Chairman of the Council of Ministers and Minister of Agriculture of the RSFSR, Pavel Lobanov, and the head of the State Committee for Building Affairs, Vladimir Kucherenko. The Praesidium or inner Council of Ministers, now consisted of fourteen members: the Chairman, Bulganin, the five First Deputy Chairmen, Kaganovich, Mikoyan, Molotov, Pervukhin, and Saburov, and the eight Deputy Chairmen, Malenkov, Malyshev, Kosygin, Tevosyan, Kucherenko, Khrunichev, Lobanov, and Savenyagin.

At the same time changes took place in the Council of Ministers. Among those dismissed were the Minister of State Farms, Alexei Kozlov, who was succeeded by Benediktov, the Minister of Culture, Georgi Alexandrov, who was succeeded by Nikolai Mikhailov, and the Minister of the Coal Industry, Alexander Sasyadjko, who was succeeded by Alexander Sademidko. The former ambassador to the German Democratic Republic, Vladimir Semyonov, and Nikolai Fyodorenko both became deputy Foreign Ministers; Semyonov took over the German Department and Fyodorenko the Far Eastern Department of the Foreign Ministry.

At the same time the army leaders moved into the foreground and announced their demands. On 11 March 1955 eleven new marshals were appointed, six Marshals of the Soviet Union, Bagramian, Biryusov, Grechko, Yeremenko, Moskalenko, and Chuikov, two marshals of the air force, Rudenko and Sudets, two of the artillery, Varentsov and Kazakov, and one Chief Marshal of the air force, Zhigarev.

At a conference of military writers the army chiefs demanded a revision of the historiography of the second world war.

Lieutenant-General Shatilov complained that the beginning of
the German-Soviet war was 'not infrequently idealized'.
Events were presented as if the Soviet High Command had
planned and calculated an active defence in advance. 'In
reality, however, because of the surprise attack of the enemy
and his numerical superiority in tanks and planes, the initial
period of the war was unfavourable for our country and its
army, which, in spite of the steadfastness and braveness of the
fighters who defended every inch of native soil, had to experience the bitterness of retreat.' The over-simple account
hitherto provided could not, he said, be allowed. The army
leaders issued a warning against under-estimating military
knowledge in the non-Soviet world, for this might cause
complacency. It was important 'carefully to study the development of technical weapons and the way in which they were
used'.[1]

At the same conference there were complaints that no biographies of Soviet military leaders existed. It was suggested
that books should be published about the Soviet marshals,
Koniev, Zhukov, Bagramian, Govorov, Rokossovsky, and
Chuikov. But things went even further: Why, it was asked, are
the memoirs of opponents not also published, of such men as
Denikin and Yudenich, who during the civil war had been on
the side of the Whites? Even Guderian's memoirs should be
published.[2]

The new pre-eminence of the economic and military chiefs
had unfortunate consequences for the First Party Secretary,
Nikita Khrushchev. In November 1954 and January 1955 he
had, it has been seen, personally signed two Party resolutions.
Now he was publicly put in his place. 'Lenin taught us the
collective nature of work. He often reminded us that all members of the Politburo are equal and that the secretary is chosen
to execute the resolutions of the Central Committee of the
Party,' wrote *Pravda* on 20 April 1955. A few days later the
Party secretary was again sharply reminded of the collective
principle: 'Lenin repeatedly stressed the importance of collective leadership in the Party and the country. To avoid any
misunderstanding, Lenin said . . . that only resolutions agreed
on by the Central Committee after they had been sanctioned by

[1] *Literaturnaya Gazeta*, 28 May 1955.   [2] *Literaturnaya Gazeta*, 2 June 1955.

the Orgburo, the Politburo or plenary session of the Central
Committee should be put into practice by the Secretary of the
Central Committee of the Party. Otherwise, the Central Com-
mittee cannot work efficiently.'[1]

THE MODERNIZATION OF THE ECONOMY

The unsuccessful experiment with the consumer goods programme had shown that the problems of modern soviet industrial society could not be solved with Stalin's economic set-up.
The modernization of the methods used to direct the economy
was now on the agenda.

Already in the spring of 1954 Khrushchev had spoken bluntly
at the Supreme Soviet about bureaucratic abuses among the
heads of the economy. As an example he mentioned a factory
making agricultural machinery in Ryazan which every year
received 2,580 detailed instructions from the economic ministry; in 1953 alone the management had to send 10,250 documents to the economic authorities to which it was subordinated.
The post-Stalin leaders were also worried by the great number
of authorities with parallel functions, the rigid planning with a
mass of unnecessary, detailed indices which deprived enterprise directors and local economic bodies of any rights, pre-
venting them from taking independent decisions. In addition,
the wage system was in a state of chaos. The same work in the
same branches of industry was differently rewarded in different
regions. The basic wage was, in many instances, no more than
half the total wage, the rest consisting of arbitrarily fixed
premia and allowances.

The first attack was directed against the centralized control
of the Soviet economy, which had been axiomatic in the Stalin
era (the official textbook for Soviet state law says: 'We Bolsheviks are centralists by conviction'). On 23 October 1954 the
government organ *Izvestia* published an article of several
columns with the unusual title 'On formalism and the harmful-
ness of exaggerated centralization'. The author was a relatively
unimportant official called P. Morosov, chairman of the town
soviet in Kemorovo in Western Siberia. It was clear to every
official, after reading this article, that it had been written by
order of the Party leaders, because, from a few examples in

[1] *Kommunist*, No. 6, 1955.

Kemorovo, conclusions were reached for the whole country.

Only a week later, on 30 October, in an article of twelve columns *Pravda* announced changes in economic policy: 'The excessive centralization of the planning system, the attempt to set a great number of detailed targets for individual localities is a mistake which harms the economic interests of the country.' The Party and state leaders of the USSR were, therefore, preparing measures for 'the correct balance between centralized direction and initiative and responsibility on the part of local bodies', in particular the slimming of the economic administration, the decentralization of economic control, a simplification of planning, a reduction in the number of index numbers reported to the government, and the greater independence of local bodies.

As early as November 1954 Zverev, the Minister of Finance, reported in *Kommunist* that the number of people employed by the central administration had fallen by 20·6 per cent. since 1952; 34,000 people had left the Ministry of Finance, and in the process of eliminating duplication 200 main administrative bodies and 4,500 different offices had been abolished. Several thousand enterprises which until then had reported to the central authorities in Moscow were to be handed over to the Union Republics. Under the motto 'return to direct production', administrative experts were transferred to productive concerns.

The simplification of the system of agricultural planning announced on 11 March 1955 was particularly important. In a joint resolution of the chiefs of Party and state 'serious mistakes and errors' in agricultural planning in the past were pointed out. Until then, every collective and every state farm had had all its sowing plans and number and types of livestock dictated from Moscow. This, it was now explained, had deprived farms of the opportunity of showing initiative. In future, only the quantities and kinds of products to be delivered were to be planned. The collective and state farms were given the right to operate according to their own discretion and were only obliged to fulfil their plan for delivery.

In the middle of April 1955 the Party and state leaders convened a conference of designers, technologists, factory directors, and chief engineers to discuss the modernization of industry. The senior leaders of the Soviet Union took part: Bulganin, Khrushchev, Kaganovich, Malenkov, Mikoyan, Molotov, Pervukhin, Saburov, Voroshilov, Kirichenko, Pospelov, and Suslov. In the middle of May the same questions were discussed at a conference of industrial officials. The Prime Minister, Bulganin, made a remarkable speech, in the course of which he admitted frankly that the quality of many Soviet products was inferior to that of foreign goods. Many Soviet economic officials resisted the introduction of modern technical methods, so that the designers were already saying it was easier to invent a new machine than to put it into service. The confusion in the wage system was to be overcome by new and clear wage scales. Industry would have to change to specialization and co-operation.

The rights of factory and other directors were also to be extended. The director of the Ural Machine Factory, Glebovsky, complained at the meeting that Soviet enterprise directors were subjected to petty interference. He objected that they lacked the right to transfer a single item in their budget from one department to another. Amid the applause of those present, Glebovsky, demanded a model statute defining the rights of enterprise directors.[1] It was characteristic of the atmosphere of those days that *Novy Mir*[2] published its own report of the meeting of industrial officials under the heading 'The masters of our country'.

Soon after the conference a number of government committees were attached to the Council of Ministers. The committee on questions of labour and wages, set up on 24 May under the direction of Lazar Kaganovich was to adapt the system of wage payment to the conditions of a modern industrial society. The committee for the introduction of modern technical methods under Vyacheslav Malyshev had the task of working out new measures for the modernization of Soviet industry in the light of foreign experience. In order to improve planning, the former state planning commission was divided into a state commission for long-term planning (Gosplan) and a state commission for current planning (Gosekonomkomissiya). Gosplan, under the direction of Nikolai Baibakov, who had for many years been Minister of the Mineral Oil Industry, was to

[1] *Pravda*, 20 May 1955.   [2] No. 7, 1955.

consider fundamental questions of long-term planning; Gosek-onomkomissiya, under the direction of Saburov, was to deal with short-term planning.

All these changes were to be considered in detail in July at the full session of the Central Committee. But at the same time another question was occupying the attention of the Soviet leaders, their attitude towards Yugoslavia.

THE VISIT OF THE SOVIET LEADERS TO BELGRADE

On 14 May 1955 it was announced in Moscow that it had been decided to send a Soviet government delegation to Yugoslavia. Its members were Khrushchev, Bulganin, Mikoyan, Shepilov, the Deputy Foreign Minister, Gromyko, and the Deputy Minister of Foreign Trade, Kumykin. *Pravda* commented in its leading article that although 'fundamental differences of opinion on a number of important problems of social development' existed between the Soviet Union and Yugoslavia, the fact that in Yugoslavia, too, the most important means of production were publicly owned provided a basis for extensive co-operation. Thus, for the first time since the beginning of the Cominform quarrel in the summer of 1948, Yugoslavia was again described as a socialist country.

The Cominform conflict and the existence of an independent socialist Yugoslavia constituted a heavy liability for Moscow. For the first time the Soviet leadership was faced with a communist country which was going its own way in domestic and foreign policy, in economic and cultural life, thus endangering Moscow's ideological monopoly. The Yugoslav theory of the right of each country to its own road to socialism and Yugoslav criticism of the degeneration of the Soviet system were echoed throughout the international communist movement. The measures which were put into practice in Yugoslavia after the break with Moscow in the summer of 1948 had attracted the greatest attention—such, for instance, as the decentralization of the economic and state apparatus, the dissolution of the machine and tractor stations, the introduction of workers' councils in the factories, the relaxation of the rigidly centralized planning system, the abolition of compulsory deliveries in agriculture, the dissolution of the unprofitable agricultural co-operatives, and the freeing of art and literature from the

strait-jacket of 'socialist realism'. Yugoslavia's independent
policy revealed to the reforming forces in the communist world
a socialist alternative to the Stalinist system, and its unyielding
resistance to Soviet claims to hegemony strengthened the
opposition in the satellite countries.

All Stalin's attempts to induce Yugoslavia to submit—the
economic blockade, frontier provocations, appeals for resistance
against the Yugoslav government, defamation of the Yugoslav
communists as traitors and fascists, provocative broadcasts,
staged trials and arrests in the East European countries—had
ended in failure for Moscow. Stalin's successors had the choice
between continuing this sterile policy or reconciling themselves
with their former comrades and thus removing the Yugoslav
question from the scene.

Soon after Stalin's death, Moscow's attitude towards Yugo-
slavia had changed. Among the slogans for May Day the usual
exhortation to fight against the 'fascist régime of the Tito-
Rankovič clique' was missing. The journal of the Stalinist
Yugoslav emigrés in Moscow was no longer mentioned, and the
Soviet press contained no more anti-Yugoslav articles.

On 22 September 1954 *Pravda* actually published a speech of
Marshal Tito's without hostile comments. On the occasion
of the tenth anniversary of the liberation of Belgrade on
10 October 1954, *Pravda* once again admitted the share of
the Yugoslav partisans in the liberation of their country.

But the restoration of normal relations between the Soviet
Union and Yugoslavia was bound to remain illusory as long
as the trials staged in Eastern Europe against 'Titoists' had not
been revoked. One of the key figures in these trials was the
American, Noel Field. He had left the American government
service at the end of the thirties because he could not reconcile
his work with his communist sympathies. During the war he
had been the head of an organization to help anti-Fascist and
anti-Nazi refugees in Switzerland. There he entered into
friendly relations with communist emigrés. After 1945, he paid
frequent visits to East European countries to see his wartime
friends who had since advanced in the world. Shortly after the
break between Belgrade and Moscow he was arrested in
Hungary as an agent of the American secret service. Thereafter, Field appeared neither as the accused nor as a witness in

any trial. But in the East European trials of 'Titoists', of Rajk in Hungary, Kostov in Bulgaria, Clementis and Sling in Czechoslovakia (during the Slansky trial), and during the great purges of 'Titoists' in Poland and Communist Germany, the connexion with him—and thus with the American secret service—was the crux of the case for the prosecution. In November 1954 Field was suddenly released and rehabilitated, thus destroying the legal myth upon which the trials of the Titoists had been based. Shortly afterwards, on 29 November 1954, the Yugoslav national holiday was again celebrated in Moscow. At a reception at the Yugoslav embassy Malenkov and Khrushchev raised their glasses to drink to the health of 'Comrade Tito' and the Yugoslav Communist Party.

Yugoslavia showed itself ready to establish normal relations with the Soviet Union. But it did not hide the fact that it had no intention of giving up the independence it had won since 1948. The most difficult problem between Moscow and Belgrade was the question as to who was to accept the guilt for the conflict of 1948. This started a public controversy.

On 8 February, Molotov tried, in a speech on foreign policy made before the Supreme Soviet, to justify the Cominform resolution of the summer of 1948. He declared that Yugoslavia had moved from the position it had adopted after the end of the second world war. At conferences in the other communist countries in the spring of 1955 the new attitude of the Soviet Union towards Yugoslavia was explained by saying that Yugoslavia was trying to make amends for past mistakes. Tito replied to this on 7 March 1955, before the Yugoslav Parliament, with a strong statement: 'In the countries of the Eastern bloc,' he said, 'they are trying to present the establishment of normal relations to their Party members and populations as if Yugoslavia had partly admitted its mistakes and was trying to make amends for them. This is nonsense and may well raise doubts in our minds as to the sincerity of these statements. . . . There is no doubt that Molotov's statements on Yugoslavia in his speech to the Supreme Soviet do not correspond with the truth. . . . We regard this as an attempt to gloss over the facts before his own people—again at our expense.'[1]

Only two days later the Soviet press dissociated itself from

[1] *Internationale Politik*, March 1955.

Molotov's statement. *Pravda* and *Izvestia* published Tito's speech—including his criticism of the Soviet Foreign Minister— without comments, and on 12 March 1955 *Pravda* declared that no one said the Yugoslavs 'had now seen the error of their ways', or were 'trying to reform'. This public disavowal of Molotov reflected, as we know from Bialer's report,[1] sharp disputes in the Soviet Party Praesidium. According to Bialer, the Party Praesidium met after Molotov's anti-Yugoslav remarks. Molotov was accused of thwarting the establishment of normal Soviet-Yugoslav relations. His attitude towards other international questions was criticized. In May 1955, before Khrushchev and Bulganin went to Belgrade, Molotov opposed the projected visit. Although he was in favour of the resumption of diplomatic relations with Yugoslavia, he rejected the restoration of Party connexions with the Yugoslav communists on ideological grounds. But Molotov remained in the minority. The Party Praesidium adopted a resolution (which was not published) approving of the journey to Belgrade. In a second resolution of the Party Praesidium (also not published) the opposing points of view of Molotov and Khrushchev on the Yugoslav question were set out, and it was decided to refer this question to the next full session of the Central Committee. The differences of opinion on Yugoslavia in the Party leadership are confirmed also by another incident. On 9 May 1955 Marshal Zhukov, writing in *Pravda*, praised the 'outstanding steadfastness of the Yugoslav peoples under the leadership of Marshal Tito', and expressed the wish that recent differences should be 'speedily removed and new friendly relations re-established between our countries'. But on the same day, Marshal Sokolovsky, in the army newspaper *Krasnaya Zyedza*, put Yugoslavia in the last place but one among those countries which had allegedly been liberated by the Soviet Union.

Khrushchev was particularly interested in the resumption of Party relations. He needed a success in Yugoslavia for the Party more than for the government, in the first place in order to consolidate his position, and secondly in order to weaken the dangerous influence of the ideological heresy of the Yugoslavs in the satellite countries.

[1] *Hinter dem Eisernen Vorhang*, No. 10, 1956.

The Yugoslav press, on the other hand, ostentatiously emphasized the official character of the visit. When the Russians arrived in Belgrade, the buildings of the Communist Party and the Socialist League were not decorated with flags. But Khrushchev had not lost the hope of obtaining a success for the Soviet Party, and for himself personally, from the visit. In his first speech, at Belgrade Airport, he made the sensational statement that he deeply regretted the anti-Yugoslav campaign since 1948, but put the blame for the conflict on Beria, saying:

'We sincerely regret what has happened, and are removing with determination everything that has accumulated during this period. In this, we, for our part, without any doubt include the provocative role which the enemies of the people, Beria, Abakumov, and the others, who have now been unmasked, played in the relations between Yugoslavia and the USSR. We have carefully examined the material on which the serious accusations and insults which were made against the Yugoslav leaders at that time were based. The facts show that this material was invented by enemies of the people, despicable agents of imperialism who had joined the ranks of our Party through deception.'

This statement lacked all credibility and was ominously reminiscent of Stalin's political style. But Khrushchev had at any rate placed the whole responsibility for the Cominform conflict on the Soviet Union, obviously thinking that he could trade this for a concession from the Yugoslavs. The Yugoslav reaction was icy. When Khrushchev's speech came to be translated into Serbo-Croat, Marshal Tito stopped it abruptly and led the Soviet representatives straight to the cars which were waiting. The cool attitude of the Yugoslav Party leaders and also of the population of Belgrade was stressed by all foreign correspondents.

THE BELGRADE DECLARATION AND KHRUSHCHEV'S VISIT TO SOFIA

The Soviet-Yugoslav discussions culminated in the Belgrade declaration which was published on 3 June 1955. This was signed by both heads of government, President Tito and the Soviet Prime Minister, Bulganin, but not by the Party Secretary, Khrushchev, although officially he was the head of the delegation. Nothing was said about relations between the two communist parties except that both governments had agreed to facilitate 'the co-operation of the social organizations of the two countries through the establishment of connexions, the exchange of socialist experience and a free exchange of opinion'. Politically, the most important part of the Belgrade declaration was the statement 'that differences in practical forms of socialism are exclusively the affair of individual countries'.

After the conclusion of the visit to Yugoslavia, the Soviet delegation went to Sofia where it had discussions with the Bulgarian Party leaders. The official communiqué merely said that an exchange of views on the international situation had taken place between the Soviet government delegation and the Bulgarian government. In reality, Khrushchev's visit to Sofia was of far greater importance than appeared from this brief communiqué. According to a reliable report which reached London shortly afterwards, but which was not published until February 1959.[1] a meeting took place in Sofia on 3 June 1955 at which members of the Central Committee and the Government, as well as senior officials of the Party—in all 300 people—took part.

At the morning meeting Bulganin gave a general report on Soviet-Yugoslav relations and explained why the diplomatic attitude of the communist bloc towards Yugoslavia should be changed. At the afternoon meeting Khrushchev made an ideological speech, containing accusations against Stalin which anticipated much of his speech at the Twentieth Party Congress. Khrushchev spoke of the break-down of 'Leninist Party practice' under Stalin and of the reign of terror after the Seventeenth Party Congress in 1934; he dealt with Stalin's role during the war and his diplomacy after it, and described the situation among the Russian leaders after Stalin's death. He declared that the case against a number of Party leaders liquidated by Stalin had been examined and that these leaders would be rehabilitated at the next Soviet Party Congress. As a particularly gruesome example of Stalin's practices he mentioned the shooting of Nikolai Voznesensky in the spring of 1949. This speech before the chief Bulgarian communists shows that, in

[1] See Richard Löwenthal in *The New Leader*, No. 6, 9 Feb. 1959.

the summer of 1955, the Soviet leaders were already preparing an open denunciation of Stalin.

After this the Soviet delegation visited Bukarest where it met not only the leaders of the Rumanian Communist Party, but also the Hungarian Party leader, Rákosi, and his Prime Minister, Hegedüs. Czechoslovak Party leaders, including the First Secretary, Antonin Novotny, were also present at these discussions. The visit was clearly intended to prepare the East European Communist parties for a reversal of policy.

THE PLENARY SESSION IN JULY 1955

From 4 to 12 July 1955 a plenary session of the Party Central Committee of the Soviet Union took place. Officially it was concerned with the modernization of the economy; Bulganin made an important speech about this. But the most important items on the agenda were debates on the Yugoslav question and on the relations between the Soviet Union and the People's Democracies.

The Soviet press was silent, but the foreign Party leaders were informed at private meetings about the course of the full session in July. Bialer saw the shorthand minutes intended for the Polish Party leadership and later described them in the West.[1] According to his account Molotov tried to justify Stalin's policy towards Yugoslavia in the following words: 'We should have had great difficulties in the other people's democracies if we had not taken such a determined stand on the Yugoslav question. . . . Let us remember Gomulka who was then an important person in Poland. If we had not remained firm in the case of Yugoslavia who knows what would have happened in Poland? Perhaps Poland would have followed in Yugoslavia's footsteps. Thus our strong reaction in the Yugoslav affair was entirely justified, since it prevented the catastrophe from assuming greater dimensions.'

After Molotov's speech there was an animated discussion. When Molotov expressed the view that Party problems should not be discussed with Tito, Khrushchev interrupted him with the words: 'But you managed to have talks with Ribbentrop in 1939.' Khrushchev then explained that it was too risky to pursue too aggressive a policy, because the Soviet Union would

[1] *Hinter dem Eisernen Vorhang*, No. 10, 1956.

then run the danger of pushing the people's democracies into a Titoist course. Thus their differences were essentially tactical. Khrushchev hoped for a more flexible policy towards Yugoslavia, whereas Molotov held the view that the old stubborn policy of Stalin would be more successful. Both, however, wished to prevent a Titoist development, that is, a complete retreat from Stalinism.

Molotov was also attacked by Bulganin, Mikoyan, Kaganovich, Suslov, and Shepilov. Though Khrushchev in his final speech emphasized that there was no personal disagreement between him and Molotov, that it was entirely a question of the Party and that as a man he had nothing against Molotov, the minutes, according to Bialer, record Khrushchev as saying: 'Vyacheslav Mikhailovich, this is all your wife's fault. It would be much better for you if you didn't listen to her. She spurs your ambition: she is your evil spirit!'

Finally Molotov yielded. He read a short statement which takes up only a page in the stenographic record. He admitted that Khrushchev's accusations were well-founded and said that he agreed with the views of the Central Committee on the Yugoslav question. Bialer says, however, 'The phrases were so stilted that in reading them I had little doubt that it was an attempt on Molotov's part to save what could be saved. Molotov wanted in this way to forestall the arguments which might have led to his dismissal.'

In the secret sessions of the July meeting the economic relations between the Soviet Union and her satellites were also discussed, in particular the mixed companies which had been established after the war in almost all the other communist countries. Anastas Mikoyan spoke on this question. Until then Soviet propaganda had always presented the mixed companies as an outstanding example of big-brotherly help. Mikoyan now described them as a clear and particularly blatant form of Soviet interference in the internal economic affairs of the satellites, and even as an example of economic exploitation. Mikoyan, however, also explained his demand to abolish the mixed companies by reference to a Sino-Soviet conflict on this question. After Stalin's death, the Soviet Union had suggested the foundation of Sino-Soviet companies to grow southern fruit in China and to export it to Russia. Mao Tse-tung had made the counter-proposal that China should export the fruit on a normal commercial basis. 'Did we need these mixed companies? Was it necessary to be snubbed by Comrade Mao Tse-tung when he refused permission for similar companies in China? Should we not learn from past mistakes and dissolve them?' Mikoyan asked, according to Bialer. And indeed this is what took place.

The controversy about Yugoslavia, the attacks against Molotov, and Mikoyan's report on economic relations between the Communist states remained secret. Only Bulganin's long report on the modernization of Soviet industry was published. It was remarkably frank. Bulganin gave many examples of Soviet industry lagging behind development abroad and criticized the isolationism cultivated in the Stalin era. Many government officials, members of scientific institutes, and enterprise directors, he said, underestimated the achievements of science and technology abroad. Research institutes wasted their time and resources in discovering things long ago made known in the foreign press. He attacked the view dear to people trying to hide their own ignorance beneath arrogant phrases that it is not worth while to study foreign experience. Everything new in the world of science and technology must be studied all the time, he said, relations with scientific institutes of research should be developed and more foreign technical literature should be published in the USSR. At about the same time, the Russian Government addressed a letter to all officials in industry on the modernization of the economy and the study of foreign experience, a letter which was, however, not published and has been mentioned only once.[1]

Bulganin demanded the introduction of new technical methods, as well as rational specialization in industrial enterprises, and more co-operation between them. The wage system also should be modernized. In particular the disproportion between rates of wages and actual earnings should be eliminated. Average wages had doubled since the pre-war years but standard wage-rates had risen only insignificantly. Managers deliberately kept norms low in order that workers could earn high wages all the same. Thus, in practice, the work

[1] *Kommunist*, No. 11, July 1955.

norms did not determine the wage, but were adjusted to it. The new wage system would have to provide material incentives to increase productivity, thereby overcoming the contradiction between norms and wage-rates.

Economic organization should be further decentralized. More use should be made of the administration of each Republic of the Union in running the economy. Bulganin announced that steps had already been taken in this direction. Many unnecessary economic organizations working parallel to one another had been abolished and the central economic administration had been reduced in size. The staff of the Council of Ministers for instance had been cut by 50 per cent. All this was only the beginning of a complicated undertaking intended to simplify the structure of the administrative machine. Bulganin also pressed for the extension of the authority and responsibility of the directors of factories and other enterprises.

This led soon after the plenary session in July, that is on 9 August, to an important 'resolution of the Council of Ministers of the USSR on the extension of the rights of enterprise directors'. These directors now received the right, subject to certain restrictions, to change quarterly plans according to their own needs, to accept orders not in the plan (as long as this did not endanger the fulfilment of the plan) and, when prices were not fixed, to determine prices and rates for certain orders. Directors were allowed to use working capital for rebuilding and expansion according to their own judgement, to obtain building material from local industry independently, to agree to new projects and, if necessary, to alter them. Within the framework of the existing regulations they were permitted to fix wages for individual categories of workers and in agreement with the trade unions to adapt the wage system to the needs of the enterprise.

Further, Bulganin expressed himself as in favour of encouraging the trade unions to be active. Party, industrial, and trade union officials should 'come to terms with the needs and demands of the employees. . . . Officials who failed to reckon with the feelings of the simple worker must be called to account as bureaucrats.' From an article which was published later in *Partinaya Zhizn*[1] it emerges that the July meeting had directed

[1] No. 16, 1955.

the trade unions to see that the needs of the workers were heeded. It would be a serious mistake if the trade unions 'agreed to every action on the part of the management because the enterprises were state enterprises. Such an attitude would be useful only to the bureaucrats.' The trade unions, too, were to become more independent.

Bulganin's remarks on the delicate subject of relations between Party organizations in the factories and their directors were of interest too. They reflected the frequent conflicts, in the framework of the individual concern, between the economic and the Party apparatus. Bulganin criticized the 'petty supervision' by the Party committees which frequently delegated to themselves the work of the managers.

At the same time, the ideal type of modern manager was described in innumerable articles. *Kommunist*[1] demanded that every manager should have an inherent feeling for new things. He should rely more upon the initiative of his collaborators. The Soviet manager should not shut himself up within the four walls of his office, but should work closely with the whole community of his workers.

In some undertakings in Moscow, lectures were given at that time on the topic of 'what should a Soviet manager be like', which led to lively discussions. In the Moscow enterprise 'Kaliber' the workers complained that managers swore freely and addressed the workers with the familiar second person singular, while demanding respect and politeness in return. A certain Novikov made the remarkable suggestion 'that a special journal should be published for us managers, in which the factory and mine managers can exchange their experiences'. As an example he quoted the English journal, *The Director*, 'which is instructive for us in many respects'.[2] *The Director* is the organ of the British Institute of Directors.

The July meeting not only initiated far-reaching measures for the modernization of the economy, but was also the overture to the Twentieth Party Congress which it resolved to convene on 14 February 1956. Changes in Party positions were also announced. To the nine members of the Party Praesidium two new ones were added: the Ukrainian Party Secretary, Alexei

[1] No. 10, 1955.   [2] *Partinaya Zhizn*, No. 13, 1955.

Kirichenko,[1] and the Party ideologist, Mikhail Suslov.[2]

At the same time the Secretariat of the Central Committee was enlarged. Until then, it consisted of Khrushchev, Suslov, and the Party theorist, Piotr Pospelov. The new members were the Party organizer, Averky Aristov,[3] the Party secretary of the Altai Region, Nikolai Belyayev,[4] and the editor of *Pravda*, Dmitri Shepilov,[5] all of them close to Khrushchev.

MOLOTOV'S SELF-CRITICISM

The political controversies at the July meeting over the Yugoslav question, in which Molotov was defeated, had a curious sequel. In the middle of October, *Kommunist*[6] published a self-critical statement by Molotov made on 16 September 1955, and intended not merely to weaken Molotov's position, but also to put the Party slogan 'transition to communism' back

[1] Alexei Kirichenko first appeared after the end of the war as secretary of the regional Party committee in Odessa. In September 1952 he became Second Secretary of the Ukrainian Communist Party, and in July 1953 he was promoted to the post of First Ukrainian Party Secretary in succession to Melinkov.

[2] Mikhail Suslov, by contrast with Kirichenko, already occupied a leading position in the last decade of the Stalin period. Since September 1947 he had been Central Committee secretary for Propaganda and Agitation. He played a leading part in the foundation of the Cominform. He was also responsible for relations with the foreign communist parties. He took a leading part in the anti-Yugoslav campaign. He signed both Cominform resolutions against Yugoslavia, those of 28 June 1948 and November 1949. In other questions, too, he had been prominent in the last years of Stalin as a firm and unyielding Stalinist.

[3] Averky Aristov, formerly director of the Mignitosgorsk steel works, had already been employed in the Central Committee Secretariat for a short period in 1952–3; now he was to be responsible particularly for questions of Party organization.

[4] Nikolai Belyayev, from 1950 to 1955 First Party Secretary of the Altai Region, had in 1954 and 1955 worked with Khrushchev in a responsible position in the organization of the virgin lands campaign. He was probably brought to the Central Committee Secretariat to work on agricultural questions.

[5] Dmitri Shepilov, appointed head of the Central Committee Department for Propaganda and Agitation in 1947 and head in 1948, became editor-in-chief of *Pravda* in 1952 and in the spring of 1954 chairman of the foreign affairs commission of the Council of Nationalities of the Supreme Soviet. He was a member of the government delegation which visited Peking in October 1954: in his article of 24 January 1955 he provided the ideological justification for the return to the priority of heavy industry; in April 1955 he delivered the speech in memory of Lenin, and in the summer of 1955 he accompanied the Soviet leaders to Belgrade.

A number of facts suggest that Shepilov was appointed to the Central Committee Secretariat at that time to counter-balance Suslov. In the Secretariat he was to work on ideological questions, and he was also to deal with questions of foreign policy, possibly as a counter-weight to Molotov.

[6] No. 14, 1955.

into the centre of things. In his self-criticism Molotov said:

'In my report of 8 February 1955 to the Supreme Soviet I used an inaccurate formulation with reference to the question of the building of a socialist society in the USSR. It says in the report: "Besides the Soviet Union where the foundations of socialist society have already been laid, there are also some people's democracies, which have taken only the first, but most important, steps towards socialism." This faulty formulation leads to the misconception that a socialist society has not yet been set up in the USSR, but only the basis for a socialist society, that is to say the foundations of socialist society. This is not in accordance with the facts and runs contrary to the repeated evaluations of the results of the setting up of socialism in the USSR which are found in Party documents.'

Molotov then explained at length that the Seventeenth Party Congress (1934) had already declared that the foundations of a socialist society had been established, that the Eighteenth Party Congress in March 1939 had noted that the Soviet Union had entered the phase of gradual transition to a communist society and that the Nineteenth Party Congress in October 1952 had incorporated this formulation into the new Party statutes. In conclusion, Molotov said:

'The political danger of this formulation lies in the fact that it brings confusion into ideological questions, that it is contrary to the resolutions of the Party on the question of the setting-up of a socialist society in the USSR and that it puts in doubt the establishment of a socialist society in our country.'

This was no scholarly dispute, but an important political issue. Since Khrushchev had succeeded in the promotion of a number of officials who were close to him, the Party apparatus had gained in influence. Khrushchev used this increase in his power to give to recent Soviet policy, all too much influenced by economic expedients, an ideological direction which was bound to strengthen the Party machine.

Molotov's self-criticism was also of importance in relation to satellite countries. In the Belgrade declaration the Soviet leaders had recognized the right of different countries to choose different roads to socialism. It was difficult to reconcile this with the earlier thesis about the leading role of the Soviet Union. But if the Soviet Union was already on the road to communism, while the satellites were still engaged in the construction of socialism, the leading role of the Soviet Union followed automatically: the other socialist countries might be entitled to the same rights, but the Soviet Union was already at a more advanced stage of development and the other countries thus had to follow its lead.

Since Stalin's death, no Soviet leader had mentioned the 'transition to communism'. Theoretically, therefore, all the officials of Party and state were due for self-criticism. But this was neither expedient nor necessary. Molotov, who had been opposed to the visit of the Soviet leaders to Belgrade and probably also to other political measures, was the scapegoat for the others in his self-criticism; it was bound to damage his position. After Beria and Malenkov, Molotov was the third prominent member of the leadership formed after Stalin's death who was deprived of authority in the Party.

The tendency to replace the leaders of the Stalin period by younger officials became still clearer during the preparations for the Twentieth Party Congress. In the autumn of 1955 very many changes of office took place. According to a Yugoslav report,[1] in Georgia alone 2,589 secretaries of the basic organizations were moved and in the Ukraine as many as 95,000. In the Party secretariats of the towns, regions, and Republics also, many officials were changed. Let us mention only three examples, because they affected officials who were later to play important parts. The First Party Secretary in Kazakhstan, Ponomarenko, was replaced by Leonid Brezhnev, the First Secretary of the town of Gorki, Smirnov, by Nikolai Ignatov.[2] Finally, in December 1955, the First Secretary of the Party of Uzbekistan, Nyasov, was replaced at a Party conference, in the presence of Khrushchev, by Nuritdin Mukhitdinov. It may be assumed that a large number of the new officials were followers of Khrushchev who were being launched by him, for only two years later they belonged to the leading bodies of the Party.

THE PREPARATIONS FOR THE TWENTIETH
PARTY CONGRESS

In the period between the meeting of July 1955 and the Twentieth Party Congress of February 1956 a number of

[1] *Borba*, 13 Feb. 1956   [2] *Pravda*, 5 Nov. 1955.

important measures obviously intended to prepare the Soviet population for a new policy were taken.

The first step in this direction was the amnesty for Soviet citizens who had collaborated with the German occupation forces during the German-Soviet war; this was decreed by the Praesidium of the Supreme Soviet on 17 September.[1] All Soviet citizens who had been sentenced during the war to ten years' or less deprivation of liberty 'for giving aid to the enemy' were to be released from detention. All persons who had been sentenced 'for serving in the German army, the police or German special units' were to be released, regardless of the length of their sentence. But the amnesty was not to apply to those prisoners 'who had been sentenced for murder or maltreatment of Soviet citizens'.

It is interesting to note that a special article referred to Soviet citizens living abroad. The amnesty promised that those who during the war had surrendered to the German army or who had been active in the German army, police, or special units would not be prosecuted. All those who had occupied 'leading positions in the police, gendarmerie, and propaganda units' of the German occupation forces during the war and who had worked in anti-Soviet organizations after the war would not be called to account 'if they had subsequently expiated their guilt through patriotic action for their country or had confessed their guilt'. For Soviet citizens living abroad 'who had committed serious crimes against the Soviet state' a confession was to be regarded as a mitigating circumstance. They should be sentenced at the most to five years' banishment. The amnesty was clearly intended to induce Soviet citizens living abroad to return to the USSR. But it must have appeared as a sign of retreat from the Stalin period.

In September 1955 a big trial of officials of the Georgian state security service took place; the public was, however, not informed about this until a radio announcement from Tiflis on 22 November. The accused were the former People's Commissar for the Interior, Rapava, the former Head of the Investigation Department, Rukhadze, the former deputy Minister of the Interior, Tsereteli, and the former examining magistrates of the Georgian NKVD, Krimyan, Savitski,

[1] Published on 4 Oct. 1955 in *The Communications of the Supreme Soviet.*

Khazan, and Paramonov. Like Ryumin and Ignatiev in April
1953, Beria in July and December 1953 and Abakumov in
December 1954, the Georgian state security officials were
accused of 'having forged investigation dossiers and of having
employed criminal methods of investigation strictly prohibited
under Soviet law against detained persons', as well as 'having
committed terrorist acts of vengeance against honest Soviet
citizens, by accusing them falsely of counter-revolutionary
crimes'.

This trial was of great importance. Not only did it again
focus attention on the terroristic measures of the post-war
period, but for the first time officials were rehabilitated who
had been victims of the great purge of 1936 to 1938. The
accused were said to have participated actively in 'collecting
damaging' material', which Beria had used in his intrigues
against the former member of the Politburo, Serge Ordzhonikidze. They were also accused of 'terroristic acts of vengeance'
against some Georgian officials, among them the former Party
secretary of Transcaucasia, Mamiya Orashelashvili. Ordzhonikidze had committed suicide in February 1937. Orashelashvili,
a close friend of Ordzhonikidze, who as early as the twenties
moved into the central 'apparatus' in Moscow, was sentenced
to death and executed in December 1937 together with
Yenukidze and Karakhan. The rehabilitation of Ordzhonikidze
and Orashelashvili heralded an early rehabilitation of other
victims of the great purge.

On 10 November 1955 Stalin's ornate architecture was
officially condemned. In 1954 there had been veiled suggestions
pointing in this direction. Now a resolution of the Party and
Council of Ministers stated that a 'pompous style of architecture, full of vulgar excrescences . . . was not in character with
the line of the Party and the Government in architecture and
building'. Architects and engineers were asked to concentrate
their attention on economical methods of building, comforts
for the population, and the provision of parks in the residential
areas. Soviet architecture should be marked by simplicity of form.
Architects should 'be bolder in their use of modern achievements in building methods at home and abroad'.

The press and the architects immediately took up the official
criticism. The journal *Ogonyok* made fun of the 'fashionable

disease of decorative embellishments which had even penetrated below the ground', a clear reference to the Moscow underground. Until then, this had been particularly praised. In the Large Soviet Encyclopaedia,[1] the Moscow underground was still described as an 'outstanding work of Soviet architecture' which 'expressed in striking fashion the nobility and beauty of the socialist age'. Professor Nikolaiev criticized the architecture of the Volga-Don Canal. 'Many million roubles had been thrown out of the window' for towers, rows of pillars, sculpture, and triumphal arches.[2] Three years earlier, the Volga-Don Canal had been praised by *Pravda*,[3] as 'an architectonic achievement reflecting the greatness of the Stalin era. . . .'

On 29 November 1955 the Praesidium of the Supreme Soviet issued a decree reversing that of 27 June 1936 against abortion. But pregnancies were only to be terminated artificially in hospitals 'in accordance with the directives of the Minister of Health of the USSR'. The responsibility of doctors and unqualified persons who carried out abortions unofficially remained. The decree was obviously issued because the ban on abortion was driving women to people without medical training. This led to innumerable deaths and many cases of serious damage to health.

In ideology, too, new tendencies could be discerned in the autumn of 1955. The journal *Voprosy Ekonomiki*[4] criticized dogmatism and foolish memorizing. There was too little creative discussion. The journal openly admitted that 'this situation is partly caused by the desire for reinsurance among some leaders and their fear to let controversial questions be discussed'. A study of the new phenomena of capitalism was urgently demanded. 'Many scientists take up a dogmatic and oversimplifying attitude towards the economic situation of present-day capitalism. This finds expression in an unexplained rejection or a suppression of the achievements attained in the capitalist countries in the development of production, science and technology.' *Kommunist*[5] also gave a warning against 'oversimplifying ideas about the decay of capitalism which are in vogue in our propaganda'.

The historians were asked to strengthen their links with

---

[1] Vol. 27, p. 331.   [2] *Izvestia*, 23 Nov. 1955.
[3] 21 July 1952.   [4] No. 10, 1955.   [5] No. 14, 1955.

scholars abroad. This was connected with an indirect criticism
of the nationalistic Russian historiography of the later years
under Stalin: 'All the peoples of the world—the great and the
small—make their own contribution to culture. Soviet historiography aims at bringing out as fully as possible the contribution of every nation to the history of the struggle for freedom
and civilization.'[1] In the same number pre-revolutionary
Russian historians and—which was even more important
politically—the Marxist historian M. N. Pokrovsky, who had
been banned by Stalin, were again referred to with praise.
At the same time the preparation of a new textbook of Party
history was announced.

Interesting—if conditioned by foreign policy—was a new
assessment of Gandhi. In the Large Soviet Encyclopaedia[2]
Gandhi was still described as the 'founder of a reactionary
political doctrine' who took 'the side of British imperialism' and
started an agitation in the interest of the upper middle class
and the big landowners of India. Now he was described as a
famous 'patriot and friend of the people', and the Soviet press
printed Bulganin's speech in Bombay in which he had said:
'We, the pupils of Lenin, do not share Gandhi's philosophical
views, but we consider him an outstanding personality who
contributed much to the development of the peace-loving
views of your people and to its struggle for independence'.[3]

Authors who had been banned until then were 'rehabilitated'. In the autumn of 1955 Dostoievsky and the poet, Sergi
Esenin[4], who was very popular with students, came back into
favour. The seventy-fifth anniversary of Dostoievsky's death
was celebrated in a fashion which would have been unthinkable under Stalin. *Crime and Punishment* was described as 'one of
the most powerful works of world literature', and Dostoievsky's
importance for the present was indicated with reference to the
complexity and contradictions of his art. The publication of his
collected works in an edition of 300,000 copies was announced.[5]

In modern literature, too, certain relaxations became noticeable in the autumn of 1955. *Literaturnaya Gazeta* complained
that so many authors praised what was new, but ignored
abuses. 'For example magazine writers often describe parts

---

[1] *Voprosy Istorii*, No. 8, 1955.   [2] Vol. 10, 1952.   [3] *Pravda*, 26 Nov. 1955.
[4] He committed suicide in 1925.   [5] *Pravda*, 6 Feb. 1956.

which resemble the magnificent town districts of Norilysk or Magadan. Whereas one still on occasion (and this is by no means a secret) comes across miserable huts with cockroaches and nasty smoking oil lamps . . . we still have hardly any magazines in which those avaricious, corrupt individuals and boasting bureaucrats who go on working with soulless formalism, sometimes even using malicious taunts, are castigated and even lose their lives.'[1] The well-known Soviet writer, Ovechkin, even said that in many Soviet books 'the truth of life was outraged'.[2]

After the first prominent victims of the years of the great purge had been rehabilitated in September 1955 in the trial of the Georgian state security officials, there followed the most important rehabilitation of all in December 1955 in a most peculiar manner. In a survey of Soviet publications about the second world war[3] Voznesensky's book *The war economy of the Soviet Union during the period of the Great Patriotic War* was without any further explanation again praised.

Two weeks before the opening of the Party Congress the dismissal of the Soviet Minister of the Interior, Sergei Kruglov, was announced; he had become Beria's deputy in 1938, and, according to certain unconfirmed statements, was head of the notorious organization 'Smersh' (short for 'death to spies') during the war. At the conferences in Yalta and Teheran he had been responsible for the security of the Soviet and Allied statesmen and was decorated with Soviet as well as British and American orders. More important than his dismissal was the fact that he was not replaced by a state security official, but by a Party official, Nikolai Dudorov, who had formerly been deputy chairman of the Moscow City Soviet and head of the building department under the Central Committee.

THE SOVIET UNION IN FEBRUARY 1956

When the Twentieth Party Congress met in the middle of February 1956, only three and a half years after the Nineteenth Party Congress, the Soviet Union had changed very considerably. In the place of a dictator glorified in Byzantine fashion, a collective leadership had emerged, whose members,

---

[1] *Literaturnaya Gazeta*, 20 Oct. 1955.   [2] *Literaturnaya Gazeta*, 26 Oct. 1955.
[3] *Voprosy Istorii*, No. 12, 1955.

even if they had not equal rights, had at least been strong enough to prevent the emergence of a new autocrat.

Only a few months after Stalin's death the police cordon from the Kremlin to the Moscow villas where the Party leaders lived had been considerably reduced, a change which the population of Moscow had noted carefully. At the turn of the year 1953 to 1954 the Soviet Ministers moved out of the Kremlin, some of them into houses in Moscow. Whereas the leaders in Stalin's day had remained in a closely guarded Kremlin, Khrushchev, Bulganin, and other leaders now travelled about the various regions of the Soviet Union, came into contact with officials of all ranks, visited local Party conferences, factories and collective farms, and went on more journeys abroad in one year than had their predecessors in the whole of the preceding decade. They had much more social contact with foreigners and for the first time for many years cocktail parties were given for foreign diplomatists and journalists living in Moscow. In 1954 the Kremlin had been open for special occasions, but in May 1955 it was thrown open to all visitors.

Thus within the short period of three and a half years the new rulers had deviated in many important fields of public life from Stalin's fundamental principles. Before long this indirect retreat from Stalin would have to be completed by direct criticism. This is not wisdom after the event, as I expressed the same view three months before the Twentieth Party Congress.[1]

[1] See *SBZ Archiv*, No. 24, 1955, p. 378.

CHAPTER IV

THE TWENTIETH PARTY CONGRESS

THE Twentieth Congress of the Communist Party of the Soviet Union opened on 14 February 1956 in the Kremlin and closed in the afternoon of 25 February after twenty sessions. According to the official report, 1,355 delegates with voting status and 81 delegates with consultative status represented 6·8 million full Party members and 420,000 candidate members. Delegates from 55 foreign communist parties also took part in the Congress. It must be mentioned as astonishing that among the Soviet delegates there were five who had been excluded from the Party for several years, and later readmitted, but probably completely rehabilitated only shortly before the Party Congress.

Mikoyan said of the Congress that it was the most important since Lenin's death. In fact it differed fundamentally from all Party Congresses in the days of Stalin. For once a Party Congress had been summoned at the time laid down in the statutes. Changes of great importance were made, and differing conceptions and tendencies found expression, if only in a concealed way.

THE CRITICISM OF STALIN

The most important characteristic of the Congress was its open criticism of Stalin whose photograph had been removed from the Congress Hall. In his opening address, Khrushchev asked those present to rise from their seats in memory of Stalin, Gottwald, and Tokuda. Thus he put Stalin, who had been idolized for over a quarter of a century, on the same level as the Czechoslovak President and a Party leader who was hardly known outside Japan. In his seven-hour report Khrushchev mentioned Stalin only once and then it was only by the way: after his death, he said, the enemies of the Soviet Union had speculated on disagreement among the Russian leaders. In the next sentence Khrushchev turned to the 'unmasking' of Beria, an instructive association.

All the leading Communists criticized Stalin's autocracy, referred to in Soviet usage as the cult of personality, and contrasted it with the principle of collective leadership proclaimed after his death. Malenkov said that the cult of personality made it impossible to dispute the decisions of a single individual and led to arbitrary action. Suslov complained that ordinary mortals were left with the task of popularizing whatever Stalin had proclaimed. Mikoyan went furthest of all for he attacked Stalin's last book because it did not explain the complicated phenomena of modern capitalism. He appealed to Soviet economists to criticize the theories it expounded. The historian, Anna Pankratova, condemned with strong words the effects of the cult of Stalin's personality on the writing of Party history. Khrushchev called for a new textbook on the history of the Party to be based on historical facts; he thus made it clear what he thought of *The History of the CPSU* attributed to Stalin. Nikolai Belyayev spoke of serious mistakes made in agricultural policy before 1953. Only Kaganovich was noticeably restrained. One might almost discern a certain criticism of Stalin's successors when he referred to development since the Nineteenth Party Congress (i.e. Stalin's death) as a difficult period in the history of the Party.

The remarkable change of *décor* was revealed in *Pravda* on two anniversaries during the period from 1953 to 1956, that is to say, on Stalin's birthday, 21 December, and on 5 March, the day of his death. On 21 December 1953 Stalin was not mentioned at all, *Pravda* merely referring to the distribution of the Stalin peace prizes. On the first anniversary of Stalin's death *Pravda* published a leading article entitled 'J. V. Stalin, worthy heir to Lenin', a big photograph[1] on the front page, and a three-column article in honour of Stalin by G. Alexandrov. On the seventy-fifth anniversary of Stalin's birth in 1954 *Pravda* carried a large picture of the dead dictator on its front page and also mentioned him in its leading article. It also published another article called 'Stalin, worthy heir to Lenin'. The second anniversary of Stalin's death was commemorated in a much more restrained fashion. Stalin was not mentioned

[1] 7½ by 10¼ inches.

on the front page, *Pravda* merely publishing a cautious article by Konstantinov called 'J. V. Stalin and the establishment of communism'. On 21 December 1955 *Pravda* published his photograph[1] on the front page together with a commemorative article 'on the occasion of the seventy-sixth anniversary of Stalin's birth'.

The fact that the memory of Stalin was still stressed in this fashion only seven weeks before the opening of the Twentieth Party Congress permits the deduction that the decision to criticize Stalin at the Congress can have been taken only a short time beforehand. This conclusion is supported by further evidence. In the year before the Twentieth Party Congress a number of Soviet leaders had celebrated their sixtieth birthday, including Bulganin on 10 July and Mikoyan on 24 November 1955. In the official telegram of congratulations from the Central Committee they were described—as had been customary hitherto—as Lenin's faithful pupil and Stalin's comrade-in-arms. But when Voroshilov, the Chairman of the Supreme Soviet, celebrated his seventieth birthday on 3 February 1956, this formula was cut down: thus Voroshilov was merely congratulated as the faithful pupil of the great Lenin, without any mention of Stalin. It follows that the decision to criticize Stalin directly at the Twentieth Party Congress must have been taken between 21 December 1955 and 3 February 1956. But the date of this important political change can be still more exactly determined, because it is known from reliable reports that at a meeting of representatives of all the communist countries on 27 and 28 January 1956 they were informed that Stalin was about to be criticized. It follows from this that the Soviet leaders must have decided on direct criticism of Stalin between 21 December 1955 and 27 January 1956.

Open criticism of Stalin's despotism was necessary for two reasons. In the first place the principle of collective leadership needed further emphasis in order to prevent the emergence of a new autocrat. Secondly, it was desirable to destroy the myth of Stalin's infallibility so that the new leaders should not be tied by Stalin's policy. New measures required new theories.

The new principles of the Twentieth Party Congress aimed

[1] Only 7 by 8 inches this time.

at adapting the ideology of the Party to the changed conditions of the period since Stalin. The most important innovations involved the issues discussed above. An effort was made, too, to resuscitate faith in Lenin and to return to his gospel and carry out what it preached.

THE THEORY OF 'DIFFERENT ROADS TO SOCIALISM'

The most important ideological change was comprised in the theory of different roads to socialism. The fact that not only Khrushchev but also Suslov, Shepilov, Kaganovich, Molotov, and Kuusinen expressed themselves about it at length shows what importance was attributed to the matter.

Since the break with Yugoslavia in the summer of 1948, the very idea had been regarded as utter heresy. After 1948 all the communist states had been brought into line with the slogans 'We follow the example of the Soviet Union' and 'To learn from the Soviet Union means to learn to conquer'. All quotations from Marx, Engels, and Lenin about different roads to socialism had been severely suppressed.

At the Twentieth Party Congress the Party leaders not only conceded national idiosyncrasies in socialist development, but Khrushchev even spoke of the possibility of reaching socialism by the parliamentary road. He said in his report that the transition to socialism was by no means 'always bound up with civil war'. The parliamentary road to socialism was closed to the Russian bolsheviks, but since then 'fundamental changes have taken place which make it possible to approach this question in a new way'. In a number of capitalist countries today there existed the real possibility of defeating 'the reactionary forces hostile to the people' through a parliamentary vote. Supported by a mass movement the achievement of a stable majority in a number of capitalist states, as well as in formerly colonial countries, would 'create the conditions for carrying out fundamental social change'.

How far the rulers of the USSR intend to go in an ideological reorientation of this kind can usually be gathered from the extent to which quotations from the classics, Marx, Engels, and Lenin, are used in justification. In this case it was easy to find suitable quotations, because Marx and Engels, as well as Lenin, repeatedly stated that the road to socialism differs from country to country, and that in certain conditions the transformation could be achieved by taking the parliamentary road. At the Twentieth Party Congress Mikoyan was the only one who quoted a remark from a speech by Karl Marx, at a workers' meeting in Amsterdam in September 1872, which had been taboo in the Stalin era: 'We did not say that the paths to this goal (a socialist society) are the same everywhere. We know that different institutions, customs, and origins must be taken into account and we do not deny that there may be various countries, such as America and England, and if I knew your institutions better I might perhaps add Holland, where the workers can reach their goal by peaceful means.'[1]

There are, however, more far-reaching statements by Marx and Engels on this subject. Marx, for example, in his *Analysis of the debates on the anti-socialist law* at the end of September 1878 said: 'If the working class in England or the United States were to win a majority in Parliament or Congress it could remove constitutionally the laws and institutions which stand in the way of its development.' In his preface to the English edition of *Das Kapital* of 1886 Engels said that in England 'the inevitable social revolution could be carried out completely by peaceful and legal means'. In the eighties of the last century Engels also included France among those countries in which a peaceful transition to socialism appeared possible to him. In his pamphlet *Criticism of the social-democratic draft programme of 1891* he says: 'One can imagine that the old society could grow into the new one peacefully in countries in which the people's representatives hold all power, in which one can, constitutionally, do what one wants, as soon as one has a majority of the people behind one. This might be possible in such democratic republics as France and America or in such monarchies as Great Britain where the dynasty is powerless against the will of the people.'

All these statements went too far for the Soviet leaders who are otherwise so fond of quotations. In his speech to the Party Congress Mikoyan queried whether the Party was not beginning to slip down the slope of revision. He denied this, however, drawing a sharp distinction between himself and the revisionists or 'apologists for capitalism'; the possibility of peaceful

[1] Karl Marx, *Collected Works*, Vol. 13. Moscow 1940, pp. 668–9.

development, he declared, should never be confused with reformist ideas, and one should not forget 'that the revolution, whether peaceful or not, will always be a revolution'.[1]

Thus the Soviet leaders considered a peaceful transition to socialism as a *possibility*, nothing more. As concrete examples they quoted only the East European countries under Soviet influence; socialist tendencies in the non-Soviet world, Scandinavia, India, Burma, Israel, were not mentioned, and even Yugoslavia was dismissed in a few words.

In spite of these reservations the theory of different roads to socialism was of great importance. It provided the oppositional forces in Eastern Europe with an ideological justification for their attempts to secure independence. The unforeseen results forced the Soviet leaders to annul essential parts of their own thesis only a few months later.

But why did the Soviet leaders proclaim this dangerous view at all? They had three aims in mind. In the first place, they wished to facilitate a political and ideological *rapprochement* with Yugoslavia; secondly they wanted to forestall any oppositional tendencies in the other communist countries by this admission and to prevent the emergence of independent communist forces; thirdly, they wanted to make possible a *rapprochement* with the social-democratic parties abroad and with the nationalistic movements of Asia and Africa.

Both Khrushchev and Suslov hoped that communists and social democrats would stop their mutual recriminations and search for possibilities of co-operation. Their conciliatory offer was not, however, echoed back as they had expected. Since it was accompanied by sharp attacks on 'reformists' it failed to overcome the deep and well-founded distrust of Western socialism.

The Russian leaders showed greater readiness to compromise over their desire to co-operate with the revolutionary movements of Asia and Africa. Otto Kuusinen, who for many years had occupied a leading position in the Comintern, devoted the greater part of his speech to this question. He admitted that the Communist International had made serious mistakes. In particular the role of the middle class had not been correctly analysed in these countries, and it was very regrettable that

[1] Italicized in the official record.

until recently Gandhi's real achievements had been denied, for he had 'played an outstanding part in the history of the Indian people'. The conquest of 'sectarianism'—by which was meant the distinction between the communists and the nationalistic movements of Asia and Africa—was demanded also by Suslov. It was necessary, he said, 'to unite into an anti-imperialist stream' movements of all shades and colours in the Arab, Asian, and Latin-American countries; he appealed to 'Catholics or Protestants, followers of Buddhism or Islam', an indication of how far the Soviet leaders were prepared to go.

THE IDEOLOGICAL JUSTIFICATION OF CO-EXISTENCE

The second important ideological change was a new attitude towards the economic development of foreign countries and an acceptance of the view that wars might be avoided in the age of imperialism.

At the Twentieth Party Congress Mikoyan demanded above all an objective attitude towards the economic development of foreign countries. He expounded the new ideas of the Soviet leaders à propos Stalin's last book. 'This work does not explain the complicated phenomena of modern capitalism or the fact that capitalist production has increased in many countries since the war.' Soviet economic science was behindhand in the investigation of the present stage of capitalism. 'We do not subject the facts and figures to a thorough examination and we are often satisfied for purposes of propaganda to select isolated facts which suggest an impending crisis or illustrate the poverty of the workers, but we do not provide any comprehensive assessment of life in other countries.' Closely connected with the new attitude towards the West was the attempt to provide an ideological justification for the policy of co-existence, a phrase which has become the *leitmotiv* of the Soviet rulers since Stalin's death. In contrast with the theory of different roads to socialism that of co-existence cannot be supported by quotations from Marx, Engels, or Lenin. On the contrary, Lenin in his book *Imperialism as the Final Stage of Capitalism* said that wars are inevitable in the age of capitalism. Thus Lenin needed revision. Khrushchev said that Lenin's proposition that imperialism made war inevitable had been worked out at a time when imperialism was an all-embracing world system; the social and political forces without interest in war were then too weak to be able to force the imperialist powers to abandon it. This view had been justified during the first and a part of the second world war, but since then the socialist cause had become powerful. There was also a large group of other states—Khrushchev was clearly referring to the neutral countries of Asia and Africa—who had no interest in war; finally the 'workers' movement' and the 'movement for world peace' had become influential factors. Thus strong forces existed today which could prevent the imperialists from unleashing a war. All the speakers repeated the key sentence from Khrushchev's report 'that countries with different social systems can not only exist side by side, but beyond that must strive for an improvement of relations, a strengthening of confidence and mutual co-operation'.

There was, in fact, a tendency among the intellectuals and the planners, and probably even among Party officials, to push the policy of co-existence further than was agreeable to the Party chiefs. This is confirmed by Khrushchev's statement that some officials had tried 'to transplant into ideology the wholly correct conception of the possibility of the co-existence of countries with different social and political systems'. This was a 'dangerous mistake'. The fight against Western liberalism must by no means be abandoned; on the contrary, it was the duty of the Party untiringly to denounce the West.

Thus the Twentieth Party Congress had reduced several ideological absolutes, sacroscant until then, to a generous relativity, and had prepared the way for new political measures. In this sense the new formulations were to be seriously taken. On the other hand it must not be forgotten that the Soviet leaders wished to apply them with strict limitations. Thus they did not break with Stalinist ideology but adapted it to new conditions.

THE REVISION OF THE HISTORY OF THE PARTY

Soviet publications on the history of the Party have never been intended to suggest what really happened, but only what should have happened in accordance with Party policy at the time. In many ways Stalinist history no longer corresponded with the wishes of the new leaders: it had now to be adapted to new conditions. For this, too, the Party officials were prepared in good time.

The *Short Course in the History of the CPSU*, originally published in 1938 as the basic political textbook of the USSR, was mentioned less and less after the spring of 1953. On 26 July 1953 the Propaganda department of the Central Committee published a number of propositions on the fiftieth anniversary of the Second Party Congress. In these Stalin, who until then had been the central figure in Party history, was hardly mentioned.

This was the first step towards the revision of official Party history. In January 1954 a new edition was published of all the Party resolutions and decisions from 1898 to 1953. It contained a number of documents which were not in the collected volumes of the Stalin period. This material became the basis for the teaching of Party history in place of the *Short Course*. The revision of the history of the Party had thus begun long before the Twentieth Party Congress.

At the Party Congress the *Short Course* was publicly criticized for the first time. Khrushchev gave the signal for this in his report. Without directly attacking the *Short Course* he passed a devastating judgement on the book, as the author of which Stalin had let himself be glorified. 'The glorious history of our Party must be kept as one of the most important sources of political education. Hence we need a popular Marxist textbook of Party history based on historical facts; in it a general moral must be drawn from the Party's struggle for communism; it must deal with events up to our own days.'

Mikoyan declared roundly that historical research was 'the most backward section of our ideological work'. Until recently books 'in which facts are falsified, in which some people are arbitrarily praised, and others not mentioned at all, in which minor events are praised to the skies and other more important ones are played down' were described as 'unimpeachable standard works'. There were 'no really Marxist works on the period of the civil war', many history books had no scientific value, they had even done harm. Some historians had explained complicated historical events 'not by changes in the relative strengths of different classes in the various periods of history, but by the allegedly destructive activities of the individual Party leaders of the time, who many years after the events as described were wantonly branded as enemies of the people'. Such 'historical scribbling' had nothing in common with the Marxist view of history. It was unpardonable that there was no full history of the Party in the last two decades, and that almost forty years after the October Revolution there existed neither a short nor a detailed Marxist and Leninist textbook on the history of the October Revolution and the Soviet state to display, without glossing over things, not only the façade, but the whole of Soviet life. Mikoyan asked the historians to study the history of the Party thoroughly and 'to burrow in the archives and not only in the newspapers of the period'. Then they would be able 'to throw more light from the Leninist point of view on many events explained in the *Short Course*'.

Anna Pankratova attacked the habit of glossing things over under Stalin. She complained that some historians dressed up historical events or over-simplified them. They represented the road which the Party had taken as one long march of triumph. The historical literature of the Stalin era was too dry, she said. The memoirs of the old Bolsheviks must be utilized. And in particular a fight must be fought against a subjective attitude to history.

During the Twentieth Party Congress, the second issue that year of the periodical *Voprosy Istorii* went into print. It contained a report of a conference of 600 historians and history teachers which had taken place at the end of January, that is, shortly before the Twentieth Party Congress. At this conference Anna Pankratova and the deputy editor-in-chief of *Voprosy Istorii*, E. N. Burdzhalov, had been in favour of a new look at Party history. In this they had gone far beyond the demands of the Party Congress: it was impossible, they had said, that historians should write about Party Congresses, as had been the case until then, without using the stenographic records. The history of the Party must be freed from falsifications. By 'falsifications' were meant the three most important official writings on the history of the Party in the Stalin period: The *Short Course of the History of the CPSU*, Beria's book *On the History of Bolshevik Organization in Transcaucasia*, and Mir Dzhafar Bagirov's *History of the Bolshevik Organization in Azerbaidjan*.

In the following issues of *Voprosy Istorii* criticism was not restricted to the period after 1934—as at the Twentieth Party Congress—but the events of the year 1917 and even the period before the revolution were put in a new light. In the publications on the revolution of 1917 and the Civil War, Stalin's role was said to have been in part misrepresented, in part exaggerated. For this purpose the fighting at Tsarytsin (later Stalingrad) had been made into the most important event of the Civil War, whereas in reality the fighting on the Eastern front was of greater importance. In this connexion the real leaders of the Civil War, whose names had been suppressed for almost three decades, were mentioned again for the first time.

The revision of Party history was also dealt with in other publications. *Kommunist*[1] criticized the history of the Party as presented hitherto in the Soviet Encyclopaedia, and it later published a new interpretation of Plekhanov.[2] In the leading article of the March number of *Partinaya Zhizn* it was announced that the archives of the Foreign Ministry and the Ministry of the Interior would, as far as possible, be put at the disposal of historians. All documents dealing with past events, except those relating to current affairs of state, would, after examination, be made generally available within the next two years. The times in which historians had been hindered in their research through bureaucratic measures and exaggerated secrecy, belonged to the past. The journal asked Soviet historians 'to study the facts of history conscientiously and objectively and to correct the many errors of historical science'. The monthly journal of the Ministry of Defence, *Voyenny Vestnik*, demanded, in the second half of April, a thorough examination of all descriptions of the war. Soviet military science must be cleansed of the personality cult, and the part which the people, the Party, and the armed forces had played during the war must be correctly gauged.

THE REHABILITATION OF FORMER 'ENEMIES OF THE PEOPLE'

The rehabilitation of Stalin's victims was closely connected with the revision of the history of the Party. Already between 1953 and 1955 old Bolsheviks, who under Stalin had been

[1] No. 3, 1956.   [2] No. 6, 1956.

forced out of public life or even arrested, had been silently rehabilitated and decorated with orders and medals.

At the Party Congress these rehabilitations were freely mentioned and well-known Bolshevik leaders were referred to by name. Mikoyan in his speech of 17 February referred with praise to Stanislav Kossior, a member of the Central Committee from 1918, for many years First Party Secretary of the Ukraine and from 1930 a member of the Politburo, who disappeared in 1938; he also spoke of Vladimir Antonov-Ovseyenko, a famous leader who had been Secretary of Trotsky's Military Committee which organized the rising of October 1917. Later Antonov-Oveseyenko was head of the Political Administration of the Red Army. Under Stalin he was robbed of all power and was sent in 1936 to Barcelona as Soviet Consul; after his return to Russia he was arrested.

The Polish Communist Party was also 'rehabilitated' at the Party Congress. In a joint declaration the Party leaders of the USSR, Poland, Italy, Bulgaria, and Finland condemned the decision of the Communist International of January 1938 to dissolve the Polish Communist Party and stated that the assertion of the Comintern that there were 'hostile agents' among the Polish Party leaders was false. In reality the Polish communists had fought creditably both before and after the dissolution of the Party. In this connexion the Soviet press paid tribute to the refounding of the Polish Workers' Party in 1942 in which Wladislaw Gomulka played a decisive part. This was the first step towards the rehabilitation of Gomulka. On 21 February 1956 followed the rehabilitation of Bela Kun, the founder of the Hungarian Communist Party, who was executed in Russia in 1938. In an article signed by Eugene Verga he was described as one of the most important leaders of the international workers' movement. After the Party Congress, countless other victims of Stalin's wave of persecution were rehabilitated and, if they were still alive, released from prisons and camps. After the Twentieth Party Congress, the names of those who had been arrested or even shot during the Great Purge were again mentioned by every kind of writer without any further explanation. Some writers were said to have died 'too young'. Several old Bolsheviks were rehabilitated through the publication of their former books, which, however, had been partly revised. Thus the memoirs of Vladimir Antonov-Ovseyenko were now published in a large edition. A book by the former Commissar for Justice, Nikolai Krylenko, another victim of Stalin's great purge, was allowed to reappear.

Voprosy Istorii[1] published historical articles in which, without further explanation, three former members of the Politburo, Yan Rudzutak, Pavel Postyshev, and Yakov Chubar were again mentioned with approval. Rudzutak had been branded as an 'enemy of the people' at the Moscow 'trial' in March 1938, and Postyshev, who had rebelled against the continuation of the purge, was recalled from the Ukraine in April 1937 and disappeared shortly afterwards.

Among the most prominent of Stalin's victims who came back into favour was the former Secretary of the Siberian Party Committee, Robert Eikhe, who had been arrested in April 1938, the former Secretary-General of the Komsomol, Alexander Kosarev, who in the late autumn of 1938 became a victim of the purge of the Komsomol leadership, and the old Bolshevik, Andrey Bubnov, in 1917 a member of the Central Committee and of the Revolutionary Military Committee,[2] who until his arrest in 1937 had been People's Commissar for Education in the RSFSR. Nikolai Zkrypnik, too, one of the leading Ukrainian Party leaders, who had committed suicide in 1933, was again mentioned with approval.

The posthumous rehabilitation of these and other prominent Party characters—even if only by way of praise in some article—was something which had wide repercussions. The political fall, the arrest or the shooting of one of these leaders during the thirties usually affected thousands, and sometimes even tens of thousands, of people; their posthumous rehabilitation thus meant the rehabilitation of all those who had been prosecuted in connexion with them. For those who were still alive this meant release from the camps.

Apart from Party leaders, former People's Commissars—or Ministers—and army leaders who had been arrested during the Great Purge were praised again; among them were the former Minister for Health, G. N. Kaminski, the former Under-Secretary for War. J. S. Unshlikht, and M. Rukhimovich, a military leader in the Civil War who, until his arrest, had been

Minister for the armaments industry, Yan Gamarnik, too, who had for ten years been the head of the main Political Administration of the Red Army, and who had committed suicide on 31 May 1937 shortly before the Tukhachevsky affair, were now rehabilitated in similar fashion.

Among the army leaders who were rehabilitated, the following should be mentioned: the former supreme commander of the armed forces in the Far Eastern Republic, Marshal Blücher, and Marshal Yegorov, for many years Chief of the General Staff of the Red Army and Under-Secretary for War. Both vanished after 1938.

The rehabilitations also included some writers and publicists. Mikhail Koltsov, contributor to *Pravda* and *Krokodil*, who had been arrested after his return from Spain, was again spoken of with approval. The Academy of Sciences began to publish books by Professor Vavilov, the former President of the Agricultural Academy, who had been purged as an enemy of Stalin's favourite, Trofim Lysenko. At about the same time, in April 1956, Lysenko lost his office as President of the Academy for Agricultural Research.

Some of the historians who had been banned in the days of Stalin were again approved, among them the much abused Mikhail Pokrovsky, whose books Lenin had valued highly, as well as Knorin, the author of a Party history which had appeared earlier. Finally, the great producer, Vsevolod Meyerhold, who had been arrested in 1939 and probably murdered, was also at least partially rehabilitated. The publication of his literary works was announced.

An exceptional form of indirect rehabilitation was used in the case of the former member of the Politburo, Alexei Rykov. On 22 April 1956, *Pravda* published a letter of 1922 from Lenin to Rykov, one of the oldest and most prominent Bolsheviks. Rykov had been a member of the Central Committee since 1905. After Lenin's death, he succeeded him as Chairman of the Council of People's Commissars or Prime Minister. From 1925 to 1928, together with Bukharin and Tomsky, he led the 'right-wing opposition' which was directed against Stalin. With Stalin's rise, his own decline began: in 1929 he was expelled from the Politburo and the Central Committee for 'rightist opportunism', in 1931 he was degraded to the post of

Minister for Posts and Communications, on 27 September 1936 he was relieved of this post also, on 5 March 1937, together with Bukharin, he was expelled from the Party and in March 1938 sentenced to death.

The rehabilitations belong to the most important events of the first years after Stalin's death. But they, too, had their limits. These former 'enemies of the people' were again mentioned with approval, but in no case was it said when and how they had died. As a rule those were rehabilitated who had actively supported the Stalin faction until 1934 and had been arrested later. The leaders and supporters of the anti-Stalinist groups of the twenties—such as Trotsky, Bukharin, Kamenev, Zinoviev, Shlapnikov, and Tomsky continued to be banned.

THE 'RETURN TO LENINISM'

Both criticism of the personality cult and ideological changes were justified by saying that the Party leaders were allowing 'the directives of the great Lenin' to guide them. The farther the new rulers of the USSR departed from Stalin's assumptions, the more Lenin and his writings were pushed into the foreground. An interesting change was made over the celebration of Lenin's anniversaries. Lenin had hitherto been commemorated on 21 January, the day of his death. On 10 January 1955 the ruling authorities decided to change the commemoration to Lenin's birthday on 22 April. This gave it a different character. Formerly the celebrations were focused on the last period of Lenin's life, when Stalin already played a role in the Party, and the time thereafter when Stalin took over the leadership of the Party and the Government. The celebrations had, in fact, not so much glorified Lenin as Stalin. During the thirties the following riddle went round Moscow: 'What is it that starts with Stalin, continues with Stalin and ends with Stalin?' Answer: 'A commemoration of Lenin!' By changing the date, the period of Party history when Lenin was leader and Stalin played no noteworthy part was emphasized. No longer was Lenin's death, and thus the end of the Lenin era, commemorated, but its beginning, its flowering, in order, according to the resolution of 10 January 1955, 'to give this day an importance which corresponds to the whole spirit of Leninism as an ever-living, life-affirming doctrine'.

At the Twentieth Party Congress Khrushchev announced that in connexion with the fourth edition of the thirty-five volumes of Lenin's collected works a new biography of Lenin was to be published. Madame Pankratova remarked critically that the publication of Lenin's legacy of doctrine 'was not completely satisfying'. Many important books by Lenin had not been published; some of Lenin's articles and letters which were contained in the second and third edition of Lenin's works 'had for some reason or other not been incorporated in the fourth edition'. This was obviously directed against Stalin, because this edition had been prepared in the time of Stalin and a large part of the volumes had appeared before his death. Mikoyan, too, lamented that 'in the last fifteen to twenty years very little of the wealth of Lenin's ideas had been utilized'.

It is probable that some of the Soviet chiefs, particularly those who had themselves been threatened by Stalin and his staff, were quite honest in their professions of belief in Lenin. Great applause at the Party Congress showed that this applied even more to the delegates who attended it. But the tribute paid to Lenin by no means implied a return to the practices of the Lenin period. The Twentieth Party Congress, with its unanimous resolutions, its carefully read speeches, and solid unanimity even over the most delicate questions, was much more like a Party Congress of the Stalin era than the Bolshevik congresses of the first years after the revolution. The retreat from some Stalinist principles was a first hesitant step, but by no means a return to Leninism.

Nevertheless, the importance of the fact that between March and June 1956 many important Lenin documents appeared, which had hitherto been suppressed, must not be under-rated. The most important publication of this kind was a collection of seven documents in *Kommunist*.[1] It included a letter (generally known as his *Testament*) written on 25 December 1922 to the Party Congress in which Lenin described the most important Bolshevik leaders of the day, Trotsky, Bukharin, Stalin, Zinoviev, Kamenev, and Pyatakov. About Stalin, Trotsky and Bukharin he wrote:

'Having become Secretary-General Comrade Stalin has acquired immense power, and I am not sure that he will always

[1] No. 5, 1956.

know how to use this power with sufficient caution. On the other hand, Comrade Trotsky, as already shown by his struggle against the Central Committee on the question of the People's Commissariat for Transport, is distinguished not only by outstanding abilities. Personally he is no doubt the ablest man in the present Central Committee, but at the same time he is possessed by too much self-confidence and an excessive inclination towards the entirely administrative solution of problems. . . . Bukharin is not only a most valuable and most eminent Party theorist, he is also regarded as the favourite of the whole Party; but it is very doubtful whether his theoretical views can be regarded as wholly Marxist, because there is something pedantic in them (he never studied and, in my view, has never fully understood dialectics). . . .'

Another Lenin document published in *Kommunist* showed the differences between Lenin and Stalin on the nationalities question. In an article published in December 1922, Lenin gave a warning against Stalin: 'I believe that Stalin's haste and administrative impetuousness, as well as his stubbornness over the famous "social-nationalism" played a fatal part in this. In politics there is nothing worse than such stubbornness. . . .'

Finally, *Kommunist* in the same number also published Lenin's famous 'postscript' to his testament of 4 January 1923, in which he attacked Stalin sharply and proposed his dismissal:

'Stalin is too rude and this failing which is bearable in our circles and in the relations between us communists, becomes quite intolerable in the office of the Secretary-General. Therefore I propose to our comrades that they should think of a way of removing Stalin from this post and appointing to it another man who should distinguish himself from Stalin by being more patient, more loyal, more courteous, more attentive to our comrades, less capricious. . . .'

Kommunist commented upon the publication of these Lenin documents, which had been kept secret until then, as follows: 'J. V. Stalin flagrantly disregarded the Leninist principle of collective direction, allowed the misuse of power and infringements of socialist legality, and committed serious mistakes in the organization of agriculture, in military questions, and in foreign policy.' The reference to Stalin's mistakes in foreign policy, which had never been officially mentioned until then, suggested that the Soviet Party leaders were thinking of a criticism of Stalinism in this respect, also, in June 1956.

It is characteristic that even at this stage the Soviet leaders did not mention the fact that these documents had long been published abroad or announce anything about the fate of the colleagues whom Lenin had valued so highly. Zinoviev and Kamenev, who had defended Stalin so passionately in May 1924, were arrested in 1935 and shot after a staged trial on 25 August 1936. Vishinsky, Public Prosecutor at the time, abused them at this trial as 'mad dogs'. Pyatakov, to whom Lenin in his testament attributed outstanding abilities, was tried with thirteen other old Bolsheviks in January 1937; he was denounced by Vishinsky as 'leader of this gang of bandits' and shot on 20 January 1937. Nikolai Bukharin, called by Lenin the 'favourite of the whole Party', was insulted by Vishinsky at the trial from 2 to 13 March 1938 as an 'accursed mongrel, half fox and half swine', and shot on 15 March 1938. Leo Trotsky was expelled from the Soviet Union in 1929 at Stalin's instigation and murdered on 20 August 1940 in Coyoacan (Mexico) by the NKVD agent, Jacques Mercarder. On the occasion of his death *Pravda*[1] published an article headed 'Death of an international spy'.

The limited publication of the Lenin documents, no doubt carefully thought out by Stalin's successors, shows the split mind of the Soviet Party leaders at that time: in the desire to free themselves from Stalin and some of his methods, they went so far as to publish papers in which Stalin was sharply attacked and Stalin's victims were referred to with approval. On the other hand, the rulers of Russia were not, even at the climax of de-Stalinization, prepared to admit serious political discussion of the struggles inside the Party before 1934, because this would have made inevitable an at least partial rehabilitation of the anti-Stalin faction in the Party opposition. They themselves, moreover, would have been discredited, since they had risen to power thanks to their support of Stalin.

STATE, JUSTICE, AND NATIONALITIES POLICY

The central bureaucracy of the state was sharply criticized at the Party Congress. According to Khrushchev, 750,000

[1] 24 August 1940.

people had been dismissed from the administration since Stalin's death. But in spite of this, it was still 'excessively large'. The main thing was to simplify the administrative structure, cut down the number of posts, and to come closer to the public. The Ministry of State Control, which had as one of its tasks the supervision of the execution of Party and governmental decisions was to be 'fundamentally reorganized'.

Voroshilov was critical of the fact that meetings of the Soviets were not called for the appointed dates. This was an infringement of the constitution. The Soviets, he complained, were bureaucratic in their working methods and had no contact with life; deputies should take an active part in the administration of the state.

Khrushchev said that the Party leaders had in recent years 'paid great attention to the consolidation of socialist legality'. Apart from the Leningrad Affair, they 'had also examined a number of other dubious trials' and had 'taken measures to restore legality'. Innocent people who had been sentenced had been rehabilitated and the state security organs had been placed 'under the necessary Party and governmental control'.

About the state security service, Khrushchev said: 'It must be said, as a result of the rescinding of the verdicts in some cases, a certain suspicion of the members of the state security service has arisen among some comrades. This is, of course, very unfortunate. We know that the overwhelming majority of the members of our state security service consists of honest officials who are devoted to our common cause, and we trust them.' This explanation had a double meaning. On the one hand, it saved the honour of the state security service, and, on the other, the hint that not all members of the secret police were honourable people left open the possibility of further trials of state security officials. In fact, the next one—of Bagirov—took place only three weeks after the Twentieth Party Congress.

Soon after the Party Congress, important changes in the administration of justice were announced. A resolution of the Praesidium of the Supreme Soviet of the USSR of 19 April 1956 dissolved the special tribunals of the Ministry of the Interior which played such a fateful part during the great purge and after it. All investigation procedures which had formerly been under the direction of the special tribunals were passed to the judicial authorities which were in future to observe the procedures laid down in the penal codes. A second decree extended the duties of the public prosecutors. A judicial commission for the codification of the law was also appointed. The central Ministry of Justice was dissolved and its functions handed over to the Union Republics. The assumption made in Stalin's day, in particular by Vishinsky, that an accused person could be sentenced if there was only a probability of his guilt, was condemned. The practice of arriving at verdicts solely on the basis of the personal confession of the accused was officially described as 'an offence which cries to heaven against the principle of socialist legality and the foundations of jurisprudence'. Further legislation concerning social and economic matters was announced.

The drive against the power of the state security service was continued with the trial of Mir Dzhafar Bagirov and five high officials of the Caucasian state security service.[1] Bagirov had occupied a leading position in the Caucasian state security service from 1920 to 1931. In 1933 he became First Secretary of the Communist Party of Azerbaidjan. He was prominent as an obstinate Stalinist, both in the ideological field, thanks to his *History of the Bolshevik Organization in Azerbaidjan*, and, between 1950 and 1953, in the fight against 'cosmopolitans' and 'bourgeois nationalists'. At the Nineteenth Party Congress in 1952 he had made the strongest speech in this direction. Shortly after Beria's fall in July 1953 he was relieved of all his offices. Now he was sentenced to death together with three high officials of the state security service, while two other accused were sentenced to twenty-five years' deprivation of liberty.[2]

The Twentieth Party Congress also confirmed the new nationalities policy. Whereas the Nineteenth Party Congress had still emphasized the 'leading role of the Russian people' and demanded an intensified struggle against 'bourgeois nationalism',[3] at the Twentieth Party Congress the leading role of the Russian people was no longer mentioned. Instead, Khrushchev declared that the Party was guided in its nationalities policy by Lenin's view that only a very careful regard for

[1] 12–26 April 1956.   [2] Bakinsky, Raboshy, 27 May 1956.
[3] Meaning the movements in the non-Russian Union Republics which resisted Stalin's russification.

the interests of the different nations can remove their mutual distrust. Madame Pankratova spoke particularly strongly against the nationalistic version of Russian history. But the theory propagated since the forties that the annexation of the non-Russian populations by (tsarist) Russia had been progressive she still described as 'completely correct'. It was important, however, to pay attention 'to the other side of the question': 'Tsarism subjugated nations in a cruel fashion and hindered their political, economic, and cultural development.' She recalled that Lenin had described tsarist Russia as a 'prison of the peoples'. The history of nationalist movements must be studied more thoroughly, and the battle, not only against the nationalism of the non-Russian nations, but also against Great Power chauvinism (this, of course, referred to Russia) must be continued, because they 'were two sides of the same medal'.

Soon after the Party Congress *Voprosy Istorii* published a series of articles on the abuses which had been denounced. It condemned the tendency to pre-date the beginnings of the Russian state, the idealization of Ivan the Terrible and the Russian army leaders Suvarov, Kutusov, and Admiral Nakhimov, and the justification of the tsarist annexation of non-Russian peoples. The history of the non-Russian nationalists, of their thinkers, and their revolutionary movements was re-emphasized. The famous nineteenth-century champion of Caucasian freedom, Shamil, whom Bagirov had described in 1950 as a British agent, was 'rehabilitated'!

THE ECONOMIC DIRECTIVES

The major portion of all the speeches at the Congress was concerned with economic policy. In contrast with the Nineteenth Party Congress abuses were much more openly mentioned. A number of new measures were announced which were intended to modernize the direction of the economy. The size of the administrative machine was to be reduced; the economy was to be profitably run. Thus material incentives were to be provided; authority was to be distributed at lower levels, enterprise directors and trade union officials were to be given greater rights, and the interest of manual and office workers in production was to be stimulated by giving them a

THE FIFTEEN REPUBLICS OF THE USSR

Armenia
1·8 m. inhabitants
Capital: Erivan

Azerbaidjan
3·7 m. inhabitants
Capital: Baku

Georgia
4 m. inhabitants
Capital: Tbilisi (Tiflis)

USSR

Union of Soviet Socialist
Republics

Estonia
1·2 m. inhabitants
Capital: Tallinn

204 m. inhabitants

Capital: Moscow

Latvia
2·1 m. inhabitants
Capital: Riga

Lithuania
2·7 m. inhabitants
Capital: Vilna

White Russia
Bielorussia
8 m. inhabitants
Capital: Minsk

Turkmenistan
1·5 m. inhabitants
Capital: Ashkhabad

Uzbekistan
8 m. inhabitants
Capital: Tashkent

Tadzhikistan
1·9 m. inhabitants
Capital: Stalinabad

Kazakhstan
9·3 m. inhabitants
Capital: Alma-Ata

Kirgisia
2 m. inhabitants
Capital: Frunze

Moldavia
2·9 m. inhabitants
Capital: Kishinev

RSFSR

Ukraine
41·9 m. inhabitants
Capital: Kiev

Russian
Federal Soviet Socialist Republic

117·5 m. inhabitants

Capital: Moscow

limited right to express their views and by offering social improvements. The essential principle for the future was to be the priority of heavy industry together with greater attention to the production of consumer goods. The production of goods for the needs of the masses was to be increased almost threefold between 1950 and 1960. The location of Soviet industry was to encourage the development of Siberia, the Soviet Far East, and Kazakhstan. Industry was to be mechanized and automation introduced.

The egoistical management of Russia's concerns was described as the most dangerous phenomenon in the Soviet economy. Pervukhin said that quite a few Soviet economic officials suffered from such a narrow, egocentric attitude towards their own enterprise that 'they were incapable of looking further than the end of their nose'. Saburov, who made one of the most remarkable speeches, did not restrict his criticism to local shortcomings in Soviet planning as had been customary until then, but spoke of a lack of proportion in the state as a whole. In the past Five-Year Plan he said the development of mining had lagged behind the requirements of the coal-consuming industries because of faults in planning; this had had serious consequences for the Soviet economy. The larger the scale of production the more dangerous were the consequences of ill-co-ordinated planning.

The decentralization of the control of the economy was generally welcomed. Khrushchev said that centralization had been necessary earlier and that only now had a transition to decentralization become possible because in the meantime a sufficient number of specialists had been trained in the Union Republics.

After the Party Congress the non-Russian Union Republics were given new economic competence. For instance, the duties of the central ministries of transport, roads, and river traffic were handed over to the Union Republics. On 4 June 1956 *Pravda* commented that it was high time 'to end the petty supervision of the Union Republics'. The Union Republics must be given the right, within the general framework of the Soviet Union, 'to decide concrete questions of economic development for themselves'. In the short period between 1 January and 1 July 1956,[1] 5,600 enterprises which had formerly been under

[1] This emerges from the textbook *The Economy of the Industry of the USSR*, published in 1957.

central control were handed over to the Union Republics concerned.

Less clear was the attitude of the Soviet leaders to the role of the enterprise directors. At the Twentieth Party Congress Khrushchev interestingly enough made no mention at all of the important decree on the extension of these functionaries' rights, and Bulganin glossed it over with a brief remark. Pervukhin, on the other hand, particularly stressed it. He complained that a number of central institutions had resisted this order. Almost as if he were resigned to it, he remarked: 'We take many decisions over the various economic problems, but they are often carried out badly and late.'

Some speakers, in particular Bulganin, Kaganovich, and Shvernik, explained what demands the Party made of a modern director of a concern. Bulganin said that he must not only be a good technician and organizer, but that he must also be in close contact with those he employed and pay attention to their criticism. Shvernik was critical of the fact that so many managers did not, in fact, discuss questions of production with the workers at all.

In the discussion of agriculture particular emphasis was laid on the difference since Stalin's time. There was hardly a prominent speaker who did not refer to the weakness of agricultural policy up to 1953 and who did not report on the difficult heritage which the post-Stalin leaders had been left. The most important measures since Stalin's death—the increase in procurement prices, the dispatch of specialists from the administration to do practical work at the collective and state farms and machine and tractor stations, as well as the sending of Party officials to direct collective farms, the virgin lands campaign and the relaxation of agricultural planning—were, as might have been expected, generally welcome. There were complaints, however, that the administrative machine was still too big.

In future, the collective farms were to be encouraged to set up their own ancillary services, for example, brickyards or small power stations, as well as buildings for general use, for nurseries, homes for old people, clubs, and maternity homes. This was a remarkable retreat from the Nineteenth Party Congress, at which Malenkov had said in his report that a stop must be put to such practices.

Agricultural administration was to be simplified. 'We do not need a central machine which takes over the duties of local bodies,' said Khrushchev. The agricultural authorities should limit themselves to the study of progressive methods and to their introduction; for this a small staff of highly qualified specialists was enough. The observations of Nikolai Belyayev, who spoke strongly in favour of working at a profit and the recognition of the price factor in agriculture, were particularly interesting. He attacked the system of administrative prices— procurement prices, contract prices, and bonuses—and demanded that prices for agricultural products should be 'brought into line with the use of material and labour per unit of production'.

TRADE UNIONS AND SOCIAL POLICY

The Twentieth Party Congress devoted more attention to social questions than any of its predecessors. It dealt with the role of the trade unions, the changing of the wage system, the consultation of factory and office workers over internal questions, and social and political measures to benefit the population. Never before had so much emphasis been put on the implementation of the trade unions.

Khrushchev complained that many enterprises did not keep collective contracts, 'but the trade unions are silent, as though everything were all right'. In future trade unions should attack the bureaucratic attitude of the managers and work for the material interests of the workers more vigorously. He even encouraged the trade unions 'to have a real fight' with the managers. At the same time, however, it was demanded that the trade unions should subordinate themselves unconditionally to the Party. Shvernik promised that the Soviet trade unions would continue to obey the directives of the Communist Party and to be its faithful allies.

To make factory and office workers take a greater interest in the production of their enterprise, production councils should be called together more often than before and be given greater authority. Kaganovich even described the production councils as the true centre of the enterprise. The system of 'socialist competitions', so favoured under Stalin, was cautiously criticized. Kirichenko complained that competitions resulted in superfluous gatherings at which 'much, very much, was only talk'. Often commitments were entered into which nobody believed would be fulfilled; this threatened to become a 'mass phenomenon'. There was also a popular form of competition which committed no one to anything; 'Quite often it happens like this: Two collective farms have a competition. Both show bad results at the end of the year. Neither has fulfilled its commitments or even its plan. But one can show slightly better figures and is acclaimed the victor. The thing has been a failure, but there must needs be a winner.'

A reform of the wage system was also demanded at the Twentieth Party Congress as it had been at the Plenary Session in July 1955. Higher wages were promised for work on the new buildings in the Eastern and Northern regions of the USSR. The demand for the abolition of big wage differentials was significant. Most speakers justified them as having been a practical necessity, but Mikoyan advanced a political argument: the big difference in wages had been justified in the period of industrialization when workers had to be encouraged to become skilled quickly. Now that a highly skilled body of workers existed it was possible to reduce differences in wages.

Khrushchev announced that it had already been decided in principle to raise the wages of the less well-paid workers. Kaganovich, who was responsible as chairman of the committee for questions of labour and wages, tried almost desperately to explain to the Party delegates how difficult it would be to carry out this decision. Twice he pointed out that he needed time. Four months after the Party Congress, on 6 June 1956, he was dismissed and replaced by Alexander Volkov, chairman of the Council of the Union of the Supreme Soviet of the USSR, who on 9 February 1955 had read Malenkov's request to be relieved of his duties.

Still more important was the labour code announced by Khrushchev at the Party Congress; in particular, the rescinding of one of the most unpopular orders of the Stalin period. The working day was to be reduced to seven hours for manual and office workers, and for underground workers in coal and ore mining and juveniles of sixteen to eighteen years of age to six hours. On Saturdays and any day before a public holiday, only six hours should be worked. The transition to the short-ened working day without loss of wages was to be completed in all branches of the economy by the end of the sixth Five-Year Plan, i.e. by 1960. An improvement in pensions was also indicated; rates for the lowest paid pension groups were to be raised, but unjustifiably high pension rates were to be reduced. An improvement in the provision for old age and disablement and an extension of paid maternity leave were also announced. From the beginning of the new educational year, i.e. 1 September 1956, fees[1] at universities and technical teaching institutions as well as in the three highest classes of the Soviet ten-class schools were to be abolished.

This time there were not only promises. Several of the measures announced were put into effect only a few weeks after the Twentieth Party Congress. On 8 March 1956 the Praesidium of the Supreme Soviet decided to reduce the hours worked on days preceding Sundays and public holidays to six hours. On 10 March a joint resolution of the Central Com-mittee and the Council of Ministers laid down that members of the collective farms must be paid monthly advances—though at the same time the number of compulsory labour-days was fixed. On 28 March paid maternity leave for pregnant women and breast-feeding mothers was increased from 77 to 112 days.

On 25 April followed the most striking measure of all, that is to say the official withdrawal of the order of 26 June 1940 according to which workers were not allowed to leave their place of work; for arriving more than twenty minutes late they were no longer liable to a period of up to six months compul-sory corrective labour at their place of work. The order that a worker could give notice only with the consent of the authori-ties was also rescinded. All penalties imposed for leaving a place of work without permission were abolished. Workers who had been sentenced on these grounds were to be released and all proceedings pending against persons who had left their place of work were to be dropped. A fortnightly period for giving notice was introduced.

On 9 May 1956 followed the resolution cutting working hours for juveniles from eight to six. On the same day the draft

---

[1] Introduced in autumn 1940.

of a new pensions law was published, laying down a minimum pension of 300 roubles and a maximum of 1,200 roubles. In the case of those who had been earning up to 350 roubles a month, pensions were to go up to the full amount of the former monthly wage; in the case of incomes larger than this, they were to amount to up to 50 per cent. of what had been earned. Finally, on 9 June 1956, compulsory educational fees were abolished.

EDUCATIONAL POLICY

Questions of popular education, science, and art also occupied a considerable amount of time in the Party Congress debates. The introduction of technical instruction in the schools was the central item of interest. Khrushchev criticized the teaching in schools for being out of touch with life. The policy decreed by the Nineteenth Party Congress on the introduction of technical education had only been carried out hesitantly. It was wrong to prepare pupils only for the transition to further education; the main task was to educate them for practical work, because the majority of those leaving school would work in industry. The Chairman of the Komsomol, Alexander Shelepin, too, remarked critically that Soviet schools 'did not do justice to the demands of life'. This led 'to sad results'. Out of 3 million school leavers during the fifth Five-Year Plan (1951–5) 1·38 million had gone on to further education 'and what are the rest doing? Many of them don't work at all.' This was the fault of the schools which did not impart to their pupils the necessary practical skills.

Khrushchev demanded also the establishment of boarding schools which were to be set up in suburbs and on suitable sites in the country. In these boarding schools 'all the conditions for an all-round physical and intellectual development of the young citizen of the Soviet Union will be created'. Admittance to such boarding schools was to be exclusively at the request of the parents. Fees were to be adapted to the circumstances of the family. For children of poorer families the state would take over the costs, parents with higher incomes would have to pay a certain amount and 'a certain number of parents'—by which were meant of course the senior state, Party, and economic officials—would have to be responsible for the whole cost of a

child's education. Khrushchev keenly supported these boarding schools: 'Here we must not stint money nor effort for they
will be repaid a hundredfold.'

The Soviet universities, too, were accused of lacking contact
with practical life. Education always lagged behind the level of
technology. The universities were still too much confined to
Moscow and Leningrad: thus it was necessary to transfer them
to the centres of production, where the demand for specialists
was particularly great. Bulganin announced that in the period
of the sixth Five-Year Plan (1956–60) 4 million specialists were
to be trained, almost as many as in the preceding ten years.

In the Party Congress debates interesting differences of
opinion emerged on the relation between pure and applied
science. The president of the Academy of Sciences, Professor
Alexander Nesmeyanov, spoke against an excessively 'practical
approach'. It should not be the main task of the Academy of
Sciences to search for results of immediate practical importance.
On the contrary, it should be to 'discover and investigate new
phenomena in nature and society and to trace the logical
sequence of phenomena, and utilize this in the interest of
socialist society'. Even *Pravda's* leading article of 6 February
1956 had not put sufficient emphasis on the importance of
theory. For example, it was wrong that the Ministry of Trade
should order the Academy of Sciences to instal on the doors of
the 'Prague' restaurant a device which automatically opened
them at the approach of a guest. The Academy of Sciences
should not be overwhelmed with practical tasks of this sort.
Technical progress could not be guaranteed without a general
extension of theoretical research.

T. S. Maltsev, a member of the Party since 1939 and an
honorary member of the Academy of Agriculture, in a grandi-
loquent speech interpreted the relationship of theory and
practice quite differently. Maltsev criticized those scientists who
were only rarely to be seen on collective farms or machine and
tractor stations. Many had not taken up a scientific career for
love of science 'but because they hoped to obtain a degree in
science and to secure their material position at the expense of
the state'. He went so far as to demand close collaboration
between philosophers and collective farmers: 'Comrade philosophers, more contact with representatives of the natural

sciences, in particular the representatives of the agronomic sciences, the practical men of the collective farms, state farms, and machine and tractor stations!' Nesmeyanov's and Maltsev's speeches revealed tendencies which are likely to influence future developments. It was noticeable that Trofim Lysenko, who in the Stalin era had played the part of a dictator in biology, exercised the utmost restraint in his speech to the Congress. Lysenko described himself as a scientist without Party allegiance and refrained from all polemics, restricting himself to a factual presentation of a number of specialized agricultural problems.

The Twentieth Party Congress confirmed the renunciation of ostentatious architecture. Khrushchev said that it could no longer be tolerated 'that millions of roubles be spent on point-less decoration'. Buildings should offer people 'a maximum of comfort' and 'be solid, practical and beautiful'. It was desirable that small, modern settlements should be built in the vicinity of big towns. The building of private houses should be en-couraged side by side with municipal housing.

It was striking that the problems of Soviet literature were little mentioned at the Twentieth Party Congress. Khrushchev complained that in spite of many achievements literature and art lagged behind Soviet reality. Creative activity must be permeated 'by the spirit of the struggle for Communism'. Bobodzhan Gafurov, Party Secretary of Tadzhikistan, accused the writers of having been surrounded by the people with love, respect, and care without having given the people anything in return in the last few years. The feeling of responsibility which was to be found among the officials of industry and agriculture was missing in the 'workers on the cultural front'. Gafurov's comparison between writers and economic officials remained unanswered. But his slur on the former was too much even for Alexei Surkov, Secretary of the Writers' Union and a faithful supporter of the Party line. In reply to Gafurov he said that 250 Soviet writers had been killed during the war. The achieve-ments of Soviet literature after the war could be judged from the fact that the number of new books produced by the pub-lishing house 'Sovietski Pisatel'[1] had risen from 104 in 1953 to 131 in 1954 and to 173 in 1955.

[1] The Soviet Writer.

In style and form Surkov's speech was almost indistinguishable from that of a minister of the fuel industry. The well-known writer, Mikhail Sholokhov, described this kind of literary success report as 'hoodwinking'. The development of literature could not be measured by the number of newly published books. 'Comrade Surkov should have said that the good books which have been published here during the last twenty years can be counted on the fingers of one hand, but that there is an abundance of colourless stuff.' It was the ivory-tower writers who were responsible for the fact that literature lagged behind, but so too were the Party organizations and the Writers' Union. The latter had transformed itself 'from an organization serving those who create, which it should be, into an administrative organization. Although the technical machine was running at full speed and couriers travelled backwards and forwards, no books were being written.' Sholokhov condemned the bureaucratic working methods of the Union by quoting the example of Fadeyev, who had been Secretary-General of the Writers' Union for fifteen years. 'Should not Fadeyev have been told that a disposition to give orders in the business of writing is something which leads nowhere,' he asked. 'The Writers' Union is not a military unit and certainly not a fatigue squad, and no writer will stand to attention before you, Comrade Fadeyev. . . . Fadeyev has for many years taken part in discussions about creative writing, made speeches, provided writers with housing and written nothing. He has had no time to occupy himself with such "minor matters" as writing books.' Sholokhov demanded that writers should above all be freed from having to dash needlessly from meeting to meeting and 'from everything which prevents them from writing books'.

THE PROBLEM OF THE YOUNGER GENERATION

The Twentieth Party Congress had to deal with a problem which had never seriously been considered by any Party Congress in the days of Stalin—the problem of the younger generation. Under Stalin the young were always praised and all difficulties attributed to the failures of local officials. At the Twentieth Party Congress this was no longer possible. It could no longer be concealed that political consciousness, a sense of duty, and enthusiasm for work were by no means as firmly implanted in the younger generation as Stalinist propaganda had asserted.

After the Old Bolsheviks and the Stalin generation a third generation had grown up, young people who had been born in the late twenties or even since then. They knew revolution, civil war, collectivization, and industrialization only by hearsay, while their first important experience had been the wave of arrests between 1936 and 1938. They had reacted in various ways. One reaction was to run away from politics and take refuge in specialized learning, another was to run after a career. Sons and daughters of high officials, used to a pleasant, and by Soviet standards wealthy, way of life, sought refuge in distraction and drink. The more thinking members of this generation, in particular those whose parents had been arrested in the great purge, became increasingly opposed to the system— whether as a protest against the spiritual uniformity, or for political reasons, or out of the realization of how great the contradiction was between the aims of the October revolution and the reality of the Stalinist system.

A few exceptional cases apart, the real problems of the third Soviet generation were not discussed even after Stalin's death, though some aspects were talked about. In the autumn of 1953 there began the big campaign against the 'gentlemen's sons'. *Literaturnaya Gazeta*,[1] spoke of 'precocious gentlemen's sons' who were distinguished by their 'parasitical habits'. Out of consideration for the merits of their fathers these young ne'er-do-wells were usually treated leniently. The organ of the Soviet League of Youth, *Komsomolskaya Pravda*,[2] said that many sons and daughters of high officials and scientists were hanging about in bars, behaving as though they had 'come out of an American gangster film'. On 15 January 1954 the same paper attacked the superior airs and the aristocratic behaviour of the children of privileged parents. The article appeared under the significant title 'Aristocrats'. Soon afterwards, the satirical journal, *Krokodil*, published a caricature in which an adolescent of about fifteen is sitting on a bar stool, looking arrogantly bored. Before him stands a domestic servant in a submissive attitude: 'I beg your pardon, but your mother rang up to ask whether you have done your homework!'

[1] 15 Nov. 1953.   [2] 19 Nov. 1953.

It is interesting that almost all books of the 'thaw' period deal with the contrast between the generation which grew up under Stalin and the older people who had fought in the revolution and the Civil War. In Ehrenburg's *The Thaw*, the Old Bolshevik, Pukhov, is contrasted with his son, Volodya, a cynical painter who adapts himself to the circumstances of the moment and who is completely corrupted by the system and has nothing but contempt for ideals. In Zorin's *Guests* three generations are contrasted. The old Alexei Kirpinchev, a friend of Dzherzhinski and a hero of the first Five-Year Plan, sees with bitterness what has happened to the Soviet Union under Stalin. 'Did we fight for this?' he asks. His son, Piotr, a typical Stalinist bureaucrat, replies: 'Who talks of aims? The country is different; we are different!' Piotr's son and Kirpinchev's grandson, Tema, is an irresponsible young man, officially registered as a student, but who really belongs to the teddy-boys who are called *stilyagi* in the Soviet Union.

Nor could the difficulties created by young people be avoided at the Komsomol Congress in March 1954. Alexander Shelepin, then First Secretary of the Komsomol, complained openly of the absence of discipline and political interest among the younger generation and of their unfitness to share in the government of the country. The fight against egoism, immorality and drunkenness, against 'alien moods', and shirking, must be intensified.

In the autumn of 1954 began a big campaign to persuade those who had completed a secondary school education to do practical work in production. Vladimir Semichastny, then Shelepin's deputy in the Komsomol[1] said, 'Among some of the younger generation one finds the view that only employment in institutes or offices is worth having and that productive work is only a second-rate occupation.'[2]

Demoralization also became apparent in the schools. *Komsomolskaya Pravda*[3] found it necessary to denounce cheats who took examinations for other pupils and forged examination papers. In the entrance examinations for universities, too, forgeries became increasingly frequent. *Sovietskaya Belorussaya* reported on 21 August 1955 that for a consideration which

---

[1] From March 1958 to March 1959 he was First Secretary of the Komsomol.
[2] *Komsomolskaya Pravda*, 2 Oct. 1955.   [3] 6 Oct. 1955.

amounted to thousands of roubles, students with forged papers were taking entrance examinations for failed candidates.

But the authorities were worried not only about those who shirked physical work, the pleasure-seeking sons and daughters of privileged families and the *stilyagi*, but also the serious, thinking members of the younger generation who were searching for independent solutions of problems and who were often in opposition to the Party leadership. Naturally, only a little was and is written on this in the Soviet press. The problem was hinted at in *Literaturnaya Gazeta*.[1] A correspondent described the life of young workers in a community in Novo Tagil. He had the following conversation with one of the young people:

'It would be interesting to get scarce books as well,' he said unexpectedly.

'What do you mean—scarce?'

'Well, Esenin, Pushkin . . . banned writers.'

'Why banned—after all, they are published.'

'Don't think I'm so stupid. . . . I have heard that there are still unpublished poems in the museums. It would be interesting to read all poetry. Some things by Esenin I have written down in an exercise book. By Lermontov too. You can't get them in Tagil. When I go to Moscow for my holidays I shall try there.'

Afterwards, the writer had a talk with the secretary of the Komsomol of the town, who was quite aware that a number of things must be changed in youth work. 'One should, of course, speak frankly to the young people. But I doubt whether they would be sincere. . . . They have got out of the habit.'

At the Twentieth Party Congress Khrushchev confined himself to some general remarks. But he found fault with ideological education and said that the Komsomol organization sometimes had no understanding of how to interest the young people in practical work.

Voroshilov, Pervukhin, and Shelepin went into the youth problem in greater detail. Voroshilov spoke of 'unpleasant phenomena'. The Komsomol often did not understand how to organize the free time of the young and how to direct their exuberant energies into the right channels. Pervukhin said roundly that 'young people are wrongly educated at our universities and colleges of technology'. The young specialists

[1] 1 and 6 Oct. 1955.

rushed to find 'clean work', insisted on working in research institutes and drawing offices, and considered it a particular misfortune to be put into a production department in a factory.

Shelepin held the economic authorities responsible for what was wrong. The managers did not take sufficient interest in the life and studies of the young workers. No housing was provided for them. In this connexion Shelepin made the interesting proposal, which was, however, dropped, 'to abolish the organized recruitment of labour altogether'. Managers paid no attention to the needs of the workers because they knew in advance 'that they would get as many workers as they asked for'. The abolition of the organized recruitment of labour would force them to look after the workers better.

The Komsomol had already taken steps to limit the paper war within the organization and to give the young people more chance to use their own initiative. The training work was so boring that some of the young were drifting away from the Komsomol and escaping from its influence.

INTERNAL PARTY QUESTIONS

Khrushchev, Suslov, and Aristov, Central Committee Secretary for organizational questions, spoke on internal Party problems. Khrushchev denounced every attempt 'to reduce or weaken the leading role of the Party in the system of the Soviet state'. The importance of the Party in the whole political, economic, and cultural life of the country 'had become still greater' in the past few years. The Party must be strengthened in the future also. It should always have the last word. What this means in practice can be seen from the following sentences of his speech: 'It must be said that some comrades have the wrong attitude to the growing of feeding stuffs. There are cases where clover is no longer planted in old clover-producing regions. Such behaviour is contrary to the directives of the Party.'

As at the Nineteenth Party Congress the transition to communism was proclaimed as the general political aim of the Party, though with a new emphasis. In his report Khrushchev attacked two forms of deviation in this question. He rejected the 'incorrect' theory that only the foundations of socialism had been laid in the Soviet Union. The socialist system had already been victorious when the new constitution of the USSR was adopted in 1936. The contention that the Soviet Union was still in the stage of the construction of socialism meant a 'disorientation of communists and all Soviet people in the extremely important question of the long-term development of our country'. This was directed against attempts to develop the country through economic methods, pushing ideology, and with it the power of the Party, to one side.

As the 'other extreme' Khrushchev regarded the view that the theory about the gradual transition to socialism was a demand 'for the immediate realization of the principles of communist society at the present stage'. Some 'hotheads' and 'visionaries' had already begun to 'draw up a timetable for the transition to communism'. On the basis of these utopian ideas there was growing a disparaging attitude to the socialist principle of the material interest of the workers in the results of their work. Unjustified suggestions were made to speed up the substitution of Soviet trade by direct exchange of products. This proposal, it should be recalled, came from Stalin. Khrushchev, and with him the majority of the Party leaders, had evidently decided on a middle course directed equally against the economic reformers and the dogmatic Stalinists.

Closely connected with this were Khrushchev's and Suslov's remarks about the relation between the Party and the planners, a question which was to play a big part after the Twentieth Party Congress. The measures introduced in 1953 to modernize planning had considerably increased the power of the managers. There was a danger that the Party 'apparatus', with its officials ideologically trained but practically inexperienced, would be forced out of its leading position. The Party officials were, therefore, asked to concern themselves more than before with economic problems. Khrushchev described economic development as one of the most important aspects of Party work: 'The activity of a leading Party official must in the first place be judged by results in the development of the economy, for whose success he is responsible. Leading officials who do not understand this, who are incapable of leading the fight for prosperity, must be speedily replaced because they are insufficiently prepared for Party work.'

Khrushchev proposed that the pay of Party officials in

economic undertakings should depend on how the concern fulfilled its plan. To the objection that this was impossible
because Party officials dealt with problems of Party ideology,
but not with economic problems, he replied: 'But can the
organization of the Party be described as successful if it does not
increase production?' The full implications were to become
clear only during the big changes in 1957.

Besides this central question the Party Congress dealt with the
social structure of the Party. Khrushchev and Suslov demanded
the 'improvement of the social composition' of the Party. This
Soviet expression means that the number of workers and collective farmers in the Party should be increased. In fact, the
number of Party members working in the administration was
(and is) extraordinarily large, and the number working in
factories and collective farms very small. According to the report of Averky Aristov, the Communist Party of the Soviet
Union at the time of the Twentieth Party Congress had
6,795,896 full members and 419,609 candidate members.
Compared with 1 October 1952, that is immediately before
the Nineteenth Party Congress, the number of full members
was up by 782,637, and the number of candidate members
down by 449,277. The Party consisted of 350,000 cells, 43,061
of them in industry (3,870 more than in 1952), and 80,015 in
the collective farms (5,666 more than in 1952). With a total of
slightly more than 87,000 collective farms in February 1956
this meant that there were still over 7,000 collective farms
without a Party cell. In February 1956, 1,877,773 specialists
with a higher education were members of the Party. In the
main, they formed the framework of the administration in
which, obviously, the Party was strongly represented. Among
industrial workers the influence of the Party was much smaller.
According to Khrushchev, in all, 90,000 Party members were
employed in the coal industry, of whom only 38,000 worked
underground. More than 3 million full and candidate members
were engaged in agriculture, but less than half worked on
collective farms, state farms or machine and tractor stations.

The most important change in the organizational structure
was a 25 per cent. reduction of the personnel of the Central
Committee 'apparatus'. Suslov announced a further reduction
of staff in the Party machine. Of the other organizational

changes the following were of fundamental political importance: the independent Central Committee agents for Party
Control, who had been installed at the Nineteenth Party Congress, were abolished; full sessions of the Central Committee
were once more to meet every four months, not every six, as
had been laid down at the Nineteenth Party Congress; the
political sections in the system of transport were abolished.

For the third time since 1939, it was decided to prepare a
new Party programme. A programme which did not fulfil its
task had already been drawn up at the Eighteenth Party
Congress. In October 1952 the Nineteenth Party Congress
instructed a new commission to work out a programme, but it,
too, failed to do so. The Central Committee was now directed to
prepare and publish the draft programme in time for the Twenty-
first Party Congress. Khrushchev demanded that the draft of
the Party programme should be directly related to the long-
term economic and cultural plan for the whole country. This
also indicates that the Party's chief tasks were to be economic.[1]

THE COMMUNIST WORLD AND INTERNATIONAL COMMUNISM

The more the Soviet Union freed itself internally from the
rigidity of the Stalin régime the more its relations with other
communist countries were transformed. From 1948 until Stalin's
death Poland, Eastern Germany, Czechoslovakia, Hungary,
Rumania, Bulgaria, and Albania were in the truest sense of
the word satellites of the USSR. Soviet representatives transmitted detailed directives for every sphere of social life which
were accepted by their leaders unconditionally. There were
signs, moreover, that Stalin wanted to transform the satellite
states into Union Republics of the USSR.

In the period between Stalin's death and the Twentieth
Party Congress, Soviet control was relaxed. Moscow confined
itself to general directives without, as before, interfering in
every detail. The Soviet Union tried in particular to 'legalize'
military relations. On 14 May 1955 it concluded the Warsaw
Pact with Albania, Bulgaria, Hungary, Eastern Germany,

---

[1] In fact, at the Twenty-first Party Congress in January 1959, no new programme was submitted either—the question was postponed until the Twenty-
second Party Congress planned for 1961.

Poland, Rumania, and Czechoslovakia, officially for twenty years. The member countries committed themselves to consult on all important international questions which affected their joint interests, in particular 'when in the opinion of one of the contracting parties the danger of an armed attack on one or more members of the Pact arises' (Article 3). In case of armed attack all members bound themselves to provide assistance to the member attacked 'with all means which they deem necessary, including the use of military force'. Their action would, however, be suspended if the Security Council of the United Nations were to take the steps necessary to preserve peace. In accordance with Article 5 of the Pact, a joint command of the armed forces was set up. In addition, a consultative political commission was formed. All members of the Pact committed themselves not to join alliances whose aims were in contradiction with the Warsaw Pact. Marshal Koniev, who had been commander-in-chief of the armies which captured Prague and Dresden in the spring of 1945, was appointed Supreme Commander of the united armed forces of the Warsaw Pact. Since 1956 Koniev has been Deputy Minister of Defence of the USSR and a member of the Central Committee of the CPSU; he had been a candidate member of the Central Committee since 1939. The ministers of defence 'or other military leaders' of the other member states became deputies of Marshal Koniev. Moscow was made headquarters of the general staff of the united armed forces of the Warsaw Pact.

The most important changes in the relations between the Soviet Union and the East European states were of an economic kind. Until Stalin's death every satellite state had the task of developing all branches of production as fast as possible, regardless of its own economic traditions. Mixed companies, in which Russia formally had a fifty per cent. interest, were formed in each country. In reality, the Soviet representatives completely controlled these companies and used them to exploit the rest. The trade treaties which dictated to the other communist countries what goods they had to deliver to the Soviet Union and at what prices formed another instrument of exploitation. The 'Council for Mutual Economic Aid' (usually called 'Comecon' in the West), which was founded in January 1949, was, in fact, a huge Soviet trade organization.

Soviet experts occupied important positions in all satellite countries. Their chief task was to speed up deliveries to Russia.

A few months after Stalin's death, changes became noticeable. The mixed companies were dissolved and the Soviet experts recalled. In 1954 there began a fundamental reorganization of the planning system of the other communist countries in order to effect their economic integration. Details about this were published for the first time in the West in a series of articles by Fritz Schenk and Richard Löwenthal.[1] From 1952 to July 1957, Fritz Schenk was the personal adviser of the Chairman of the State Planning Commission and Deputy Prime Minister of Eastern Germany, Bruno Leuschner, who represents the DDR on the Council for Mutual Economic Aid. Until his flight Schenk took part in all the meetings of this Council.

According to his report Stalin's system of exploiting the satellite countries was openly criticized for the first time at the meeting of the Council in 1954 in Moscow at which a rational economic collaboration between the East European countries and the Soviet Union was proposed. In the summer of 1954 Soviet economic experts visited Eastern Europe, not as controllers from the Soviet embassy, but as consultants in the true sense of the word. They had been seconded to the planning chiefs of the various countries, behaved very politely, did not interfere in questions of detail, and were only expected to acquire a general picture in order to prepare the co-ordination of the economic plans. They recommended that the co-ordinated new Five-Year Plans of the various countries should all begin on 1 January 1956.

The next meeting of the Council took place in Budapest in December 1955; it was the first to be held outside the Soviet Union. This was symbolic of the fact that Soviet exploitation was to be replaced by new forms of economic collaboration. The Council decided to treat Eastern Europe as a unified economic region, in which each country took over certain production tasks for the whole region. Poland, for example, became the main country for the production of bituminous coal, East Germany for lignite and chemicals, and Czechoslovakia for motor-cars. The various branches of armaments production

[1] *Observer*, Nov. 9, 16, 23, 1958.

were also divided. The system of specialization and co-operation which was being introduced inside the Soviet Union at that time was thus extended to the whole Eastern bloc.

Questions of international communism were dealt with relatively little at the Twentieth Party Congress. Stalin had devoted his last speech at the Nineteenth Congress to this subject, but Khrushchev hardly touched on it in his report. It was noticeable that in their greetings several leaders of foreign communist parties, for example, the Chinese representative and Walter Ulbricht, used definitely Stalinist slogans which were out of tune with the Twentieth Party Congress. In the West this was for a long time regarded as indicating that the foreign parties had not been made aware of the intentions of the Soviet leaders. But since then it has become known that in January 1956 a number of Communist Party leaders (Ulbricht included) from the most varied countries had been summoned to a private conference in Moscow at which they were informed of the political aims of the Twentieth Party Congress. In the light of these facts the Stalinist speeches of some of the leaders of foreign communist parties must be regarded as an expression of opposition to Russia's policy of de-Stalinization.

In fact the East European leaders Novotny (Czechoslovakia), Bierut (Poland), Ulbricht (Eastern Germany), Gheorghiu-Dej (Rumania), Rákosi (Hungary), and Enver Hoxha (Albania), assured the Russians of their gratitude for the help they had received and promised to follow the example of the Soviet Union. Ulbricht fell into line at the last moment. On 14 February, *Neues Deutschland*, published a telegram of greeting from the East German Communist Party to the Congress which ended with exaltation of Stalin. When Ulbricht read the message at the evening meeting of the Party Congress on 16 February, he replaced this with 'Long live Marxism-Leninism'. How little the success reports of the Eastern European Communist Party leaders corresponded to the facts is shown by Rákosi's speech; six months before the Hungarian revolt he declared: 'The whole of our nation is impregnated with a deep love for the Soviet Union.'

Not one of the leaders of the East European and Asian communist countries referred to the theory of different roads to socialism. Among the representatives of the west European

parties, only Togliatti and Thorez mentioned it. Togliatti said
that the Soviet road could not be compulsory in every respect
for other countries. 'The Italian communists,' he added, 'are
faced with the task of finding an Italian road to socialism. This
must take into account the historical development of the
country, its social structure, the mentality and aims of the broad
masses of the workers, and must make it possible to find the
forms which are suitable for Italy so that the majority of the
people can be won over to a socialist re-organization of society.'
Thorez recalled that already on 18 November 1946 a representative of the French Communist Party had said in an interview
with *The Times* that the French road to socialism might be
different from that of Russia; he did not mention that he himself had given this interview. Thorez promised that the French
Communist Party would always be faithful to the great ideas
of Marx, Engels, Lenin, and Stalin. It was interesting that
Khaled Bagdash, in the name of the communist parties of
Syria and Lebanon, was the only Party leader of the non-
European countries who mentioned 'an independent Arab
road to socialism'.

What was new was the attitude towards Yugoslavia. At the
Nineteenth Party Congress a Yugoslav emigré living in the Soviet
Union had appealed to the Congress 'to suppress the fascist
régime of Tito'. At the Twentieth Party Congress there
was no criticism of Yugoslavia at all. The Chairman of the
Communist Party of Trieste, Vittorio Vidali, one of Tito's
bitterest opponents, though present, did not speak. The telegram of greetings from the Communist Party of Trieste was
read by a Soviet speaker; it referred only to the sixth Five-Year
Plan of the USSR. The Yugoslav League of Communists had
sent no representative; only a telegram of greetings from Tito
was read, saying that the Yugoslav communists were able to
appreciate the trials which the Soviet Union had had to under-
go in order to reach its present stage of development. One
should be satisfied with the general improvement of relations
between Yugoslavia and the Soviet Union, because this was the
healthiest way to restore confidence and offered an opportunity 'to eliminate from every-day practice all the elements
which might prevent our mutual confidence'. Tito's message
was received with 'prolonged and stormy applause'.

THE NEW SOVIET LEADERS

Three days after the end of the Twentieth Party Congress, on 28 February 1956, the composition of the new committees of the Party was announced. The eleven members of the Party Praesidium remained unchanged,[1] but there were important changes among its candidate members. After the Twentieth Party Congress, Shvernik, Brezhnev, Zhukov, Shepilov, Furtseva, and Mukhitdinov[2] were candidate members of the Party Praesidium. Except for Shvernik, all of these became candidate members of the Praesidium only after Stalin's death or after the Twentieth Party Congress. They were a new set of leaders who were later to play an important part.

A number of new officials were also admitted to the Central Committee Secretariat. After Stalin's death the Central Committee Secretariat, which is officially responsible for carrying out decisions taken by the Party Praesidium, had at first lost importance. After the plenary session of July 1955, when the influence of the Party on the government again increased, it moved into the foreground, and at the Twentieth Party Congress it was increased to eight members, Khrushchev, Suslov, Pospelov, Aristov, Shepilov, Belyayev, Brezhnev, and Furtseva.

The political importance of the individual leaders at that time can be judged by whether or not they belonged simultaneously to both the Party Praesidium and the Central Committee Secretariat. Khrushchev and Suslov were full members of both while Shepilov, Brezhnev, and Madame Furtseva were candidate members of the former and full members of the latter.

The fact that no changes were made in the composition of the Party Praesidium suggests that there was an equilibrium of forces at the top of the Party and the continuity of the leadership was preserved. This gave special authority to the decisions of the Party Congress. The changes among the candidate members and in the Central Committee Secretariat on the

[1] Khrushchev, Bulganin, Molotov, Kaganovich, Mikoyan, Voroshilov, Malenkov, Pervukhin, Saburov, Suslov, Kirichenko.
[2] Nuritdin Mukhitdinov, formerly Chairman of the Council of Ministers of the Union Republic of Uzbekistan; from December 1955, after Khrushchev's return from India, Burma, and Afghanistan, First Secretary of the Central Committee of the Communist Party of Uzbekistan.

other hand, showed that the Khrushchev faction had gained ground.

THE CHANGES IN THE CENTRAL COMMITTEE

The Central Committee was increased in size to 133 full members and 122 candidate members.

Of the ministers of the Soviet government who were members of the Central Committee the most important were probably Dudorov (Internal Affairs), Zverev (Finance), Mikhailov (Culture), and Professor Kovrigina (Health). The army was represented by Marshal Zhukov, the Deputy Ministers of Defence, Marshal Vasilevsky and Marshal Koniev, the Chief of the General Staff, Marshal Sokolovsky, the Supreme Commander of the Coastal Defence Region, Malinovsky, the Supreme Commander of the Moscow Defence District, Moskalenko. Of those concerned with foreign affairs the following were members of the Central Committee: the Deputy Foreign Ministers, Gromyko and Kuznetsov, the Minister of Foreign Trade, Kabanov, and the Ambassadors, Grishin (Czechoslovakia), Ponomarenko (Poland), and Yudin (China). The representation of the state security service was strikingly small. Only General Ivan Serov, Chairman of the Committee for State Security, became a member of the Central Committee. Victor Grishin, who had been appointed Chairman of the Soviet trade unions shortly after the Twentieth Party Congress, and the First Secretary of the Komsomol, Alexander Shelepin, were also members of the Central Committee. The strongest group was formed by the district Party secretaries. Twenty-eight first district Secretaries were members of the new Central Committee, among them the Party secretaries of Moscow, Ivan Kapitonov, of Leningrad, Frol Kozlov, and of Gorki, Nikolai Ignatov. Semyon Ignatiev,[1] was confirmed as a member of the Central Committee.

Forty-seven members of the old Central Committee had disappeared. Four of them had died: Stalin, Shkiryatov, former Chairman of the Party Control Commission, Vishinsky, former Foreign Minister, and Mekhlis, former chief of the main Political Department of the Red Army. Beria had been shot in December 1953, Shatalin, former Central Committee Secretary,

[1] See above.

had been dismissed in the spring of 1955, and Kruglov, former Minister of the Interior, had been dismissed at the beginning of January 1956. Among other important officials not re-elected at the Twentieth Party Congress were Kuznetsov, former Deputy Minister of Defence, Poskrebyshev, former head of Stalin's private secretariat, and Cheznokov, former editor of *Kommunist* and *Voprosy Filosofi*. The former Secretary of the Writers' Union, Fadeyev, was degraded to a candidate membership of the Central Committee. Others worthy of mention are the former head of the Leningrad Party Organization, Andryanov, who had been removed from his position in November 1953, and Arutinov and Bagirov, the former Central Committee Secretaries of Armenia and Azerbaidjan respectively, who had both been purged after Beria's fall.

Among the 122 candidate members of the Central Committee the administration, industry, and the army were more strongly represented than among the full members; a smaller proportion of candidate members than full members were District Secretaries and other pure Party officials, that is, paid employees of the Party machine.

The Committee for Party Control (CPC) had its rights curtailed by the change in the statutes decided on at the Twentieth Party Congress, but it remained an important factor in the Party. Nikolai Shvernik became its head; Pavel Komarov, who scarcely appeared in public, became deputy. Later Ivan Boitsov was also mentioned as deputy chairman of the Committee for Party Control.[1] The names of the other members of this Committee were, as usual, not published, and no clues were provided by the press as to its composition.

THE NEW CENTRAL COMMITTEE BUREAU FOR THE RSFSR

On 29 February *Pravda* reported on its front page that a special bureau of the Central Committee of the CPSU of the RSFSR (Russian Union Republic) had been set up under the leadership of Nikita Khrushchev. This was an innovation in the structure of the CPSU. Until 1956 only the fifteen non-Russian Union Republics—the USSR then consisted of sixteen Union Republics—had their own Central Committees.

[1] *Pravda*, 19 March 1958.

Already in 1954 or 1955 separate departments had been established in the RSFSR for agriculture and for personnel questions. But this was apparently not enough. Ten Party officials were now appointed members of the new Central Committee Bureau: Khrushchev, Belyayev, Mikhail Yasnov,[1] Kozlov, Kapitonov, Victor Churayev,[2] Vladimir Mylarschikov,[3] Alexander Pusanov,[4] Ignatov, and Andrei Kirilenko.[5]

In the middle of March, the Central Bureau for the RSFSR was enlarged by the inclusion of Aristov and Pospelov; this had been decided at the first large congress of regional secretaries convened by the Central Committee Bureau.

Khrushchev was now First Secretary of the whole Party of the USSR and head of the Party apparatus in the RSFSR. Most of the members of the new Bureau were his followers from the Ukraine or Moscow where he himself had worked for many years. The increase in his power could no longer be overlooked.

THE IMPORTANCE OF THE TWENTIETH PARTY CONGRESS

The Twentieth Party Congress has become the symbol of de-Stalinization. At it the Party leaders acknowledged and justified the measures which had, since 1953, changed the system inherited from Stalin. Both actions constituted a withdrawal from important principles and methods with which Stalin was identified.

The terror was reduced, control of the state and of the economy was decentralized, freed from administrative coercion, and switched to effective methods of direction. Stalin's nationalities policy was revised, his aggressive attitude to foreign countries and to international socialism abandoned. Many branches of learning and in particular the natural sciences were

[1] For many years active in the Moscow Party Organization, appointed Chairman of the Council of Ministers of the RSFSR in January 1956, a few weeks before the Party Congress.

[2] Head of the Department for Party Organs of the RSFSR of the Central Committee for the CPSU.

[3] Head of the Department for Agriculture of the RSFSR of the Central Committee of the CPSU.

[4] First Deputy of the Chairman of the Council of Ministers of the RSFSR.

[5] For many years a Party official in the Ukraine, since December 1955 First Secretary of the Party in Dniepropetrovsk and then in Sverdlovsk.

given extensive scope for objective research, ideological pressure was reduced, and a certain degree of freedom to criticize was granted.

The system was changed, but it was not abolished. The Twentieth Party Congress not only made clear the extent of de-Stalinization, it also laid bare its limitations. The frontiers of de-Stalinization were drawn where the domination of the Communist Party was threatened.

All the speakers at the Party Congress renounced the cult of a leader, but the place of the leader was taken by the 'collective wisdom of the Central Committee'. Faith in authority was not criticized, but the type of authority was changed.

The Party leaders rehabilitated some of Stalin's victims such as Bela Kun, Antonov-Ovseyenko, and Kossior, but Trotsky, Bukharin, Shlapnikov, and their followers continued to be described as enemies of the Party. Only the accusation that they had been agents of foreign powers was dropped.

A number of speakers, in particular Khrushchev, Mikoyan, and Madame Pankratova, rejected some of Stalin's theses, but the principle of the 'leading role of the Party'—in the Stalinist, not in the Leninist sense—was not touched. On the contrary, the Party was proclaimed the sole authority, not only in political life but also if it were a matter of the details of cement production or of the quality of Beethoven or of choosing the best method of growing clover.

The promised increase in pensions and the reduction of working hours were certainly to be welcomed, but they came as a gift from above. Although greater activity on the part of the trade unions was asked for at the Party Congress, this was to be under the absolute control of the Party machine, and there was no mention of any form of workers' self-government such as the workers' councils in Yugoslavia. The return to Leninism which had been proclaimed could—perhaps—be considered as an aim, but its serious realization was out of the question.

CHAPTER V

KHRUSHCHEV'S SECRET SPEECH

'NERO was a product of his time. Nevertheless, when he was dead his statues were destroyed and his name everywhere erased. The revenge of history is greater than that of the most powerful secretary-general. I dare to take consolation from this.'

Trotsky was unable to finish the biography of Stalin in which he uttered these words; in August 1940 he was murdered by one of Stalin's agents. His prophecy, however, came true. Scarcely three years after Stalin's death, on 25 February 1956, Nikita Khrushchev appeared before the delegates of the Twentieth Party Congress and read his so-called secret speech, 'The Cult of personality and its consequences', with which the Soviet leaders emphatically dissociated themselves from Stalin.

This speech has not been published in the communist world. In the West it exists in a version published by the State Department of the United States. Today there remains no doubt of the authenticity of this document. It has never been denied by Moscow and was even indirectly confirmed by *Pravda* which, on 27 June 1956, published an article by the American communist leader, Eugene Dennis, referring to Khrushchev's secret speech. *Pravda* explained this to its readers in the following footnote: 'The author is referring to the material which was published in the press by the U.S. State Department and which was described as a report by Khrushchev to the Twentieth Party Congress of the CPSU.' In addition the revelations contained in the American version tally with the reports and articles on the personality cult published by foreign communist leaders after the Party Congress; for example, by Palmiro Togliatti on 17 June in *Unità* and Walter Ulbricht on 4 and 18 March 1956 in *Neues Deutschland*.

The American document is possibly a version prepared by the Central Committee of the CPSU for other communist parties and censored accordingly. Boris Nikolayevsky, to whom we owe the most thorough analysis of the secret speech,[1] pointed out that the version published in the West contains only a few facts about foreign policy and nothing about the struggles in the Comintern, although on 19 February 1956— that is, six days before the secret session of the Party Congress— the Communist Party of Poland, which had been dissolved in 1938 by the Comintern leadership as a 'party of foreign agents', was rehabilitated.

But even the censored version was enough to throw the communists of all countries into the utmost confusion and to cause a sensation in the non-Soviet world. Khrushchev's reports reveals a number of facts about the Stalin period which had been unknown until then, and confirms others known only from unofficial sources or rumours. Khrushchev paints a picture of Stalin's personality which might have been concocted by the most malevolent anti-communist propagandists. Stalin is accused of the basest crimes, of organized mass murder of the extermination of whole peoples; he is represented as a megalomaniac, an hysterical dictator who glorified himself in the most repulsive fashion, gave a free hand to criminals, delivered his closest collaborators to the torture chambers of the secret police, and treacherously drove his best friends to suicide. Khrushchev criticized in Stalin his 'flagrant misuse of power', his 'moody and despotic character', his 'intolerance', his 'brutal wilfulness', his 'abuse of socialist legality', his 'irresponsible behaviour', his 'disregard of obvious facts', his 'incorrect leadership of state and Party', 'stubbornness', 'haughtiness', 'self-deification', and 'refusal to recognize the facts of life'. Stalin had been 'pathologically suspicious'; 'his persecution mania knew no bounds'.

This speech of Khrushchev's undoubtedly comprises an important step in the withdrawal from Stalin's falsification of history. Stalin was described in a manner far more in accordance with the actual course of Bolshevik Party history than anything in the historical writings of the thirties and forties. The forces of reform throughout the communist world conceived the hope, at that time not unfounded, that Khrushchev's speech was the beginning of a fundamental revision of Stalin's ideology and of a withdrawal from Stalinism in political practice.

[1] In *Sotsialistichesky Vestnik*, No. 5–6. *The New Leader*, 16 July 1956.

On the other hand, it could not, and should not, be overlooked that Khrushchev limited his criticism. This was certainly
not unintentional. Essentially he accused Stalin of two things:
the abolition of collective leadership in the Party—the so-called
personality cult—and the crimes which he committed in order
to establish and preserve his personal dictatorship.

Concerning the first point, Khrushchev made comparisons
with the days of Lenin when Party democracy was still intact, the
Party statutes observed and Party congresses and full sessions
of the Central Committee convened regularly. He quoted Lenin's
testament and letters he exchanged with Krupskaya from which,
as we know, it emerges that Lenin wanted to dismiss Stalin,
and finally broke off personal relations with him. Khrushchev
contrasted Lenin's personal modesty with Stalin's byzantine cult
of leadership and cited a number of grotesque examples of
Stalin's self-glorification.

On the second point, Khrushchev reported fearful details
about the terrorism of the secret police in the thirties, from the
murder of Kirov, the Secretary of the Leningrad Party, at the
end of 1934, to the great purge of 1936 to 1938. He described
the mass extermination of Old Bolsheviks and Party stalwarts
from whom false confessions were obtained by inhuman tortures, and the intrigues of the secret police chiefs, Yezhov and
Beria, for the removal of their personal enemies.

In Khrushchev's opinion, Stalin's main fault was that he
substituted his own dictatorship for that of the Party. If
Khrushchev wrote off the person of Stalin, he did not write off
his policy. He rejected the latter only in part and only from the
moment when it was directed against his own people, that is,
from about 1934. Khrushchev's concept of the Party meant
the Stalin faction of the twenties; he regarded Trotsky's group
as enemies. He approved of their destruction although they
had been Lenin's closest brothers-in-arms; he did, however,
deplore their physical annihilation.

THE 'YEZHOVSHCHINA'

Khrushchev, therefore, was concerned in the main not with
fundamental political questions but with Stalin's misrepre-
sentation of the conception of an enemy and, as we shall see,
with his mis-timing of his reign of terror. It follows logically

that Khrushchev's revelations about the period of the great
purge of 1936 to 1938, the 'Yezhovshchina', are the most
revealing part of the secret speech. We do not indeed get from
Khrushchev a history of the Yezhovshchina, only incidents
taken out of their context. In one of these, however, Nikolayevsky believes he has discovered the key to the purge. This
is the telegram, quoted by Khrushchev, which Stalin and
Zhdanov sent on 25 September 1936 from Sochi to Kaganovich,
Molotov, and other members of the Politburo:

'We deem it absolutely necessary and urgent that Comrade
Yezhov be nominated to the post of People's Commissar for
Internal Affairs. Yagoda has definitely proved himself to be
incapable of unmasking the Trotsky-Zinoviev bloc. The GPU
is four years behind in this matter. This is clear to all Party
workers and the majority of the representatives of the
NKVD.'

Khrushchev emphasized that the formulation that the GPU
was four years behindhand had also been forced upon the
full session of the Central Committee which met in February
and March 1937. (Khrushchev already belonged to the Central
Committee at that time.)

Nikolayevsky has examined the importance of this phrase.
Why was the OGPU four years behind? Four years earlier,
from 28 September to 2 October 1932, a meeting of the Central
Committee took place at which the punishment of Riutin's
opposition group was considered. This group had worked out a
programme which was clearly aimed against Stalin. In it[1]
Stalin was 'represented as a kind of evil spirit of the Russian
revolution, who, moved by personal love of power and revenge,
has brought the revolution to the edge of the abyss'. Stalin
described this as a challenge to murder him and demanded the
death penalty for Riutin and other Party officials.

Yet neither in the Praesidium of the Central Control Commission, nor in the Politburo, nor in the plenary session of the
Central Committee was Stalin able to get his way. Only
Kaganovich supported him unconditionally. All the others
opposed the imposition of the death penalty against communists
or avoided any expression of opinion. Stalin's main opponent
was Kirov, who was very popular in the Party.

[1] See letter from an old Bolshevik in *Sotsialistichesky Vestnik*, Dec. 1936–Jan. 1937

This was Stalin's first heavy defeat in the Central Committee. Nikolayevsky describes the September plenary session in 1932 as the 'beginning of Stalin's conspiracy against the collective leadership', which at that time still existed formally. There were more profound reasons for the controversy over the use of the death sentence against Riutin. Stalin and his supporters held the view that the class struggle in the Soviet Union was increasing and that sharp measures were necessary against all those whom they chose to regard as hostile elements. At that time collectivization was in full swing, being forced through with mass arrests, deportations, and shootings. In the countryside there was an unbelievable famine and the whole economy was disorganized; there were spontaneous outbreaks of unrest among the workers and a Kronstadt mood[1] was spreading. There were heated discussions at the next full session of the Central Committee in January 1933 about the cause of the desperate situation and the steps needed to overcome it. Stalin's policy was sharply criticized, but a retreat from collectivization would have threatened the authority of the Party. Nikolayevsky recounts a characteristic episode in the discussion. While Kaganovich was speaking a member called out from his seat: 'But we have already begun to eat people in my part of the country.' Kaganovich replied: 'If we lose our nerve we shall both be eaten—is that better perhaps?' Collectivization was continued, but at the same time special commissions were sent to the most important agricultural regions to examine the situation and to stop mass reprisals against the peasants.

Stalin used the situation to justify his views about the intensification of the class struggle and stubbornly demanded more terroristic measures against 'class enemies'. Kirov, on the other hand, was of the opinion that with the consolidation of the economic basis of socialism (i.e. the nationalization of the means of production and the collectivization of agriculture), there would also have to be a gradual change in the ideological superstructure. Since the class enemy had been deprived of his economic basis, it was the duty of the Party, in the coming period, to re-educate the masses by persuasion, not persecution. It is interesting that Khrushchev in his secret speech

[1] Such as led to the naval mutiny in 1917.

rejected Stalin's use of terror with the same arguments as Kirov had used. For he said that Stalin had used the Party and the NKVD to establish a reign of terror of which there was no need since the exploiting classes had already been exterminated.

At the Seventeenth Party Congress in January 1934 Kirov won over the majority of the members to his point of view. In the following years bread-rationing was stopped, and the political departments of the machine and tractor stations, which Stalin had managed to establish as instruments of political repression, were abolished. The success of this new attitude was most clearly expressed in the new Soviet constitution of 1936 which proclaimed the victory of socialism. Its author was Bukharin.

The Seventeenth Party Congress is described as the 'Congress of the Victors' in histories of the Stalin period, and Khrushchev, too, used this expression in his secret speech. But the victor was not Stalin, the victor was the faction which under his leadership had gained control of the Party, had eliminated Trotsky and Bukharin, and had carried out industrialization and collectivization and thus established 'socialism in one country'. This faction favoured dictatorship, but the dictatorship of the Party, which, under collective leadership, was gradually to change over to moderate methods. Stalin could no longer work with the Central Committee but only against it. Khrushchev confirmed this in a cautiously worded paragraph:

'How can it be explained that after the Seventeenth Party Congress mass reprisals against activists kept on increasing? Stalin had raised himself so far above the Party and nation at that time that henceforth he considered neither the Central Committee nor the Party. Whereas before the Seventeenth Party Congress, Stalin still took the opinion of the collective leadership into account, after the complete political liquidation of the followers of Trotsky, Zinoviev, and Bukharin—when the Party had achieved unity through this struggle and the victory of socialism—he increasingly disregarded the views of the members of the Central Committee and even of the members of the Politburo.'

Stalin's first victim was Kirov. He was murdered on 1

December 1934. Khrushchev now expressed the suspicion that Kirov's murderer 'was helped by somebody whose duty it should have been to protect Kirov's person'. On the very same day the so-called Lex Kirov was enacted. It instructed the police and judicial authorities to deal very quickly with cases in which the defendant had been accused of the preparation or execution of terrorist acts, and to carry out the death sentence immediately after announcing the verdict; the Praesidium of the Central Executive Committee would not consider appeals for clemency from criminals in this category. The Lex Kirov deprived the accused of every possibility of a proper examination of their case. It was, as Khrushchev expressed it, 'the basis for the massive abuse of socialist legality'.

The result of this abuse of power was, as Khrushchev admitted in another part of his speech, that of the 139 full and candidate members of the Central Committee elected at the Seventeenth Party Congress, 98 were liquidated during the Yezhovshchina, and of the 1,966 delegates to the Party Congress, 1,108 were arrested for counter-revolutionary crimes.

Khrushchev provided a wealth of detail on the period of the Yezhovshchina, particularly about the fate of a number of well-known Party chiefs. The purge in the army leadership, on the other hand, he mentioned only briefly and in very general terms. The names were given only of those army leaders 'who survived despite severe tortures in prisons, and who from the first days of the war showed themselves to be real patriots, fighting heroically for the glory of the fatherland'; these were Rokossovsky, Gorbatov, Meretskov, and Podlas. The best known victims of this purge, Marshals Tukhachevsky, Blücher, and Yegorov, he did not mention, although Blücher and Yegorov had been rehabilitated shortly before the Party Congress.[1]

STALIN DURING THE WAR

Khrushchev gave a number of examples of Stalin's military failure during the war. Among other things, he accused Stalin of not paying attention to the numerous warnings from allied and Soviet quarters about Nazi Germany's impending attack;

[1] See *Voprosy Istorii*, No. 3, 1956.

he also mentioned in this connexion a German citizen who deserted to the Soviet troops at the last moment and betrayed the German order to attack.

The name of this German citizen was Alfred Liskow. He came from Kolberg, having worked in a furniture factory there. His unit was stationed in Tulyash on the Pruth, opposite to Sokaly in Russia. When he heard about the order for the attack, he swam across the Pruth to inform a unit of the Red Army. The unit, as we now know from Khrushchev, immediately transmitted this news to Stalin. Walter Ulbricht announced these facts at a meeting of German emigrés in Moscow on 23 June 1941. On 27 June the Soviet communiqué from the front reported Alfred Liskow's desertion and on the same day *Pravda* published his photograph with a long statement. At first Liskow was fêted and is even said to have spoken at public meetings in Kharkov and Kiev. In the late autumn of 1941 he disappeared without trace. His name was mentioned neither in the publications of 'Free Germany' nor in the publications of East Germany, nor was it mentioned by Khrushchev.

Khrushchev's description of the deportation *en masse* during the war of Soviet national groups whom Stalin accused of high treason was also incomplete. He mentioned the deportation of the Karachai and the Kalmucks at the end of 1943, of the Balkars in April 1944 and the Chechenzi and Ingushi whose autonomous republic was dissolved in March 1944. But he kept silent about the liquidation of the autonomous republics of the Volga Germans (1941) and the Tatars (1944) of the Crimea whose populations were deported to Siberia and Kazahkstan. (This resettlement was directed by General Ivan Serov.) That there were deeper reasons for this silence of Khrushchev became clear a year later. On 11 February 1957 the Kalmucks, Balkars, Karachai, Chechenzi, and Ingushi were 'rehabilitated' by a decision of the Supreme Soviet; they were allowed to return to their former homes, and their national autonomy was restored. But the decision did not mention the Volga Germans and the Tatars of the Crimea. They still live in Siberia and Kazahkstan, and their autonomy was not re-established. Since the spring of 1954 the Crimea no longer belongs to the RSFSR, but has become part of the Ukraine.

THREE POST-WAR INCIDENTS

Khrushchev's speech dealt with three events in the post-war period: the Leningrad Affair of 1949,[1] the Mingrelian Case of 1951–2, and the Case of the Kremlin doctors.[2] The clarification of the background of these affairs would undoubtedly provide important clues to the controversies between the Soviet leaders before Stalin's death. But Khrushchev's statements about them were incomplete. It is clear that it was greatly to his interest to draw a veil over these affairs. He explained them only as arbitrary acts of Stalin who, during the last years of his life, had been full of pathological distrust, and, out of fear of imaginary conspiracies, had liquidated faithful Party members as enemies of the people. The vile and abject Beria had used this feeling of panic; with the help of the former Minister of State Security, Abakumov, he had fabricated false accusations and extorted confessions by using criminal methods of investigation.

There is something to be said for this explanation. That Beria and Abakumov shared in Stalin's guilt needs no proof. As far as Stalin's distrust of his surroundings is concerned, Khrushchev quoted examples of it in another part of his speech when he spoke of Stalin's suspicion of Voroshilov, Molotov, Mikoyan, and Andreyev. But careful study of Khrushchev's remarks shows that he made Beria and Abakumov personally responsible only for the Leningrad Affair. This is the more remarkable as Khrushchev sought to denounce Beria as the embodiment of evil. If he did not link two such important cases as the Mingrelian conspiracy and the case of the Kremlin doctors directly with Beria, and did not name anybody else as being responsible (apart from Stalin), one is inclined to think that other people might be at the bottom of these two cases and that Khrushchev had reason to keep silent. An examination of the three post-war affairs from this angle provides some support for the view that they were really organized by different groups intriguing against one another.

The Leningrad Affair was clearly directed against the supporters of Zhdanov. Stalin probably had a personal interest in the Leningrad purge. Apart from his general distrust he had

[1] See above. p. 72.   [2] See above.

reasons to be particularly suspicious of the Party functionaries
there. In 1925 Zinoviev succeeded in mobilizing the Leningrad
Party organization against Stalin and his nominees. At the
Fourteenth Party Congress in December 1925 the whole
delegation from there was opposed to Stalin. Only after a
struggle did Stalin succeed in bringing the Leningrad Party
under his control. In 1934 it was again the Secretary of the
Leningrad Party, Kirov, who was the head of an anti-Stalinist
opposition until he was murdered. After the war, according to
unconfirmed rumours, the Party leaders there are supposed to
have demanded that Leningrad be made the capital of the
RSFSR in place of Moscow. The most powerful Soviet leader
of the time apart from Stalin, Andrei Zhdanov, came from
Leningrad and still had close links with this town which he had
successfully defended against the Germans during the war. He
died in August 1948 in mysterious circumstances, but Leningrad remained in the hands of his supporters until they were
purged in 1949.

According to Khrushchev, it was Beria who started the
Leningrad Affair. But the person who benefitted most from
the liquidation of Zhdanov's supporters was Malenkov, who,
thanks to his position as head of Stalin's private secretariat,
moved increasingly into the foreground after the death of
Stalin's favourite, Zhdanov, and finally at the Nineteenth
Party Congress in October 1952, appeared as the predestined
heir. In this connexion, it is interesting that in August 1953,
when Malenkov was the undisputed leader of the Soviet Union,
the anniversary of Zhdanov's death, contrary to usage, passed
unnoticed. But the next year, when Malenkov's days as Prime
Minister were already numbered, Zhdanov's name was spoken
of with approval in the press.

After Stalin's death, the Leningrad Affair came up on
several occasions and always at crises in Khrushchev's struggle
against Malenkov. After the secret circular in July 1953 in
which Beria alone was held responsible, the Leningrad Affair
was mentioned for the first time in the press in December 1954
in connexion with the trial of Abakumov, who had collaborated
with Malenkov for many years. Two months later Malenkov
had to resign as Prime Minister, and shortly afterwards an
internal Party circular openly accused Malenkov of sharing

the responsibility for the Leningrad Affair. Finally, in July 1956, when Malenkov had been removed from the leadership of the Party, Khrushchev at a mass meeting described the Leningrad Affair as an outstanding example of the violation of socialist legality. But as in his secret speech of 1956 he did not mention Malenkov in this connexion.

All this supports the view that Malenkov was one of the instigators of the Leningrad Affair. But Khrushchev in Sofia in the summer of 1955 gave another version in which he, together with Malenkov and Molotov, appears courageously interceding for the disgraced Voznesensky. The account of the Sofia conference given by Richard Löwenthal[1] says on this point:

'According to Khrushchev, Voznesensky (shortly before the Leningrad purge) went to Khrushchev, Malenkov, and Molotov and said that he had spent a long session with Stalin explaining his draft for the new Five-Year Plan. Part of this provided for some relaxation of over-centralized planning and for certain NEP-style measures to restore the economy. Stalin had then said: "You are seeking to restore capitalism in Russia."

'This, said Khrushchev, was enough to cause Comrade Voznesensky serious concern, and he came to us asking us to intercede with Stalin. The three of us asked for an interview with Stalin and were received by him at noon. We stated that we had seen and approved the measures proposed by Voznesensky. Stalin listened to us and then said: "Before you continue you should know that Voznesensky was shot this morning."

'There you are. What could you do? A man is prepared to be a martyr but what use is it to die like a dog in the gutter? There was nothing we could do while Stalin lived.'

The Mingrelian Affair, that is a purge in 1951–2, was directed against a nationalistic organization which allegedly existed in Georgia with the aim of separating Georgia from the Soviet Union and making it part of Turkey. In his secret speech, Khrushchev went to great lengths to prove that there was, in fact, not the slightest danger of any Georgian separatism at the time and that there was even no nationalistic organization. But six months after the secret speech, in August 1956, a meeting of the Central Committee of the Communist Party of

[1] *New Leader*, 9 Feb. 1959.

Georgia took place in Tiflis at which the First Secretary of the Central Committee, V. P. Mzhavanadze, said: 'During the long time that they had control of the Republic in their hands, Beria and his henchmen tried to instil a feeling of national exclusiveness into the Georgian population in order to tear the Georgian people away from the fraternal family of peoples of the Soviet Union and to isolate it. . . . Beria secretly and by every possible means supported and helped the activities of the nationalist elements which existed in the Republic.'

Mzhavanadze said in the same speech that the consequences of the 'Beria régime' had not yet been overcome in 1956. This arouses considerable doubt about Khrushchev's account. Even greater doubts appear on reading the new Soviet history textbook published in February 1958, which says about Beria:

'In 1951–2 the so-called Mingrelian Affair came up, as the result of which many honest Georgian Party and Soviet officials were oppressed. Beria tried to undermine the friendship of the peoples of the Soviet Union, to sow discord between the Russian and other fraternal peoples of the USSR and to foster bourgeois-nationalist elements in the Union Republics. Beria and his followers, who for a long time controlled the Central Committee of the Georgian Communist Party, tried to innoculate the Georgian population with a feeling of national exclusiveness, to confine it within a narrow national framework, in order to isolate the Georgian people and to tear it from the united family of the peoples of the USSR.'

The introduction is phrased as in Khrushchev's secret speech, so as to create the impression that Beria had been the initiator of the Georgian purge. But here, too, he is not directly held responsible. Then he is suddenly accused of the very crimes which were the reason for the purge. Thus from executioner Beria is abruptly transformed into victim.

If one follows up the theory that Beria really was the victim, and not the initiator, of the Georgian purge, one discovers the interesting fact that no Soviet source gives the date on which Beria's supporter, Abakumov, was succeeded as Minister of State Security by Beria's enemy, Ignatiev. Officially, Ignatiev is mentioned for the first time as Minister of State Security in January 1953, in connexion with the proceedings against the Kremlin doctors. But the change must have taken place earlier.

Nikolayevsky puts it at November 1951,[1] and concludes that the Georgian purge was a blow against Beria, whose position it weakened. This theory is supported by the deliberately vague official phrases about Beria's part in the Mingrelian Affair, as well as the fact that in the trial of December 1954 Abakumov was not held responsible for the Georgian purge, which he obviously would have been if at the time of it he had been Minister of State Security. Finally, this theory is also borne out by the fact that in April 1953, when Beria and Malenkov were in power, the Georgian state security officials who had carried out the purge were dismissed and sentenced, whereas a number of purged government officials were re-instated. To explain this, it was even said that the rehabilitated ministers had been 'trained and hardened in the Georgian Party organization . . . which had for many years been directed by Georgia's best son, Lenin's highly gifted pupil and Stalin's comrade-in-arms, the outstanding leader of the Communist Party and the mighty Soviet state, Comrade Lavrenti Pavlovich Beria'. Ignatiev was also dismissed in April 1953 and sharply attacked. His dismissal must, however, be considered primarily in connexion with the affair of the Kremlin doctors.

In his secret speech, Khrushchev did not name Beria as responsible for the arrest of the Kremlin doctors either, nor do later statements about Beria contain any such accusation. But Khrushchev did mention two other people by name: Dr. Lydia Timashuk, who denounced the doctors to Stalin and according to Khrushchev was a secret member of the state security service, and Ignatiev, Minister of State Security at the time, who had been entrusted with directing the investigations. According to Khrushchev, Stalin threatened Ignatiev with the words, 'If you do not obtain confessions from the doctors, we shall shorten you by a head.' Khrushchev also says that Stalin had sent for the examining magistrate and given him exact instructions on the methods of investigation he should use. 'These methods were simple; to beat up and beat up and beat up again.' The investigating magistrate was the then Deputy Minister of State Security, Ryumin. In April 1953, together with Ignatiev, he was relieved of his post, and in July 1954 he

[1] *New Leader*, 16 July 1956.

was sentenced to death. But his chief, Ignatiev, who had been responsible for the proceedings against the Kremlin doctors, became Party Secretary of Bashkiria in March 1954, in which capacity he took part in the Twentieth Party Congress.[1] Khrushchev now used him as a witness of Stalin's order to the investigating authorities to extort the desired confessions by torture. No explanation was given by Khrushchev of the strange favouritism shown to the chief accused in the 'vile affair', as Khrushchev called the case of the doctors. But the answer to the question against whom the doctors' case was directed is informative. The doctors' alleged victims, whom they were said to have murdered or planned to murder, were, apart from Stalin, Marshals Koniev, Vasilevsky, Govorov, and Zhdanov and his follower, Shcherbakov. Apparently, therefore, the proceedings against the Kremlin doctors were intended to strike a blow against the persecutors of the Zhdanov group. But the most important of those were Beria and Malenkov. Since Stalin's death, Khrushchev has always been eagerly on the side of Zhdanov's followers, who were liquidated in the Leningrad trial, whereas he has always shown himself to be an implacable enemy of Malenkov and Beria. It is, therefore, not very surprising that he has protected those who took action against the persecutors of Zhdanov's followers. It is also possible that there were disagreements about the sentence on Ryumin, for he was not executed until a year and a half after Stalin's death, with Malenkov still in power.

The material which is available today does not permit any absolutely definite conclusions on the three affairs. But it clearly points to a struggle between the supporters and opponents of Zhdanov. It would only be logical for Khrushchev not to reveal the whole truth because he wanted to conceal this state of affairs.

STALIN'S COLLABORATORS

Khrushchev barely mentions the men who, after Stalin's death, were his colleagues in the Soviet Government. It is, therefore, interesting to see in what connexion he does mention them and in what light he makes them appear.

Molotov and Kaganovich are named as recipients of

[1] See above.

Stalin's telegram of 25 September 1936 from Sochi. He holds them partly responsible for the appointment of Yezhov as People's Commissar for Internal Affairs and throws some blame upon them indirectly for the purge.

Malenkov is mentioned twice pejoratively and on each occasion it is implied that he is Khrushchev's opponent. At the beginning of the war, Khrushchev, by telephone from Kiev, demanded more weapons for the army which Malenkov refused on the ground that all available arms were needed in Leningrad. In 1942 the Soviet troops at Kharkov were in danger of being encircled by the Germans. Khrushchev telephoned to Stalin to obtain a change in the operational plans. Stalin refused to speak to him and asked Malenkov to tell him that he did not want any change. The result was the encirclement and defeat of the Russian troops at Kharkov. Khrushchev used both examples to illustrate Stalin's military mistakes, but at the same time he revealed Malenkov as Stalin's closest confidant and therefore his accomplice.

Mikoyan is praised because he told Stalin after the war that Khrushchev's plan of operation had been right and thus aroused Stalin's displeasure. About Marshal Zhukov Khrushchev quotes his own remark to Stalin that Zhukov was a good general, to which Stalin refused to agree. He quotes this remark from Bulganin to prove his dislike of Stalin: 'One may accept an invitation from Stalin as a friend; but when one sits down with him one has no idea whether one will be sent home or to prison afterwards.'

Voroshilov is addressed directly by Khrushchev when he refers to Stalin's role in the civil war and challenges Voroshilov: 'Let our dear friend Kliment Yefremovich find the necessary courage to write the truth about Stalin; after all, he knows how Stalin fought! It will be difficult for Comrade Voroshilov to undertake this, but it would be a good thing if he did.' This obviously refers to Voroshilov's *Stalin and the Red Army* which glorified Stalin's role in the civil war.

In conclusion, Voroshilov, Molotov, and Mikoyan are represented as victims of Stalin's persecution mania during the last years of his life. Stalin is said to have forbidden Voroshilov for years to attend meetings of the Politburo and to have expressed the suspicion that he was a British agent. He is even said to have installed a tapping device in Voroshilov's home. Andreyev is also mentioned here as one excluded from the work of the Politburo. Stalin is said to have accused Molotov and Mikoyan of some kind of mistake. Khrushchev's comment is: 'It is possible, had Stalin remained at the helm another few months, that Comrades Molotov and Mikoyan would not have delivered speeches at this Congress.'

About Beria Khrushchev is really abusive. He calls him the 'rabid enemy of our Party, an agent of a foreign intelligence service' who wormed his way into Stalin's confidence. 'It has now been established that this villain had climbed up the government ladder over an untold number of corpses.' For most of the crimes after 1938 Beria is held entirely responsible while Stalin almost appears as someone misled who often let himself be influenced by Beria without himself knowing what was going on.

HOW COULD IT HAPPEN?

Khrushchev's task was delicate and he appears to have been aware of this. For decades Stalin had been the unquestioned leader of the Party. Khrushchev could not reveal these monstrous crimes without explaining how it had been possible for Stalin to commit them in the name of the Party, unopposed. But Khrushchev is in the first place the spokesman of the Party; he must make it seem innocent not only in order to protect himself and all other Party leaders personally, but above all in order to preserve its authority and to justify the policy which only Stalin's personal dictatorship had made possible. Therefore, he gives the following 'dialectical' reply to the question why the Party leadership did not fight against the cult of personality in good time:

'First of all we have to consider that the members of the Politburo viewed these matters in a different way at different times. Initially, many of them backed Stalin actively because he was one of the most powerful Marxists and his logic, his strength, and his will greatly influenced the essential Party membership and its work. It is known that Stalin, after Lenin's death, worked hard for Leninism against the enemies of Lenin's theory and against those who deviated from it. Beginning with this theory, the Party, with the Central Committee at its head,

started the massive industrialization of the country, the collectivization of agriculture, and the cultural revolution. At that
time, Stalin gained great popularity. The Party was bound to
fight those who attempted to lead the country away from the
true Leninist path; it was bound also to fight the followers of
Trotsky and Zinoviev, the extreme Right, and the bourgeois
nationalists. . . . Later, however, Stalin, abusing his power
more and more, began to fight eminent Party and government
leaders with terroristic methods.'

In this explanation criticism of Stalin is carefully limited.
The catastrophic crimes which were the outcome of his policy
are attributed to Stalin's faults of character. Khrushchev con-
demns Stalin's actions, but as Stalin cannot be completely
distinguished from the Party, he concludes with the following
justification of the dictator's motives:

'Stalin was convinced that all this was necessary for the
defence of the interests of the working classes against hostile
plots and the attacks of the imperialist camp. . . . We cannot
say that these were the deeds of a despot who had lost his
bearings. He considered that all this should be done in the
interest of the Party, of the working masses, in the name of the
defence of the Revolution's aims. This was the tragedy.'

In conclusion, Khrushchev demands that the Party should
'abolish' the cult of personality once and for all and draw the
proper conclusions, both theoretical and practical. Any attempt
to reintroduce the personality cult must be stubbornly fought;
it must be eradicated from historiography, philosophy, science,
and literature. The Soviet national anthem should be re-
written, Lenin prizes should be reintroduced, towns, factories,
and collective farms should no longer be named after living
persons. The Party statutes must be observed, and collective
leadership firmly established.

THE DELEGATES' REACTION

Little is known about the feeling of the Party delegates at the
secret session. The report that some fainted has not been
confirmed but the minutes provide some clues as to their re-
actions. They mention, for example, 'commotion in the hall'
after the reading of Lenin's statement on breaking off relations
with Stalin and after Khrushchev had carefully hinted at the

suspicion that Stalin had shared in the responsibility for Kirov's murder. 'Indignation in the hall' occurred after Khrushchev's announcement that 70 per cent. of the members of the Central Committee elected at the Seventeenth Party Congress were later arrested and that Stalin had a tapping device installed in Voroshilov's home. The record registers 'tumult in the hall' when Khrushchev quotes Stalin's instructions to Ignatiev. Laughter was said to be the reaction to the news that Stalin had described Voroshilov as a British agent and—this is particularly interesting—also when Khrushchev described General Poskrebyshev, as Stalin's 'loyal shield-bearer'; it was the relieved laughter of the leading men of the Soviet state who need no longer fear Stalin's private secretariat. There was 'tempestuous and prolonged applause' when Khrushchev said that victory in the war had been achieved not by Stalin but by the heroic Soviet army, its talented leaders and brave soldiers, and the whole Soviet people, and 'tumultuous, prolonged applause' broke out when Khrushchev announced that Lenin prizes were to be reintroduced.

Most significant of all was the reaction of the congress delegates to Khrushchev's declaration at the end of his speech that the revelations must not go beyond the Party: 'We must not mention all this outside the Party, particularly not to the press. . . . We must recognize limits, and not give ammunition to the enemy; we must not wash our dirty linen before his eyes. I think that the delegates to the Congress will gauge all that I propose correctly.' After these words the record again shows 'tumultuous applause'. This was the delegates' way of thanking Khrushchev for showing so much trust in them and an expression of pride in belonging to the élite of the Soviet Union.

WHY WAS THE SPEECH MADE?

Why was Khrushchev's speech necessary at all? Would not the criticism of Stalin which Khrushchev, Mikoyan, and Pankratova voiced in the open meetings of the Party Congress have been enough? Did Khrushchev make his speech as a result of a decision of the whole Party leadership, or on his own initiative in order to out-trump Mikoyan who had made the fiercest attack on Stalin at the official meetings.

To answer these questions we can but rely on guesswork.

Although accounts exist from former communist officials who were familiar with the secret letter about Beria of 1953 and knew what happened at the plenary session of July 1955, there is as yet no authentic information about the secret session of the Twentieth Party Congress. There are clues, however, to help answer the question.

In the first place, there are some important sentences at the beginning of Khrushchev's speech to which, until now, little attention has been paid. Khrushchev announced that at the earlier full sessions of the Central Committee 'much had been said about the cult of personality and its harmful effects'. The 133 full members of the Central Committee, but probably also the 122 candidate members, were therefore already more or less completely *au fait*—but not the delegates to the Congress. Former communist officials who have fled to the West have reported that as early as the second half of 1955, particularly in connexion with the visit of the Soviet leaders to Belgrade, there was talk within the Party of major attacks upon Stalin. One of these reports, published by Richard Löwenthal, makes it fairly certain that the leaders had planned a settling up with Stalinism long before the Party Congress. But it had probably not been intended for the forum of the Party Congress. This suggested that the Congress programme was changed during the session. Originally a mass demonstration had been planned in the Red Square in Moscow for 25 February, the day Khrushchev made his secret speech. On 23 February Radio Moscow was still calling on the population to attend. On the evening of 23 February a special meeting of the army delegates to the Congress took place under the chairmanship of Marshal Zhukov, who was known as an opponent of Stalin; officially this was in honour of Red Army Day. It is possible that on this occasion the army delegates demanded the rehabilitation of their chiefs. The next day the afternoon meeting of the Party Congress was suddenly cancelled and on 25 February delegates were summoned to a secret session at 10 a.m.

It is quite possible that the speeches by Khrushchev, Mikoyan, and Pankratova, in which Stalin was for the first time openly criticized had caused unrest and perhaps even opposition among the delegates, and that the leaders had been forced, in the interest of Party unity, to take up an attitude to the Stalin question. This view is supported by Khrushchev's opening sentences:

'Because of the fact that not everyone as yet has fully realized the practical consequences of the personality cult and the great harm caused by the violation of the principle of the collective leadership of the Party, which results in the concentration of unlimited power in the hands of a single individual, the Central Committee considers it absolutely necessary to make the material pertaining to this matter available to the Twentieth Party Congress.'

This may mean that many conservative officials did not understand the policy of the new leaders. In that case, Khrushchev's revelations were necessary to break their resistance and to gain their support for the measures planned. The leaders of some satellite states also expressed themselves to this effect after the Party Congress. Walter Ulbricht in his first speech after the Congress spoke of a 'healthy shock'.

It is conceivable that the leaders had decided on some cautious criticism of Stalin in the official Congress speeches in order to find out how delegates would receive it. Such an experiment was often tried among communists in Stalin's day. The author knows of a number of instances when officials, with the approval of their superiors, suggested new theories which, according to the reaction of the Party, were either adopted by the leaders or dropped—in the latter case the proposer had, of course, to take upon himself the responsibility for the 'mistake' and to criticize himself. It is, therefore, possible that after Khrushchev's first critical remarks about the Stalin textbook of Party history, Mikoyan and Pankratova were given the task of voicing more far-reaching criticism. When it became clear that these attacks were causing unrest and confusion among the delegates, the leaders decided on the healthy shock. This could, of course, be administered only by the First Secretary of the Party, Khrushchev, because only a declaration by him could make it clear to all delegates that these really were the official Party views.

This plausible explanation presupposes that collective leadership still existed intact. According to another view which assumes disagreements among the Party leaders, Mikoyan and Anna Pankratova had put forward more far-reaching criticism of Stalin on their own responsibility and had thus over-trumped the First Secretary in some way. With his secret speech Khrushchev regained the initiative, represented himself as the chief architect of de-Stalinization, and at the same time answered the question of how much others were implicated in Stalin's crimes.

Khrushchev left no doubt that he regarded the settling of scores with Stalin as an internal Party matter. He ignored the fact that Stalin's terror was not directed only against Party officials, but that ordinary Party members too, the whole nation and, after the war, also a number of other nations had suffered from it. The discussion of these things was to take place strictly within the limits which he had set. Perhaps he foresaw what actually happened shortly afterwards: That the discussion once it had got out of control, of the Party, would no longer stop at a condemnation of Stalin's dictatorship.

Three months after the Party Congress the whole record of the Party Congress was published in an edition of half a million copies. In this it was officially announced that the Party Congress, at a closed session, had heard a report by Khrushchev and unanimously adopted a resolution on it. This is probably the shortest resolution in the history of the Bolshevik Party; it merely says that after listening to the report, the Congress had instructed the Central Committee consistently to carry out measures 'to put an end to the cult of personality which is alien to Marxism-Leninism, to liquidate its consequences in all spheres of Party and state activity and of ideological work, and to ensure the strict maintenance of the standards of Party life worked out by the great Lenin and of the principles of collective Party leadership'.

THE DIFFUSION OF THE SECRET SPEECH IN THE USSR

There are various answers to the question how far Khrushchev's secret speech is known to the Soviet population. According to most reports, a shortened version of the speech was read at closed Party meetings. But there are also reports that the speech was made public at Komsomol meetings and even at meetings in the universities attended by persons not belonging to the Party. William C. Just, who was in Moscow in 1956, asked many Moscow students how the contents of Khrushchev's speech were spread and what effect they had on the students.[1] One student describes the course of such a meeting at his university:

'We already had some idea before. One day a special meeting was announced which was to take place in the conference room of our university. We all had to show our Komsomol cards. The room was crowded; the atmosphere was tense and excited. The chairman, a member of the Komsomol committee, rose and announced that he was now going to read an historic document of the Twentieth Party Congress. He emphasized that this document came from a closed meeting and that it was intended for the personal information of the Party and Komsomol members. Then he read the speech without comment.' In answer to further questions, Soviet students told Just that the full text of the speech was read at some universities and even at general meetings of students.

All the accounts given by foreign observers in Moscow at the time indicate that Khrushchev's speech had the effect of a shock and that many tongues were loosened. According to Klaus Mehnert, while the official Party Congress was still meeting, that is before Khrushchev's speech became known, there were almost no open political discussions. The population had taken little notice of the opening of the Congress. While it was taking place and all the newspapers appeared in enlarged editions with the speeches published, mostly verbatim, people could be seen in the streets engrossed in reading the Congress speeches. At meetings, in factories and schools, the material was 'worked over'. Dr. Mehnert, who attended a meeting of the kind, said that he did not notice the slightest attempt at a discussion of the problems touched on in the speeches.

After Khrushchev's speech became known the atmosphere changed quickly. Tosa Popovsky, the permanent Moscow correspondent of the Yugoslav newspaper, *Borba*, reported that it seemed as though a weight were lifted from many people's minds. For the first time he again heard political remarks in the streets of Moscow. In the Lenin-Stalin mausoleum Popovsky heard visitors murmuring words of respect and sympathy at Lenin's coffin, but uttering curses at Stalin's. In Moscow, dis-

[1] See *The Observer*, 7 Oct. 1956.

cussions could already be heard in which the mistakes of the past were attributed not to Stalin's person but to the system which had made possible a single man's rule.[1]

The reaction of the population to criticism of Stalin varied greatly. Just tells of discussions which took place after the reading of Khrushchev's speech. Some students said: 'According to what we have heard, Stalin is to be forgotten. How can we continue to honour his memory at all?' Another student tried to belittle the criticism and spoke the whole time of 'Stalin's little mistakes'. Others again appeared unable to cope with the problem. 'It was as if we had suddenly been hit over the head,' said a girl student. 'We simply could not deal with it. For weeks we wrote or discussed nothing else among ourselves.' The French novelist, Vercors, who visited the Soviet Union at the end of 1956, reported similar impressions. He was continually meeting writers who were deeply affected by the revelations at the Twentieth Party Congress and who 'had not yet managed to come to terms with them'. Even poems on this subject were passed from hand to hand. 'We built on granite, but now the stone crumbles, dissolves, and melts away at my feet,' says one.[2]

But there were also other opinions. Some young people, in particular, were angry, and made a show of demonstrating their loyalty to Stalin. In the Union Republic of Georgia, he was regarded by many as a Georgian national hero who ruled over Russia. Thus in Georgia there were open demonstrations in favour of Stalin. Louis Fischer, who visited Moscow in the summer of 1956, in his book *Russia Revisited*, reports a conversation with a Soviet youth, a dyed-in-the-wool Stalinist as follows:

'What do you think of Stalin now that you have heard what Khrushchev said about him?'

'I love Stalin,' he asserted aggressively.

'You love the man who butchered millions of people before and after the war, broke up lives, and caused mountains of casualties in the fighting with Hitler?'

'Stalin was a great statesman and he built up our country.'

'And what about the millions whom he ordered to be shot?'

'Since they were Trotskyists they had to be shot.'

[1] *Borba*, 26 March 1956.   [2] *Die Politische Meinung*, August 1957.

'And Bukharin, the philosopher of communism, popular leader, beloved of Lenin and the youth?'

'If he was harmful to the state he had to be shot.'

However, aggressive professions of faith in Stalin were probably exceptional. The characteristic reaction was the feeling of being unable to deal with the new situation and, above all, the hope that now the worst was over and that better times would come. The feeling of relief and hope probably predominated, particularly among educated people—including part of the ruling class. Louis Fischer continuously met people who received the condemnation of Stalin with relief, full of hope that things would get better now. 'If it goes on like this, we might even become free,' he quotes from his conversations, and 'Now the nightmare is over'. He sums up the mood of those weeks in the following words: 'They are inclined to be sceptical but they are full of hope. One would think that they must hate the political system which is responsible for the massacres and reign of terror. Some do, but most of them are grateful for the new moderation.'

THE NEW GENERAL POLICY

The Party leaders were alarmed by the reaction of the population, including intellectuals and Party officials, to Khrushchev's speech. They had to make their position clear in order to direct public discussion into the right channels. This happened in two *Pravda* articles in which policy was defined. The first appeared on 28 March under the heading 'Why is the cult of personality alien to the spirit of "Marxism-Leninism?" ' and the second on 5 April under the heading 'The Communist Party continues victorious thanks to its loyalty to Leninism'. Both articles are no less important than Khrushchev's secret report in order to interpret Soviet policy. A comparison between the speech and the two articles shows the difference between criticism of Stalin for the élite and for the people.

The task of the first *Pravda* article was to bring some of the essential conceptions of Khrushchev's speech to the notice of wide circles of the population in a diluted form. Stalin's activities were again divided into a good and a bad period. Taken almost literally from Khrushchev was *Pravda's* assertion that Stalin had rendered 'great services to our Party, to the working class and the international workers' movement'; he had been 'one of the strongest Marxists' and 'his work, his logic, and his will had great influence on the shape and the work of the Party'. Industrialization, collectivization, and the fight against all the Soviet state's enemies were of course enumerated again.

The characteristics of Stalin which led to the cult of personality are said to have appeared only gradually; the successes of the Soviet Union had been wrongly attributed to Stalin alone and explained as due to his qualities of leadership. Without giving examples, the abuses of the Stalin period were then condemned in the spirit of Khrushchev's speech.

On the other hand, the article contained a hint which was not in Khrushchev's speech. The criticism of the personality cult and of one-man rule was restricted to the Party. *Pravda* expressly stressed that 'the Communist Party has advocated and continues to advocate the principle of single control in industrial enterprises and in the army'.

As in every article in which policy is declared, certain conclusions were also drawn in this one, and certain tasks set. The remains of the cult of personality were to be eradicated. This was 'one of the most important tasks of the Party'. Administrative measures alone were not enough. A big propaganda campaign and a reorientation of ideological work were announced.

In the second article published on 5 April the basic themes were repeated, but the main emphasis was already on ways and means of overcoming the cult of personality. In this connexion, *Pravda* pointed to the necessity of fighting two harmful tendencies. On the one hand, the cells were called upon boldly to criticize those who had not freed themselves from bureaucratic methods of work. This obviously referred to the forces which opposed de-Stalinization, the 'apparachiks' who clung to old Stalinist practices. On the other hand, the Party cells were warned against rotten elements which were trying to 'use criticism and self-criticism for a variety of slanderous attacks and anti-Party assertions'. This was aimed at those who wanted to carry de-Stalinization further than the post-Stalin leaders wished. In particular, *Pravda* criticized members of a certain scientific laboratory, participants in a meeting of Party activists in Chkalov, and—this is probably the most important example —a Party meeting of the Statistical Administration in Moscow which had attacked Yaroshenko[1] for challenging anti-Party statements, without, however, in the opinion of the Party leaders, condemning him in sufficiently strong terms.

The importance of the *Pravda* article of 5 April 1956 cannot be overestimated; it proclaimed for the first time the fight against two trends, against Stalinist 'apparachiks' on the one hand, and the reformers who were moving too fast on the other. Thus *Pravda* adopted a middle course, opposed to both 'deviations'.

---

[1] He had been attacked by Stalin in 1952. See above.

CHAPTER VI

THE YEAR OF HOPE AND CONFUSION

(February 1956 to June 1957)

THE Twentieth Party Congress was hardly over before a wave of meetings swept over the Soviet Union. At first practical and especially economic questions were in the foreground, but during the second half of March the centre of gravity shifted to the fight against the cult of personality. At the end of March, Dr. Klaus Mehnert[1] reported that at meetings criticism of Stalin was supported with many concrete accusations. Frequently bewilderment was created because the material condemning Stalin did not exist in print, but was spread by word of mouth and handed on in a distorted form.

In some places the photographs of Stalin had already disappeared. In March 1956 the big paintings of Stalin were removed from the Tretyakov Gallery. The Museum of the Revolution founded in December 1949 on the occasion of Stalin's seventieth birthday contained gifts from all over the world exhibited in ten rooms; now it was not closed, but the descriptions of all the presents were changed. Instead of 'to the great Stalin on the occasion of his seventieth birthday from factory X', one found 'jubilee gift from factory X'. According to reports from foreigners who were in the Caucasus at the time, there were serious disturbances in Georgia, since many Georgians regarded Stalin as their compatriot now under attack from 'foreigners'.

The difficulties which the Party leaders faced in Georgia were admitted only several months later, and then indirectly. On 23 August *Sarya Vostoka*, the central organ of the Communist Party of Georgia, published in Tiflis, carried a report of a plenary session of the Central Committee of the Georgian Communist Party at which a number of leading officials had been strongly attacked because of their policy immediately

---

[1] In a series of articles in *Die Welt*.

after the Twentieth Party Congress. It was said that the Georgian Party leaders had insufficiently appreciated 'that the cult of Stalin's personality was deeply rooted in the consciousness of the population of Georgia, and that it had attained particularly exaggerated dimensions among us and been given a nationalist complexion'. The Party organizations had taken very little trouble to point out the 'tremendous damage which the cult of Stalin had done to our Party and to the Soviet people'. The Party organizations, it was said, had been too tolerant towards nationalistic demonstrations among Georgian intellectuals.

The Soviet leaders had decided on open criticism of Stalin primarily for domestic reasons. Khrushchev's speech to the Twentieth Party Congress was intended to shock the officials into changing their ways of thinking and to remove ideological obstacles in the way of further reforms. But it soon became clear that once people's thoughts had been freed from Stalinist shackles they could no longer be led into predetermined channels. Particularly in the countries of Eastern Europe, the Kremlin lost control over political developments.

THE REACTION OF THE COMMUNIST WORLD

As early as March 1956, something very unusual emerged: the statements of the various national parties differed strikingly from one another. The majority tried to limit and minimize criticism of Stalin. But others—particularly the communist parties of Poland and Italy—welcomed the Twentieth Party Congress as the beginning of a new policy which would give them greater independence.

One of the first Party leaders to dissociate himself publicly from Stalin was Walter Ulbricht in East Germany. But it was obvious that he intended not to encourage de-Stalinization, but to put a brake on it. In two articles of 4 and 18 March in *Neues Deutschland*[1] he repeated some of what Khrushchev had said against Stalin in his secret speech. Ulbricht criticized Stalin's excessive self-flattery and the perversion of the history of the Party in the Stalin biography. 'Comrade Stalin offended against Leninist standards and also made serious mistakes in executing the policy of the Party; one cannot say that he

[1] The newspaper of the East German Communist Party.

belongs to our classics. Stalin has now been put in the place which corresponds to his role.' Nor was Stalin the brilliant commander who led the Soviet Union to victory over Fascism: 'This is what Comrade Stalin himself wrote into his biography.'

Neither Ulbricht nor his colleagues nor the press of East Germany published their own comments on the question of Stalinism, although they drew theoretical and practical conclusions from the Twentieth Party Congress. The Third Party Conference of the SED, which took place in March, dealt with economic questions and ignored the ideological problems thrown up by the Twentieth Party Congress.

In Poland, on the other hand, the Twentieth Party Congress provided the stimulus for a far-reaching ideological and political transformation. The Polish Party paper, *Trybuna Ludu*, said as early as March that the cult of personality was irreconcilable with the spirit of socialism, because socialism 'tries to bring about relations based on the equality, liberty, and fraternity of everyone'. Not only was Stalin's autocracy condemned, but also Stalin's way of treating certain questions as taboo. Instead of Party discipline, 'blind faith in the omniscience of one man had become customary'. The cult of personality had had serious consequences for Poland, among them 'the strangulation of democracy within the Party, abuses on the part of the state security service, and the petrification of many branches of our sciences'. The Twentieth Party Congress was 'the beginning of . . . the cleansing of the reality of our life of everything not in harmony with the liberating aims of socialism'.

On 12 March the leader of the Polish Party, Boleslav Bierut, died; he was succeeded by Edvard Ochab. Soon afterwards, Gomulka, Spychalski, and Komar, leaders who had been purged earlier, were released from prison and rehabilitated together with a number of their supporters. Members of the state security service and officials known as violent Stalinists lost their posts. In the second half of April a comprehensive amnesty was promulgated; 40,000 prison sentences were reduced and 36,000 prisoners, mainly political, were released.

The Party leaders of Czechoslavakia, Hungary, Rumania, and Albania faced a difficult situation after the Twentieth Party Congress. In the years 1949 to 1952 big trials of 'Titoists' had taken place in these countries, in the course of which high officials and thousands of Party members had been arrested and shot. The most famous of these trials were those of Kochi Dzodze in May 1949 in Albania, of Traicho Kostov in the autumn of 1949 in Bulgaria, of László Rajk at the end of 1949 in Hungary, and of Slansky in December 1952 in Czechoslovakia. The revision of these trials, the rehabilitation of innocent people who had been sentenced, and the punishment of those responsible were now on the agenda. But those responsible were still in office and tried to restrict the rehabilitation to a minimum.

In Hungary the Communist Party leader, Mathias Rákosi, said that the Hungarian Party leadership had arrived at the conclusion 'that the Rajk trial had been based on provocation'.[1] The Central Committee had therefore decided 'to rehabilitate Comrade László Rajk'. This laconic statement did not even form part of a Party resolution, but was made by Rákosi at a Party meeting in a small Hungarian town. In Czechoslovakia nothing was said at first about a revision of the Slansky trial. The Party leaders confined themselves to the rehabilitation of some survivors, among them Arthur London and Hajdu, without mentioning the others. In Rumania the cult of personality was condemned at a full session of the Central Committee at the end of March, and it was proposed that the streets and towns called after living people should be renamed. In Bulgaria the Party leader Viko Chervenkov, who had lived in the Soviet Union from 1923 to 1944 and who was known as one of the keenest antagonists of Titoism, was relieved of his post. He was succeeded by Anton Yugov, who did not belong to the Moscow group of emigrés, but who had been a member of the Bulgarian resistance movement. Kostov, who had been executed in September 1949, was rehabilitated. The Bulgarian Party Secretary, Todor Zhivkov, announced the withdrawal of the charges against Kostov of Yugoslav connexions, and the rehabilitation of all the accused in Kostov's trial.

In Albania, however, Kochi Dzodze, one of the founders of the Albanian Communist Party, and after the war Deputy Prime Minister, Minister of the Interior, and Deputy Chairman of the Party, who had been executed in May 1949, was not

[1] *Szabad Nep*, 27 March 1956.

rehabilitated. The Stalinist Party leader of Albania, Enver Hoxha, merely said that the Albanian Party leaders had been deceived by Beria.

The Communist Party of China adopted a strange attitude towards the Twentieth Party Congress. On 5 April the Chinese Party organ *Jen-min Jih-pao* said that Stalin had made a number of serious mistakes during the last decades of his life. 'He became conceited and careless,' it continued, 'and began to think in subjective terms: consequently, he made wrong decisions on a number of important questions, and this had very harmful consequences.' At the same time, however, Stalin was described as a 'world-famous and highly honoured leader', the study of whose works would have to go on; 'Some people think that Stalin did everything wrong. This is a great mistake. Stalin was a great Marxist-Leninist, who made a number of mistakes without recognizing them as such. We must look at Stalin from the perspective of history and weigh up carefully what he did right against what he did wrong, drawing salutary lessons from this. His achievements and his mistakes were typical of the international movement and bear the stamp of their time.'

Jen-min Jih-pao published some Chinese Communist Party resolutions from earlier days to prove that the Communist Party of China had long been fighting against what was now condemned in the Soviet Union. There was no mention at all of any Chinese cult of personality, nor was it suggested that any change was due in China.

The two big West European communist parties, the French and the Italian, also reacted differently. In the name of the Communist Party of France, Duclos and Thorez in *Humanité* of 10 and 17 March stressed almost nothing but Stalin's merits. Like no other communist party outside the Soviet bloc the French Communist Party leaders tried to minimize the importance of the new decisions.

Togliatti, on the other hand, said[1] that the Twentieth Party Congress had created a new situation. Stalin, with his view of the intensification of the class struggle in socialist society had reached 'the fundamentally desperate prospect of never-ending mutual persecution' not only between the parts of society which opposed each other but also within the organization of

[1] *Unità*, 15 March 1956.

the working class. Thus Stalin's suspicion was bound to extend in all directions and to all circumstances. This led, Togliatti continued, to 'unjustified measures of repression and to infringements of socialist legality, to a situation, that is, where mere confessions were accepted as valid proof without supporting evidence'. It was now the business of the Soviet comrades to be more specific in their criticism.

THE 'EXPLOSION OF TRUTH'

Soon after the Twentieth Party Congress another phenomenon became noticeable: some Party members tried to become more independent. Typical of the mood after the Congress are the letters published by the London *Daily Worker* in the last week of March: 'Why don't we recognize once and for all that the communists in Moscow, whoever they may be at the moment, are not the fount of all truth and that we, as creative Marxists, should and must develop our own ideas', wrote one correspondent on 21 March.

'If it is true that innocent people were killed as a result of Stalin's mistakes, then we must state emphatically that these actions are inexcusable', wrote four Party members on the following day. On 23 March, someone wrote: 'Let us remember our own position. If we are honest, we must admit that our hymns of praise for Stalin were always ridiculous and most of us knew it all the time.' On 26 March another correspondent of the *Daily Worker* wrote: 'The attitude that, right or wrong, I am on the side of the Soviet Union today does only harm to our Party. It induced us to approve of practices which are indefensible.'

In the communist world these feelings were probably still stronger, but they found little expression in the Party press, except in Poland.

On the 27 March the newspaper *Zycie Warszawy* reported that the editor had been inundated with letters; many questions were asked about a general re-appraisal. In reply to the frequent plea: 'Don't tear Stalin from our hearts!' *Zycie Warszawy* replied: 'It is the truth which tears Stalin from our hearts, the truth which is gradually working its way to the light of day; it works without an anaesthetic, without the precision instruments of the surgeon.' It was not a question of the cult of personality under Stalin, but of the fact that in his day 'signs of the corruption of the man and of Party life appeared side by side. . . .'

Two days later *Trybuna Ludu*, under the significant heading: 'Where does the truth lie?' published the following letter: 'I have followed the course of the Twentieth Party Congress with attention. Every day brought interesting news. But the more I read the more I became worried by one question—the Party Congress announced a great change in policy about which one can only be glad. But aren't these new revolutionary things yet another mistake?'

The editorial reply was: 'What is true, what is false? This question need not surprise one. There are many who think like this today. If I could believe in lies and could think they were the truth, who can guarantee to me that what is given out as truth today will not again be a lie tomorrow. . . . This brings us to the conflict faced by many communists today. . . . The conflict of conscience has increased in the last few years. As time passes, it becomes clear that this conflict was not normal, that it was the result of illness, of those abscesses which had grown on the body of the Revolution. It emerged that on the occasions when there was a marked conflict between the practice of the Revolution and its humane character, it was not the result of tactical requirements, but of excesses, of deviations from the true path of the Revolution.'

Such sentences were formerly found only in books by people in opposition, who had turned their back on the Party. Now they were reproduced in the central organ of a ruling Communist Party. And what was the way out of this conflict of conscience? The hopeful answer of the Polish paper was:

'Today we are searching for an answer to a great number of worrying questions. To many we have not got one yet, to many we shall—who knows?—perhaps no longer be able to give one. But to the question where lies the truth and where falsehood, or what guarantee is there that the Twentieth Party Congress was not a new mistake, we can reply that the removal of this conflict, the restoration of harmony between the conscience, words, and deeds of a communist means a return to truth.'

THE DISSOLUTION OF THE COMINFORM

Soon after the Party Congress rumours suddenly spread about the dissolution of the 'Information Bureau of the Communist and Workers' Parties', 'Cominform' for short. The first news of the impending dissolution of the Cominform did not come from Moscow, but from the Yugoslav radio station at Zagreb on 11 March; the source was a Communist Party conference in Rome. The dissolution of the Cominform was announced officially in Moscow by Mikoyan on 17 April. The following day all communist papers carried the news.

Although the dissolution of the Cominform was a logical result of the new development, there appear to have been differences of opinion about it among the Soviet leaders. Without any apparent need, Khrushchev, before the Supreme Soviet on 29 December 1955, after his return from India, still expressed himself strongly in favour of its continued existence. Three months later, the Soviet leaders decided on dissolution after all. This was chiefly due to the hope that it would facilitate a rapprochement with the social-democrats of Western Europe, and with the Yugoslav communists. The Yugoslav communists had repeatedly expressed themselves against the continued existence of the Cominform; among the communist movements of the world, it appears to have been the Italian one in particular which pleaded for dissolution, and it was at a conference of the Italian Party that the impending dissolution was mentioned for the first time.

The communist press justified the dissolution by the official explanation that the Cominform had fulfilled its function, and stressed its alleged importance. Only Togliatti[1] referred to some of the mistakes of the Cominform, the interference, for instance, in 1948 and 1949 in the affairs of the Yugoslav Communist Party. The composition of the Cominform leadership had been heterogeneous and accidental and its activity less and less fruitful. The dissolution of the Cominform, it was emphasized in the official commentaries, would encourage the independence of the individual communist parties. *Pravda* said on 18 April that the communist parties must be asked 'more than ever ... to pay careful attention to the idiosyncrasies of national

[1] On 18 April 1956.

conditions in their countries'. It was important to develop a policy in accordance with the traditions of each nation.

Togliatti went still further in his statement. Reality, he said, was always richer, more many-sided, and surprising than any model. He hoped that there would now be 'a greater degree of independence in the critical evaluation of progress and mistakes'.

The hopes which the Soviet leaders had placed on the dissolution of the Cominform did not, however, materialize as the Russian rulers had hoped. At a press conference given by the Yugoslav Party theorist, Mose Pijade,[1] the Yugoslav communists welcomed the dissolution of the Cominform, but protested against its wording. 'A serious historical analysis of this organization (the Cominform) in the future will show,' said Pijade, 'that it played no constructive part at all.'

With the dissolution of the Cominform the Soviet leaders had renewed their offers of a united front to the social-democratic parties of Western Europe. Boris Ponomaryov, who was in charge of questions concerning the international workers' movement, published an article in *Pravda*, in which he declared official policy, describing 'practical collaboration between the communist and social-democrat parties' as one of the most important tasks. It was not a question of philosophical problems, but of reaching practical agreement. This offer was, however, rejected by the social-democratic parties. In the first half of April the Bureau of the Socialist International announced that the condemnation of Stalin had not fundamentally altered the character of the communist régime. The most recent statements of the communist leaders provided no reason for any change in the attitude of democratic socialists.

The Party leaders in Moscow did not, however, abandon their efforts to achieve a united front. On 20 April *Pravda* again demanded collaboration. On 23 April during the state visit by Khrushchev and Bulganin to Great Britain, a meeting took place between the Soviet representatives and the British Labour leaders.

As long as Bulganin was talking to the latter in the House of Commons all went well. But when Khrushchev for over an hour threw out unjustified accusations against British pre-war

[1] See also *Borba*, 19 April 1956.

policy, the situation deteriorated quickly. After his speech, Gaitskell rose and recalled the many Social Democrats imprisoned in the communist countries: he handed Khrushchev a list of 200 of them. Khrushchev, however, refused to accept the list; in Russia, he said, there were no Social Democrats and he was not in a position to speak for the other countries. The first attempt of the Soviet leaders to achieve closer relations with Western European Social Democrats thus ended in failure.

POST-HASTE DE-STALINIZATION

After the dissolution of the Cominform in April 1956 de-Stalinization measures followed one another in quick succession. On 19 April the dissolution of the special tribunals of the state security service was announced in the Soviet Union. Soon afterwards the order of 26 June 1940 was rescinded according to which workers who arrived twenty minutes late were sentenced after the first offence to six months' corrective training at their place of work. On the same day, 25 April, workers were given the right to give notice and freedom to choose their place of work. The state security service was deprived of more of its power through the trial of two leading state security officials of Azerbaidjan;[1] criticism of Stalin was continued, and in particular the part he played in 1941 was scrutinized.[2] A law increasing pensions was promulgated on 14 July, working hours for young people were reduced from eight to six hours on 26 May, decentralization was continued through the transfer of all light industry and textile concerns, as well as of shipping, to the Union Republics on 31 May, and at about the same time a commission of jurists was appointed to examine the penal code. These and many other measures during the spring of 1956 fostered the hope, fully justified at the time, of a fundamental change in the system.

Of the countries of Eastern Europe, Poland went furthest in de-Stalinization. Thousands of officials who had been arrested or outlawed returned to public life, while well-known Stalinist officials, Jakob Berman for example, were relieved of their posts. Accounts with the past were mercilessly settled in the press and at meetings. Attacks were not restricted to official

[1] On 26 April.   [2] On 29 April.

criticism of the cult of personality, but soon spread to the principles of the Stalinist system.

In the other countries of Eastern Europe as well, the political climate changed. In Czechoslovakia 235 of the rank-and-file Party organizations demanded, against the wish of the leaders, that an extraordinary Party Congress should be convened. Turbulent scenes took place at the Congress of Czechoslovak writers in the second half of April, for the latter declared that in future they wanted to write only what was true. President Zapotocky commented that these remarks frightened him, since they implied that the writers had suppressed the truth until now. The universities were in a state of ferment. The students passed resolutions demanding objective information about life abroad from the press, that foreign radio stations' broadcasts should no longer be jammed, that Parliament should no longer be a rubber stamp but should have proper debates, that the trials of the past should be re-opened, those responsible punished and the innocent rehabilitated, and that in the libraries the 'poison cupboards' with forbidden books should be opened and made available to the students.

The Czechoslovak Party leaders tried desperately to control this movement. The leading article in the Party organ, *Rudé Pravo*, on 1 May almost begged its members not to lose confidence in the Party: 'Much has happened this year. Much that was dear to us has been smashed,' it wrote. 'Our souls are full of pain because strings have suddenly been touched which we thought inviolable and feelings which were dear to us. Side by side with joy about the recent rapid developments many an old communist will feel sadness. He may even feel very bitter.

'We too feel in the same way, comrades, but the one is unthinkable without the other. And if we believe in the Party we believe in it firmly! Only a Party for which revolutionary truth is everything is in a position to plunge the knife of self-criticism so deeply into its own flesh. . . . Let us believe in the Party! Let us believe in it because it has the stuff in it to say quite openly: We made a mistake—we shall correct it.'

In Hungary the reform movements were particularly strong among intellectuals and young people. On 18 May Rákosi felt compelled to criticize himself: 'It is true that I tolerated and frequently encouraged the cult of personality. I must frankly admit this, otherwise comrades might have the impression that we were beating about the bush.' Rákosi also admitted responsibility for illegal actions and promised to restore legality. But it was obvious that he only yielded to public pressure reluctantly.

In Rumania and Bulgaria, also, the Party leaders were forced to make concessions; only in Albania did things remain unchanged. At the Third Party Congress of the Communist Party of Albania, at the end of May 1956, Enver Hoxha even justified the execution of Kochi Dzodze. Apart from announcing an amnesty for 520 persons and a reduction of the sentences of 813 political prisoners, there was no self-criticism in Albania, nor were any Stalinist officials dismissed or rehabilitations announced.

At the beginning of June 1956 the American State Department published Khrushchev's secret speech. It was no longer possible to evade the problems it raised. The Soviet leaders were faced with the alternative of putting themselves at the head of the anti-Stalin movement or of trying to restrain it. Until the end of June it seemed as though Moscow had chosen the first course.

JUNE 1956: THE CLIMAX OF DE-STALINIZATION

In the Soviet Union the main event of June 1956 was the visit of Marshal Tito, who arrived in Moscow on 2 June. *Pravda* published his photograph and his biography together with a long theoretical article by the Yugoslav Vice-President, Edvard Kardelj, who introduced the Russian population for the first time to the authentic ideas of the Yugoslav communists. On the same day, Molotov, who had signed the Cominform resolution against Yugoslavia and who, after Stalin's death, had been known as a supporter of the anti-Yugoslav line and a representative of the conservative forces, was relieved of his post of Foreign Minister and replaced by Dmitri Shepilov. Four days later, Kaganovich,[1] a second pro-Stalinist, was dismissed from the post of Chairman of the State Committee on Labour and Wage Questions.

In many ways Marshal Tito's visit cannot be compared with the visit of any other foreign statesman, however important.

[1] Replaced by Alexander Volkov.

It was of exceptional significance both in the eyes of the Soviet public and in its effect on Party circles and even on the Party leaders. During Tito's visit the publication of Lenin's testament was prepared. In Soviet factories workers' councils were introduced experimentally, and in the last week of June, according to Reuter's correspondent, John Rettie, the Soviet leaders considered whether, at elections to the local soviets, instead of the usual single-candidate system, several candidates should be nominated. This was the system used in Yugoslavia in the election of workers' councils, and introduced in Poland after the events of October. That such tendencies really existed in the second half of June was later confirmed by a campaign in the course of which these ideas were violently attacked.

At the end of the Yugoslav visit a declaration was signed on 20 June on the relations between the League of Yugoslav Communists and the Communist Party of the Soviet Union; this confirmed the Belgrade declaration of 2 June 1955 and went even further. Both parties stated 'that the roads to socialist development in different countries in different conditions are different', and that 'diversity in the development of socialism helps to strengthen it'. Thus the Soviet leaders acknowledged even more clearly than in the Belgrade Declaration the Yugoslav theory of different roads to socialism. The agreement also stated emphatically 'that neither one side nor the other has any inclination to push forward its own conceptions in determining the methods of socialist development'. Collaboration must be completely voluntary and based on equality, friendly criticism, and a comradely exchange of views.

The importance of the Soviet-Yugoslav Party declaration was all the greater because at that time violent discussions were taking place inside the world communist movement on de-Stalinization. The climax of these discussions was an interview with Togliatti in the periodical *Nuovi Argumenti*, an interview which was later also published by *Unità* and other Western European communist papers.

Whereas Khrushchev had spoken only of Stalin's failings, Togliatti linked them with the system of society in Russia. For he said that in the Soviet Union the rapid increase of bureaucratic, authoritarian methods and flagrant violation of law had half suffocated democratic life. Togliatti said openly that the responsibility was shared by the whole leading group 'including those comrades who have now taken the initiative in revealing the wrong done, in putting an end to it and in removing its consequences'. The attitude of the Party Congress to Stalin's mistakes was not satisfactory. The Soviet leaders remained under the spell of the personality cult as long as they represented Stalin's faults of character as the source of all evil. The real problem was how and why Soviet society 'could and did deviate to the point of degeneration' from its path. Togliatti considered that Stalin's mistakes were connected with an excessive increase of bureaucracy in the life of the Party and the country.

He expressed the hope that 'in the course of the new road which the Soviet Union had taken, important new discussions will take place in which the extent of the old mistakes will be examined'. It was to be hoped 'that corrections will be made unhesitatingly and courageously, so that socialist society will be provided with a stimulus to further progress on a broad, sound, democratic basis, full of new and living impulses'.

In the international sphere Togliatti, as we know, demanded greater independence for the individual communist parties. The situation had changed, he said, to such an extent that the Soviet example 'can and must no longer be compulsory'. A 'polycentric system' was being developed and even inside the communist movement it was no longer possible to speak of a unified leadership. This was the most significant declaration in the communist world since the Yugoslav communists broke with Moscow. For the first time Stalinism was attacked from the communist side as a system and not only as the sum of individual mistakes.

The Togliatti interview immediately influenced other communist parties in Western Europe. Even the French, the most Stalinist of all parties in Western Europe, now criticized the Soviet leaders. It was admitted in *Humanité* on 19 June that the publication of Khrushchev's speech had caused understandable excitement among French Party members. It was very regrettable that French communists had been informed of the contents of the speech through the non-communist press. Soviet statements so far about Stalin's mistakes could not be regarded as satisfactory; a thorough Marxist analysis of the facts which had made Stalin's autocracy possible was essential. Three days later the British communist leaders echoed the views of their French colleagues.

At the same time, George Lukács, in a lecture which caused excitement at the Budapest Academy, demanded a thorough reorientation in philosophy and literature. In his speech which was published in the June to July number of *Tarsadelmi Szemle*, Lukács said that it was necessary to make socialism attractive instead of a spectre which frightened people in the West away. It was undeniable that the majority of workers, peasants, and intellectuals in the West 'recoiled from the form which socialism takes today'. It was important to make socialism more humane: 'The more humane we make socialism, humane for ourselves, for our own purposes, from the point of view of our own development, the more we help the final victory of socialism in the international field.' It was desirable, he continued, 'to come into contact with the representatives of opposite views and to engage in free discussion'.

Lukács condemned the Stalinist attitude towards literature. For decades mediocre literary productions had been praised uncritically. This had undermined the reputation of socialist realism and gradually the view had developed 'that by socialist realism were meant those mediocre, mechanical works that our critics are accustomed to praise to high heaven'. One would at last have to consider books without prejudice; hitherto criticism had known only the extremes of praise and condemnation.

Lukács further expressed the hope that the Twentieth Party Congress had done away completely with Stalinist dogmatism. Now it was important that serious international talks should start among communists and that these should also be extended to the social democrats and the opponents of Marxism. . . . 'It is our duty,' he said, 'to break energetically with the past.' These statements by Togliatti and Lukács were typical. They went far beyond what was published at the same time in the Soviet Union.

Up to the end of June 1956 the reformers among the Soviet leaders seemed to have the upper hand. Although Togliatti's interview and Lukács' lecture were not published in Russia, *Pravda* on 27 June carried a long article by the American communist leader, Eugene Dennis, which showed similar tendencies. It contained the most far-reaching criticism of Stalin that had ever come out in the Soviet Union. Eugene Dennis took as his point of departure Khrushchev's report on Stalin which was thus for the first time directly mentioned in the Russian press. However depressing and shocking the facts which Khrushchev announced had been, they represented a part of history, and 'communists must have the courage to look these things in the face, to analyse them and to draw the appropriate conclusions'. The cruelties which had overshadowed the last period of the Stalin era were unforgivable and could not even be justified as political or historical necessities. 'Nothing,' wrote Dennis, 'can justify the use of torture and defamatory verdicts, of mass deportations, or of provocative and chauvinist actions, as for example against Yugoslavia, or the persecution of the Jewish doctors. A socialist society cannot admit that such hideous injustices should not be revealed and repaired.'

Dennis tried to explain Stalinist developments by the difficult situation of the Soviet Union during the Civil War, the wars of intervention and the blockade and, finally, at a later stage, by the destruction caused by Hitler's armies during the war. The industrialization which had been carried through with great sacrifices at the beginning of the thirties led to a centralization of power which had in turn led to an increase in Stalin's authority and had finally resulted in Stalin's absolute rule. This had impaired the creative and cultural life of the Soviet Union. The organs of the state security service 'were given excessive and dangerous powers and took criminal liberties with the Soviet Constitution'. The results, such as the false confessions and manufactured evidence, were a dreadful result of the atmosphere of distrust and hysteria which Yezhov and Beria had exploited.

Eugene Dennis also criticized Stalin's successors. 'Had any of them during the past three years tried to change anything? Could the evils which were developing not have been removed before?' We hope, added Dennis, that the material now published reflects only a part of the investigations which are being made and which will probably continue to be made for many years by the Russian Communist Party.

Dennis attacked not only the leadership cult, but also a

superstitious faith in authority generally. 'No one can maintain,' he wrote, 'that new mistakes of a different kind are not being made in socialist countries. To rely on the infallibility of any one group of leaders means to repeat the fundamental mistakes of the past, and to learn nothing from the dreadful elevation of Stalin to the status of a demi-god.' The publication of this article in *Pravda* made its argument official Party doctrine. Thus the Party leaders must have been in agreement on 27 June 1956 with Dennis's arguments, and even with his criticism of those who were trying to minimize the errors revealed.

THE CHANGE IN POLICY

Dennis's article was the climax of de-Stalinization: it was the last publication of the kind. Only a few days later a reversal of policy became noticeable in Moscow, for criticism of Stalin and the Stalin period was suddenly cut down. The material available at present suggests that the causes of the change are to be found less in Russia than in the other communist countries. On 28 June 1956, one day after the publication of Dennis's article in *Pravda*, a strike which developed into a rising took place in Poznań. At first it was presented by the press as the work of 'imperialist agents'. The Poles and Yugoslavs, however, quickly changed their approach and focused attention on the bad social conditions of the workers, admitting that their demands were justified. The Soviet Union and the other communist countries, on the other hand, kept to the theory of foreign provocation. It is probable that the Soviet leaders were more worried by the fact that the Polish and Yugoslav communist parties had sided with the Poznań strikers than about the rising itself and that this led to a quick change in the Party line.

On 30 June 1956, the Central Committee of the CPSU adopted a resolution on 'The cult of personality and its consequences' which was published by the Soviet press on 2 July. This resolution, too, criticized Stalin, for it condemned his theory of the intensification of the class struggle; it also mentioned Lenin's criticism of Stalin and described the great purges as 'mass repression'. The important tasks of the Party were said to be to overcome the personality cult, to observe the Party statutes and to restore the reign of law.

The resolution, however, contained unmistakable signs of a reversal of de-Stalinization. The followers of Trotsky, Bukharin, Rykov, and Tomsky were described as enemies of Leninism and it was said that the realization of their ideas would have led to the restoration of capitalism in the USSR. This indicated that the revision of the history of the Party was to be kept within narrow limits. The new tendency became even clearer in the condemnation of Togliatti's interview and the sharp rejection of the view that Stalin's autocracy had resulted from social changes in the USSR. The post-Stalin leaders were obviously trying to prevent the discussions of the personality cult from spreading to the fundamental principles of Stalin's system. The resolution repeatedly stressed that the effects of hero-worshipping Stalin had already been removed. It was also stated emphatically—this was clearly added shortly before the resolution was printed—that the Poznań rising was reactionary and had been financed from abroad. Lastly, the theory of different roads to socialism was considerably watered down and it was insisted that ideological solidarity between the communist parties was essential.

A *Pravda* article of 6 July had already suggested that Stalin's terrorism had been necessary. The Party had been forced 'to conduct a merciless struggle against the enemies of Leninism'. The statement that the foundations of democracy had been undermined was a 'hostile accusation'. One could merely say that in the last period of Stalin's life the cult of his personality had to some extent weakened the Party's action. The article also dealt with one-party rule in the USSR. The mere formulation of the unusual question of 'Why is there only one party in the Soviet Union?' shows that this problem was being discussed at the time and that a plural party system had perhaps been envisaged—at least for local government. This was now rejected. The Soviet Union was on the road to communism and the Communist Party was the only voice of socialist hope.

The *Pravda* article, 'The unshakeable unity of the countries of the socialist system', of 24 July, went further still. Not 'reformist back-yards', but 'Marxism-Leninism' was the criterion. The development towards socialism was a homogeneous historical process which had nothing to do with the fantasies of certain theorists who wished to achieve socialism in their own special way. 'Homogeneous unity' was as necessary as 'stern opposition to all manifestations of revisionism'. After this it was no longer surprising that at the end of July, in an article by Bugayev, 'When the scientific point of view is lost', it was declared that the Twentieth Party Congress had called for an 'intensification of the struggle against bourgeois ideology'. Soviet historians—particularly Burdzhalov—who only some weeks before had tried, with the approval of the Party leadership, to bring the presentation of the history of the Bolshevik Party nearer to the truth, were now accused of a nihilist attitude.

The Party resolution of 30 June and the *Pravda* article of July 1956 brought to an end the period of post-haste de-Stalinization. Criticism was no longer directed against the forces which were unable to free themselves from the old forms, but against those going in the other direction.

WRITERS AND STUDENTS IN THE AUTUMN OF 1956

The general relaxation of the system, as we have seen, had made itself felt in literature. Criticism of Stalinism, frank discussions, the rehabilitation of such well-known writers as Isaak Babel, Boris Pilnyak, of the publicist Mikhail Koltsov, and the distinguished producer, Meyerhold, the announcements about facilitating the publication of books by foreign writers, the foundation of new literary periodicals—*Neva*, *Moskva*, *Nash Sovremennik*, and *Inostranaya Literatura* which published only translations of foreign writers—strengthened the conviction of Soviet authors that the time had come when at last they could touch forbidden problems and write about what had been on their minds for a long time and what their readers were waiting for.

Short stories, poems, and novels which had been written in the hopeful months after the Twentieth Party Congress had been published by now. Policy had changed in the meantime, but neither writers nor readers, least of all the students, were prepared to bury their hopes of far-reaching change so quickly.

David Burg, a Russian student, who emigrated to West Berlin in 1956, wrote about this period in the weekly, *Das Parlament*:[1] 'Many, very many, at that time were expecting

[1] 29 Oct. 1958.

fundamental changes in the life of the people, democratization, workers' self-government, spiritual freedom. Many people were convinced that fundamental reforms were about to come, and some even believed that these reforms had originated in the wishes of the communist leaders. In this way the meaning of changes was misunderstood for a long time.' Burg quotes the allegorical poem 'Dawn' by the young Russian poet, Robert Rozhdestvensky, which characterizes this mood:

'The town with its wide streets is asleep.
Everything in it—from the aerials to the locks,
to the advertising hoardings—
Everything is full of expectation: soon
Soon you will hear the birds sing,
The mists are dissolving and vanishing.
Darkness creeps into cellars, archways and empty pockets,
bends over, watches, looks on with faded eyes,
None of that can help it any longer.'

This poem ends with the words:

'Day is breaking,
Day is breaking,
I love this hour,
I love to be alive,'

In the poem 'Railway Station Winter' also quoted by Burg, which was published in *Octyabr*,[1] the poet Yevtushenko admits:

'What do I want.
I want to fight bravely
And in a way that always in everything for which I fight
One and only one truth shall burn,
which I shall never know.'

The short stories, and novels which appeared in the Soviet Union between July and December 1956 varied greatly, but they all had one thing in common: they touched on problems hitherto forbidden.

The first story of this kind was Daniel Granin's 'A Personal Opinion.'[2] Granin describes an engineer, the head of a research laboratory, Minayev, who is also the editor of a scientific

[1] *Novy Mir*, Aug. 1945.   [2] No. 10, 1956.

journal and who knows his way about in the new Soviet society. He refuses to publish an article by a young man called Olkhovsky, in which the latter criticizes a motor built by a famous academician. Olkhovsky continues to try in vain to get his article published. Minayev, the editor, rather likes the young man who reminds him of his own youth. But since then he has adapted himself to the power of authority. Earlier, Minayev now recalls, he found himself in a situation similar to Olkhovsky's and always hoped to rise so high one day and to be so powerful that he could defend a good cause. But now he recognizes that he will never have enough influence or courage, however high he rises in the Soviet technocracy. The bureaucratic system has broken him.

A month later there appeared Semyon Kirsanov's poem 'The Seven Days of the Week'[1] which was much discussed later. The hero of this poetic fantasy, which is recounted in the first person, invents a new heart to replace the steel hearts of the inhuman, unfeeling bureaucrats. The bureaucrats' answer at the end of the poem is: 'We do not need such hearts . . . we need useful hearts like iron locks, hearts which do what they are told.'

In the same period Vladimir Dudintsev's novel *Not by Bread Alone* was published in serial form.[2] This novel was later the focal point of controversy. It has been translated into most European languages. Dudintsev tells the story of the inventor, Lopatkin, who tries desperately to push through, against the power of the managers and bureaucrats, an invention necessary to Soviet development. The first part of the novel takes place in a small industrial town in Siberia, whose public life is controlled by Drozdov, the head of the big industrial combine. The name of this man has since become a synonym in the Soviet Union for all narrow-minded, power-grasping bureaucrats. Drozdov, domineering, cold, self-satisfied, has nothing but contempt for Lopatkin. He is afraid of unpleasantness and extra work and therefore refuses to help the inventor. Lopatkin's miserable way of life is contrasted with that of the powerful, wealthy Drozdov: 'The guests arrived at the house of the director. The first to come was the head of the coal-mining concern, an imposing figure in a fur-lined leather coat with a

[1] *Novy Mir*, Sept. 1956.   [2] *Novy Mir*, Aug.–Oct. 1956.

new fur collar. Then came the Ganichevs, he and his made-up wife in a black lace dress, imported from Eastern Germany.' When his wife, Nadya, wants to invite her teacher colleague to a party, Drozdov refuses because 'She would only envy us.' But the hero of the novel, the engineer Lopatkin, lives in a poor house. He lives on bread, dry potatoes, and fish oil and even has to get his drawing paper under the counter. The second part describes Lopatkin's efforts to get his invention accepted in Moscow, his vain attempts to arouse the interest of some competent person among the many different central authorities. It seems impossible to break through the 'conspiracy' of the bureaucracy. Through complicated intrigues the officials even succeed in getting Lopatkin arrested by the state police. He is sentenced to eight years' hard labour and only rehabilitated in the end, almost by accident, and released from the camp. When the industrial combine gets into difficulties Lopatkin expresses his willingness to help his old enemy Drozdov. Drozdov's former wife, who from the start had taken a great interest in Lopatkin's fate, cuts herself off from her husband and his world and openly declares her support for Lopatkin. Lopatkin finally succeeds, but his bureaucratic opponents retain their positions, Drozdov even becoming a deputy minister.

In November 1956 there appeared the miscellany *Literatur-naya Moskva*.[1] The material had been collected before 1 October, but the printing was delayed, so that the book appeared only after the defeat of the Hungarian rising, at a time, that is, when the post-Stalin leaders were further than ever from encouraging new ideas.

The contributions in this miscellany go beyond anything that had been published in the Soviet Union before or after this period. The critic A. Kron openly expressed himself as in favour of freeing creative work from the distortions of Stalinism and the pressure of the Party: 'every cult by its very nature contradicts Marxism-Leninism . . . wherever a cult spreads scientific life has to give way to blind faith, creative work to dogma, and public opinion to arbitrary action. A cult creates a hierarchy of its own servants . . . it tolerates no criticism . . . by its nature it is directed against the people. A cult humiliates the people, making them believe that everything for which

[1] = *Literary Moscow.*

they pay a high price with the work of their hands and their blood is a present "from above". . . . It is a degradation of the individual. In reality the leader should be the servant of the people. But the fact that millions of pupils have had to jump up from their seats at the mere mention of their teachers' name, is a phenomenon which is alien to the democratic traditions in which we have been trained by the Revolution and the structure of its society. . . .'

Kron did not confine himself to an analysis of the consequences of Stalinism, but also made demands; 'Literature and art could not avoid the pressure. The creative work of the artist, however, is linked with social conditions, with the fight for new things. An inventor, in whatever period he is living, will always be in some way ahead of the ideas of his contemporaries . . . but a bent head cannot look forward.'

Nikolai Zhdanov's short story, *Journey Home*, was an interesting criticism of society contributed to this anthology. A high official returns to his native village after an absence of many years. Zhdanov shows the gulf between the life of the official and the surroundings from which he has risen. While former acquaintances tell him about the deprivations in his native village the official is thinking with shame of the environment in which he now lives. A peasant on a collective farm asks him for his opinion. She tells him how the authorities had demanded that crops should be delivered before the date fixed: 'Couldn't the state have waited for one week?' she asks. 'We should have made our delivery, once we had finished the other work! As it was, we delivered the produce, but our harvest was destroyed in the meantime. We fulfilled our delivery quota first and now we have no bread for ourselves. Was that fair?' The official unwillingly mumbles something about 'political questions' and that the demands of the state take precedence. The *kolkhoz* peasant agrees in resignation. She knows the phrases and finishes off his explanation for him. Soon afterwards the official returns to Moscow, to his own atmosphere. He is glad to be back, but he has nevertheless a slight feeling of guilt. On the way home the miserable village rises before his mind's eye and he hears again the peasant's 'Do you think they treated us fairly?' With this question the story ends.

Alexander Yashin's *The Lever* is set on a collective farm.

Four *kolkhoz* officials, all Party members, are sitting together. They complain about lack of understanding on the part of the Party authorities. 'At the top they don't wish to understand. They only say, "Carry out the Party line, convince the people, you are the lever of the Party!" . . . They think that the Party will lose its authority if they talk to the people like human beings. They know exactly that on the collective farm we get 100 grams per working unit, but they repeat their refrain: "Prosperity grows daily!" We have no more cows in the village, but they go on talking about strengthening the collective animal husbandry. All the leading officials can think about are figures. How people are to live does not interest them.'

The collective farm officials complain that everything comes 'from above. . . . The plans come from above, the chairmen come from above, productivity comes from above', they say bitterly. But suddenly they shrink in fear: They notice an old charwoman who has been sitting behind the stove all the time listening to their conversation! There is an embarrassed silence until one says to the others: 'What are we frightened of, friends? We are even frightened of ourselves.'

Soon afterwards the Party meeting starts in which these same four people take part. They are joined by a young woman teacher. But at the moment when the Party meeting begins they have changed. They no longer speak in simple, comprehensible words, but use the phrases of the Party press and official meetings: To mobilize, to practice self-criticism, to take measures, to execute the decisions demanded from above. From living beings they have turned into 'levers'. After the Party meeting, on the way home, they become human again and resume their former conversation.

In November 1956 *Octyabr* published a poem by Margarita Aliger, one of the editors of *Literaturnaya Moskva*; it was called 'The Most Important Thing' and expressed the human conflict which Stalinism had caused. It described Soviet man, who tempered steel, hewed rocks, built houses, dug canals, wrote countless books, fought the fascists, and created a socialist world. 'But suddenly a false note could be heard. He lied without reason, lost his self-confidence, betrayed his friends. The flicker of fear in his eyes showed that he would hide himself in stormy weather.'

In the autumn of 1956 not only Soviet writers but also the most varied circles of the population, particularly students, increasingly demanded reforms. Young Russians who had grown up in the age of Stalin learnt after the Twentieth Party Congress from the documents and memoirs which were published, including even John Reed's famous book *Ten Days that Shook the World*, that in reality things had happened very differently from what they had learnt at school. Prisoners returned from the camps, Old Bolsheviks arrested and murdered in the days of Stalin were rehabilitated. Much that young people had learnt to regard as 'historic truth' during Stalin's lifetime, was now questioned. Much that had hitherto been discussed in whispers in small circles was now said openly at the universities.

William C. Just, an Englishman who speaks fluent Russian and who spent a considerable time in Moscow in the autumn of 1956, had long discussions there with Soviet students. In a series of articles in the *Observer*[1] he reported that to his question: 'How would you like to see your country in the future?' which he put to many Moscow students, the desire for reforms was expressed time and again: 'We think we should have a real workers' democracy,' said one student, 'all workers should be free to form their own political organization, for example the peasants. They are workers and they have their own special interests. They should be allowed to have their own party to look after those interests.' Another suggested that the electoral system introduced in the Stalin period,[2] under which only one candidate may be proposed in each constituency, should be changed. 'We need more than one candidate for every constituency. We want to be able to choose. All different groups of workers should be able to put up their own candidates.' The principle of collective leadership should not be confined to the Central Committee; the Supreme Soviet should meet regularly and the leading Party and government officials should 'not live in a special quarter outside the city in luxury villas heavily guarded; they should live among the people and be in constant touch with them'. Others wanted to have a system of voluntary co-operatives in place of the collective farms. 'If I were asked what I want, I would first advocate the abolition of the

[1] Oct.–Nov. 1956.   [2] Still in force today.

collective farm system. We want conditions as in Yugoslavia.
. . . In Yugoslavia there are no collective farms. . . . Each works
his own plot or there are free co-operatives of a number of
households, voluntary in fact and not just on paper.'

All the Moscow students to whom William C. Just spoke in
the autumn of 1956 wanted these changes to be realized
through reforms: 'We don't want a new upheaval, more
catastrophe, more bloodshed. We have had enough. What we
hope and pray for is slow but continuing change, a gradual
evolution and reform towards a free and better life.'

EASTERN EUROPE IN FERMENT

In the autumn of 1956 the Soviet leaders were less worried
about the thaw among the Soviet intellectuals than about the
growing unrest in the other communist countries. Policy had
changed already at the beginning of July 1956, but the movement in the other countries had assumed such proportions
that some Party leaders no longer followed the directives from
Moscow. The contrast between the Russian and Polish parties
became clear in their attitudes to the Poznań rising. On 20
July the Polish Party leader, Edvard Ochab, said that it was
wrong to concentrate attention on the machinations of foreign
agents and that it was desirable to discover the social causes of
the revolt which had been a danger signal. Democratization
must be carried further.

The next day Marshal Bulganin, who was visiting Poland at
the time on behalf of the Soviet Party leaders, said that the
events in Poznań had been 'provoked by enemy agents'; he
spoke of 'mad plans of international reactionary elements'.
It was inadmissible under the banner of 'a very doubtful extension of democracy to endanger the unity of the socialist
camp'. In Poland 'fickle circles among our own ranks had
played themselves into the foreground'.

The Soviet press demanded severe punishments for the
Poznań strikers. But on 22 September it was announced from
Warsaw that 169 of the participants in the rising had already
been released without trial. The majority of the remaining
accused were acquitted at the trial, which was fairly conducted;
the sentences were unusually mild. There was no mention of
imperialist agents or class enemies. There were no confessions

or self-accusations. Foreign observers were allowed to attend the trial.

Whereas democratization in Poland was supported, or at least not hindered, by some of the Communist leaders, the movement for democratization in Hungary met with strong resistance from the leadership. Although the hated Rákosi was dismissed in the middle of June, he was not replaced by Imre Nagy, the leader of the reformists, but by Ernö Gërö, who essentially continued Rákosi's policy. The hub of the reform movement was the Petöfi Circle. The writers, Gyula Hay and Tibor Déry and many others, came out increasingly strongly for further reforms. Losonczy, a former member of the Central Committee who had been arrested in 1951 and only rehabilitated in the summer of 1955, on 2 September demanded the punishment of those who had been responsible for Stalinist practices: 'They are still in leading positions. . . . In particular, there are those who crowned their mistakes by refusing to make a fundamental change in their attitude after the Twentieth Party Congress.' On 8 September Gyula Hay in *Irodalmi Ujsag* demanded the liberation of literature. 'Let us say it calmly: Yes, we mean complete, unrestricted freedom. Writers must have unrestricted freedom to speak the truth, to criticize everything and everybody, to be sad or in love, to think of death . . . to believe in Almighty God or to deny God, to doubt the accuracy of some plan figures, to follow the paths of non-Marxist ideas. . . . They must be permitted to dislike certain statesmen or to say that the standard of living is too low, even that of people whose wages the competent authorities do not think of increasing.'

In the other countries of the Eastern bloc, too, the movement spread, and the Party chiefs found it difficult to keep it within bounds. In Rumania the labour laws were considerably relaxed late in the summer, but the government proved strong enough to exclude from the Party authors and economists who were keen supporters of reform. In Bulgaria Kostov and his co-accused were officially rehabilitated. Kostov's widow was granted a pension and his son sent to Russia to be educated.

The Czechoslovak Party leaders also announced relaxations in the labour laws, reductions of work norms, and greater autonomy for the Slovaks; but they left no doubt that bigger political reforms were not intended. This policy—social and political concessions to the workers but increased control over the intellectuals—was later described in Moscow as the 'Czechoslovak solution'; it became the leitmotif of Soviet domestic policy.

In the second half of August the Russian leaders considered themselves already strong enough to prevent a 'Titoist development' in Eastern Europe. On 23 August the Soviet leaders sent out a secret circular warning the Party leaders in Eastern Europe against following the Titoist example. The Yugoslav communists, it was said, could not be regarded as real communists; they were, in fact, left-wing social democrats. Care and restraint towards Belgrade were recommended.

But for Poland and Hungary it was far too late. Only three weeks later, on 19 September, Khrushchev thought it necessary to visit Tito in person. Officially this visit was described as a holiday, but in fact Khrushchev tried to gain Tito as an ally in the controversy inside the Russian Party. In Moscow it had meanwhile been recognized that Khrushchev's 'secret speech' and the reforms after the Twentieth Party Congress had created the danger that the Kremlin might lose control over the countries of Eastern Europe. The Stalinist faction, led by Molotov and Kaganovich, was regaining influence and Khrushchev's position was in danger. The rumour even went round Moscow that Khrushchev was being obliged to justify himself before the other Party leaders for his attack upon Stalin. Khrushchev needed the authority of the Yugoslav Party leaders, while the Yugoslav communists hoped that a strengthening of the Khrushchev faction would speed up the de-Stalinization of the whole communist world.

Khrushchev remained in Belgrade until 27 September. After that Tito, the Yugoslav Deputy Prime Minister, Ranković, and the President of the National Assembly of Bosnia, Pucar, went to Yalta where they were welcomed not only by Bulganin and Voroshilov, but also by Khrushchev's followers, Kirichenko, Brezhnev, Madame Furtseva, the head of the state security service, General Serov, Marshal Grechko, Admiral Gorshkov, and the Soviet ambassador in Belgrade, Firyunin. According to an official announcement, hosts and guests wanted to have a few days' holiday on the Black Sea. But in his speech in Pula in

THE YEAR OF HOPE AND CONFUSION 221

November 1956, Tito said that Soviet relations with Poland, Hungary, and other East European countries were discussed. The Soviet leaders had held mistaken views, he said, but this had not been the attitude of all of them! 'We saw that this attitude had been imposed by those people who took up and today still take up a fairly strong Stalinist stand, but that there are still possibilities that those elements will be victorious in an internal evolution of the leadership of the Soviet Union which support a stronger and faster development in the direction of democratization, the abandonment of all Stalinist methods and the establishment of new relations among socialist states.'

The Soviet leaders had staged an 'accidental' meeting in Yalta with Gërö who, according to Tito, 'appeared in sackcloth and ashes' before the Yugoslavs and promised to undo the mistakes of the past. It was agreed that a Hungarian delegation headed by Gërö should visit Yugoslavia. Khrushchev and his friends hoped that the Hungarian Party leaders, covered by the authority of the Yugoslav communists, might gain the confidence of the Magyar people.

After Tito's return from Yalta on 5 October, Yugoslavia's key position had become clear. A great number of communist delegations visited Belgrade to seek advice and moral support. Shortly before his journey to Yalta, Tito had received Polish and Czechoslovak parliamentary delegations, as well as a delegation from the Polish Central Committee. On the day of his return an Italian communist delegation, led by Togliatti's deputy, Longo, was waiting for him, as well as a Bulgarian delegation led by the First Party Secretary, Todor Zhivkov. The new Polish trade union chairman was also in Belgrade and on 15 October a Hungarian delegation arrived led by Gërö and the Prime Minister, Hegedüs. On 20 October a Rumanian delegation arrived, led by Gheorghiu-Dej and the Prime Minister, Stoica.

While Belgrade was becoming the meeting place of the Communist Party leaders from many countries, astonishing reports came in from Poland and Hungary. In Hungary a funeral ceremony was held in honour of Rajk, Palffy, Szönyi, and Szalai, who had all been unjustly executed in 1949. *Szabad Nep*[1] wrote of them as martyrs; they had not been the victims of a

[1] Chief organ of the Hungarian Communist Party.

counter-revolution; the tragedy lay in the fact that they had been sentenced to death in the name of the people and of socialism. Their trials had caused painful wounds which had not yet healed. The article appeared under the title: 'Never again!'

In Poland, Gomulka's old opponent, Hilary Minc, the economic dictator who had the rank of a member of the Politburo and Deputy Prime Minister, was relieved of his post on 9 October. In the middle of October it was announced that Gomulka was to be readmitted to the Central Committee at the opening of the eighth full session of the Central Committee on 20 October. It was also announced that Marshal Konstantin Rokossovsky, the Minister of Defence who had been appointed by Moscow, was not to be re-elected to the Polish Politburo.

'OCTOBER IN POLAND' AND THE HUNGARIAN REVOLT THROUGH SOVIET EYES

While de-Stalinization was moving towards its revolutionary climax in Poland and Hungary, in Russia Stalin's good points were more and more emphasized. The editor of *Kommunist*[1] announced that he had received a large number of letters asking 'whether Stalin's writings could be used in the study of Marxist-Leninist theory and the history of the CPSU, and if so which?' Others asked whether Stalin's works should not be renounced altogether. This, he wrote, was of course, quite wrong. Stalin had been a great Marxist theorist; his writings before 1934, particularly *The Foundations of Leninism* (1924), *Problems of Leninism* (1926), *On Industrialization and the Rightist Deviation in the CPSU* (1928) must, without question, be studied as training for the Party.

The Stalinist faction in the Russian Party leadership had by now unmistakably gained ground. Kaganovich, who had been relieved of his post at the beginning of June, rejoined the government on 22 September as Minister of the Building Materials Industry. Two months later, on 22 November, the even more significant appointment of Molotov as Minister of State Control was announced. The People's Commissariat[2] for State Control, which had been established in 1940, was a Ministry with far-reaching powers. Among other things it controlled government expenditure in all branches of the economy

[1] No. 14, Sept. 1956. [2] Renamed Ministry in 1946.

and supervised the execution of all government decisions; it had the right to inflict disciplinary punishment, though only with the consent of the Council of Ministers, on all those who did not carry out official decisions, or wasted material and financial resources. The appointment of Molotov as Minister of State Control suggested that state control was to be increased and that within the ruling class there had been a change in the balance of power, by which the state had been strengthened at the expense of the Party machine controlled by Khrushchev.

When it became known in Moscow that in Poland the reformist communists under Gomulka were going to take control and that the Stalinists were to be excluded from the leadership, the Russian leaders decided to step in. On 19 October, one day before the opening of the full session of the Central Committee in Poland, a delegation of Soviet Party chiefs which included Molotov and Kaganovich as well as Khrushchev and Mikoyan, arrived in Warsaw. But the intervention misfired. Gomulka threatened to appeal to the population of Warsaw for help. The Soviet delegation returned to Moscow without having achieved anything. On 21 October *Pravda* published a short announcement that the talks had been conducted in an atmosphere of frankness befitting to Party members and friends, a formula which had never been used before. On 20 October *Pravda*, under the heading 'Anti-socialist attacks in the columns of the Polish press' had accused the Polish newspapers of poisoning 'the thoughts of readers, through an imported ideology, alien to the workers'. The revisionists who had lost all decent reticence and who were misusing the Polish press for their 'filthy purposes' must be called to order.

But neither the interventions of the Russian leaders nor the threatening *Pravda* article were able to prevent 'October in Poland'. The reform movement was actively supported by both workers and intellectuals. Gomulka was appointed leader of the Party, Rokossovsky lost his place in the Politburo, and the Polish Stalinists were defeated. For the first time since the breach between the Yugoslav communists and Moscow the reform movement of a party had been victorious over the Stalinists.

The Russian rulers now tried to prevent Polish ideas from spreading in the Eastern bloc, and in particular to the Soviet

Union. Whereas the whole world press was full of news about events in Poland, the Russian press was silent. It mentioned only those things which were in accordance with the policy of Moscow, so that the Russian public was unable to grasp the importance of the Polish plenary session in October.

The Hungarian revolt presented the Soviet leaders with even greater difficulties. The Kremlin had to prevent or at least to hold within bounds any repercussions elsewhere in the communist world, and to take care that neither the character of the Hungarian revolt nor its extent should become known to the Soviet population. Events in Hungary were, therefore, completely misrepresented by the Russian press.

Until 25 October no Soviet newspaper mentioned what was happening in Hungary. The Russian public, therefore, did not know that already on 21 October the students of Budapest had demanded the freedom of the press, the abolition of the death penalty, and the restoration of self-government to the universities, and that on 22 October rallies of sympathy for Poland had taken place all over Hungary. Nor did the Soviet press mention the demonstrations which took place in Budapest on 23 October or the demands of the demonstrators for national independence, for the freedom of the press, the withdrawal of Russian troops, the trial of Rákosi, and the reinstatement of Imre Nagy. Neither the press nor the radio told the Soviet population that the rising had begun on the evening of 23 October, that the Hungarian Party Secretary, Gërö, had called upon Russian troops for help and declared martial law, that the Prime Minister, Hegedüs, had resigned and that Imre Nagy had become Prime Minister. The Soviet press was silent over events in Hungary in the hope that the revolt would be suppressed before the Russian public heard about it.

But on 24 October the rising spread, the workers began to strike, and street fighting took place in the Hungarian towns. All attempts by the government to persuade the rebels to lay down their arms failed, and the ultimata of the government had repeatedly to be extended. It was no longer possible to pass events over in silence. On 25 October, *Pravda* on its fourth page announced under the heading 'Collapse of an adventure directed against the people in Budapest' that 'insolent fascist gangsters' had tried to bring about a counter-revolutionary rising. 'The Central Committee of the Hungarian Workers' Party and the Government are receiving telegrams from all parts of the country in which the Hungarian workers express their angry disgust at the criminal actions of the counter-revolutionaries,' *Pravda* said.

While the peasants in Hungary were dissolving the collective farms, while the factories were being taken over by workers' councils, and the Hungarian army joined the rebels, *Pravda* still wrote about *coups de main* by counter-revolutionary insurgents.

Not till 28 October did the paper publish its first commentary. In a three-column article, entitled 'The collapse of the adventure against the people in Budapest', *Pravda* stated that the most recent events in Hungary had been the result of well-prepared subversive activities by the imperialist powers. The counter-revolutionary underground movement had been supplied with arms from abroad. But, on the other hand, serious economic mistakes had been made; the Party had been mismanaged, and socialist legality violated. Enemies had made use of these mistakes for their own purposes. But now a new government had been formed and the Hungarian workers were ready to protect the people's power against enemy attacks.

When this article appeared in *Pravda* the revolution in Hungary was approaching its climax. On 28 October at 6 p.m. the Russian soldiers declared that they were willing to shoot only if they were attacked. The Central Committee of the Hungarian Communist Party appointed a new Party Praesidium of six people including Nagy and Kádár. On 29 October this body reversed Hungarian policy. It vehemently denied *Pravda's* statements that the rebels were 'counter-revolutionaries' or 'agents', and spoke of the 'heroic fight of young Hungarians for democracy'. At midday on 30 October the new government announced that single Party rule had been abolished in Hungary. It approved the re-establishment of all the Parties which had existed in 1945. The national liberation committees, revolutionary councils, and workers' councils were recognized. From members of the re-established Parties a new Cabinet was formed to prepare free elections and a coalition government. Apart from the Communists, Nagy, Kádár, and Losonczy, the Cabinet consisted of two members of the Small Farmers' Party and one member each from the Peasants' Party and the Social Democrats. In the afternoon Imre Nagy announced that the government was negotiating the withdrawal of Russian troops and that they were already being moved. In the evening the Minister of Defence asked the Soviet army to move out of Budapest by the morning of 31 October. On 1 November all the Russian soldiers had left Budapest.

Pravda was silent about all these events. On 29, 30, and 31 October it confined itself to short reports on the last page, which now, however, appeared under the heading: 'The situation in Hungary.' The reports emphasized that the situation was becoming normal; on 31 October it was said that the situation had become 'more difficult'.

Until 31 October the Soviet leaders apparently hoped to come to an agreement with the government of Imre Nagy. This assumption is supported by the hastily prepared declaration on the relations between the Soviet Union and the East European countries which was published on 31 October. The Soviet government announced a number of concessions. It promised that relations between the communist countries should be based on national equality, and state sovereignty. It was openly admitted that there had been 'many difficulties' and 'outright mistakes' in the relations between Russia and her—hitherto—satellites. The declaration supported the Warsaw Pact, but stated that the question of Soviet troops in the other communist countries could be discussed.

Over events in Hungary the Soviet government declared that 'the justified and progressive movement of the workers' had been joined by reactionary and counter-revolutionary forces which were trying to exploit dissatisfaction, to undermine the popular democratic order, and to restore the capitalist system. At the request of the Hungarian government the Soviet government had sent Russian military units to Budapest to restore order. As their remaining in Hungary might strain the situation further the Soviet government had instructed its military command to withdraw its troops from Budapest 'as soon as the Hungarian government considered it necessary'. At the same time the Soviet government expressed its readiness to negotiate with the Hungarian government and other members of the Warsaw Pact about the stationing of Soviet troops on Hungarian territory.

In retrospect this declaration appears as a major concession by Moscow. But the Hungarian revolt could no longer be confined within the limits desired by the Russians. On 31 October leading Hungarian Stalinists, including Hegedüs and Gërö, fled from Hungary. In spite of assurances to the contrary, fresh Russian troops marched into Hungary on and after 29 October. On 1 November Nagy protested against this to the Soviet ambassador, proclaimed the neutrality of Hungary and asked for its guarantee by the four Great Powers. At the same time he asked the United Nations to put the Hungarian question on the agenda of the next General Assembly. In spite of this, Russian soldiers continued to move into Hungary.

A change was clearly noticeable in the Soviet press. Whereas before events had been played down, *Pravda* on 3 November spoke of the 'licentiousness of the counter-revolutionary gangs' as well as of the murder of Party and government officials in Hungary.

The Soviet representatives there continued to declare their readiness to withdraw the Russian army from Hungary. But the Russians occupied all strategic points and formed a circle around Budapest. On 3 November Soviet troops closed the Austrian frontier. The new troop concentrations were explained as security measures to cover withdrawal.

On 4 November, under the heading 'Barricade the path of reaction in Hungary', *Pravda* published the strongest commentary up to that point. The Hungarian rising had been staged by counter-revolutionary forces directed by Horthy elements in West Germany and Austria. Workers were being murdered and books were being burnt. The reactionary terror had assumed unheard-of dimensions. Imre Nagy had shown himself to be the 'accomplice of reactionary forces'. The government had, in fact, collapsed and handed over to elements hostile to the people. There was said to be chaos in Hungary. Events in Hungary showed the need for greater revolutionary vigilance. Hungary was facing the question whether it should continue on the road of socialist development or whether reaction was going to gain the upper hand. There could, however, be no doubt that forces would be found in Hungary to destroy the counter-revolution. By the time this commentary appeared the Hungarian negotiators at Soviet headquarters had already been arrested and the Russian army had started a big offensive.

POLICY HARDENS

The Russian intervention gave a shock comparable with that provided by the Twentieth Party Congress to the Western European Communist Parties. There were mass resignations from the French and Italian parties; even officials of long standing left in protest. In the smaller Communist Parties too—the British, Swiss, Dutch, and Danish—the leaders had to contend with serious difficulties. In a number of countries dissident groups were formed which produced their own publications and built up their own organization. There were also serious conflicts in the communist world. In the SED Wolfgang Harich drew up a political programme in which he favoured a reformist line: soon afterwards he and a number of his closest collaborators were arrested.

Moscow continued to repeat the claim of counter-revolution in Hungary and committed all the Communist Parties to it. The most important Soviet pronouncement on this subject was Suslov's speech on 6 November 1956 at the ceremony in honour of the thirty-ninth anniversary of the October Revolution. He repeated all the Soviet lies about the Hungarian revolt, without even trying to justify them or to explain how it could have been possible for a few enemy agents to start a general revolt in the whole of the country. He stressed the need for the unity of the communist world movement and postulated four common principles of Soviet development.

Among other things, Suslov demanded 'the establishment of the political power of the working class with its most progressive members to lead it'; by this he meant the rule of the Communist Party in the form in which it had been realized in the Soviet Union. He also demanded 'the determined defence of the achievements of the socialist revolution against the attacks of the former exploiting class', a formulation which covered an internal reign of terror as well as armed intervention abroad in a case like Hungary. Although Suslov qualified his formulation so as to admit national differences of tempo and of method, it was clear that his principles were intended to bring all Communist Parties back to the Soviet fold.

Soon afterwards attempts could be discerned to resuscitate the Cominform. On 28 November *Neues Deutschland* stated that reactionary attacks 'made it desirable to find new forms of consultation'. The unity of the communist world movement should be promoted and all Communist Parties required a clear answer to this problem. On the same day the Austrian Communist Party organ, *Die Volksstimme*, also expressed itself in favour of 'the creation of an international organ of the Communist Parties' and announced that the Austrian Party had 'taken steps in this direction, but in a number of Communist Parties differences of opinion still exist on this question'. The Moscow periodical, *Mezhdunarodnaya Zhizn*[1] also demanded that new forms of relations between the Communist Parties of different countries should be firmly established and that experiences should constantly be exchanged. The communist world movement was a homogeneous, ideological movement; its strength lay in sharing the same ideology and in the 'unity of its strategic aims'. Roads to socialism should not lead apart but should 'take the same direction'.

The defeat of the Hungarian revolt, the official version of counter-revolution and foreign agents, the retreat from the principles of the Twentieth Party Congress, and the new bringing into line of the communist movement under the leadership of Moscow led to a fresh conflict with the Yugoslav communists about whom the Soviet leaders has made such efforts since 1955. At conferences of functionaries from the communist world, Moscow had already held Yugoslavia responsible for the Hungarian revolt. On 8 November *Pravda* published an article by Enver Hoxha, which opened the new anti-Yugoslav campaign.

On 11 November Tito, in his speech in Pula, commented on the change in Russian policy. He said that thanks to Stalin the Soviet Union had reached a dead-end in domestic as well as foreign affairs. The leaders since Stalin had recognized the main causes of these difficulties and had condemned Stalin and his policy at the Twentieth Party Congress, but had mistakenly interpreted the whole affair as a question of the cult of personality and not as a matter of the system. Bureaucratic methods and the disregard of the aspirations of the workers were

[1] No. 11, 1956.

the real problems, Tito said. It must also be recognized that a number of Communist Parties in Western Europe as well as in the communist countries 'opposed democratization and the decisions of the Twentieth Party Congress'. After the events in Poznań in the summer of 1956 the attitude of the Soviet leaders towards Yugoslavia had already become cooler. Tito welcomed the eighth full session and 'October in Poland', but strongly condemned Russian policy in Hungary. The Hungarian rising had become a rising of the whole people; it had been directed against Rákosi's methods and only during its course had other forces become effective. The Soviet leaders were responsible for this because they had supported Rákosi for so long and had prevented other forces 'in whom the workers and the whole people had confidence' from taking over the leadership. The question now arose 'whether the new spirit which originated in Yugoslavia and of which there are quite a number of signs in the decisions of the Twentieth Party Congress, will triumph in the Communist Parties . . . or whether the Stalinist line will be victorious again'.

On 19 November *Pravda* sharply rejected Tito's views. His speech, it was said, contained declarations which contradicted the 'principles of proletarian internationalism' (in other words, subjugation to the Soviet Union). In particular *Pravda* attacked Tito's statement that it was important which policy would win and his view that the personality cult had been the product of a particular system. This was the beginning of a bitter campaign against the Yugoslav communists and all reformist efforts in Eastern Europe as well as in the communist movement in general. De-Stalinization had come to an end.

THE RE-ASSESSMENT OF STALIN

It has been seen that 'October in Poland' and the Hungarian revolt had found an echo in the Soviet Union as well. Even the Soviet press admitted—and it was again and again confirmed by foreign visitors—that strong feelings of opposition existed among the educated classes in Russia. At many polytechnics and universities, including the Lomonossov University in Moscow, there were open protests against lecturers who took the official Party line, as for example during lectures in which it was attempted to justify the suppression of the

Hungarian revolt. On 3 December 1956 many students were expelled from Moscow University, but the protests did not stop.

At Leningrad University an illegal mimeographed journal appeared at the beginning of December, entitled *The Blue Flower*, in which problems of modern Marxism and questions of creative socialist work were discussed in a new, independent manner. This was not the only illegal publication. It emerges from the Soviet press, particularly *Komsomolskaya Pravda*, that mimeographed journals were also being distributed at other universities, including *Figleaf* at Vilna University, *Culture* at the Leningrad Technological Institute, and *Fresh Voices* at the Transport Institute of Leningrad. Particularly interesting were the titles *The Bell* (a reference to Alexander Herzen's revolutionary paper), a journal which circulated in a number of institutes in Moscow, and *Heresy*, a mimeographed sheet which was distributed in the Institute for the training of librarians in Leningrad. There were even leaflets demanding reform, and in Moscow rumour had it that these were inspired by an illegal student organization which called itself 'The Real Communist Party'. There were signs in the Soviet press that reformist tendencies were at work even within the Party organizations.

As early as 9 November Khrushchev felt compelled to speak openly about 'errors' among certain students. At the beginning of December the campaign began against the enthusiastically critical writers. It began with a *Pravda* report of a Party meeting of Ukrainian writers in Kiev at which 'harmful, anti-Party' views were expressed. Such reports were now frequently to be found in the Soviet press. In the second half of December a series of plenary meetings of the Party in the most important Russian centres took place which dealt exclusively with the political education of young people. The Moscow Party conference which set the tone was addressed by Yekaterina Furtseva and the Minister of Higher Education, Yelyutin.

At the same time Stalin was rehabilitated step by step. On 23 December 1956 *Pravda* denied that there had ever been any Stalinism in the Soviet Union. Stalin had been an important Marxist and had been guided in his doctrines by Marxism. Stalin's mistakes had been criticized by the Russian Communist

Party and the battle against the effects of the personality cult would be continued, but this had nothing to do with a fight against Stalinism which was nothing but 'an imperialist offensive against the achievements of the Soviet Union'.

At the New Year reception in the Kremlin on 31 December 1956, only ten months after his notorious speech, Khrushchev went one step further: 'If it is a question of fighting against imperialism we can state with conviction that we are all Stalinists in fact. We can be proud that we have taken part in the fight for the advance of our great cause against our enemies. From that point of view I am proud that we are Stalinists.'

This first pro-Stalin statement by Khrushchev was not published in the Soviet press. Its tendency was confirmed by a second statement that he made at a reception at the Chinese Embassy in Moscow on 17 January 1957. According to an account in *Pravda* on 19 January Khrushchev then said 'that in our opinion Stalinism, like Stalin himself, is inseparable from communism. Where it was a question of the revolution, of the defence of the class interests of the proletariat in the fight against the enemies of our class, Stalin defended the cause of Marxism-Leninism bravely and unyieldingly'. Stalin had, of course, made mistakes, but he had been convinced that they were necessary for the defence of the Revolution. In fundamental matters, such as the cause of Socialism, 'God grant, as the saying goes,' exclaimed Khrushchev piously, 'that every communist may fight as Stalin fought.' *Pravda* recorded 'tempestuous applause' after these words. Senior Chinese and Russian officials attended the reception. Was the tempestuous applause a sign of relief that no dangerous ideological experiments need now be feared from Khrushchev? Or were his words an indication to those present that the differences among the leaders which existed at that time had been overcome and that Khrushchev had adhered to the views of those then in the majority?

Historians and philosophers were now taken to task because of their critical publications in the spring and summer of 1956. *Pravda* accused Soviet philosophers of—among other things—not having conducted the fight against Western ideas with sufficient vigour and not having taken enough part in the fight against 'revisionism and national communism'; the fact that,

'under the pretence of the fight against the cult of personality'
the Party leadership had been attacked in art and literature
was particularly condemned.

Of striking importance was the change in the official Party
line as to whether with the development of socialism the class
struggle was intensified or not. The principle of the intensification of the class struggle had been proclaimed by Stalin during
the Great Purge of March 1937 as an ideological justification
of his reign of terror. The rejection of this thesis had been one
of the most important events of the Twentieth Party Congress.
In December 1956 *Partinaya Zhizn*[1] said that the fact that there
was no longer class antagonism in Russia did not mean 'that
there were no more manifestations of the class struggle in
Soviet society'. In the Soviet Union the hostile influence of
capitalist countries was still noticeable. 'Against the enemies of
the socialist system our fight must now as ever be firm and
merciless'; the Communist Party and the Russian state must
not 'allow any leniency towards bourgeois ideology and its
influence on individuals'.

These examples can be increased at will. They prove that
the drive against Stalin was systematically stopped by the
Soviet leaders from July 1956 onwards and even to some extent
reversed. But this happened only in the political sphere. Social
and economic policy was unaffected. At the beginning of
September the lowest rates of wages were raised by an average
of 33 per cent. At the same time minimum wages of 300
roubles in towns and 270 roubles in the country were fixed, and
the tax-free limit was raised from 260 to 370 roubles. At the
beginning of November the trade unions were called on to
prevent all infringements of the labour laws and vigorously to
defend the material interests of the workers. In the same month
a new wage system was introduced in coal-mining which gave
underground workers a considerable rise in wages; in December
an improvement in the law protecting young workers followed.

THE PLENARY SESSION OF DECEMBER 1956

Economic and social changes on the one hand, a retreat from
the principles of the Twentieth Party Congress, tighter control
over the intellectuals, and the checking of all attempts at

[1] No. 20, 1956.

political reform on the other, were from the autumn of 1956 onwards the policy of the Soviet leaders. It is extremely probable that this represented a compromise between two political opinions held by the ruling classes.

The plenary session of the Central Committee from 20 to 24 December 1956 reflected both the policy of the period and the new balance of power. If official statements are to be believed, neither the Hungarian revolt nor events in Poland were discussed, no political question in fact. Saburov, Chairman of Gosekonomkomissiya, and Nikolai Baibakov, Chairman of Gosplan, reported on the sixth Five-Year Plan; then Prime Minister Bulganin spoke on his favourite topic, 'Better economic direction'.

The priority of heavy industry continued to be emphasized, but the practical measures taken indicated a relaxation of this principle. The full session of the Central Committee decided, for example, to postpone a number of building projects in heavy industry, to pay greater attention to the consumer goods industry and to grant additional funds for housing. The decentralization of the economy was to be continued, the Union Republics were to be given new economic responsibilities and the rights of local authorities, enterprise directors, and managers, were to be extended. The trade unions were made responsible for labour legislation and housing. They were to organize discussions of production and regular workers' meetings.

The decisions of this session followed logically on those taken in July 1955. They aimed at a further modernization of the economy, but—and this is probably the most interesting point—under the direction of the functionaries of the state. The Party was mentioned only in passing in the December resolutions. Neither Khrushchev nor any other Party official, such as Kozlov, Kirichenko, Furtseva, Brezhnev, Belyayev or Ignatov, spoke at this session—or at any rate their speeches were not mentioned. All those who had risen to the top of the Party since the autumn of 1955, with Khrushchev's assistance, appeared to have been pushed into the background.

The advance of the civil servants also showed itself in the new appointments announced on 25 and 26 December. The plenary session decided to remove Khrushchev's protégé,

Shepilov, from the Secretariat of the Central Committee. Saburov, who had always supported a realistic economic policy and whose expert knowledge of economic questions was generally esteemed, was relieved of his post as head of Gosekonomkomissiya. He was replaced by Pervukhin, who was less popular in economic circles because of his authoritarian method of work and his ambition. In practical policy he was strongly in favour of centralized economic control, but in public he expressed himself repeatedly in favour of extending the rights of enterprise directors.

Even more important was the strengthening of the new Gosekonomkomissiya under Pervukhin. It was to consist of seven well-known economic leaders, Alexei Kosygin, Vyacheslav Malyshev, Mikhail Khrunichev, Vladimir Kucherenko, Vladimir Matskevich, and Ivan Benediktov: except for Benediktov, all of these were deputy premiers of Russia. The Gosekonomkomissiya under Pervukhin thus became a sort of second government. For the first time there was created a *leading economic body* which consisted of almost the same people as Bulganin had brought together when he became Premier in the spring of 1955.

THE PLENARY SESSION OF FEBRUARY 1957

Only six weeks later, on 13 February, the Central Committee met for another full session: economic reforms were again on the agenda.

Khrushchev made the main speech on further improvements in industry and building. His demands went far beyond all plans so far published for reorganizing the direction of the economy. He criticized not only centralization, but the whole system of ministries for running the economy. It was impossible, he said, for centralized specialist authorities in Moscow and the capitals of the Union Republics to direct 200,000 enterprises and 100,000 organizations scattered over the vast territory of the USSR. The existing form of administration had inhibited both the co-operation of enterprises in the same regions and the active participation in economic matters of the local Party organizations.

Khrushchev proposed to divide the USSR into a number— not yet specified—of regions, each under an economic authority which would control all its factories and farms. These new economic authorities would be called People's Economic Councils, *sovnarkhozy*, as they were in Lenin's time. They would be able to tackle all the problems in their region on their own responsibility; all the specialized ministries for industry and building would thus become superfluous. Pervukhin's State Commission for current planning was to be dissolved and the Ministry of State Control, headed by Molotov, was to be thoroughly reorganized, basing itself on the new *sovnarkhozy*.

Khrushchev's proposals were not immediately accepted. The Central Committee instructed the Party Praesidium and the Council of Ministers to prepare proposals on these lines and to submit them to the Supreme Soviet. The February full session also decided to re-appoint Shepilov, who had been dismissed in December 1956, to be Secretary of the Central Committee. Kozlov, who since February 1956 had been a member of the Central Committee Bureau for the RSFSR headed by Khrushchev, was made a candidate member of the Party Praesidium.

The Party leaders tried to present the February session as continuing and supplementing the December one. In fact, however, the plenary meeting in February once again changed both the Party line and the balance of power among the leaders. At the December meeting, the economic reforms were announced by Bulganin and Pervukhin, in February by the First Secretary of the Party, Khrushchev; in December Shepilov had been removed from the Central Committee Secretariat, in February he was restored. The December session decided to relax the centralized direction of the economy by transferring authority in the economic sphere to the economic ministries of the Union Republics and the enterprise directors: the February meeting announced the abolition of the economic ministries in favour of territorial economic authorities, that is, the complete reorganization of the economy. In December the Party had hardly been mentioned, in February it was always mentioned first. In short, in February Khrushchev succeeded in taking economic reform out of the hands of the economic leaders and putting it under the direction of the Party.

The political changes in the Soviet leadership which made this result possible took place in the six weeks between the meeting in December 1956 and that in February 1957. Did Khrushchev achieve his success by mobilizing the provincial apparatus of the Party and with the support of the army leadership? Did his group receive the support of the Chinese delegation which—apart from a short break—was in Moscow from 7 to 19 January? Were Khrushchev's two speeches of 31 December 1956 and 17 January 1957 in favour of Stalin the result of a compromise with the majority of the Party Praesidium, which had enabled him to strengthen the Party apparatus? Evidently all the more powerful authorities in the country were prepared to fortify the Party because it was the political clamp of the system needed to check the forces seeking independence and reforms, both in Russia and her East European satellites.

KHRUSHCHEV'S REFORM OF THE RUSSIAN ECONOMY

Evidently Khrushchev had strong hostility to overcome. The decisions of the February full session were published on 16 February, but Khrushchev's speech became public only on 30 March 1957 and then in a form which, for the Soviet Union, was very unusual. It was stressed that Khrushchev's assertions only indicated the general direction to be taken and did not provide answers to every concrete question. A 'general people's debate' was to be held on the subject. The whole Russian press was asked to provide 'a maximum of space' for the great discussion on these questions.

The debate began on the very next day. From 31 March to 4 May the second page of all Soviet papers was exclusively devoted to the reorganization of the control of the economy. Within this period, according to Khrushchev, more than 500,000 meetings took place at which over 40 million participants busied themselves exclusively with these questions, and more than 2 million people put forward suggestions. Almost 70,000 people commented in the press. *Pravda* and *Izvestia* alone received more than 8,000 letters, over 800 of which were published. Admittedly, no views opposed to the Party theses were expressed but there was a great variety of opinions as to how economic reform should be carried out. One thing was immediately to be observed: not a single member of the leadership—Molotov, Kaganovich, Bulganin,

Mikoyan, Voroshilov, Pervukhin, and Saburov—commented in the press. Their silence was a clear sign of resistance, or at the least that they were waiting to see how Khrushchev's project would develop. There were also elements in Russia which regarded Khrushchev's economic measures as the starting point for further reforms.

For example, demands were heard for workers' self-government in industry. The Soviet press considered it necessary several times to oppose such proposals. *Kommunist*[1] stated in a leading article that demands had been made to 'replace the principle of appointment of managers from above by election from below'. Other readers had suggested that the directors should be elected in the enterprise, justifying this by saying that it was in accordance with Lenin's ideas. 'Social self-government' in industry had also been demanded.

Views differed most as to whether all ministries should be dissolved or whether some should remain, and where and how many people's economic councils should be set up. In spite of all their Party training the attitude of the Soviet officials was not very different from that of politicians and industrialists in other social systems. Almost every Minister tried frantically to prove that his ministry was essential and must therefore continue to exist. The members of the State Planning Commission were in favour of putting the newly created *sovnarkhozy* under strict supervision of the Gosplan while the leading officials of the Union Republics demanded closer links between the *sovnarkhozy* and their governments. The Party secretaries of the non-Russian Union Republics desperately resisted any possible splitting up of their territories. But once a division had been decided on—as for example at the beginning of April 1957 in the Ukraine—there was no way of stopping it. Now every district and every region wanted its own *sovnarkhozy*.

The influence of these circles was so strong that Khrushchev increasingly gave way to their pressure. He needed the support of local Party officials to carry out the reorganization at all, and also—and that was his second political aim—to break up or at least paralyse the machinery of the central economic ministries. Initially twenty to twenty-five economic regions

[1] No. 3, March 1957.

had been envisaged, but at the beginning of May 1957 there was already mention of twenty-nine *sovnarkhozy*. Whereas on the one hand, to please the Party more *sovnarkhozy* were established than originally intended, on the other, Khrushchev had to make concessions to a number of ministries too. As a result not all the industrial ministries were dissolved as had originally been planned.

When the great economic reform was discussed in the Supreme Soviet at the beginning of May 1957, the programme of reorganization too had changed to a great extent. On 10 May the 'law on the further improvement of the organization of industry and construction' was passed, and the very next day it was published. The territorial principle in the control of the economy was officially introduced, and twenty-five economic ministries were dissolved. Ten of them were central ministries which had been responsible until then for the manufacture of motor-cars, machinery, haulage machines, heavy machinery, the electro-technical industry, tool manufacture and automation, and the manufacture of machine tools and road-making machines. All enterprises which were subordinate to these ministries now came under the control of the newly established regional *sovnarkhozy*. The other fifteen economic ministries which were dissolved were in the Union Republics. They included the ministries for light industry, timber, oil, non-ferrous metals, and quartz metallurgy.

However, a number of economic ministries, for example the Union ministries for ship-building, chemicals, medium machines, power stations, and the manufacture of transport equipment, continued to exist. A complicated situation thus arose in that some industries continued to be directed centrally while the majority of enterprises came under the control of the regional economic councils.

In spite of several compromises, those forces which wanted the Party to direct the modernization of the economic system finally won. The economic officials were forced to retreat. The Gosekonomkomissiya was dissolved, and Pervukhin, who still appeared so powerful in December 1956, was on 30 April 1957 degraded to the post of Minister of Medium Machine Building.

The only central economic organ which remained, the State

Committee for long-term planning, was placed under the direction of Yosif Kuzmin, a Party official until then hardly known to the public. He had been a member of the Party since 1930, had studied at the Academy for Electrotechnology and in 1939, after some years of practical experience in a searchlight factory, was moved into the Commission for Party Control of the Central Committee and employed there as the controller in charge of the industrial division. In 1940 he was the official representative of the Commission for Party Control in the Kuibyshev district, and from the end of 1940 until 1946 he was Deputy Chairman of the Commission for Party Control, one of the senior Party positions. Since the membership of the Party Control Commission is not as a rule made public it was easy to explain that his true importance had remained hidden from both the Russian and the international public. From 1947 to 1950 Kuzmin was a member of the Council of Ministers of the USSR and since 1950 Deputy Chairman of the Bureau of Agriculture and Procurement directly under the Council of Ministers. As Khrushchev occupied a leading position in the direction of Soviet agriculture at the same time, it may be assumed that Khrushchev and Kuzmin had known each other at least since then. In 1952 Kuzmin became deputy head of the department for industry and transport of the Central Committee, in 1953 he was promoted to be head of this department, and was then until April 1957 head of the department for machine-building of the Central Committee of the Party. At the beginning of May 1957 he took over the Chairmanship of the State Planning Commission and at the same time became First Deputy Prime Minister of the USSR, a further sign of the fact that the influence of the Party apparatus on the direction of the Soviet economy had increased.

In the hierarchy of the Gosplan Kuzmin as First Deputy Chairman ranked with Kosygin, the expert on consumer goods questions. The former minister of the aircraft industry, Lieutenant-General Mikhail Khrunichev was appointed a deputy chairman of the Gosplan; so were Vassili Sotov and Nikolai Strokin, formerly ministers of the food and car industry respectively. Most of the well-known Soviet economic leaders whom in the spring of 1955 Bulganin had made deputy prime ministers and who were in Pervukhin's office in December

1956[1] were forced out of the central economic leadership: so was Pervukhin himself.

The great economic reform not only brought with it a profound change in economic leadership, but also—and this was very soon to show itself dramatically—a fundamental change in the balance of power. Above all, the reform, whether looked at in terms of the allocation of functions or of personalities, meant a strengthening of the Party machine. The Party, however, presented this transformation in a way which let the hope arise among junior functionaries that they would be given greater scope to conduct their own affairs. The army paper *Red Star*, too, several times expressed itself as in favour of the formation of the *sovnarkhozy*. In spite of the contradictions which emerged during the debate, and in spite of differences in ideas on questions of detail, it became increasingly clear that for the reform of the economic leadership a successful alliance based on common interests had been formed between the Party, the army, and the smaller officials.

On the other hand, the staff of the economic ministries which had been dissolved lost its influence and had, at the best, the opportunity of finding jobs in one of the regional economic councils—by no means a rosy prospect. The retarding, pro-Stalinist forces probably also expressed their reservations, both on principle because they wanted to preserve Stalin's economic structure, and also for reasons of power politics because the new economic régime would sooner or later threaten their position. There thus developed in the spring of 1957 a strange coalition between the pro-Stalinist forces, whose spokesmen were Molotov and Kaganovich, and the central planners under Malenkov, Pervukhin, and Saburov. Both groups had united against Khrushchev's programme— the one, because it was against any reform whatsoever, and the other because though it favoured a reform of the economy, it wanted it to take place under its own leadership and not, as proposed by Khrushchev, through the Party.

[1] They included Kucherenko, Matskevich, Benediktov, and of course Saburov, the chief planner for many years.

CHAPTER VII

KHRUSHCHEV DOMINATES THE SOVIET SCENE

(July 1957 to January 1959)

THE EXCLUSION OF THE 'ANTI-PARTY' GROUP

AN event which apparently had little to do with the impending crisis excited the attention of the public. On 30 June 1957, Soviet Air Force Day was due to be celebrated as usual. On 15 June the officer commanding the Air Force parade Colonel-General Loginov, announced that the fly-past would last very much longer this year and that new types of aircraft would be shown. A few days later the traditional fly-past was cancelled, the reason given being that the meteorological conditions were bad—which was not true.

At about the same time a meeting of the Party Praesidium was about to take place. On the proposal of Malenkov and Molotov it had been convened for 18 June. According to a report, unconfirmed until now, an unpublished decision had already been taken to relieve Khrushchev and the other members of the Central Committee Secretariat from their positions. At the meeting of the Praesidium on 18 June the ceremonies in connexion with the celebration of the 250th anniversary of the City of Leningrad were to be discussed. The celebration seemed out of place since every Russian school book gives 1703 as the year in which St. Petersburg was founded: the anniversary should, therefore, have been celebrated in June 1953.

During these decisive days Khrushchev and Bulganin were in Finland and Khrushchev's supporter, Kirichenko, was also away. On 14 June Khrushchev and Bulganin came back from their journey: their return was like a great state occasion. On 15 June *Pravda* published on the front page a large photograph showing their reception by Malenkov, Molotov, Kaganovich, Mikoyan, and Suslov, amid a sea of flowers.

But appearances belied reality. It became known soon

afterwards that serious disagreements which had nothing to do with the celebration of the 250th anniversary of Leningrad were expressed at the session of the Praesidium which had opened on 18 June. Khrushchev was sharply attacked both on account of his reorganization of the economy and of his ideological escapades. 'Talk less, and give the people more to eat' was said to have been Molotov's taunt. Among other things, Khrushchev is said to have been accused of deviating from the decisions of the Twentieth Party Congress about the liquidation of the personality cult and the strengthening of collective leadership. According to some reports, demands were made at this session of the Party Praesidium, which lasted until 21 June, that Khrushchev should be dismissed from the position of First Party Secretary and degraded to the position of Minister of Agriculture, Molotov becoming First Party Secretary and Malenkov Prime Minister. But Khrushchev and his group, with the help of their supporters in the Central Committee, were successful in mastering the grave danger to them. Khrushchev demanded that the question should be discussed not in the closed circles of the Praesidium but before the whole Central Committee. He gave the alarm to the Party officials in the provinces and brought them to Moscow in army aeroplanes made available by Marshal Zhukov. Thus Khrushchev and his followers needed to gain time. They even took refuge in filibustering speeches; Madame Furtseva is said to have made a six-hour speech to hold up the progress of the session until the arrival of more of Khrushchev's followers in Moscow.

After 22 June the Praesidium no longer met alone, but there was a plenary meeting of the Central Committee at which— apart from the 133 full members and 122 candidate members of the Central Committee—the members of the Central Revision Commission were also present. According to *Trybuna Ludu* of 9 July, in all 309 people were present at the full session, of whom 215 asked for the floor.[1] More than sixty persons actually spoke, the others making their statements in writing.

At first Malenkov, Molotov, Kaganovich, and their supporters were on the offensive. Khrushchev was accused of wanting to create a new personality cult. With his 'milk and butter' speeches, they said, demanding greater attention to

[1] See *Unità*, 8 July 1957.

agriculture Khrushchev had been guilty of a 'rightist peasant deviation'.[1]

But things soon began to change. The provincial officials stood firmly by Khrushchev and his policy. They now accused Malenkov, Molotov, and Kaganovich of having torpedoed the decisions of the Twentieth Party Congress. Their silence during the discussion of the great economic reform was—undoubtedly correctly—interpreted as hostility to it. According to some reports, confirmed indirectly later, Zhukov spoke strongly in favour of Khrushchev at this full session. He reproached Malenkov, Molotov, and Kaganovich with their attitude during the Great Purge of 1936 to 1938 and even threatened to publish documents of the year 1937.

During this bitter struggle Shepilov, who until then had been regarded as a follower of the Khrushchev faction, apparently went over to the other side. He was not the only turncoat. Mikhail Suslov, who had always been a Stalinist, but now guessed better than Shepilov who would win, joined the Khrushchev wing, saving himself from the fate of Molotov, Malenkov, and Kaganovich. For the controversies at the plenary session in June resulted in a clear victory for the 'united front' of Party, army, and smaller officials over the Stalinists and central planners.

The resolution of the June session was published on 4 July 1957, the conflict being only indirectly implied. According to the usual method the victorious majority now described itself as 'the Party'. The defeated minority was presented as the 'anti-Party group' of Malenkov, Molotov, and Kaganovich, which was said to have tried to 'change the political line of the Party', and to achieve changes in its leadership 'through anti-Party, fractional methods'.

More exactly, the 'anti-Party group' was accused of having worked against the extension of the rights of the Union Republics as well as against a greater local participation at the expense of the central authorities. The group was said to have tried to thwart the reorganization of economic controls and the formation of regional economic councils; it had resisted the reorganization even after this had been approved by the Supreme

---

[1] In May and June he had made several speeches to the effect that the Russians would be better fed than the Americans in a few years' time.

Soviet. They were, in fact, said to have opposed everything that Khrushchev had supported. Old errors were dug up too. Molotov—mentioned more frequently than Malenkov and Kaganovich—was accused of having for a long time opposed an improvement in relations with Yugoslavia and a reduction of general international tension.

All three were accused of 'conservatism', a political deviation which became the focal point of the campaign which followed. They were caught up in old ideas and clung to outmoded methods of work which did not correspond to new conditions— an accusation which undoubtedly applied to Molotov and Kaganovich, but hardly to Malenkov. They had indulged in group intrigues, their aim being to change the policy of the Party. It was said that they had plotted with Shepilov, thus offending against the Statutes of the Party. After a detailed presentation of these accusations, it was announced that the Central Committee condemned as irreconcilable with the Leninist principles of the Party, the intrigues of the anti-Party group, Malenkov, Molotov, Kaganovich, and Shepilov. Further, the Central Committee decided 'to remove Comrades Malenkov, Molotov, and Kaganovich from the Praesidium of the Central Committee and the Central Committee itself, to relieve Comrade Shepilov of his responsibilities as secretary of the Central Committee of the CPSU and to remove him from the ranks of candidate members of the Praesidium of the Central Committee as well as from the ranks of full members of the Central Committee'.

THE KHRUSHCHEV FACTION TAKES OVER THE PARTY LEADERSHIP

On the same day the most far-reaching changes in the two dominant organs of the Party leadership, the Party Praesidium and the Central Committee Secretariat were announced.

It was not only Malenkov, Molotov, and Kaganovich who left the Party Praesidium: Saburov was also expelled from it and Pervukhin was degraded to the rank of candidate member. Thus at one stroke five of the eleven full members of the Party Praesidium were removed. They were replaced by nine new officials, most of whom belonged to the Khrushchev group, people who had appeared at the Twentieth Party Congress as

candidate members of the Praesidium and members of the
Party Secretariat such as Aristov, Belyayev, Brezhnev, Ignatov,
Kozlov, and Yekaterina Furtseva, who was moving increas-
ingly into the foreground. There was also Otto Kuusinen, the
veteran of the Comintern leaders, who from 1940 to 1956 had
been chairman of the Supreme Soviet of the Carelian (Finnish)
Union Republic, Nikolai Shvernik, the chairman for many
years of the Soviet trade unions, and finally the Minister of
Defence, Marshal Zhukov, hitherto a candidate member of the
Party Praesidium.

Six of these nine new full members of the supreme body of
the USSR, the Party Praesidium, came from the Party apparatus. They had come into greater prominence only after Stalin's
death and had been promoted by Khrushchev. Two of them—
Kuusinen and Shvernik—belonged to the older generation
and had obviously been promoted for reasons of tradition and
at least a pretence of continuity. Marshal Zhukov's advance-
ment showed the pressure from the army.

At the same time there were a number of changes in the
candidate members of the Party Praesidium. Of the six candidate members at the time of the Twentieth Party Congress,
Furtseva, Zhukov, Brezhnev, and Shvernik became full members; Shepilov was excluded. Thus, as a result of the sudden
change in the leadership in July 1957 only one candidate
member of the Praesidium remained, Nuritdin Mukhitdinov.
Eight new candidate members were appointed: the Party
theorist, Pospelov; the Chairman of the Supreme Soviet of the
Ukraine, Demian Korochenko, who had been Central Committee Secretary in the Ukraine from 1939 to 1947; the First
Secretary of the Communist Party of Latvia, Jan Kalnbersin;
the Party Secretary of Sverdlovsk, Andrei Kirilenko; Alexei
Kosygin, expert on consumer goods, who was at the same time
appointed Deputy Chairman of the Council of Ministers of the
USSR; the First Secretary of the Party of Bielorussia, Kyril
Masurov; the First Secretary of the Union Republic of Georgia,
Vassili Mzhavanadze; and finally Mikhail Pervukhin, now
degraded from full membership.

It is no exaggeration to consider this change of leaders as
important as the fall of Beria or the Twentieth Party Congress
with Khrushchev's secret report. Its extent becomes evident

if the membership of the Party Praesidium before and after the plenary session in June are compared:

Before the Plenary Session
in June 1957   After it

Full Members of the Party Praesidium

Before	After
1. Khrushchev	1. Khrushchev
2. Bulganin	2. Aristov
3. Kaganovich	3. Belyayev
4. Kirichenko	4. Brezhnev
5. Malenkov	5. Bulganin
6. Mikoyan	6. Furtseva
7. Molotov	7. Ignatov
8. Pervukhin	8. Kirichenko
9. Saburov	9. Kozlov
10. Suslov	10. Kuusinen
11. Voroshilov	11. Mikoyan
	12. Shvernik
	13. Zhukov
	14. Suslov
	15. Voroshilov

Candidate Members of the Party Praesidium

Before	After
1. Brezhnev	1. Kalnbersin
2. Furtseva	2. Kirilenko
3. Mukhitdinov	3. Korochenko
4. Zhukov	4. Kosygin
5. Shepilov	5. Masurov
6. Shvernik	6. Mukhitdinov
	7. Mzhavanadze
	8. Pervukhin
	9. Pospelov

The Praesidium of the Council of Ministers was profoundly affected by these changes. Molotov, Kaganovich, Saburov, and Pervukhin who were now dismissed had been First Deputy Prime Ministers of the USSR. Molotov, who had to give up his post as Minister of State Control was made Ambassador of the USSR in Outer Mongolia, Kaganovich director of an enterprise in the Urals, and Malenkov, until then a Deputy Prime

Minister and Minister of Power Stations, lost both these posts and took over the direction of a power station in Ust-Kameno-gorsk in East Kazakhstan. Pervukhin at first fared best of all those who were degraded for, although he lost his position as First Deputy Prime Minister, he was put in charge of the Committee for Foreign Trade under the Council of Ministers.

Five Deputy Prime Ministers were expelled, but only one new appointment was made to the Praesidium—that of Kosygin. Thus the Praesidium of the Council of Ministers, once so powerful, after the plenary session of June 1957 con-sisted at first only of four people; the Chairman, Bulganin, the two First Deputy Chairmen, Mikoyan and Kuzmin, and Kosygin newly appointed as Deputy Chairman.

This was the most important shift of power since Stalin's death. At one stroke the chief Stalinists, Molotov and Kagano-vich, together with the leading representatives of the economic bureaucracy linked with Malenkov, were driven out. The change of cast showed the emergence of those forces within the Soviet government Party which were pressing for further 'reforms from above' and wanted a modernization of the system under the absolute domination of the Party.

Immediately after the fall of Molotov, Malenkov, Kagano-vich, and Shepilov, a big propaganda campaign was started. The Moscow Party organization alone held 8,000 meetings on 3 and 4 July. It is instructive that the dismissal of Saburov and the down-grading of Pervukhin were not mentioned at all. Attention was focused mainly on the accusations against Malenkov, Molotov, and Kaganovich and, as always on such occasions, on the unity of the Party.

The campaign reached its climax with the celebrations of the 250th anniversary of Leningrad, at which Khrushchev, Yekaterina Furtseva, Bulganin, Kozlov, Kuusinen, and Shvernik produced more accusations against the 'anti-Party group'. Khrushchev said that Molotov had pursued a foreign policy of 'tightening the screw'. Malenkov was responsible for the so-called Leningrad Affair. Shepilov, once his protégé, Khrushchev called a shamelessly double-faced person who had committed treason to further his career. Frol Kozlov, now a member of the Party Praesidium, accused those expelled of having during the last two or three years shown 'permanent resistance' to the new policy of the Party, and Kalchenko, Prime Minister of the Ukraine, said that Kaganovich when he was Party Secretary in the Ukraine had cast suspicions on honest Party officials and intellectuals and had clearly intended to prepare a new purge. Only Bulganin, in his speech, was noticeably reticent.

The expulsion of the 'anti-Party group' was not without effects in the other countries of the Eastern bloc. In Rumania two Politburo members, Josif Chisinevshy and Miron Constantinescu, were expelled from the Party leadership as early as the beginning of July. Soon afterwards the Bulgarian Party leaders expelled Georgi Chankov, member of the Politburo and First Deputy Prime Minister, as well as the Central Committee officials Dobri Terpeshev and Jonko Panov, from their midst.

From 9 to 16 July Khrushchev visited Czechoslovakia. In Prague, and afterwards in Moscow, he had discussions with representatives of the Bulgarian, Italian, French, and Albanian Communist Parties.

During Khrushchev's absence, on 15 July, Zhukov made an important speech to the workers of the 'Bolshevik' enterprise in Leningrad in which he gave his own interpretation of the latest changes. He asserted that Molotov and Kaganovich did 'not want to give up the privileges that they had enjoyed thirty years ago'. This was a reference to events in the late twenties when Stalin's rise began. Thus Zhukov touched on questions which had not even been mentioned in Khrushchev's secret speech. He accused the fallen leaders of sharing responsibility for Stalin's reign of terror.

'In particular', he said, 'they were opposed to the idea of unmasking and calling to account those people who bore the main responsibility for the violations of legality which used to occur . . . it had become clear why they had been against revealing the illegalities which had occurred. They were afraid to accept, before the Party and the people, responsibility . . . for their illegal actions.'

It was clear that Zhukov was referring to the part played by Malenkov, Molotov, and Kaganovich during the Great Purge of 1936 to 1938. But apparently he went even further in this speech, because *Pravda* on 16 July finished its report with the following words: 'after this G. K. Zhukov mentioned details of the offences against legality committed by the members of the anti-Party group, Malenkov, Molotov, and Kaganovich.'

Neither then nor later did the Soviet press say what further details Zhukov had mentioned. But it deserves to be noted that as early as 16 July 1957 *Pravda*, which is controlled by the Party apparatus, censored a speech of Zhukov's who since the beginning of July had also been a member of the Party Praesidium, because he had touched on things about which the Party leaders wished to keep silent.

The impression of Mr. Montgomery Hyde, a British M.P., who was in the Soviet Union at the time and took part in the Leningrad celebrations, was that the 250th anniversary celebrations aroused more interest than the news of the dismissal of the Party leaders. Young men to whom he spoke in the street merely shrugged their shoulders at the mention of Malenkov: they appeared to take no interest in the matter. Although Montgomery Hyde stressed that Khrushchev received a great ovation on his arrival in Leningrad, it seemed to him that Malenkov and Molotov would have been given an equally warm welcome had they won the last struggle for power in Russia.[1]

In many political circles outside Russia, particularly in Belgrade and Warsaw, the changes were welcomed. The determined support that the victorious leaders had given to the decisions of the Twentieth Party Congress and the condemnation of Stalinist methods awakened hopes of further de-Stalinization. But there were also other voices. Mr. Desmond Donnelly, M.P. who was in the Soviet Union shortly afterwards, reported—and this was confirmed from several sides—that the dismissal of Malenkov had caused anxiety. This is easy to explain as the peasants connected Malenkov's name with a considerable alleviation of their lot. Khrushchev had to take account of these feelings. On 5 July, one day after the expulsion of the 'anti-Party group,' an important concession was made to the peasants: compulsory deliveries from personal plots were abolished for all agricultural products. Among the intellectuals many probably preferred the cultivated Malenkov to Khrushchev. There were even several instances of open opposition to the advance of the Khrushchev wing. An Austrian who

[1] *Observer*, 14 July 1957.

returned from Russia in 1958 told the author that at the beginning of July 1957 the workers of the electrical appliances factory in Kursk stopped work. They asked for an explanation of the dismissal of Molotov, Malenkov, and Kaganovich, and demanded that the fallen leaders should comment over the radio on the events at the full session of the Central Committee. The Party officials of the factory implored the workers to stop the strike: 'Remember, Molotov, Malenkov, and Kaganovich themselves admitted that they were guilty,' they said. Only after an hour did work start again. In other enterprises, too, there was unrest. Workers openly abused the Party leaders which officials pretended not to hear.

Khrushchev and his supporters were naturally very anxious to get old Bolsheviks to declare their support for the change. But the old Bolsheviks were very difficult to win over. Not until 24 July was *Pravda* able to publish the first declarations. Others followed on 1 and 4 and finally 13 August. Later reports bear witness that every means of persuasion had to be used to bring about these favourable comments. Most of them had no particular feeling for Malenkov, Molotov or Kaganovich, but they were afraid that the recent change might set a precedent for future purges.

THE BLOW AGAINST THE WRITERS

With the plenary session in June 1957 the period of compromises between the different groups of leaders was over. The Khrushchev faction began to change the system according to its own ideas. It tried to create the impression in Russia and all Eastern Europe that de-Stalinization would be continued with increased speed; but soon a greater harshness in cultural affairs became apparent.

Since the autumn of 1956 the Soviet leaders had been trying to regain control over the forces which they had unchained. They succeeded in many directions, but their tussle with the writers and artists continued for many months. In May 1957 the Party leadership interfered. The Central Committee called a conference of writers and a reception was held in the Kremlin for them and for painters and composers at which all the Party leaders, including Molotov, Malenkov, Kaganovich, and Shepilov, were present. But this had no success. At the third full session of the Union of Soviet Writers there was open resistance to the criticism and self-criticism demanded by the authorities and against the acceptance of 'Party-mindedness' and 'social realism'. In spite of a direct demand, neither editor nor contributors to *Literaturnaya Moskva* were willing to criticize themselves. The Soviet press spoke of a 'conspiracy of silence'. The demand that the writers should decide either for the Writers' Union or to be silent also met with no success at first. At later meetings of the writers, particularly in Moscow, Leningrad, and Armenia, strong opposition was renewed. In Leningrad Party criticism concentrated on the unpublished collection of writings, 'The Flood', which was to be issued under the literary guidance of Vera Panova. Madame Panova, who had already drawn attention to herself with a critical novel, *Companions of the Road*, replied to the criticism by resigning her post, an event without precedent in the Soviet Union. Speakers loyal to the régime had to admit that in Leningrad her 'notoriously heroic silence had found a response'.

On 28 August there appeared under the title 'For a close linking of literature and art with the life of the people' a collection of Khrushchev's speeches that he had made at the conference of the Central Committee with the writers and at the Kremlin reception. Since then Khrushchev's speeches have always been referred to as 'the document' or 'the historical document'. Undoubtedly they provide the most important cultural directive since Stalin's death, being to some extent a modernization of Zhdanov's directives of the years 1946 to 1948.

Like almost all declarations of the post-Stalin period Khrushchev's directive was aimed against two 'deviations'. On the one hand he used strong words against 'scholars who learnt by rote', 'parrots', 'hair-splitters', and 'quotation maniacs' who did not recognize new conditions and tasks, who 'juggled with quotations from the classics of Marxism-Leninism at every suitable and unsuitable moment' and who could not free themselves from the old, outmoded methods. It was noteworthy that Khrushchev described these neither as right nor left deviations, Trotskyism or Bukharinism, but as 'conservatism'. The main blow of the Party, however, was not aimed against the conservatives, but against the refractory writers and artists.

Khrushchev accused them of too greatly emphasizing the

darker sides of Soviet life in their works. They lost contact with the ground under their feet, wandered off the right path and expressed the erroneous opinion that literature and art existed only to discover defects. In this connexion Khrushchev criticized particularly Dudintsev's *Not by Bread Alone* which he declared to be 'fundamentally wrong', and the miscellany *Literary Moscow*, which he regarded as unhealthily pessimistic. Above all Khrushchev condemned the writers' demand for creative freedom. And he was concerned over the writers' notion that the principle of the Party-mindedness of art (which in practice degraded art into a propaganda instrument) should be replaced by the concept of proximity to the people: this interpreted the social duty of the writer to the people as unaffected by power politics and linked up with the best traditions of Russian literature in the last century.

Khrushchev did not deny the need for criticism, but demanded that it should 'start from the right positions and pursue the right aim'. Criticism was a means of discovering mistakes and of removing obstacles with the aim of further 'consolidating our Soviet order and the position of the Communist Party'. Creative work must not be bound up with the people, but Party-minded. Party-mindedness showed itself not in formal Party membership, but in an artist's convictions. To the objection raised by Khrushchev himself that some 'liberally-minded people' might accuse him of issuing a call to battle he replied that the communists had never pretended not to make an ideological call to arms.

This made the basis of Khrushchev's cultural policy unmistakably clear: literature and art, which since Stalin's death had threatened to slip away from Party control, were to be brought back to do the Party's bidding. Authors had the right to criticize certain manifestations of the Stalinist past, but only in so far as this was in the interest of the Party. They must support the modernization of the system but had no right to go a step further independently.

MARSHAL ZHUKOV'S FALL

After the full session of June 1957 the army leadership remained as the only serious rival of the Party apparatus. Relations between the army and the Party had played a decisive part in every phase of Soviet development. Time and again Stalin felt forced, on the one hand, to make concessions to the army and on the other, through Party control, to prevent the army from becoming too strong.

After Stalin's death, however, there was a clear tendency to reduce the direct political influence of the Party over the army. The activity of the political administration and the Party organizations which according to Article 64 of the Party Statutes had to direct political work in the army, was reduced. Particularly from 1955 onwards the army leaders expressed the view—Zhukov with special frankness—that the influence of the Party should be restricted to strengthening the authority of the army commanders. At the end of 1955 the political officers at company level, that is, those who were in immediate contact with the troops, were disbanded. Just before the Twentieth Party Congress Marshal Zhukov said at the Party conference of the Moscow defence district: 'One or two attempts have been made in the district to criticize the service activities of officers at meetings. Such attempts must be punished. It is our task to strengthen the officers' authority by all means.' At a meeting of leading political officials of the Soviet armed forces at the end of April 1956 Zhukov repeated his demands more clearly and with greater confidence: 'Within the armed forces ideological work must be directed to providing comprehensive knowledge, strictest discipline, training for good fighting morale, and the further development of Soviet military science.' He was supported by Marshal Timoshenko, who on 27 April 1956, in an interview in *Krasnaya Zvezda*[1] demanded the unconditional support of army officers by the Party organizations: 'Communists and Komsomols must play the same tune as the officers.'

In April 1957 the Party functionaries made a further important concession to the chiefs of the army. In 'Instructions for the Organization of the CPSU in the Soviet Army and Navy' the political activity of the Party organizations was officially put under the unit commanders. The instruction said: 'The regimental or the naval commander (that is, the officer in command of the unit) directs the work of the Party organization both personally and through his political deputy.' This

[1] *Red Star.*

was qualified, however, by the statement that 'to set tasks for the Party organizations does not mean to control them, but merely to direct their work'. It is interesting that these concessions were not at first made public. Only on 12 May was the instruction mentioned by *Krasnaya Zvezda* and *Sovietski Flot*,[1] the papers of the army and the navy. On 17 July the quotation given above from the instruction was published.

On the one hand the Party was losing influence within the army between 1953 and 1957, while on the other the increasing influence of the army chiefs on the political development of the country was clearly to be seen. At all decisive points— the fall of Beria in July 1953, the resignation of Malenkov in February 1955, the meeting with Tito in the summer of 1955—the voice of the military leaders could not be ignored. The first criticism of the falsified Stalinist presentation of the war came from the army—it was uttered by General Shatilov at a conference convened by army circles in May 1955. On 23 February 1956 during the Twentieth Party Congress, the meeting of army delegates mentioned earlier took place under the chairmanship of Zhukov, who probably pressed for intensified criticism of Stalin. In the composition of the leading Party organs more attention than before was paid to representatives of the army. Six marshals, Zhukov, Vasilevsky, Sokolovsky, Koniev, Malinovsky, and Moskalenko, were full members of the new Central Committee, and another twelve representatives of the army and navy were appointed candidate members. It is significant that the then head of the main political administration, General Zheltov, did not join the Central Committee.

The increasing importance of the army within the dominant political group after Stalin's death also found expression in Marshal Zhukov's meteoric career. Zhukov was recalled in the autumn of 1946 from being head of the Soviet military government in Germany and Commander-in-Chief of the Army, and was then for several years not mentioned in the Soviet press. Immediately after Stalin's death, however, he was appointed Deputy Minister of Defence, and on 31 December of the same year a bust of him was unveiled in his birthplace, Ugodski Savod, near Kaluga. After Malenkov's resignation in February

[1] *Soviet Fleet.*

1955 he was promoted to be Minister of Defence; it has been seen how thanks to his support of the Khrushchev faction he then advanced in June 1957 to become a full member of the Party Praesidium.

But Zhukov's appearance at the plenary session in June was probably the reason for his fall. Immediately afterwards reports from Moscow said that Marshal Zhukov had emerged there as the sharpest accuser of the anti-Party group and had threatened during the discussion that he would publish documents regarding the activities of Malenkov, Molotov, and Kaganovich during the Great Purge of 1936 to 1938. This threat was probably extremely effective and must have contributed notably to Khrushchev's victory. But it was a two-edged weapon. It could also be used at any time against other Party leaders, for example Khrushchev, who, although he did not play a part comparable with that of Malenkov or Molotov during the Great Purge, could also be seriously discredited by such revelations. When Zhukov on 15 July accused the members of the 'anti-Party group' of sharing the responsibility for the terror of the thirties, no doubt could remain that he wished to drive the Party officials led by Khrushchev to a further indictment of Stalinism. *Pravda* published his speech on 16 July 1957 in a censored version, after which the *Krasnaya Zvezda* on 17 July published that part of the internal Party instruction which referred to the subordination of the Party organizations to serving officers.

In the weeks that followed there were signs of great political activity in the army. It had been obvious for a long time that the military chiefs were interested in rehabilitating the marshals shot during the Great Purge in 1937, among them Marshal Tukhachevsky and Marshal Blücher. Khrushchev had mentioned neither of these marshals in his secret speech. It was all the more noticeable, therefore, when on 10 August *Krasnaya Zvezda* published a detailed biography of Marshal Blücher and thus rehabilitated him as a hero of the Civil War. Three days later *Krasnaya Zvezda* criticized Party propaganda and demanded more lectures on military topics and the history of the war; more military experts should be employed for this purpose, as their lectures would 'guarantee closer contact with life and be characterized by a wealth of factual material'.

It remains obscure why Zhukov, who had thus provoked a crisis, was prepared to leave the Soviet Union at the beginning of October and to visit Yugoslavia and Albania. Apparently he did not believe that the Party leaders would be strong enough to prepare his fall in his absence. In fact the Soviet press from 12 to 25 October 1957 reported almost daily on Zhukov's journey—always with insistence upon his position as Minister of Defence. On 25 October *Pravda* announced the appointment of Marshal Rokossovsky as commander of the trans-Caucasian defence region. Whether or not this had anything to do with the preparations for Zhukov's fall must be left undecided. Two days later, on 27 October, *Pravda* announced on its front page that Marshal Zhukov had left Tirana by air and arrived in Moscow, and on its last page that he had been relieved of his post. On the following day *Pravda's* leading article was headed 'Unshakeable unity of the Party and people'—a phrase which is always used on the occasion of important political conflicts. *Pravda* declared that it was only thanks to the leadership of the Party and its Central Committee that the Soviet people and the armed forces had been victorious in the war.

The most varied rumours circulated in Moscow at this time. It was generally assumed that Zhukov had not fallen, but had merely been transferred to another high position. According to the most popular version Voroshilov was to retire from the Chairmanship of the Supreme Soviet on account of his age, Bulganin to succeed him, and Zhukov to succeed Bulganin as Chairman of the Council of Ministers. Only on 3 November, almost a week after Zhukov had been dismissed, did *Pravda* announce that at the end of October a full session of the Central Committee had dealt with the improvement of the Party's political work in the army. The Central Committee had criticized the unsatisfactory political work of the Party in the army. It must be said unequivocally, *Pravda* stated, that the organizations of the Party had an important part to play in the army. The directives of the Party and its Central Committee must form the foundation of the policy of the military authorities and of all other offices. Recently the former Minister of Defence, Zhukov, had pursued a policy aimed at removing Party control over army and navy. Zhukov had encouraged a cult of his personality and had exaggerated his own role during the war. He had shown himself to be a politically unsound person and a bit of an adventurer in his approach both to foreign policy and questions of defence. The plenary session had decided to exclude Marshal Zhukov from the Party Praesidium and to provide him with another task. According to the official announcement this decision met with the unanimous approval of the members and candidate members of the Central Committee and the representatives of the armed forces who had attended the meeting.

On the same day, 3 November, Zhukov's self-criticism was published, which in many respects recalled that of Molotov in February 1955. It was as follows: 'This plenary meeting was a good piece of Party schooling for me. To my great regret I only here fully recognized the importance of the mistakes that I had committed in leading the armed forces, particularly recently, the political mistakes that I made as a member of the Central Committee and of the Praesidium of the Central Committee of the CPSU which were mentioned here at the plenary meeting. The criticism made of me I recognize to be essentially accurate and regard it as comradely help from the Party to me personally and to other members of the army for the proper understanding of the demands of the Party as to the correct leadership of the army and the navy and the right political education of the armed forces. When some comrades proposed a punishment they said that, once before, during Stalin's lifetime, in 1946, I had been expelled from the Central Committee and that I did not recognize the need to correct the mistakes for which I had been expelled. At that time, Comrades, I could not consider my exclusion from the Central Committee to be right and did not do so. . . . Now it is different. I confess my mistakes, I admitted them in detail during the course of the plenary meeting and I give the Central Committee of the Party my word that I shall correct my errors completely.'

As on the occasion of the expulsion of Malenkov, Molotov, and Kaganovich, immediately after the fact had been published the usual Party campaign was started with the slogan 'The strength of the Soviet army and navy lies in the leadership of the Party'. In all important centres of the USSR meetings of Party activists took place. Leading representatives of the Khrushchev faction made suitable explanatory speeches:

Kozlov in Leningrad, Furtseva in Moscow, Kirichenko in Kiev, Mukhitdinov in Uzbekistan, Ignatov in Gorki, and Aristov to the Party activists of the Pacific fleet in the Soviet Far East.

In place of Marshal Zhukov, Marshal Rodion Malinovsky became Russian Minister of Defence. Malinovsky, who was born in 1898, was during the first world war one of those Russian soldiers who fought side by side with the Allies in France, including the Americans at Château-Thierry. After the October Revolution he returned to Russia, joined the Red Army and took part in the Civil War, though he joined the Party only in 1926. He attended the Frunze Military Academy, was a major-general as early as 1940 and at the beginning of the German-Soviet war commanded an army corps on the Bessarabian front. In 1942 he took part in the battle of Stalingrad as a general, in 1943 he became supreme commander on the South-western front, in 1944 supreme commander on the Second Ukrainian front and as such took a leading part in the capture of Budapest. After the war he became a commander of the armoured units on the Transbaikal front in the Far East and took part in the short campaign against Japan. After that he was in command of the army in the Far East. At the Nineteenth Party Congress he was appointed a candidate member of the Central Committee of the Party, at the Twentieth Party Congress a full member. Since 1946 he had uninterruptedly been a member of the Supreme Soviet of the USSR.

Marshal Koniev, the First Deputy Minister of Defence and supreme commander of the armed forces of the Warsaw Pact, who in 1953 had been chairman of the military tribunal which sentenced Beria, now led the attack upon Zhukov. Koniev's accusations against Zhukov went beyond the official declaration in the Party resolution. He accused Zhukov of not having allowed the Party organizations in the army to co-operate with the other Party organizations. In Marshal Zhukov's case it was not a matter of a whole 'system of mistakes', military as well as political. As he had been chief of the general staff since January 1941, Zhukov as well as Stalin was responsible for the bad preparation of the army for the war. He had made the mistake of having big motorized units formed without ensuring that there were sufficient supplies of equipment and an adequate number of specialists. The victory at Stalingrad was by no means to be attributed to him, but to the army leaders, Yeremenko, Vatutin, Rokossovsky, and Vasilevsky. Above all, Koniev criticized Zhukov's self-glorification. He was said to have given instructions to exhibit in the Museum of the Red Army a picture of himself on a white horse in front of the burning Reichstag and the Brandenburg Gate. On his instructions the famous Stalingrad film had been changed, but only in order to replace the Stalin cult of the earlier version by a Zhukov cult. This, however, was the only attack of the kind on Zhukov; in the days that followed, marked as they were by the second 'sputnik' and the imminent celebrations of the fortieth anniversary of the October Revolution, the campaign was called off.

THE INTERNATIONAL COMMUNIST CONFERENCE

The fortieth anniversary of the October Revolution on 7 November 1957 was celebrated with special festivities. The leaders not only of all the countries of the Eastern bloc but also of the communist world movement were present in Moscow. A week later, from 14 to 19 November 1957, the biggest international communist meeting since the summer of 1935 took place there with delegations from sixty-four Communist Parties. It was an attempt by the Khrushchev leadership to restore the shaken unity of the communist world movement.

The leaders in Moscow had been preparing this conference step by step for a year. Shortly after the Hungarian revolt *Neues Deutschland* in East Germany, the *Volksstimme* in Austria, and the Soviet periodical *Mezhdunarodnaya Zhizn* had expressed themselves in favour of closer contact between the Communist Parties. But there were many difficulties to overcome. In Poland and in the Italian Communist Party—not to mention the Yugoslav communists—doubts about a new centralization were particularly strong. In China, too, tendencies towards independence had become evident. Moscow could, therefore, proceed only cautiously. In December 1956 Yekaterina Furtseva, the representative of the Soviet Party leadership at the Eighth Party Congress of the Italian Communist Party, proclaimed that contacts between Communist Parties should 'become increasingly close'. The Communist Parties of Eastern Germany, Czechoslovakia, and France in particular, who toed the Moscow line acted as spokesmen for closer collaboration. On 15 April 1957 the East Berlin radio declared that it was only a question of time before the search for new forms of collaboration between Communist Parties 'will be brought to a suitable conclusion'. In the middle of June 1957 the Czechoslovak Party leader, Hendrych,[1] expressed himself in favour of 'joint negotiations among a large number of Parties' and suggested the publication of an international communist theoretical periodical. At the beginning of July the Rumanian Party leadership also expressed itself in favour of an international communist journal. After these preparations Ponomariov described the 'further consolidation of the international collaboration of the Communist Parties' as the most important condition 'for the success of the communist movement as a whole and of each Party in particular.'[2] With special reference to the efforts of other Communist Parties, Ponomaryov expressed himself in favour of 'periodic international conferences of communist and workers' Parties on a broad basis'.

At this time the Soviet leaders were still hoping to win over the Yugoslav communists to international collaboration. Moscow's anti-Yugoslav campaign, which had been revived after the Hungarian revolt, was diminished after Khrushchev's 'come-back' and then completely abandoned. At the beginning of August a meeting took place between Khrushchev and Tito in Rumania which in fact suggested that relations had improved. The Yugoslav communists were then hoping for a further de-Stalinization, and were, therefore, prepared to make further concessions, provided their hard-won independence remained untouched. In the middle of October Yugoslavia was the first non-communist country to establish diplomatic relations with Eastern Germany; but in the weeks just before the November meeting it became clear that the cessation of the anti-Yugoslav campaign and Moscow's prudent attitude were mainly tactical and were aimed at discrediting Yugoslavia in Asia and Africa so that it could then by means of cold war methods be incorporated in the communist world. Tito refused to go to Moscow for the fortieth anniversary of the October Revolution and Kardelj and Ranković went in his place. In spite of being invited the Yugoslavs did not attend the first

[1] *Rudé Pravó*, 19 June 1957.   [2] *Kommunist*, No. 12, 1957.

session (from 14 to 16 November) to which only the representatives of the ruling Communist Parties were admitted; they also refused to sign the declaration providing a new basic programme for international communism. Later Tito justified the Yugoslav refusal by saying 'that we refused for well-known reasons—because of our opposition to a division of the world into "blocs"—to join the so-called socialist camp'.[1] The Yugoslavs only signed the 'peace manifesto' which was adopted at the second session (16 to 19 November) by all the Communist Parties present in Moscow.

From press reports[2] it emerged that there were considerable differences of opinion at the first session, particularly on the question whether the declaration should mention the leading role of the Communist Party of the Soviet Union and what form the collaboration of the Communist Parties in the various countries should take in the future.

The Soviet leaders represented by Suslov, had won over Mao Tse-tung to the view that the leading role of the Russian Communist Party should be particularly emphasized. Mao, who was the first speaker, said that the world communist movement, like every little Party group, must have a head. The Chinese Communist Party was not worthy of this position. Although China had had great experience in building up socialism, the Soviet Union had been at work for forty years. Apart from that, China had little industry and not even a quarter of a sputnik, whereas the Soviet Union had two sputniks. According to the report from Eastern Germany the 'leading role' of the Soviet Communist Party was also emphasized by Ho Chi Minh (North Viet-nam), Enver Hoxha (Albania), Hendrych (Czechoslovakia), Todor Zhivkov (Bulgaria), Dashin Damba (Mongolia), Civo Stoica (Rumania), Kim Ir-sen (North Korea), and Walter Ulbricht (East Germany). As only the names of Kardelj (Yugoslavia), Gomulka (Poland), and Kádár (Hungary) are missing from this list it must be assumed that they were opposed. In the declaration, a compromise was reached: instead of the leading role of the Communist *Party* of the Soviet Union, the leading role of the Soviet Union (as a *state*) in the communist world was indicated.

[1] *Borba*, 16 July 1958.
[2] See *Trybuna Ludu*, 29 Nov. 1957, and *Neues Deutschland*, 30 Nov. 1957.

Another bone of contention was the form of future international collaboration. From Polish sources it appears that Suslov proposed periodic global conferences, similar to the earlier world congresses of the Communist International. The Polish delegation led by Gomulka opposed this on the ground that experience with such centralized organizations as the Communist International and the Cominform had not been entirely satisfactory. He would agree only on condition that such global conferences should not interfere in the internal affairs of the affiliated parties and should pass resolutions only with the consent of all parties. Gomulka stipulated that the elected Party leaders only should participate—he obviously wished to prevent Moscow from excluding oppositional Party leaders while passing off its own followers as the 'true representatives' of the Party in question. Finally Suslov's demand for a global conference was weakened; apart from bilateral meetings more comprehensive consultations of communist and workers' Parties were recommended.

In spite of these concessions the 'declaration of the representatives of the Communist and workers' Parties of the socialist countries' adopted on 16 November 1957 was an undoubted success for Moscow. It was a policy which bound all the Communist Parties except that of Yugoslavia. The declaration demanded the consolidation of the unity of the socialist camp, ordered Communists 'to defend their historical, political, and social achievements . . . against all the intrigues of the enemy', to strengthen the Warsaw Pact, and to wage a 'determined struggle to conquer the remains of bourgeois nationalism and chauvinism'.

Thus the thesis of different roads to socialism lost prestige. Although the declaration still spoke of the 'variety of national peculiarities and traditions' it went on to say that it would damage socialism 'if under the pretext of national peculiarities there were a deviation from the universal truth of Marxism-Leninism about socialist revolution and the construction of socialism'. This made it clear that in future every attempt by a communist country to reach socialism by another road would be regarded as damaging to socialism.

The declaration contained eight 'universal laws' which provided an ideological sanction both for the bolshevisation of all the countries of the Eastern bloc and for any armed intervention such as that in Hungary.

The Communist Parties were committed anew to fight 'dogmatism' and 'revisionism'. Dogmatism replaced the study of concrete situations by quotations and learning by heart and led 'to the detachment of the Party from the masses'. Revisionism covered all reformist communist movements which denied the 'historical necessity of the proletarian revolution and a dictatorship of the proletariat', the leading role of the Party', the 'principles of proletarian internationalism'—in other words, subordination to the Soviet Union—and 'Leninist principles for the construction of the Party', that is, the principle of centralized leadership. Dogmatism was only 'condemned', while 'revisionism' was declared the main danger 'in present circumstances', 'a form of expression of bourgeois ideology which paralyses the revolutionary energy of the working class and demands the preservation or restoration of capitalism'. This apodictic formulation was, however, qualified, probably at the request of the Poles, by the addition that each Communist Party would decide which danger at a given moment was the main one.

The November declaration did concede the possibility of 'seizing state power without civil war, and ensuring the transfer of the most important means of production to the hands of the people'; but as a means of achieving this it still admitted only a 'determined fight against opportunist elements', the transformation of parliament into an 'instrument of the people' and pressure by the masses outside parliament which would break the resistance of reactionary forces and thus create the prerequisites 'for the peaceful realization of the socialist revolution'. If this should not succeed 'another possibility must be borne in mind: that of the non-peaceful transition to socialism'.

The 'peace manifesto' which was signed by the sixty-four Communist Parties, while supporting the declaration of the twelve ruling Parties, was less radical in its formulation and more in line with the needs of the fellow-travelling organizations, such, for example, as the World Peace Movement.

THE SOVNARKHOZY

After the plenary meeting in June 1957, there was no force which could prevent the Khrushchev faction from completing the reorganization of the economy announced in the spring of 1957. In July there were already 104 peoples' economic councils; seventy of them were in the RSFSR (almost every Region of the Russian Republic had its own *sovnarkhoz*), eleven in the Ukraine, four in Uzbekistan, and nine in Kazakhstan. The remaining Union Republics (White Russia; Moldavia; the three Baltic Republics, Lithuania, Latvia, and Estonia; the Caucasian Union Republics, Georgia, Azerbaidjan, and Armenia; and the central Asian Union Republics, Kirgisia, Tadzhikistan, and Turkmenistan) formed one economic unit each.

Of the *sovnarkhozy* chairmen about 30 per cent. were former central economic ministers or deputy ministers, almost 35 per cent. came from the ministries of the Union Republics, about 20 per cent. were former directors of large enterprises, and 15 per cent. Party officials.

In reality, however, the influence of the Party was greater, because most key positions in the new *sovnarkhozy* were occupied by Party officials and the regional secretaries of the Party had the right to direct the *sovnarkhozy* chairmen even over economic questions.

Data about the size, competence, and structure of the *sovnarkhozy* vary. From the different reports it appears, however, that on the average a *sovnarkhoz* is responsible for 200 to 800 concerns with a yearly turnover of 5 to 30 million roubles. The *sovnarkhozy* had correspondingly different structures. The Leningrad people's economic council consisted of five general main administrative units (technology, planning, transport, supply, and sales) and twenty branches all with 70 to 80 members. According to Mr. Desmond Donnelly, M.P., the members of a *sovnarkhoz* varied from 265 in Alma Uta to 2,220 in Moscow.

In July and August technical and economic councils were set up in the *sovnarkhozy*. They consisted of specialists, so-called innovators, representatives of the construction and production departments as well as officials of the local Party organizations, the administration, the economy, and the trade unions. The formation of these consultative organs was the first indication of the fact that the reorganization made it necessary to include wider circles in the economic leadership. Demands appeared in the press that the rights of enterprise directors should be further increased and that the trade unions should be given greater rights.

At the end of August the Ministry for State Control was dissolved and 'Commissions for Soviet Control' (CSC) were established under the Council of Ministers of the USSR and the Councils of Ministers of the Union Republics. At the end of September the Party and government leadership published a decision announcing an important change in the Soviet planning system. Planning too should no longer be conducted vertically according to enterprises but horizontally on the basis of the *sovnarkhozy*. At the same time it was decided to prepare a Seven-Year Plan (1959–65) in place of the hitherto Five-Year Plan (1956–60), the former to be ready by 1 July 1958.

In December 1957 four further ministries were dissolved; those of the aircraft industry, the defence industry, the radio-technical industry and of ship-building. Their duties were handed over to the *sovnarkhozy* and otherwise they were re-placed by so-called committees with a small staff which were to have only co-ordinating duties. Thus almost all the economic ministries were dissolved by the end of 1957. Instead of 55 ministries there were now only 19, of which only 7 were central Union ministries (transport, chemical industry, medium machine building, haulage machine building, power stations, foreign trade, and maritime shipping).

THE TRADE UNIONS RE-HARNESSED

With the economic reorganization the Soviet trade unions, which under Stalin had led a shadowy existence, gained new importance. The Party leaders now tried to use them against the managers.

To start with, the organizational structure of the trade unions had to be adjusted to the new system of economic direction. At the sixth full session of the Soviet trade unions in June 1957 it was decided to reduce the number of industrial unions from forty-seven to twenty-three. In future they were to restrict themselves to the preparation of overall agreements on systems of wage-payments, piece-rates, length of holidays, &c.; the main body of trade union work was to be handed over to local trades councils which would deal with all practical questions, including the conclusion of collective agreements within the framework of the *sovnarkhozy*. After a prolonged campaign of preparation a plenary session of the Central Committee was held at the end of December, which determined the duties and powers of the trade unions in the new conditions.

It was the first time for more than twenty years that trade union problems were dealt with at a full session of the Central Committee. This alone shows the importance which the leaders attached to the question. The main speech was made by Victor Grishin, since the spring of 1956 President of the trade unions. The December meeting decided that the trade unions should take a greater part in public life. The participation of factory and office workers in the direction of production was to be particularly encouraged. Meetings were to be held regularly at which production planning, the organization of production, technical norms, investment, and questions of internal management would be discussed. The trade unions should see to it that collective agreements between economic authorities and trade unions—which had become a mere formality since the end of the twenties—should again be taken seriously and be respected not only by the workers but also by the management. Officials who failed to fulfil their obligations under the collective agreements and who offended against the labour laws should be called to account. The yearly plans of the *sovnarkhozy* should be decided only in the presence of representatives of the trade unions. The state committee for labour questions also had a duty to solve its tasks in collaboration with the trade unions.

At the same time the trade unions were exhorted to exert themselves more than before to satisfy the material demands of the workers. Accommodation for factories and other institutions was in future to be allocated only after joint decisions by the administration and the trade union committees. Finally, the trade unions were asked to concern themselves with communal services for factory and office workers. The trade unions should also 'express their views on the cadres picked out for managerial posts' and not permit the dismissal of factory and office workers without union consent.

Thus the trade unions were for the first time for thirty years given back many of the rights taken from them in the Stalin period. On the other hand, the decision of the December plenary session left no doubt that the trade unions would have to work under the control of the Party.

BULGANIN'S FALL

In March 1958 elections to the Supreme Soviet were held. As usual, there was only one candidate for each constituency. The star candidates, that is the outstanding political leaders, were said to have been spontaneously nominated in several constituencies. But they had changed considerably. In place of the army's candidates nominated in the spring of 1954— Marshals Zhukov, Vasilevsky, and Budienny—and leaders such as Malenkov, Molotov, and Kaganovich associated with the administration, there appeared in February 1958 new Party officials, promoted by Khrushchev, such as Aristov, Belyayev, Kirichenko, Kozlov, Mukhitdinov, and Madame Furtseva.

When the new Supreme Soviet met on 28 March the deputies were surprised at the start by the formal resignation of Prime Minister Bulganin. The Chairman of the day, Pavel Lobanov, read Bulganin's statement.

In itself this was a matter of routine as formally the Council of Ministers resigns after every new election of the Supreme Soviet. But contrary to normal usage Bulganin was not proposed again as Chairman of the Council of Ministers. Voroshilov, as Chairman of the Praesidium of the Supreme Soviet, said, 'On behalf of the Central Committee of the Communist Party of the Soviet Union and the Council of Nationalities, I propose Comrade Nikita Sergeyevich Khrushchev as chairman of the Council of Ministers of the USSR,[1] and invite him to submit to the Supreme Soviet the composition of the Government of the USSR.'

In a long speech Voroshilov described Khrushchev as an 'outstanding member of the Communist Party and the Soviet Government' and as a 'glorious son of the working class' who

---

[1] At this point there was loud applause, and everyone stood up.

for forty years had served the interests of the Soviet people and the Party with indefatigable energy and fidelity to principle. An outstanding share in the successes of the Communist Party and the Soviet state was due to 'our dear Comrade Nikita Sergeyevich Khrushchev'. Then he announced that the Central Committee had decided that Khrushchev should continue to hold the position of First Secretary of the Central Committee. The Supreme Soviet unanimously adopted the following resolutions:

'1. To appoint Comrade Nikita Sergeyevich Khrushchev Chairman of the Council of Ministers of the USSR;

'2. To entrust the Chairman of the Council of Ministers of the USSR, Comrade Nikita S. Khrushchev, with the submission of the proposed composition of the government of the USSR to the Supreme Soviet for examination.'

Khrushchev expressed his thanks for his nomination as Prime Minister and promised that he would do everything to justify the confidence which had been placed in him: 'I shall serve my people and my Party faithfully and shall spare neither strength nor health nor my life in the struggle to accomplish the great aim which our Party and our people have set themselves—the construction of a communist society in our country.'

The new government again consisted of sixty members, although altogether twenty-eight economic ministries had been dissolved. The Praesidium of the Council of Ministers had seven members; the new Chairman of the Council of Ministers, Khrushchev; two First Deputy Chairmen, Mikoyan and the newly appointed Frol Kozlov; and four Deputy Chairmen, Kosygin, Alexander Zasyadko,[1] Kuzmin, and Dmitri Ustinov.[2] The government also included nineteen specialist ministers, among them Dudorov (Interior), Gromyko (Foreign Affairs), Malinovsky (Defence), Matskevich (Agriculture), Zverev (Finance), and Nikolai Mikhailov (Culture). Apart from Kuzmin seven other leading officials of the Gosplan were members of the Council of Ministers showing that the influence of Gosplan was growing. The ten chairmen of the so-called state committees or commissions were also members of the Government, among them General Serov (State Security),

---

[1] Former Minister of the Coal Industry.
[2] Former Minister of the Defence Industry.

Konstantin Rudniev (Defence Technology, i.e. armaments industry) and Georgi Yenyutin (Soviet Control). Finally the members also included Bulganin, degraded to the position of Chairman of the State Bank, Vladimir Starvosky, head of the Central Statistical Administration, and the Prime Ministers of the fifteen Union Republics.

Still more far reaching changes took place in the Praesidium[1] of the Russian Supreme Soviet which promulgated the laws drawn up on the initiative of the Party leadership between its sessions. Voroshilov was confirmed as chairman and thus at the same time as nominal Head of State of the USSR. Of the remaining members of the Praesidium ten were newly appointed, mainly Party Secretaries promoted by Khrushchev in the last few years, among them Kirichenko, Belyayev, Mazurov (White Russia), Podgorny (Ukraine), Spiridonov (Leningrad), and Ustinov (Moscow).

The leading posts in the government were thus almost completely in the hands of Party officials who supported Khrushchev. The separation of the senior state and Party posts, which since Stalin's death had been part of the principle of collective leadership, was abandoned. Khrushchev, as First Secretary of the Party and Chairman of the Council of Ministers, occupied both the two most important political positions.

On 16 August 1958 it was announced that Bulganin had been dismissed from the chairmanship of the State Bank and degraded to the chairmanship of the *sovnarkoz* in Stavropol in the Northern Caucasus. In September he was expelled from the Party Praesidium and on 12 November 1958 he was in an unusual way branded as an enemy of the Party. At the full meeting of the Central Committee considering the Seven-Year Plan and educational reform Khrushchev, without further explanation, included him in the anti-Party group: 'the full session in June 1957 of the Central Committee of the CPSU discovered and smashed the anti-Party group of Malenkov, Kaganovich, Molotov, and Bulganin with their adherent Shepilov, who had resisted the Leninist policy of the Party.'

A plenary meeting of the Central Committee took place six weeks later from 16 to 21 December. On the third day Bulganin asked to be allowed to criticize himself at length.

[1] It had thirty-eight members.

'And now comrades,' he said, 'about my own attitude. For objectivity's sake I must say honestly that until June 1957 I was not on the side of Malenkov, Kaganovich, and Molotov over the question of the changes in the running of industry and building, the development of the virgin lands or other questions. I was on the side of the majority in the Central Committee Praesidium and the Central Committee, and spoke and fought for the line of the Party, and carried it out in my practical work. But however sad it may be for me the fact remains that when Malenkov, Molotov, Kaganovich, and Shepilov began to develop their anti-Party work actively I joined them. . . . I not only became their collaborator, but also as Chairman of the Council of Ministers at the time, nominally their leader. The anti-Party group met in my office, where it made arrangements about its anti-Party work. Thus, while during a certain period my attitude was correct and in line with the Party, I later essentially joined in their unclean intrigues.

'At the June meeting of the Central Committee in 1957 I voted honestly in favour of its decision about the anti-Party group and agreed, and still today agree unreservedly, with this decision and agree with everything that has been said, at the present plenary session. All the subsequent decisions with respect to my person I accept as what I deserve, and as necessary to the Party. . . .

'I honestly recognize my mistake and ask the Central Committee to help me to return to the Party fold. . . . I am striving to do this sincerely and am filled with the wish to be useful to the Party and to work in its ranks. . . .'

But even this humiliation was not enough for Khrushchev. A succession of Party officials attacked Bulganin for insufficient self-criticism. The former Minister of State Security, at that time First Party Secretary of the Autonomous Tatar Republic, Semyon Ignatiev, said that Bulganin's self-criticism had been 'weak and unconvincing'. The Party Secretary of Omsk, Kolushchinsky, shouted to Bulganin: 'You were a member of this criminal and treacherous group and you should have admitted it.' Matskevich, the Minister of Agriculture, said, 'Bulganin has just maintained that he joined the group only at the last moment. That is not true. If Bulganin had honestly repented he would have to lay down his arms completely.'

The Chairman of the Committee for the procurement of cereals, Leonid Korniets, added abuse of Bulganin as a two-faced traitor.

THE DISSOLUTION OF THE MACHINE
AND TRACTOR STATIONS

The reform of the control of industry was scarcely over and the new *sovnarkhozy* had only just begun to work when Khrushchev in the spring of 1958 announced a great agricultural reform. The state machine and tractor stations, a cornerstone of Soviet agriculture, were to be dissolved and the agricultural machines sold to the collective farms.

The Russian machine and tractor stations (MTS) were founded in 1927 by the director of a state farm, A. M. Markovich, in the Odessa Region. His proposal to extend them to the whole Soviet Union was taken up by Stalin, and in 1930 and 1931 encouraged by Kaganovich. The MTS soon became an inseparable part of the Soviet system of agriculture, though their founder fell a victim to the purge of the thirties.

On the basis of contracts with the collective farms the employees of the MTS ploughed the *kolkhoz* fields: they were paid mainly in kind, but to a smaller extent in cash. In contrast with the collective farms the MTS were state organizations, 'responsible for the leading organizational activity in the development of the whole of collective agriculture'. Their directors were appointed by the Soviet Ministry of Agriculture. The deputy directors were political leaders as well and responsible for the political work of the stations.

The 'leading role' of the machine and tractor stations *vis-à-vis* the collective farms was justified by the principle of the two forms of property in a socialist society. The 'lower' form is co-operative ownership—the collective farms and artisans' and craftmen's co-operative; the 'higher' form is state ownership 'by the people', as of all factories and other undertakings, banks, means of transport, state trading organizations, and the machine and tractor stations. This principle was made part of the law: theft of state property is punished more severely than that of collective property.

The subordination of collective farmers to the functionaries of the machine and tractor stations was by no means popular under Stalin. Not only the collective farmers were opposed to it; there were also doubts in the higher spheres of the Party. In 1952 Zanina and Venzher, two of the authors of the textbook *Political Economy*, suggested dissolving the machine and tractor stations and selling the machines to the collective farms. 'It is clear that this must not be done,' replied Stalin briefly. 'With their proposal to sell the MTS to the collective farms comrades Zanina and Venzher are taking a retrograde step and attempting to turn back the wheel of history.'

At the Twentieth Party Congress Khrushchev still demanded that the MTS should be made more profitable and transformed into a model socialist enterprise. The Party Congress resolution declared that the responsibility of the MTS for the fulfilment of agricultural plans and for mechanization must be increased.

In the autumn of 1957 the rulers of Russia must have decided on a change of policy. The first indication of this came in an article by Ivan Vinichenko in *Octyabr*,[1] giving an account of a conversation with Zanina and Venzher, whom Stalin had criticized so severely, about the dissolution of the MTS. 'Would it not therefore be more expedient to concentrate the means of production which are now in the hands of the MTS in the hands of the collective farm? Is this solution not dictated by life itself?' asked Vinichenko and then described more conversations with agricultural officials who were suddenly treating the dissolution of the MTS, hitherto sacrosanct, as a matter of course. The last conversation finished with the words: 'Well, you see . . . it seems that I am not the only one who thinks like this, and that is a good sign.' Evidently Vinichenko had been chosen to prepare the new step psychologically; both the next number of *Octyabr* and the agricultural journal *Selskoye Khozyaistvo* of 29 January 1958 familiarized their readers with the same idea.

On 22 January 1958 Khrushchev in a speech to agricultural officials in Minsk officially proposed the dissolution of the MTS and the sale of their machines to the collective farms. The reorganization of the MTS was on the agenda of the plenary session of the Central Committee of 25 to 26 February 1958. In a speech on the development of the collective farms and the reorganization of the machine and tractor stations

[1] No. 11, 1957.

Khrushchev explained his proposal in detail. Just as on the occasion of the industrial reform he said that the MTS had played a useful part in the past. The proposal of Zanina and Venzher had been wrong in 1952 because at that time the collective farms were not yet firmly enough established to take over the machines. But as a result of the measures taken since 1953 the situation in the Soviet economy had changed considerably. Since then 908,000 tractors (in terms of 15 h.p. units), almost 300,000 combine harvesters, and more than 450,000 lorries had been put at the disposal of agriculture. The number of agricultural specialists with technical or higher education had risen from 83,000 on 1 July 1953 to 277,000 on 1 December 1957, the number of Party members active on collective farms had risen by 230,000 between 1954 and 1958. The collective farms were now economically consolidated and more robust politically thanks to the recruitment of these technicians and administrators. Therefore the time had come to sell the machines of the MTS to the collective farms. The MTS should be dissolved step by step and replaced by technical repair stations (RTS). The 186,000 officials and technicians employed by the MTS at the beginning of 1958 should be taken over by the collective farms on the same material conditions.

After this the so-called people's discussion about the reorganization of the machine and tractor stations began. From 1 to 25 March 1958 a total of 576,000 meetings attended by more than 49 million people took place. Three million people spoke at these meetings, the newspapers received 126,000 contributions on the reorganization of the MTS, of which 102,000 were published.

In form and tendency the campaign resembled the 'people's discussion' on the industrial reform in the spring of 1957, with the difference that this time the bulk of the participants were small officials and even ordinary *kolkhoz* members. Time and again the press contained contributions by *kolkhoz* chairmen, brigade leaders, secretaries of the Party organizations in the *kolkhozy*, accountants, engineers, and agronomists. The *kolkhoz* members and *kolkhozy* administrators demanded as speedy and thorough a dissolution of the MTS as possible, whereas a number of MTS officials, engineers, planners, and academic persons demanded the retention and strengthening of the new repair stations. The ideological importance of the change was dealt with by Mitin and Fedoseyev, who made great efforts to prove that the new theory did not contradict the theory of the two forms of property. This was also expressly emphasized at a conference of members of the Institute for Philosophy of the Russian Academy of Sciences.

At the end of March, with a meeting of the Supreme Soviet at which Khrushchev made a further long speech about the reorganization of the MTS, the discussion came to an end. Khrushchev's demands were embodied in the law passed by the Supreme Soviet on 31 March 1958, which in seven clauses authorized the sale of agricultural machines to the collective farms, provided for the setting up of repair stations (which were to operate on a commercial basis), and promised loans to financially weak *kolkhozy*.

According to official plans the transformation of the MTS into technical repair stations (RTS) was to take place gradually over a period of two to three years. Some of the MTS were to continue in order to help economically weak collective farms. The sale of the machines was to take place in an organized manner. Since the end of February valuation commissions had been travelling round the country to determine the prices to be paid for the machines.

But already after Khrushchev's first announcement on 22 January there had been celebrations and drinking parties in many villages. The sales of agricultural machines went on at great speed. The Ukrainian district Party secretary, Nikolaiev, reported in *Pravda* on 8 April: 'We have completed the sale of the MTS machinery. All 305 collective farms have taken over the machines they needed.' Similar reports were published almost daily. The valuation commissions, composed of the director and chief engineer of the MTS, the *kolkhoz* chairman, the leader of the tractor brigade, and representatives of the local branch of the agricultural bank, under pressure from the *kolkhoz* peasants, set the prices of the machines much below their real value. Machines which were difficult to sell were even priced for scrap. The MTS directors and their collaborators, formerly the rulers of the villages, found themselves deprived of their power and began to court the sympathy of their future employers, the collective-farm peasants.

Even the less prosperous collective farms which were to have been maintained by the MTS for many years to come took part in the rush to buy machinery. Collectives short of funds made haste to merge themselves with others in the same situation, and pooled their liquid resources to buy the machines.

As early as March regional Party conferences were held in various Union Republics to deal with the critical situation. On 20 April the Party and state leadership was forced to step in. In a joint resolution it was declared that 'the sale of agricultural machines at artificially low prices was against the interests of the state'. Prices must not be fixed at levels that could involve the state in a loss. State officials were to receive greater powers in the valuation commissions, in which hitherto the representatives of the MTS and the collective farms had decided the issue. The chairmen of the district soviets should preside over the commissions, and representatives of the regional authorities, the agricultural ministries, and the state banks should be co-opted. It was urgently demanded that the MTS should be transformed into technical repair stations, which were not only to repair the collective farm machines, but also to help the collective peasants in the use of their machine parks and to assist them with various jobs; in particular they were to be responsible for the loan of RTS machines to the *kolkhozy* and the supply of spare parts. In this way the authorities tried to prevent the complete destruction of the MTS and to make the collective farms dependent, as they had been before, on a state institution. But the Central Committee resolution of 20 April came too late. The dissolution of the MTS could no longer be stopped.

THE REFORM OF THE PROCUREMENT SYSTEM

On 17 and 18 June 1958 the Central Committee decided to abolish compulsory deliveries from the collective farms and to replace the multitude of administrative prices by standard ones for agricultural products. Until June 1958 there was in the Soviet Union a thoroughly confused system of state procurement of agricultural products. In the first place the collective farms were obliged to deliver fixed quantities of certain agricultural products to the state. For these deliveries they received very low 'procurement prices'. Secondly, they had to pay compensation in kind to the machine and tractor stations. Thirdly, they delivered to the state products beyond their obligations at higher prices. Fourth, there was the 'contract system', which committed the *kolkhozy* to deliver certain other agricultural products—for example, flax, sugar beet, hemp— to the state. For these, 'contract prices' were paid of which there were two kinds; normal contract prices for the quantities prescribed in the plan, and higher prices or premia for deliveries beyond this amount.

The complicated nature of this system necessitated a vast bureaucratic machine. Tens of thousands of people were engaged in the procurement agencies. As the procurement quotas usually had to be determined centrally many collective farms had to deliver or sell grain and potatoes to the state even though conditions were suitable for the cultivation of more valuable products. Prices were usually fixed very low and pro- vided little incentive to the collective farms. Those which only just managed to fulfil their plan could sell their produce only for those low procurement and buying prices, whereas the collectives which overfulfilled their plan were able to sell their produce at the very favourable contract prices with premia. Thus the procurement system caused the state to obtain its agricultural products most cheaply from the backward col- lectives and to pay most for the produce of advanced and successful collective farms.

In 1956 the central statistical administration in the Tashkent Region conducted an investigation. Twenty-seven collective farms, including eight prosperous, nine medium, and ten relatively poor farms were examined to discover what prices they received on the average for delivering 100 kilogrammes of cotton. The inquiry showed that the prosperous collective farms received 398 roubles, the medium ones 331 roubles, and the poorest 285 roubles. These differences of course affected the incomes of the individual *kolkhoz* peasants, who in the prosper- ous *kolkhozy* received 27 roubles (in cash and in kind) per unit of labour, in the medium 17, and in the poor *kolkhozy* 14 roubles.

The shortcomings of the procurement system had been obvious for many years. Yet even at the meeting in June 1958, at which its reform was announced, Khrushchev was relatively restrained in his criticism. As in introducing other reforms, he did not say that the existing system had been wrong, but that conditions had changed: the collective farms had established themselves, he said, the technical production of agriculture had been considerably improved, methods of planning had encouraged initiative, and so on. Only now were there the necessary conditions for a fundamental reform.

It was decided to abolish compulsory deliveries and payments in kind to the machine and tractor stations completely, and to carry out all procurement through purchase only by the state. The premia paid under the contract system were also abolished. The place of the four old types of procurement system was taken by a unified form of purchase, the place of the old differential prices by a uniform system of buying without premia.

The new prices were to be worked out on the basis of the production of medium collective farms. They were to be based on the average returns of several years and to be higher than the former prices, because the old prices (until 1953) did not correspond to the expenditure of labour and materials, and, as Khrushchev said, 'did not permit the minimum requirements for the development of the co-operative economy'.

The plenary session in June decreed that collective farms' arrears of compulsory deliveries, payments in kind, and contract deliveries should be cancelled. It was also decided to make collective farms advances, interest free, on produce which was due. The late arrival of money had hindered planning by collective farms and had made regular advances to their peasants impossible.

Finally the disadvantageous position of the collective farms in the purchase of machines, implements, and fuel was also abolished. Hitherto the state had sold technical products and fuel at two prices—a low price for state farms and a high price for collective ones. Uniform prices were now established.

The June meeting promoted Nikolai Podgorny and Dmitri Polyansky to be candidate members of the Party Praesidium. Both were Party functionaries closely connected with Khrushchev to whom they owed their rise. Podgorny—a Russian from the Ukraine, a member of the Party since 1930—had until Stalin's death been regional secretary in Kharkov; in March

1954 he became Second Party Secretary and in December 1957 succeeded Kirichenko (who moved into the central apparatus in Moscow) as First Party Secretary in the Ukraine. Dmitri Polyansky also came from the Party in the Ukraine; a Party member since 1939, he was at first regional secretary of the Crimea (1954–5), then in Chkalov (1955 to March 1957) and Krasnodar (March 1957 to March 1958). In April 1958 he became Prime Minister of the RSFSR.

THE PARTY APPARATUS AND ECONOMIC QUESTIONS

In the course of 1958 the Soviet leaders were again and again forced to consider the working methods of the *sovnarkhozy*. The economic effects of the reorganization were satisfactory, but the Party leaders were afraid that control over economic events in the country might slip from their hands. They constantly pointed out that the good of the state must come before local interests. In the spring of 1958 G. Yenyutin, formerly Party Secretary in Kamensk, became Chairman of the Commission for Soviet Control. This super-controlling authority was in the middle of May 1958 empowered to take strong disciplinary measures against *sovnarkhoz* chairmen who did not fall in line with the directives from Moscow. Local economic leaders could be sentenced to fines of up to three months' wages, and if they repeated the offence could even be handed over to the courts.

At the beginning of August 1958 there appeared in the Central Committee journal *Partinaya Zhizn* an article entitled 'Concerning crass violations of state discipline and appearances of localism', in which eight *sovnarkhoz* chairmen were attacked. The chief planner of Karaganda, Onika, was accused of having pruned the building projects planned by the central authorities of almost 40 million roubles and of having used the money for the building of rest homes, sanatoria, swimming pools, a theatre, a technical mining school, and a circus, as well as for rewards to his colleagues. Similar accusations were made against the chairmen of the *sovnarkhozy* of Gorki, Kuibyshev, Dniepropetrovsk, of Krasnoyarsk, and of the Altai Region. In many places the Party organizations were even said to have supported the economic leaders in their 'localism'. The Central Committee of the Party in the Union Republics were exhorted to increase their control of the economic organization, to take all 'localist deviationists' to task, 'to fight an implacable fight for the strictest preservation of state discipline' and to 'stop every attempt to put local interests above the general interests of the state'. On 13 August even *Pravda* discussed this problem in its leading article.

To counter the 'localism' of the *sovnarkhozy* central control was again strongly advocated from the beginning of 1958. A decree of the Praesidium of the Supreme Soviet of the USSR of 16 July 1958 considerably extended the authority of trade union committees. The latter were empowered to enforce, among other things, the observance of labour legislation and work norms, and without their consent managers were not allowed to dismiss factory or office workers or to fix piece-rates or productivity norms. But, most important, trade union committees were given the right to demand the dismissal or punishment of managers who did not fulfil the obligations defined in the collective contracts, who behaved in a bureau-cratic manner, or violated the labour laws. Managers and local authorities were obliged to 'take the opinion of trade union officials into account' when making senior staff appointments. By so extending the trade unions' authority the Party officials obviously intended to use them as an additional weapon against 'localist' managers. The leaders were clearly anxious to find a compromise between economic requirements, local initiative, and economic incentives on the one hand and central political control by the Party on the other.

The aim of Khrushchev and his friends—the modernization of the economy under the leadership of the Party—could, however, be achieved only if suitable people could be found for the lower official ranks. The Party 'apparachik' of the Stalin period, with his restricted knowledge of economic matters, his penchant for campaigns, agitators' speeches, and ideological training, was not up to the new tasks. The urgent need now was for all-round administrators as ruthlessly determined as were Stalin's functionaries, but with more contact with the population, more initiative, and more expert knowledge of practical economic matters.

In the spring of 1957, during the industrial reform, the Central Committee of the Party convened a conference of directors and Party secretaries of all the Party schools of the USSR: Aristov and Pospelov made the chief speeches. Remarkable facts about the change in the system of training the Party élite emerge from the report of this conference.[1]

The length of training was extended from two to four years, and the number of students at the Party staff college was to be increased to 16,000. The study of Soviet Economics, Agriculture, and Industrial Production was introduced in all Party schools. Lecture courses on the formation and structure of the Party and the Soviet state were particularly emphasized; they were to prepare Party and state officials for the managing of the economy and to organize the Party better. People were warned against both 'narrow-minded contempt for theory' and 'abstract theoretical discussions'. The aim of the Party schools should be 'not merely to provide the participants with a certain knowledge, but to train them to become ideologically sound, assiduous, high-principled Party officials who understood Party policy and were able to put it into practice'. The most conspicuous characteristics of Party officials should be 'the greatest conscientiousness, a feeling of responsibility for the field allocated to them, discipline, and modesty'. The Party leaders' aim in extending Party training was obviously to replace the officials of the old Stalinist 'apparatus' who had distinguished themselves by harshness in political discussion, but not by expert economic knowledge.

Only in the autumn of 1958, with the production of the 'Party Workers' Handbook', which contained a number of hitherto unpublished decisions of the Party leaders, did it become clear how much work had been done in this respect. As early as 1956, 29 four-year schools and 13 three-year schools had been opened. In law the Party schools rank equally with the universities and the student has to take a state examination to complete his course. From the curricula of these Party schools published in the 'Party Workers' Handbook' it emerged that the student has to attend 3,200 hours' teaching on 22 subjects. But only 1,400 hours are devoted to political and ideological subjects: Political economy (300 hours), dialectical and historical materialism (200), Party history (200), Party structure, the structure of the Soviet State, and the foundations

[1] *Partinaya Zhizn*, No. 10, 1957.

of Soviet law. The 1,800 hours devoted to practical economics cover such subjects as the planning and methods of production of a factory, an agricultural undertaking, or of a district or region, statistics, book-keeping, and the most important technical processes. One hundred hours are devoted to questions of animal husbandry alone.

However far-sighted these plans of the Soviet leaders may be the question remains whether Party officials, once they have been informed on economic questions, will not abandon their attachment to the Party and assume the attitudes of the economists.

THE CAMPAIGN AGAINST 'REVISIONISM'

In 1958, however, Khrushchev not only had to overcome domestic problems, but was also faced with great difficulties in the international communist movement. Although revisionism had been condemned at the conference in November 1957 there continued to be openly expressed opinions in the international communist movement in favour of greater independence from Moscow, a pronounced retreat from Stalinism, and a creative development of the heritage of Marxist ideas.

Well-known communists left the Communist Parties of many countries and founded their own papers and organizations. In Italy there appeared *Corrispondenza socialista* run by Eugenio Reale, and *Passato e presente*, edited by Antonio Giolitti. In France reformist ideas were presented in *Voies nouvelles* directed by Lefèbvre, and in *La nouvelle réforme*, *Tribune de discussion*, and *La Commune*. In Great Britain communists who had resigned from the Party had founded the periodical *The New Reasoner* in 1956–7, and in Brazil a reformist faction, which called itself '*Corrente renovadera*' and was led by Agildo Barrato, left the most powerful Communist Party of Latin America. Strong reformist currents were also noticeable in the Dutch and Danish Communist Parties; in Denmark Aksel Larsen, its chairman for many years, left the Party with many followers and founded his own organization.

Reformist tendencies also existed in the communist world. Dr. Wolfgang Harich and his friends in East Germany prepared a programme outlining the aims of the oppositional communists. They demanded that 'Marxist-Leninist' theory should be supplemented by the contributions of Trotsky and Bukharin and by Yugoslavia's experience. The tyranny of the functionaries must be broken and democracy restored within the Party. Workers' councils on the Yugoslav model should be set up in industry and collective farming no longer be compulsory.

At the beginning of 1958 Moscow began its campaign against all this. On 17 January 1958 *Pravda* pointed to the development of certain 'wavering elements' in the communist world movement who rejected the foundamental principles of Marxism. *Moskva*[1] wrote: 'Revisionism, like national communism, must be refuted by ideology and destroyed. . . . Either we bury revisionism, or revisionism will kill us. There is no third solution.'

In the second half of March the Yugoslav communists published the draft of a new Party programme. It was sent to all Communist Parties together with an invitation to attend the Seventh Congress of the League of Communists of Yugoslavia which was to open in Ljubljana, the capital of Slovenia, on 22 April 1958.

In April *Kommunist*[2] contained a detailed review of the Yugoslav draft programme by the well-known Soviet ideologists Fedoseyev, Pomelov, and Cheprakov, which was immediately published in translation in all communist countries. The Russians came to the conclusion that the Yugoslav programme reflected the old differences of opinion between the Yugoslav communists and the Soviet Union. On 21 April 1958, one day before the opening of the Yugoslav Party Congress, Pospelov made further accusations against the Yugoslav communists in the main speech at the Lenin memorial celebration in Moscow. Not even extracts from the draft of the Yugoslav Party programme were published in the communist world. The Yugoslavs, on the other hand, had published the article by Fedoseyev, Pomelov, and Cheprakov in a Serbo-Croat translation and given a copy to every delegate to the Party Congress.

After this, it was not surprising that not only the ruling parties of the communist world, but almost all the Communist Parties elsewhere, boycotted the Yugoslav Party Congress. The Danish and Norwegian communists were the only ones to send

[1] No. 1, 1958.   [2] No. 6, 1958.

delegations, while the Italian, Indonesian, and Tunisian Parties were represented by observers. The communist countries sent only their ambassadors—the most extreme form of disapproval they could express in the circumstances. When, on the second day of the Congress, the Yugoslav leader, Alexander Ranković, spoke of certain people in responsible positions in the neighbouring communist states 'who are again beginning to sharpen the old, rusty weapons of the Cominform', the communist diplomatists, with the exception of the Polish ambassador, left the Congress.

After several days of deliberation the Yugoslav Party Congress adopted the draft programme which was translated into sixteen languages. Since then, the programme has been the target for constantly recurring attacks from all the other Communist Parties of the world. Walter Ulbricht, at the Fifth Party Congress of the SED in July 1958, called it the 'revisionist counter-programme'.[1] In fact, the Yugoslav Party programme contains some of the most important oppositional ideas in the international communist movement.

The first thing which is noticeable about it is a new assessment of modern capitalism. The Parties obedient to Moscow take little or no cognisance of changes in capitalism and the most they speak of is a 'sharpening of the contradictions'. The Yugoslav Party programme, on the other hand, examines the changes in the economic structure of the Western world; in particular the nationalization of whole branches of industry, growth of investments by the state, the restriction of the powers of private capitalists, and the development of regional and international economic organizations. The Yugoslav Party programme appraised this as a strengthening of collectivist tendencies in capitalism; 'the state finds itself forced to take particular measures to control private capital', and as a result 'private control of capitalist property is limited'.

Development in the direction of socialism might take many different forms. In the highly developed industrial countries, for example, great importance attached to the participation of the workers in the management of nationalized industries.

In present world conditions the most varied forces had become agents of the development towards socialism—among

[1] *Neues Deutschland*, 11 July 1958.

others, trade unions, national revolutionary movements, social democratic parties. 'The view that the Communist Parties monopolize socialism and that socialism finds expression only in those Parties is theoretically inaccurate and practically harmful.' It was particularly in the activities of the Communist Parties that serious short-comings had shown themselves. They do not realize 'that the conditions of the struggle of the working class have essentially changed in the meantime'.

Much space is occupied by a discussion of relations within the international workers' movement. The Moscow thesis that the international workers' movement must be centralized is rejected. 'For a certain time,' indeed, one country or Party might play a bigger role, 'but that does not mean that that country has the right to claim a special position in the workers' movement.' The forms of collaboration in the international workers' movement cannot be prescribed in advance. Instead of the leading role of one Party, relations on a basis of equality were to be recommended between the individual Parties and organizations of the workers' movement. Collaboration on a basis of equality must not be restricted to communists, but must also extend to socialist Parties of different tendencies and to other progressive Parties and movements.

The Yugoslav Party programme enthusiastically supports the idea of different roads to socialism. The aims of socialism were realized by nations 'in different ways and with different means'. Nothing was more dangerous than 'clinging stubbornly to outmoded forms and methods'. Not only the road to socialism, but also the forms of socialism will be different in the various countries, depending on differences in historical development.

Contrary to the Soviet view that state property and central-ized economic planning provide the essential conditions for socialism, the Yugoslav communists declared that national-ization was only a transitional phenomenon; the goal was the self-government of the producers of the economy. Socialist planning did not mean 'that the whole of society should be transformed into a mechanism which prescribes for everybody in detail what he should do', a state in which 'man ceases to create'. Even the most perfect economic plan could not exhaust the innumerable possibilities which 'are offered by the spon-taneous development of economic forces'. Socialist planning must, therefore, limit itself to 'determining the fundamental proportions in production and distribution' and 'to isolated measures of regulation by the state'; within this framework it must guarantee free initiative to economic enterprises under market conditions.

In contrast to the Soviet view that a ruling Communist Party has not only the right but the duty to direct the arts and sciences the Yugoslav Party programme said that every attempt 'to transform the arts and sciences into tools of the political interests of the day' should be rejected. It could not be the task of the Communist Party to be 'a dogmatic judge with regard to tendencies, schools, and styles in science and art'.

Opinions contrary to Soviet doctrine are also contained in the section on the role of the Communist Party. The 'leading role˘ of the Party' is the core of Soviet ideology. The ruling Communist Party describes itself as the 'heart and brain of our epoch' and regulates all aspects of social life. According to the Yugoslav communists the 'proclamation of the absolute monopoly of political power by the Communist Party as a universal and eternal principle' is an 'untenable dogma'. All administrative pressure upon socialist relations should be rejected. 'Socialism cannot subordinate man's personal happiness to any higher aims, because the highest aim of socialism is precisely man's happiness.'

The publication of the Yugoslav Party programme was followed by a flood of anti-Yugoslav articles in all the leading newspapers of the communist world. The articles in the Chinese Party press were particularly sharp in tone, the Polish papers noticeably reticent at first. But press campaigns were not the end. On 27 May the Soviet Foreign Minister, Gromyko, informed the Yugoslav government that the Soviet Union would postpone the execution of the economic treaties of 12 January and 1 August 1956 for four or five years. A visit to Yugoslavia planned for the Soviet President, Voroshilov, was cancelled. On 3 June 1958 Khrushchev said at the Party Congress of the Bulgarian Communist Party that the Cominform resolution of 1948 against the Yugoslav communists had been right in principle. He accused the Yugoslav communists of having injured the cause of socialism by their attitude during the Hungarian uprising. The Yugoslav embassy in Budapest had become a refuge for traitors belonging to the Nagy-Losonczy group.

A fortnight later, on 17 June 1958—the fifth anniversary of the rising in Eastern Germany—the conclusion of the trial of the Hungarian Prime Minister, Imre Nagy, and eight of his closest collaborators was announced. In the judgment there were several references to Nagy's close relations with the Yugoslav Communists. Nagy and three of his closest collaborators were sentenced to death while the other five were given long prison sentences. The death sentences had been carried out before the sentences were published.

DIFFERENCES WITH PEKING

At the beginning of 1958 it appeared that the Chinese Party leaders, who until then had by and large kept to the Soviet model—nationalization of industry, collectivization, priority of heavy industry, five-year plans—were beginning to deviate from this course. Peking proclaimed the slogan of the 'great leap forward', which was soon followed by the slogan of 'walking on both legs'. No longer were only central enterprises and central industries to be built, but local small and medium industries should also be developed with their own resources. Millions of workers must be mobilized. The 700,000 collective farms with an average of 323 families proved insufficient for this. The Chinese Party leaders therefore decided to combine the existing collective farms into vast economic units called people's communes. These represent a completely new form of organization in a communist state, because they are not restricted, like Soviet farms, to agriculture, but combine industry, trade, mining, handicrafts, agriculture and animal husbandry, education and health, and even have their own militia. On the average thirty collective farms were combined into one people's commune. Members had to hand over the whole of the private property remaining to them, their personal plot of land, houses, fields, cattle. Work and free time were regulated in military fashion. Communal kitchens, crèches, shoe-repair, and sewing shops were established to free women from housework and to make it possible to use them in production. In some communes even money was abolished.

When on the 29 August 1958 the Chinese Party leaders

officially adopted the resolution on the formation of the people's communes,[1] the process was already in full swing. The resolution envisaged a period of from three to six years for the transformation, but as early as 30 September Radio Peking announced that 90·4 per cent. of all farms had been joined into people's communes. At the end of October the first people's communes were formed in the towns. In two important articles in *Hongqi*[2] the Chinese Party ideologist, Chen Po-ta, starting from an almost forgotten quotation from the Communist Manifesto, maintained that with the formation of the people's communes the 'transition to communism' had begun in China. In fact Marx and Engels in the Communist Manifesto had demanded—although expressly for 'advanced countries'—the 'unification of the working of agriculture and industry' and the 'unification of education with material production'. Chen Po-ta said that this was now being realized in the people's communes and that China was thus in a state of transition to the higher form of socialism, to communism.

This claim touched Moscow on the raw because the leading role of Russia in the communist world is justified principally by the argument that the Soviet Union has been in the period of 'gradual transition to communism' since 1917, whereas all other countries are only 'building up socialism'.

Thus Peking's claims were received with reserve by Moscow and the other communist countries. The Soviet press published the Chinese resolution without the comment customary on important occasions; the Chinese slogan of 'transition to communism' was not mentioned at all. But articles did appear in the Soviet press in which it was emphasized that the transition to communism could only be achieved on the level of the most modern technique. On 30 October *Izvestia* published an article by the Chinese Politburo candidate member Po-i-Po which among other things referred to the 'realization of communism' in China. *Izvestia* translated this as 'the realization of the people's communes'. And the Russian slogans to celebrate 7 November continued to describe China as a country which was 'building up socialism'.

By Soviet ideological standards the interpretation was justified. The transition to communism presupposes a level of

[1] Published on 10 September.   [2] *Red Flag*.

production which makes possible the satisfaction of all human wants. In China, where industrialization had only just begun, there could be no question of this. But the Chinese regarded communism primarily as a new ordering of social relations which would provide the techniques of production needed for the 'higher phase of socialism'. There are many indications that with their people's communes the Chinese communists hoped to create a model for all other underdeveloped countries in Asia of how to overcome social and political backwardness in one 'great leap'. This meant disputing Moscow's claim to leadership in Asia, and did not go unnoticed in Russia. In the periodical *Voprosy Filosofi*[1] the Soviet ideologist Stepanyan, noted that there were two economic zones in the socialist camp: the European and the Asiatic. The countries of both areas would enter upon the phase of communism together but—and this expresses unambiguously the Soviet claim to leadership—the European area would be the first to reach the goal.

At the beginning of December Khrushchev himself joined in the controversy. On 1 December he told the American senator Humphrey that the Chinese people's communes were retrograde. A similar attempt has been made in the Soviet Union soon after the October Revolution but it had served no purpose owing to the lack of the material incentives required by modern production.

Moscow's criticism in December 1958, of Chinese policy coincided with hesitation in China itself. So much hasty regimentation appears to have met with widespread resistance. Even among the Chinese Party leaders probably not everyone favoured the radical, military policy of communization. Of the twenty-six members and candidate members of the Chinese Politburo, Mao Tse-tung, Liu Shao-chi, and Chen Po-ta were particularly in the public eye during the campaign. Mao and Liu travelled about the country making speeches in favour of an early 'transition to communism'. Other Party leaders, like Prime Minister Chou En-lai, Vice-Premier Chu-Teh, and the Secretary-General of the Party, Teng Hsiao-ping, were noticeably reticent.

At the beginning of December it became known that hundreds of inspection groups had been sent to country districts to

[1] No. 10, 1958.

examine the situation in the people's communes and to listen to the peasants' complaints. This indicated an impending change, which was, in fact, decided upon at a meeting of the Chinese Party leaders in the middle of December in Vuchang.

There they withdrew the formula of the 'transition to communism'. It was acknowledged that the development of a modern industry would need fifteen or twenty years or longer and that communist transformation depended on the development of production and on the level of political consciousness, and not on 'the wishful thinking of some Party members'. It was openly stated in the resolution that there were differences of opinion about the people's communes. For the present it was important 'to establish', as quickly as possible, an agreed view on the people's communes both among Party members and the people. At the same meeting it was announced that Mao Tse-tung was no longer a candidate for the office of President.

Soon after the meeting in Vuchang, Moscow dropped its objections to the Chinese people's communes and recognized them as a legitimate form of Chinese communism. But the deeper causes of the differences between Moscow and Peking could not be removed. In spite of many important characteristics common to both the two great communist powers it is impossible to overlook contracts between them which may always lead to fresh conflict.

The difference between Moscow and Peking in 1958 had underlined a fact which had already found clear expression during the campaign against revisionism. There is no longer one centre of the communist movement; there are three: Belgrade, the centre of revisionism which is impelled to develop the ideas of Marx and Engels creatively and to follow new roads which deviate from Soviet communism; Moscow, still the most powerful centre, which is trying to adapt Stalin's ideas to the conditions of a modern industrial society without questioning the authority of the Party; and, finally, Peking, which offers a more radical, military variety of communism, because it aims at a more rapid social revolution.

KHRUSHCHEV'S REFORM OF THE SCHOOLS

During the summer and autumn of 1958 Khrushchev's third reform, the transformation of the educational system, was the main theme of Soviet domestic politics. He announced it at the thirteenth Komsomol congress on 18 April 1958 when he criticized the ten-class school system because it prepared the rising generation only for study and not for practical work in industry and agriculture. In 1957, Khrushchev said, 700,000 and from 1953 to 1956 about 2·2 million children leaving school had not been admitted to universities. But they had looked on work in factories, collective farms, and state farms 'as an insult'.

During the Stalin era the main purpose of Soviet schools had in fact been to prepare people for the universities. To encourage this the Nineteenth Party Congress in October 1952 decided that the ten-class school system should become compulsory for all children. It was to be introduced first in the towns and later in all rural areas as well. But the need for experts with university training was no longer so great. On the other hand the need for middle-grade specialists and for highly trained skilled workers was growing. The extension of the ten-class system, moreover, produced more students than could be absorbed by the universities. As they regarded themselves already as candidates for higher posts they felt little desire to work in a factory or a collective farm. At first the Party leadership tried to overcome this problem by a campaign. From 1953 to 1956 it was repeatedly pointed out that manual was as good as intellectual work, and those leaving ten-class schools were asked to go into factories. Those who refused were ridiculed as *bieloruchki* (white-handed).

After that technical training was included step by step in the curricula of the ten-class schools. In the first four school years one hour a week had to be spent in the school work-shops; this was doubled in the fifth, sixth, and seventh classes. Finally in the last three school years two hours a week were set aside for practical work in agriculture and industry and an additional sixty to eighty hours a year. Laboratories and workshops were set up in all seven- and ten-class schools.

The Twentieth Party Congress once again emphatically demanded that schools should concentrate more on technical training. New subjects, it was said, should be introduced to provide a basic knowledge of technology and production and pupils systematically enrolled to work in factories and farms.

While this was not enough really to prepare the students for practical work in production, technical training took up so much time that preparation for the university was neglected. Hence a change-over to an eleven-class school providing all-round education was considered already in 1956.

On 21 September 1958 Khrushchev made public a memorandum approved by the Party Praesidium 'On the strengthening of the links between school and life and the further development of the system of public education in the country'. Seven weeks later, on 16 November, the Central Committee of the CPSU and the Council of Ministers of the USSR published formulations with the same title. In essence they corresponded with Khrushchev's memorandum, but were more detailed although omitting certain passages.

The preparation of the rising generation for useful work was to be the main task of Soviet schools. They must 'train people with an all-round education, making them capable of systematic manual work and giving them a desire to be useful to society'. All children were to receive secondary education, to be given in two stages. The first was to be an eight-class school, compulsory for all, a preliminary technical school, providing general education which focused its main attention 'on the study of the foundations of the sciences, technical education, and the training of workers'. The second stage should provide full secondary education, from fifteen or sixteen onwards. Various types of teaching establishments were envisaged to combine theoretical instruction with productive work:

1. Schools for young people working in factories or on the land, so-called evening (shift) secondary schools. They were to provide those who had attended full-time schools for eight years with a complete secondary school education in evening classes and to extend their professional qualifications.

2. Further training courses to combine secondary education with specific vocational training. Theoretical teaching and work in production should alternate with periods adapted to the requirements of local industry or agriculture.

3. 'Technika' and other middle-grade technical schools, providing general and specialized secondary education for those who had attended an eight-year school.

Pupils who show special talent for certain artistic or scientific subjects should be able to attend special secondary schools providing preparation for the relevant specialized studies. The network of boarding schools should be extended and organized on the model of the eight-class schools or the further vocational training centres. (At the Twenty-First Party Congress Khrushchev cited boarding schools together with canteens and kindergartens as examples to show that a higher communist way of life was already developing.)

In his memorandum Khrushchev categorically demanded that 'all over the country all those leaving school should go into production whether in towns, villages or workers' settlements; no one must get out of it . . . neither the parents' position nor their requests shall free anybody from productive work'. Soviet institutions of higher education should in future accept only young people who had already done practical work in industry or agriculture. At most of these colleges, and in particular at institutes of technology, practical work should continue without interruption during the first terms, and tuition should be given at evening classes or through correspondence courses. Only from the third year onwards should students be freed from their practical work for three days a week, and during the last two years they might, according to the memorandum, 'possibly' devote their entire time to their studies.

The teaching of foreign languages in the non-Russian Union Republics was to be examined. Until then children in the non-Russian Union Republics had to learn three languages: their mother tongue, Russian, and one foreign language (German, English or French). Now Russian and national schools were to be set up, between which parents could choose. In the Russian schools the national language would be an optional subject and in the national schools the Russian language. In schools where 'the necessary conditions do not exist' foreign languages were no longer to be compulsory subjects.

Within the school reform, as with the other two big reforms associated with Khrushchev's name—the industrial reform of 1957 and the dissolution of the machine and tractor stations in the spring of 1958—the Party leaders tried to solve several problems at once. Immediate economic interests obviously stood in the foreground. The Soviet Union had developed into a modern industrial society in which growth would in future depend less on an expansion of the labour force in industry and more on improvements in efficiency. The economy needed a great number of highly qualified experts and middle-grade specialists who were to be supplied by giving the younger generation a general training in the skills of production.

Political considerations probably also affected the school reform. In the last two decades the universities had been attended primarily by the sons and daughters of the industrial bureaucrats, technicians, and managers who thus strengthened their own position. The school reform was intended to deprive this section of society of the privilege it had enjoyed until then. Another political motive counted. Revisionist tendencies and oppositional ideas had in recent years found expression above all among university students. The Party leaders apparently believed that young people who had already done several years practical work in industry would be less susceptible to heretical ideas. Finally, the Russian leaders' aim with the school reform was to overcome the contrast between intellectual and manual work. The transcending of this contrast in the phase of transition to communism is an integral part of Soviet ideology.

Like earlier reforms the change in education was discussed in public. It was of course impossible to speak directly against it, but the contributions to the discussion published in the press betrayed considerable doubts among the public. The main objections came from teachers and scientists, who feared a lowering of standards. Professor Versilin, in *Literaturnaya Gazeta*, pointed out the disadvantages of work in industry. As an example he quoted the pupils of the 44th school in Leningrad who were employed as workers in a rope factory nearby: 'this shows that the technical fate of students depends on where they live.' Professor Semyonov writing in *Pravda* thought that before launching educational reform one should ask oneself in what condition our economy will be in ten to fifteen years from now. There would be automatic workshops, complicated machines, electronic computers, and design offices; therefore it was particularly necessary to train engineers, technicians, and designers.

Doubts were also voiced as to whether it might be harmful to the development of young people if they left school too early. The well-known educationist Medinski, said that at fifteen young people went through a decisive phase of their development during which the smallest mistake might do great harm. However great the educational value of practical work might be, the education of the young could not be vouched for without expert direction. 'It must give a warning against too much enthusiasm'; wrote Professor Kolbanovski in *Literaturnaya Gazeta*, 'a school in which children learn for three days in the classroom and work for three days in the factory entails many organizational problems'.

The President of the Academy of Sciences, Nesmeyanov, said that all those leaving school must have the right to go to a university if they have the necessary ability.[1] Some members of Leningrad University claimed that the acquisition of theoretical knowledge demanded uninterrupted study.[2] It was particularly interesting that Ilya Ehrenburg expressed doubts.[3] Specialization was no doubt necessary in production, he said, but in intellectual life it led to stagnation. One-sided development meant the loss of the power to think critically. Advanced technology must not be an end but only a means.

The 42-clause law published on 25 December 'On the fortification of the links between school and life and on the further development of the system of public education in the USSR' differs in some important aspects from Khrushchev's original draft. The law made no mention of the schools for talented pupils or the question of the language in which lessons were to be conducted in the non-Russian Republics. The school's main task was not described only as a preparation for work in production, but was said to include a raising of the level of education and the moral, physical, and artistic training of children. Teaching at school was to combine the provision of the foundations of learning with technical training and education for work.

The principles of the three types of school of the second stage, those for young people working in industry or on the land, polytechnic schools with lessons in production, and the 'technika', were also more carefully formulated. The three

---

[1] *Literaturnaya Gazeta*, 20 Dec. 1958.
[2] *Vestnik Vyshei Shkoly*, No. 10, 1958.
[3] *Komsomolskaya Pravda*, 30 Nov. 1958.

highest classes of the old ten-class school were to be transformed over the next three to five years into the new types of
schools, during which 'no deterioration whatsoever of school
services for the population can possibly be allowed'. Universities were to continue to receive a sufficient number of students
who had attended a ten-class school and therefore 'a certain
number of the existing secondary schools must be maintained
in each Union Republic in the transition period'.

Khrushchev's demand that the first terms at a university
should be spent in evening classes and correspondence courses
was not incorporated into the law; it merely said that university correspondence courses and evening classes should be improved and expanded. Although Khrushchev's main demands
were given legal force they were thus considerably modified.
This fact shows again that Khrushchev and the Party apparatus
are not all-powerful and that they have to take the interests
of the privileged classes into consideration.

THE 'PASTERNAK CASE'

In the autumn of 1958 the Soviet leaders were put into a
difficult position when Boris Pasternak, whose book *Dr.
Zhivago* had not been published in Russia, was awarded the
Nobel Prize. But the 'Pasternak Case' was only one link in the
chain of conflicts between the Party and the country's writers.

In August 1957 Khrushchev had defined his new cultural
policy, but difficulties nevertheless continued. The Party
hierarchy obviously did not want to carry the quarrel to
extremes. On 28 May it adopted a resolution (published on
8 June) modifying the judgement passed on 10 February 1948
on three operas. This judgement had been one of Zhdanov's
notorious decisions on aesthetic questions in the period 1946–8,
condemning the 'formalist tendency' in Russian music as
'hostile to the people' and deleterious to music: it had been
very unpopular among intellectuals. Now in 1958 the Party
leaders declared the verdict of ten years earlier to be unjust.
It had been wrong, they declared, to throw together gifted composers like Shostakovich, Prokofiev, Khachaturian, Shebalin,
Popov, and Myaskovski and to condemn them as anti-
social. Faulty tendencies had rightly been criticized in Mur-
adeli's *The Great Friendship*, Dankevich's *Bogdan Khmelnitski*,

and Zhukovski's *With All My Heart*, but there had been no reason for presenting them as examples of formalism. The mistaken judgement 'reflected Stalin's subjective approach to certain of our artists' works'. Remarkable was the claim that Malenkov, Molotov, and Beria had advised Stalin on musical questions at that time. Although the Party leaders did not by any means turn their back on Zhdanov's intimidation of writers and artists, this attitude represented a concession by the Party to the intellectuals of Russia.

A few weeks later the Party again had to busy itself with the writers. In the summer of 1958 a discussion on the relation of the Soviet writer to the present had arisen, in which some writers had enunciated the 'distance theory': an author who wants to write about contemporary problems must keep his distance from the passionate, disputed, and only partly solved problems of the day. On 17 August 1958 *Pravda* criticized the 'distance theory' as an invention of 'literary idlers' who forget the social significance of literature.

The controversy about the 'distance theory' was completely overshadowed in the second half of October 1958 by the sensational events of the 'Pasternak Case'. After Boris Pasternak had accepted the Nobel Prize the Party leadership mounted a campaign which finally induced him to give it up. On 25 October *Literaturnaya Gazeta* published a letter to Pasternak from the members of the editorial staff of the literary journal *Novy Mir*, summarizing the reasons why they did not wish to print the novel *Dr. Zhivago*. They criticized 'the spiritual attitude of the novel', its 'rejection of the socialist revolution'. The story of the life and death of Dr. Zhivago was a story of the life and death of the intelligentsia through the Revolution. The novel betrayed the author's view that the October Revolution had been a mistake and that the contribution of the intellectuals who supported it had been an irreparable catastrophe. The editorial board had arrived at the conclusion that the novel was a 'political sermon', a work 'which quite openly and from A to Z served certain political purposes'. Therefore there could be no question of publishing it in *Novy Mir*.

On 26 October *Pravda* published a furious article by the aged journalist Zazlavski against Pasternak. Editor of a banking journal before 1917 and a violent opponent of the Bolsheviks during the Revolution—Lenin had called him a villain—he became a leading Party journalist under Stalin and energetically supported all Stalin's campaigns. His New Year article in 1949 in which he maintained that Russian was the 'world language of Socialism', is well-known. Now he declared that Pasternak was a 'superfluous, solitary person and individualist' who had been leading a 'kind of emigré existence' in the Soviet Union. Pasternak's *Dr. Zhivago* was a 'vicious lampoon on the Soviet Revolution and the Soviet people'. If Pasternak had only a spark of Soviet dignity he would reject 'this insulting award'. 'By the whole of his work Pasternak confirms that in our socialist country, filled with the inspiration of the construction of a shining communist society, he is nothing but a weed.'

On 28 October the executive committee of the Writers' Union expelled Boris Pasternak, complaining that the ideas of his novel had been 'picked out of a decadent dustbin'; he was accused of 'treason against the Soviet people'. The Komsomol leader Vladimir Semichastny attacked Pasternak even more violently. At a celebration in Moscow on 29 October he accused Pasternak of vile behaviour. In the same speech Semichastny—apparently on behalf of the Party leaders—asked Pasternak to emigrate: 'Let him go to his capitalist paradise. I am convinced that neither the public nor the government would put any obstacles in his way, but would, on the contrary, regard his disappearance from our midst as disinfecting.' As a result on 31 October Pasternak wrote the following letter to Khrushchev:

'Dear Nikita Sergeyevich,

'I am addressing myself to you personally, to the Central Committee of the CPSU and to the Soviet government. From Comrade Semichastny's speech I learnt that the Government will not put any obstacles in the way of my emigration from the USSR. This emigration is impossible for me. I am attached to Russia through my birth, life, and work here. I cannot imagine my fate alone and outside Russia. Whatever my errors may have been I could not have imagined that I should become the focal point of the political campaign which has been launched in the West.

'When I realized this I informed the Swedish Academy of my voluntary renunciation of the Nobel Prize.

'To leave my country would mean death for me and therefore I ask you not to take this extreme step in my case.

'To be honest: I have, after all, done something for Soviet literature and can continue to serve it.'

Pravda published this letter on 2 November together with a Tass statement confirming officially 'that the Soviet government would not put any obstacle in B. L. Pasternak's way should he express the wish to go abroad to receive the prize awarded to him'. It said that Pasternak had not applied for a visa. 'Should B. L. Pasternak want to leave the Soviet Union for ever . . . the authorities will not put any obstacles in his way. He will have the possibility of leaving the Soviet Union personally to enjoy all "the attractions of the capitalist paradise".'

At various meetings resolutions against Pasternak were adopted. He was therefore forced to comment once more in a letter to *Pravda*[1] on his book and the award of the Nobel Prize. He had, he said, at first accepted the Nobel Prize as a literary distinction, but subsequently refused it when he saw 'the dimensions the political campaign about my novel' was assuming. In spite of this statement the campaign continued. At a conference of the writers of the RSFSR on 8 December 1958 in the Great Hall of the Kremlin, at which almost all Soviet Party and state leaders were present, the Chairman, L. Sobolev, again accused Pasternak of treason.

THE PENAL LAW REFORM

On 25 December 1958 the Supreme Soviet passed a number of important laws relating to the administration of justice. They concerned the principles of the penal code, the responsibility for crimes against the state and for military crimes, the foundations of legal procedure, the rights of the military courts as well as the foundations of criminal procedure in the Soviet Union and the separate Union Republics.

The reform of the penal code essentially legalized the changes which had taken place since Stalin's death. The power of the state security service had been curtailed by several

[1] 6 Nov. 1958.

important trials of former leading state security officials between 1953 and 1958, and by other measures, and had been
placed under Party control. Its functions had been considerably reduced and the dreaded 'special courts' had been
abolished as early as September 1953.

Soon afterwards the military tribunals of the troops of the
Ministry of the Interior were dissolved (11 September 1953).
The penalty for minor embezzlements of state or co-operative
property was reduced (10 January 1955). Arrest as a penal
measure was removed from the disciplinary code of the railways,
the merchant marine, and the civil air lines (1 September 1956),
and the so-called transport tribunals were abolished (February
1957).

The judicial system was substantially decentralized; bodies
to preside over the local courts were formed in the regions and
Union Republics (14 August 1954), the functions of the former
All-Union Ministry of Justice were transferred to the individual
Union Republics (31 May 1956), and the administrative
offices of the central judicial authorities in the Union Republics
and regions were abolished (4 August 1956).

No less important was the reorganization of the concentration camp system. In May 1957 the deputy public prosecutor
Kudryavtsev granted an interview on this subject to the
American lawyer Harald J. Berman, a professor at the Harvard
Law School, from which the following emerged:[1] since Stalin's
death more than 70 per cent. of those in prison had been
amnestied, and two-thirds of the labour camps in Siberia had
been dissolved. Approximately 52 per cent. of the amnestied
prisoners had been released immediately after the proclamation
of the amnesty in the spring of 1953. Of the total prison
population in 1957 only 2 per cent. were political prisoners.
On 25 October 1956 the Council of Ministers of the USSR had
issued a decree,[2] which abolished the labour re-education
camps and limited deprivation of liberty to two forms: labour
colonies and prisons. In the labour colonies there are schools
and technical training establishments, which come under the
Ministry of Public Education. Prisoners enjoy a kind of self-
government, and are allowed to receive visits from relatives.
The new labour colonies were removed from the authority of

[1] *Neue Zürcher Zeitung*, 21 May 1957.   [2] Not published.

the state security service and placed under the Ministry of the Interior of the USSR and the governments of the Union Republics. The local Soviets set up control commissions, consisting of representatives of local government, trade union, and Komsomol organizations, to supervise the labour colonies.

Of all the criminal law reforms the Soviet press stressed particularly the extension of the authority of the public prosecutors. A decree of the Praesidium of the Supreme Soviet imposed on the public prosecutors the duty of ensuring the strictest observance of the law by all authorities, responsible persons, and citizens. They were directed to take speedy action against all violations of the law 'whoever may be responsible for them', and 'to take the strictest care that no citizen shall be unlawfully or unjustifiably prosecuted or suffer any other illegal restriction of his rights'. The public prosecutors were to be responsible for the observation, 'by the organs of the state security service as well as by others', of the law towards prisoners on remand. The guiding lines for the public prosecutor were also binding on the state security service. The public prosecutors had to see 'that no one is arrested without a court warrant or without the sanction of the public prosecutor'.

The punishment of criminal elements, on the other hand, was largely taken out of the hands of the official courts. On 30 April 1954 the death sentence was introduced for certain crimes, in particular murder. In the spring of 1957 the so-called parasite laws were passed in most of the Union Republics as 'a step to intensify the struggle against anti-social parasitic elements'. 'General meetings of citizens, called at the request of individual citizens, organizations or the press, by street committees or by commissions for the promotion of public order, were given the right to pass sentence of banishment for from two to five years on citizens who were of age and fit to work but were leading a parasitical existence. The meetings were empowered to take a decision if the majority of adult citizens within a block of flats or the street committee concerned (or in the country the majority of adult members of the village) were present. Sentence can be passed by an open public vote with a simple majority. The citizens' meetings may also confine themselves to a reprimand if the delinquent promises to reform. The sentence of such a general citizens' meeting must be submitted to the local *raion* or city Soviet, which must decide within ten days whether it is legal. The militia must carry out the sentence immediately. The parasite laws, first published as drafts, provoked considerable discussion. In some Union Republics well-known lawyers expressed serious objections. They criticized the imprecise expression 'anti-social and parasitic elements', the fact that questions which fall within the sphere of the judiciary should be arbitrarily decided by citizens' meetings, and also the regulation that a simple majority can decide on the banishment of a person. The question repeatedly arose as to what extent a meeting of citizens was entitled to pass legally valid sentences and thus to anticipate the organs of the law. This opposition may explain why the introduction of the parasite laws proceeded slowly. They were introduced first in Uzbekistan (27 May 1957), then in Turkmenistan (29 May 1957), Latvia (12 October 1957), Tadzhikistan (21 January 1948), Kazakhstan (25 January 1958), Armenia (31 January 1958), and Azerbaidjan (18 June 1958). In the spring of 1959 it was reported that the parasite laws had been introduced in the Union Republic of Kirghizia, which borders on China. By the summer of 1959 they had not yet been put into practice in the RSFSR, the Ukraine, Bielorussia, the Moldavian Republic, Georgia, Lithuania, and Estonia.

The laws passed on 25 December 1958 represent a compromise between the desire to achieve a rule of law on the one hand and the interest of the Party apparatus in preserving its ascendancy on the other. Although by comparison with the Stalin period, they represent an undoubted step forward, they fell far short of the wishes of certain circles.

The most important characteristics of the penal law reform are the following:

1. The elastic terms 'enemy of the people' and 'counter-revolutionary activity', which permitted the arrest of any number of people, are no longer to be found in the new laws. The new code of criminal law states specifically that 'Only a person who has committed a crime, that is someone who has intentionally or out of negligence committed a criminal act which harms the general public, may be brought before a court of law and sentenced.'

2. Reprisals against whole groups of persons because of their social environment or former activities, as the chairman of the Commission for Draft Laws of the All-Union Soviet, Polyansky, explained, are no longer to be used. A confession by the accused can no longer prove guilt. The verdict must rest on evidence which has been examined during the trial; the guilt of the accused must be established before the court.

3. Punishment can now only be imposed by courts. Other bodies, such as the state security service, no longer have the right to impose or carry out punishments. Only the court or the public prosecutor has the right to initiate proceedings if a law is violated, and to order an arrest. The counsel for the defence, only a symbolic figure in the days of Stalin, is given greater rights. Before this he could see the dossier of the case only after the investigation had been completed and the case handed over to the court but now has access to it during the investigation period. However, the demand made by some lawyers, after the Twentieth Party Congress, that they should be given access at any time to the sources of information of the security organs, was not accepted. Moreover, during the exposition of the new laws in the Supreme Soviet it was emphasized that 'counsel for the defence may not use any means to protect his client' for he must 'serve the defence of socialist society'.

4. The minimum age at which a person can be held responsible before the law was raised from twelve to sixteen years —in exceptional cases fourteen years. This ended the notorious 'children's decree' of 8 April 1935 (signed by Molotov), according to which children over twelve years could be 'brought before the courts and the full force of the law used'.

5. Sentences of banishment were reduced from twenty-five to ten years (fifteen years in exceptional cases), but good behaviour could no longer bring about the automatic reduction of the sentence.

6. According to the new ordinance, military courts can try only those accused of espionage and military crimes. Their powers are thereby more precisely defined. Under Stalin political cases also could be brought before military courts.

7. Stalin's thesis that, as socialism develops, the class struggle sharpens (the ideological justification of the Great

Purge) was explicitly rejected; punishments are to be gradually replaced by measures of a remedial character.

But in spite of these improvements severe punishments continue to exist for any form of political opposition. The new 'law concerning criminal responsibility for crimes against the state', lists ten 'particularly dangerous' and sixteen 'other crimes against the state'. Among the 'particularly dangerous' crimes are treason, espionage, terrorist acts, diversion, and sabotage as well as anti-Soviet agitation and propaganda.

Under the new law, treason, which heads the list of crimes, comprises desertion to the enemy, espionage, supplying a foreign state with military or other state secrets, flight abroad or refusal to return to the Soviet Union, rendering assistance to foreign states 'in their hostile activities against the USSR' and 'conspiracy with the aim of taking over power'. It can be punished with from ten to fifteen years' deprivation of liberty or by death. Spying for a foreign power carried a sentence ranging from death to seven to ten years' deprivation of liberty. 'Terrorist acts' that is, the murder of a political leader or a 'socially active official', carry the death sentence or fourteen to fifteen years' deprivation of liberty; the sentence for diversionary acts or wrecking activities, i.e. the intentional destruction of plant, buildings, communications, and other government or co-operative property, as well as all activities aimed at undermining the economy and weakening the Soviet state, varies between eight and fifteen years' deprivation of liberty.

A special clause deals with anti-Soviet agitation. The dissemination of 'calumny against the organization of the Soviet state and society', as well as the preparation, dissemination, and storage of material which serves this purpose, is punishable by imprisonment from six months to seven years or banishment for two to five years; warmongering, by imprisonment for three to eight years. The same penalties hold for membership of an anti-Soviet organization or activity which furthers similar crimes. Particularly dangerous crimes against 'other workers' states' are punishable under the same law.

'Other crimes against the state' include the propagation of racial hatred and national discrimination (prison for six months to three years or banishment for two to five years), the passing of state secrets to unauthorized persons (two to five years' imprisonment, in serious cases five to eight years), loss of state documents (one to three years' imprisonment, in serious cases three to eight years), bandit activities (three to five years' imprisonment), organizing unrest (three to fifteen years), and the refusal of military service (one to three years' imprisonment, in particularly serious instances up to five years).

On 19 February 1959 the new penal code and other laws adopted in December 1958 came into force. Many prisoners who had been sentenced on the basis of laws which had now been repealed were released from prisons, labour camps, and colonies. All persons under eighteen years of age, pregnant women, and women with children under eight years, were released, as well as all persons who had been sentenced for 'counter-revolutionary activity' but could not be tried under the provision of the new laws.

In comparison with conditions in the Stalin era the reform of the penal law is a great step forward, though the Soviet Union is still far from having achieved the rule of law. The severity with which acts of political opposition are punished, the arbitrary use of the punishment of criminal elements by the citizens' meetings provided for in the parasite law, the lack of legal guarantees in the constitution and also such expressions as 'conspiracy with the aim of seizing power' (which can always be used as an accusation of treason by a majority in the Party Praesidium against a minority) continue to permit arbitrary actions. The thing that counts is the relation of the Communist Party—and the state security service subordinate to it—to Soviet law. In no law is the Party mentioned, or its rights or powers. The Party is, however, not only *de facto*, but also according to official statements, the supreme directing force of the Soviet state.

THE STATE SECURITY SERVICE UNDER NEW LEADERSHIP

At the same time as the proclamation of the legal reform an important change was announced in the composition of the Committee for State Security attached to the Council of Ministers of the USSR. The Chairman of the Committee, General Ivan Serov, was relieved of his post on 9 December 1958. Serov's dismissal had probably been decided in the spring of 1958; on 28 December 1958, when *Pravda* published an article by him on the occasion of the fortieth anniversary of the Soviet frontier troops, he was not described as Chairman of the Committee for State Security, but merely as 'General I. Serov'. Two days later he was succeeded by Shelepin.

Alexander Shelepin was born in 1918 and had studied at the much sought-after 'IFLI' in Moscow, the university for philosophy, literature, and history. At the Twentieth Party Congress in February 1956 he was appointed to the commission set up to prepare a new Party programme. This was the first indication that he would soon become part of the central Party apparatus. In April 1958 he resigned his chairmanship of the Komsomol and took over the Department of the Central Committee responsible for Party organs in the Union Republics. Shelepin's appointment as Head of the State Security Service bore witness to a stricter control of the state security service by the Party leadership.

THE DECEMBER PLENARY SESSION 1958

It is interesting that the reform of the penal law was not, as usual on similar occasions, combined with a big campaign. On the contrary the Soviet press was almost silent about it, while Party propaganda was concentrated on other questions.

At the end of 1958 two plenary meetings took place, separated by only six weeks. At the session of 12 November, lasting only a day, Khrushchev's proposals on education and the Seven-Year Plan were adopted. In the speech which Khrushchev made he settled accounts with the 'anti-Party group', among whom, without explanation, Bulganin figured belatedly. The November meeting is also of importance because Nikolai Belyayev—until then promoted by Khrushchev—who had been responsible for agricultural questions in the top leadership, was dismissed from the Central Committee Secretariat. Officially the dismissal was explained by the announcement that Belyayev had been appointed First Party Secretary of Kazakhstan—but his disgrace was unmistakable.

Barely six weeks later—from 16 to 21 December 1958—a fresh plenary meeting of the Central Committee took place. Officially it was to deal with the development of Soviet agriculture since the meeting in September 1953; in reality, however, it was the propagandistic preparation for the Twenty-first Party Congress, a demonstration of Khrushchev's victory. The nature of the session was underlined by the fact that as well as full and candidate members of the Central Committee, those of the Central Revision Commission, and even a large number of people not belonging to any leading body were present. Speeches were made not only by thirty-six full or candidate members of the Central Committee, but also by thirty other people, including ten collective farm functionaries. Contrary to the usual custom a verbatim record of the December full session was later published in book form. Khrushchev, who spoke 'on the results of the development of agriculture in the last five years and the tasks for a further raising of agricultural production', announced new guiding lines of agricultural policy. The main emphasis lay on the restriction of the private property of the 'collective' peasants. He particularly criticized the increase in the number of privately owned cows. In the Astrakhan Region the number of cows owned by collective and state farms had fallen during the last five years from 37,000 to 35,000, whereas the privately-owned ones had increased by 17,000. In the Vologda Region the number of collectively owned cows had fallen by 5,000 and the privately-owned ones had increased by 34,000. The responsible officials of these Regions obviously did not realize which way the wind was blowing.

The 'collective' peasants should be encouraged to sell their cattle. As an example Khrushchev cited the collective farms of his native village Kalinovka which he called 'a laboratory for the transformation of agriculture'. Three years ago, at his suggestion they had decided to sell the privately-owned cows to the collective farms. Khrushchev tried to prove with figures that as a result the position of the *kolkhoz* peasants had improved.

Concerning the machine and tractor stations, too, Khrushchev made new proposals. The new technical repair stations (RTS) should be handed over to the collective farms several of which should jointly take charge of the workshops. He wanted the agricultural research institutes to become paying concerns. Khrushchev deplored the fact that many of the latter dealt with theoretical questions. He suggested that the institutes and experimental stations should make contracts with enterprises and trade associations and be paid according to the practical results of their scientific work.

Finally, Khrushchev announced that there would be changes among Party officials working in agriculture. Changes should 'not become the fashion', but 'we do not want to prevent those leading officials from being dismissed who are incapable of fulfilling the tasks they have been given'. Well-trained officials would have to be appointed 'with organizational ability, who can inspire their colleagues to fulfil the tasks set by the Party'.

Khrushchev accused the 'enemies of the Party' of having tried to hinder the progress of agriculture in the Soviet Union. Molotov, Kaganovich, and Malenkov had regarded the Soviet peasantry as hostile to socialist development. Khrushchev referred to the 'enemies of the Party' as 'a worthless group of miserable officials', and added that when one thought of the direction in which they had tried to push the Party of which they were still members it was impossible to regard them as comrades.

Khrushchev tried to represent Molotov and Malenkov not only as disruptive elements in the Party, but also as idiots who had no idea of the simplest questions of agricultural policy. Molotov, he said, had proposed that the collective farms near big towns should supply them with potatoes and vegetables and should concentrate exclusively on growing these products. Since at that time the price of potatoes was 2·5 to 3 kopecks a kilo, Molotov's plan would have been bound to lead to the ruin of the collective farms in the vicinity of big towns. Molotov's 'anti-peasant attitude' had also expressed itself in his proposal to make peasants subscribe more to the annual state loans.

Malenkov was taken to task even more severely by Khrushchev, and accused of 'deception of the Party and the people'. Khrushchev recalled Malenkov's speech at the Nineteenth Party Congress in October 1952, in which he had said that the gross grain yield in the Soviet Union amounted to 8 milliard pounds (128 million metric tons), and that this finally solved the grain problem. But the 8 milliard pounds, said Khrushchev, had not been the true output but the 'biological yield' based on estimates. In fact the collective and state farms in 1952 had produced not 8 but only 5·6 milliard pounds, and delivered 2·8 milliard pounds to the state. Western experts on the Soviet

Union had at the time considered the figures for 1952 to be 15 to 25 per cent. too high. Now it emerged that they had been as much as 30 per cent. too high.

However, Khrushchev's attack on Malenkov was something of a boomerang. Although the latter had actually described the grain problem as finally solved at the Nineteenth Party Congress, Khrushchev suppressed the fact that he himself had repeated this claim at the plenary session in September 1953: 'Our country has enough bread. We have the necessary state reserves and are able to export a certain amount too.' He omitted to mention that the method of calculating on the basis of so-called biological yields had been used in all Russian agricultural documents since 1933. Indeed Malenkov had been the first to criticize this form of calculation publicly: in his speech to the Supreme Soviet on 8 August 1953, he had said that 'one must put an end to the mistaken practice by which the production of grain and other products on the collective farm is calculated not on the basis of actual yields, but solely on that of the estimates of procurement commissions'.

Khrushchev's distortions of the immediate past were accepted by the Central Committee meeting without argument: after all he held the trump card. This was the first session of the Central Committee at which the 'wise leadership' was no longer spoken of in general terms; instead a cult of Khrushchev found open expression. Many speakers quoted him, adding to eulogies of Party policy the words 'under the personal direction of Comrade Khrushchev'.

CHAPTER VIII

THE TWENTY–FIRST PARTY CONGRESS OF THE CPSU

(27 January to 5 February 1959)

ON 27 January 1959 at 10 a.m. the Twenty-first Party Congress of the CPSU opened in the Big Hall of the Kremlin. It was announced as an extraordinary Party session, a very rare occurrence in Bolshevik history. Khrushchev evidently chose this procedure in order not to have to wait until 1960 to announce a new general policy.

The Twenty-first Party Congress was attended by 1,375 delegates with voting rights and 106 delegates with the right only to speak; each of them represented about 6,000 members of the Party, which now had eight and a quarter million members—7,622,356 full and 616,775 candidate members. Since the Twentieth Congress membership had thus increased by more than a million: in 1958 alone more than 480,000 people had joined the Party. This rapid increase is reminiscent of the 'Lenin levy' after Lenin's death, the great recruiting drive used by Stalin to reduce the average age of Party members and to overtrump difficult, old officials with the help of inexperienced novices.

Of the 1,269 delegates with voting rights, 432 were Party officials,[1] 355 officials from industry, building, and transport,[2] 175 agricultural officials, 147 state officials,[3] 91 representatives of the Army, 50 representatives of learning, art, and science, and 7 Komsomol officials.

Delegates from seventy foreign communist parties also attended.[4] The Yugoslav League of Communists had not been invited.

Of the leaders, Kozlov spoke on general questions concerning the state and the economy, Kirichenko on the Party frame-

---

[1] 506 in 1956.   [2] 251 in 1956.
[3] 177 in 1956.   [4] 55 in 1956.

work, Aristov on Party work in industry, Ignatov on agriculture, Furtseva on cultural policy, Mikoyan on foreign trade and relations with the Western powers, Suslov on ideological questions, Mukhitdinov on policy towards the nationalities in the Near East, Brezhnev on heavy industry, Ustinov on automation, Semichastny on youth questions, Marshal Malinovsky on the army, Gromyko on foreign policy, and Shelepin on the state security service.

THE SEVEN-YEAR PLAN

At the first session of the Party Congress Khrushchev presented details of the Seven-Year Plan. This was to provide the technical framework of communism. Thus the most developed capitalist countries must be surpassed not only in total production, but also in production per head of population. It was not expected that this goal would be reached in all branches of production by 1965, but the decisive step must be taken in this period. Heavy industry was again given priority. By 1965 gross industrial output was to be increased by 80 per cent.: this implied an annual rate of increase of production of 8·6 per cent., 9·3 per cent. for producer goods and 7·3 per cent. for consumer goods.

The Seven-Year Plan in fact envisages the following increases in production by 1965: iron ore from 84·2 million tons (1957) to 150–60 million tons; pig-iron from 37 million tons (1957) to 65–70 million tons; crude steel from 55 million tons (1958) to 86–91 million tons; coal from 463 million tons (1957) to 596–609 million tons; mineral oil from 113 million tons (1958) to 230–40 million tons; electricity from 233 million megowatt-hours (1958) to 500–20 million megowatt-hours; cement from 28·9 million tons (1957) to 75–81 million tons; natural gas from 30 milliard cubic metres (1958) to 150 milliard cubic metres. The production of the chemical industry is to be increased almost threefold. The proportion of energy derived from coal is to be reduced from 58–42 per cent. and the use of oil and gas increased from 30–49 per cent. Thermal power stations using natural gas, oil, and open cast coal are to be given preferential treatment in the building programme.

A comparison with the Sixth Five-Year Plan (1956–60) shows the following picture:

	Unit	1955 Production	1960 Sixth Five-Year Plan target	1965 Seven-Year Plan target
Electricity	million MWh.	170·1	320	500–20
Petroleum	million tons	70·8	135	230–40
Natural Gas	milliard cubic metres	10·4	40	150
Pig-iron	million tons	33·3	53	65–70
Crude Steel	million tons	45·3	68·3	86–91
Rolled Products	million tons	35·3	62·7	65–70
Coal	million tons	391	593	596–609

As a result of the newly discovered iron ore deposits in Siberia and Kazakhstan a 'third ferrous metallurgical base' is to be established. Forty per cent. of the total capital investment in the years 1958–65 is to be allocated to the eastern regions which are to become the centre of industrial production. By 1965 they are to be producing 50 per cent. of the USSR's coal, 48 per cent. of its steel, 88 per cent. of its copper, 71 per cent. of its aluminium, 42 per cent. of its cement, and 46 per cent. of its electricity.

On this occasion Khrushchev insisted upon the introduction of new techniques, and attached particular importance to the introduction of automation into the processes of production. Fully automatic processes were already in operation in machine building, metallurgy, and some branches of the chemical industry. The Seven-Year Plan envisages the establishment of fifty fully automatic pioneer factories. Partial or complete automation is to be introduced, in particular in the rest of the chemical industry, oil refining, the food-processing industry, power stations, and in the production of pig iron, crude steel and rolled products. Soon after the Party Congress a government committee for automation was set up. In May 1959 a big campaign for automatizing production was begun and on 24

June 1959 a plenary meeting of the Central Committee was convened to deal exclusively with these questions.

The production of light industry and consumer goods is also to be stepped up. The targets are higher than in the Sixth Five-Year Plan, but the speed is to be less. The gross output of light industry is to be increased by 50 per cent. and of the food industry by 70 per cent. The production of cotton fabrics is to be increased from 5·8 to 7·7 or 8 milliard metres, of wool fabrics from 303 to 500 milliard metres, linen fabrics from 481 to 635 million metres and silk fabrics from 845 to 1,485 million metres. The manufacture of underwear is to be raised from 398 to 780 million pieces and other clothes from 97 to 160 million pieces. The production of leather footwear is to be 510 million pairs in 1965 as compared with 356 in 1958.

Agricultural production is to be specialized in certain regions. Some Union Republics (for example those of Caucasia and Central Asia) are to be partly, later almost completely, exempt from growing grain, and are instead to plant more valuable crops like cotton, tea, wine, and citrus and other fruits. The Ukraine, whose grain production is less than that of the RSFSR and Kazakhstan[1] is to specialize in livestock rearing and the cultivation of crops, in particular sugarbeet. In the USSR as a whole, however, the main attention continues to be focused on grain production which is to be increased from 8·5 milliard *pouds* to 10–11 milliard *pouds* (164–80 million metric tons). The production of raw cotton is to rise to 5·7–6·1 million tons (an increase of 30–39 per cent. over 1958), of sugar to 76–84 million tons (an increase of 40–55 per cent.), and of potatoes to 147 million tons (from 86 million tons in 1958).

Particularly high targets are set for livestock produce in the Seven-Year Plan. The output of meat is to be increased to 8–16 million tons (slaughter weight), of milk to 100–5 million tons (an increase of 70–80 per cent. over 1958), of wool to 548,000 tons (a 70 per cent. increase), and of eggs to 37 milliard (a 60 per cent. increase). Total agricultural output is in 1965 to be 70 per cent. greater than in 1958—implying an annual rate of growth of nearly 8 per cent.

The social reformation of agriculture is to continue. The

[1] This Republic has become the second granary of the USSR since the virgin lands campaign.

assets ('indivisible funds') of the collective farms are to be increased, the private property of the peasants (especially their land and cattle) being further reduced. The total number of wage and salary earners is to be increased by almost 12 million to 66·5 million. Labour productivity is to rise in industry by 45 to 50 per cent., in building by 60 to 65 per cent., and in agriculture (on collective farms) by about 100 per cent. The total number of experts with a university education is to be increased to 4·5 million by 1965, that is by 50 per cent. as compared with 1958.

Centrally planned state investment in the Seven-Year Plan period is to be nearly 2 billion roubles—in money. This is equivalent to the sum of everything invested there since the Soviet state came into existence. Investment by the collective farms and by the public in housing swell the total figure to almost 3 billion roubles.

This extraordinarily high capital investment cannot but affect the standard of living of the population. From official Soviet sources it appears that from 1950 to 1955, average real wages rose by 6·3 per cent. per annum; the Seven-Year Plan, however, provides for an annual increase of only 4·9 per cent. The income of *kolkhoz* peasants rose by as much as 9 per cent. from 1950 to 1955. Khrushchev announced that no further price reductions could be expected during the Seven-Year Plan.

Social services, on the other hand, are to be considerably extended: for 1965 an expenditure of about 360 milliard roubles is planned. Minimum wages are to be raised from 270–350 roubles a month to 500–600 roubles, and there is to be a corresponding increase in old-age pensions. Working hours are to be cut in two stages by 1965: a seven-hour day is to be introduced by 1960 and a forty-hour week by 1962. For those working underground or in conditions detrimental to health a six-hour day is to be introduced by 1960 and a thirty-hour week by 1962. All other workers are to change to a thirty-five hour week from 1964 onwards. Income tax (which accounts for only 7·8 of Soviet tax receipts) is to be abolished.

Khrushchev expressed himself as in favour of raising standards of living not primarily by wage increases or price cuts (which would mainly affect personal expenditure) but through collective institutions—schools, cultural and medical services, and in particular, the extension of community catering, his pet scheme. Housing is to be notably increased: by 1965 about 15 million dwellings are to be made available.

The reaction of Western economists to the Seven-Year Plan varied. The prevailing view is that many of the targets are unrealistic, even though a number of inconsistencies of the Sixth Five-Year Plan have been eliminated and in some branches of activity a more moderate rate of development planned. In particular the total investment figures of 3 billion roubles and the increase in labour productivity of 40–65 per cent. are thought to be too high. Indeed, in spite of the progress to be expected in many branches of industry, the targets are hardly likely to be completely realized. The reform of the control of the economy has eliminated a number of the crassest bureaucratic excrescences of Stalinism, but the Soviet economy continues to be held back by many bureaucratic chains.

The division of the country into 104 relatively small *sovnarkhozy* has by no means proved successful economically: as early as the summer and autumn of 1958 the need to create larger economic units was repeatedly stressed, though Khrushchev did not touch on this delicate question at the Party Congress. There is still a contradiction between old-fashioned methods of direction and ambitious economic goals, a contradiction which has already made itself felt several times in Soviet development. If the Soviet leaders are determined to attain their aims they must make further changes in the economic system: among other things, decentralization, greater attention to material incentives and local initiative, greater authority within individual undertakings, and the participation of factory and office workers in the control of production. If the present shape of the economic system is preserved the fulfilment of the targets of the new Plan is very doubtful, and, as in the case of the Sixth Five-Year Plan it may have to be revised.

MOSCOW'S COMPETITION WITH THE UNITED STATES

When expounding the Seven-Year Plan Khrushchev said, 'The economic is the main field in which peaceful competition between socialism and capitalism takes place, and we are interested in winning this competition in a historically short time.' The Seven-Year Plan was to be a 'decisive step' towards 'overtaking the most developed countries in production per head of population in as short a period of history as possible'. This aim was to be achieved by 1970.

According to Khrushchev the Soviet Union's total industrial production already in December 1958 exceeded that of France, Great Britain, and the Federal German Republic together. It was admittedly only half as great as that of the USA, while its agricultural production was 20 to 25 per cent. less. In *per capita* production the difference was even greater. According to official Soviet estimates, United States' industrial output per head was rather more than double that of Russia, and America's agricultural output more than 40 per cent. greater than that of the Soviet Union. Labour productivity in the United States was still two to two and a half times that of Russia in industry, and as much as three times greater in agriculture. But the rate of growth in the Soviet Union was faster. While production in the USA rose by about 2 per cent. per annum, the annual rate of growth of Soviet industrial production averaged 8·6 per cent. Moreover, the absolute increments in a number of important branches of production (steel, cast-iron, iron ore, mineral oil, coal, cement, and wool fabrics) were greater in the Soviet Union than in the USA. This led Khrushchev optimistically to proclaim, 'Now our country is surpassing the United States both in the rate of growth and in the absolute size of the annual increases in production. We are moving forward four times as fast and are increasing production every year so that it will be much easier to catch up with the Americans.' Thus 'a qualitatively new phase of competition' had started. About five years after the completion of the Seven-Year Plan (that is in 1970), 'but possibly even sooner, the Soviet Union will be the first in the world, both in total production and in *per capita* production'.

In the west Khrushchev is considered to over-estimate Russia's chances. In the first place, the claim that the total output of Soviet industry in 1958 had already been bigger than that of the three western European industrial states—France, Great Britain, and Germany must be questioned. According to Soviet statistics[1] Soviet *per capita* steel production in 1957

[1] *The USSR in Figures*, Moscow, 1958.

amounted to only 52 per cent. of that of the German Federal Republic, 59 per cent. of that of Great Britain, and 78 per cent. of that of France. In electricity too, the output of the Soviet Union, according to Soviet figures, is only 50 per cent. of that of Great Britain, 55 per cent. of that of the German Federal Republic, and 73 per cent. of that of France. Much more unfavourable still is a comparison of consumer goods production.

Khrushchev's hopes that the rate of growth will be higher in the Soviet Union than elsewhere will probably also prove fallacious. The Soviet economy has now reached a stage where every further step requires far greater investment than before. The annual rate of growth has already fallen in the successive Five-Year Plans. According to official statistics the annual rate of growth was 19·2 per cent. of industrial production in the period of the First Five-Year Plan (1928–33) in that of the Second (1933–7) it fell to 17·1 per cent., and in the later Five-Year Plan periods up to 1955 it lay between 13 and 14 per cent.; the Sixth Five-Year Plan (1956–60) envisaged a rate of growth of 10 per cent. the figure falling to 8·6 per cent. in the Seven-Year Plan.

In his analysis of the Seven-Year Plan, Boris Meissner showed that in some basic industries the absolute difference between the output of the Soviet Union and that of the USA actually increased from 1950 to 1956. In the case of electricity the difference in 1956 was 483 million MWh (USA 675, USSR 192), whereas in 1950 it had only been 298 million MWh (USA 389, USSR 98). For oil the difference in 1956 was 270 million tons (USA 354, USSR 84) whereas in 1950 it had been only 229 million tons (USA 276, USSR 38). In the case of gas production the difference has increased from 208 milliard cubic metres in 1950 (USA 214, USSR 6) to 312 in 1956. This does not mean that the Soviet economy will not progress during the next seven years, but only that it is unlikely that the 'main economic aim' of overtaking the United States in *per capita* production by 1970 will be realized.

THE 'ANTI-PARTY GROUP'

Of the eighty-six Russian speakers to address the Congress sixty-seven referred in one form or another to the 'anti-Party group' (always in the order Malenkov, Molotov, Kaganovich, Bulganin, Shepilov). Khrushchev restricted himself to the remark that after the Twentieth Party Congress the general policy of the Party had 'met with the stubborn resistance of the anti-Party group which had tried to destroy the unity of the Party, to thwart the implementation of the decisions of the Twentieth Party Congress, and to lead Party and country away from the Leninist path'. These were almost the same words which had been used against the former Soviet leaders in June 1957. Khrushchev added that the plenary session in June 1957 had unmasked and ideologically destroyed the 'anti-Party group'. This statement was interesting because Khrushchev placed the main emphasis on 'ideological destruction' and at the same time suggested that the whole affair was over.

Speakers in discussions condemned the enemies of the Party with varying degrees of severity. On 29 January Ivan Spiridonov, Party Secretary in Leningrad, was the first to attack them fiercely. He described the former Soviet leaders as an 'anti-Party conspiratorial group', which had acted treacherously towards Party and people, and he demanded their expulsion from the Party. 'If up to now the members of this group have been severely called to account by the Central Committee of the Party, they must be called to account no less strictly and severely before the highest organ of the Party, the Party Congress,' he declared.

Another fierce opponent was Nikolai Ignatov, member of the Party Praesidium, and the Central Committee Secretariat, who referred to the former leaders as 'a miserable rabble of bankrupts'. A candidate member of the Party Praesidium, Nikolai Podgorny and others spoke of 'criminal attempts'. The Party Secretary of the Autonomous Tatar Republic, Semyon Ignatiev, a former Minister of State Security, said that the 'group of conspirators' had 'fought against the course unanimously accepted at the Twentieth Party Congress with characteristically jesuitical tricks'. Ivan Kapitonov, the First Party Secretary of Moscow (dismissed soon afterwards) and the Soviet Ambassador in Peking, Pavel Yudin, an ideologist notorious for his anti-Yugoslav activity, also spoke of 'conspirators'.

The strongest expressions were used by Alexander Shelepin, who had been appointed Chairman of the Committee for State

Security of the USSR in December 1958. 'These people have behaved like the Trotskyists and the Rightists,' he said. This implied that the 'enemies of the Party' should be treated in the same way as the Trotskyists and the Rightists who had in fact been shot during the Great Purge. Interestingly enough, these two sentences did not appear in *Pravda's* report of the speech on 5 February. They are known only from a message from the Italian journalist, Boffa, which appeared in *Unità* on 6 February. The censoring of Shelepin's speech suggests that his attitude was not in line with the opinion of the leadership at the time, but that he and his friends hoped to influence Khrushchev.

Other speakers showed a conciliatory attitude. The chief of the 'appeasers' was Mikoyan, but Aristov went so far as to name the fallen leaders as having tried to slow down the new development of the country, but without calling them an 'anti-Party group'. Suslov, Kosygin, Grishin, were also restrained in their comments.

It was noticeable that nineteen speakers refrained from taking up any attitude towards the 'anti-Party group' at all. Among them were not only scientists and artists, such as the President of the Academy of Sciences, Nesmeyanov, and the writer Tvardovsky, but also the Minister for Higher Education, Yelyutin. The Komsomol leader, Vladimir Semichastny, who only a few weeks earlier had attracted attention because of his violent attacks on Pasternak, also abstained from comment.

Most of the members of the Party Praesidium compromised. While strongly condemning the group they did not demand their expulsion or prosecution. They emphasized that this question was already solved and that the enemies of the Party had been 'removed', 'pushed aside', 'unmasked', 'washed overboard', 'ideologically destroyed', 'swept away' or 'thrown aside.'

This line was followed by Kirichenko, Kozlov, Furtseva, Brezhnev, Mukhitdinov, Kuusinen, and Shvernik, all full members of the Praesidium of the Party, as well as by candidate members Pospelov, Malinovsky, and Gromyko. Two of them, Kirichenko and Kuusinen, introduced a few new elements into the debate. Kirichenko said 'that no sooner was Stalin dead than the members of the anti-Party group at almost every session of the Praesidium of the Central Committee attacked

everything new that emerged from Lenin's teaching or was
suggested by life itself. After the Twentieth Party Congress,
in particular, they came out into the open. The anti-Party
group threw off its mask and turned against the course laid
down at the Twentieth Party Congress on 18 June 1957, that
is at a time when its members had counted their strength in the
Praesidium of the Central Committee and believed that they
had sufficient support to change the policy of the Party and
Government. How this ended is known. Thus the activities of
the 'anti-Party group' were moved forward to the period
immediately after Stalin's death, and 18 June 1957 was
officially designated as the day when the disagreements among
the leaders came to a head. The suggestion that Khrushchev's
opponents had attacked everything new—a shaft whose main
target was Molotov rather than Malenkov—is also interesting.
Kuusinen, too, directed his main attack against Molotov, 'who
did not hatch a single theoretical chicken himself, but accused
other comrades of theoretical carelessness'. He accused the
'anti-Party group' not only of endangering the unity of the
Party but also of being too conservative: 'When Comrade
Khrushchev produced new tasks for the Party these aloof,
factious creatures were baffled. Develop virgin land? What for?
—Reorganize the control of industry and building? What can
be the point of it? Grow maize? Another new thing?—Cultivate
personal contacts in foreign policy? As if we needed that!'

Some of the moderate speakers accused the 'enemies of the
Party' of factual errors. Mukhitdinov said that they had shown
'elements of chauvinism' and 'had mistrusted the officials of the
national Republics'. Gromyko accused the former leaders of
having done great harm to the foreign policy of the Soviet state
while Malinovsky reproached them similarly with regard to
the armed forces: he, incidentally, was the only one who made
a fresh thrust at Zhukov.

PERVUKHIN AND SABUROV'S SELF-CRITICISM

A certain combination of people tried on this occasion to
include the economic planners, Pervukhin and Saburov, both
disgraced in 1957, among the 'anti-Party group'. The signal
for this campaign was given on 29 January by the Leningrad
Party Secretary, Ivan Spiridonov: 'The candidate member of

the Praesidium of the Central Committee, Comrade Pervukhin . . . and the member of the Central Committee, Comrade
Saburov, have not once, in a year and a half, condemned the
anti-Party group or their part in it. How is this silence to be
understood, Comrades Pervukhin and Saburov? May one
demand that they should answer for their mistakes before the
Party Congress?'

Only on 3 February, towards the end of the Congress did
Pervukhin criticize himself. He expressed his agreement with
Khrushchev's speech and recalled that in June 1957 and later
he had supported all decisions of the plenary sessions and
condemned the 'anti-Party group'. Of his attitude before and
during the June session he said:

'Now I am going to describe how my mistake occurred.
When the reform of the control of industry and building was
discussed in the Central Committee I expressed my doubts and
objections to the reorganization planned. My wrong attitude
on this extremely important matter and my dissatisfaction
with it led me to make a big political mistake: at the meetings
of the Praesidium of the Central Committee before the plenary
session in June I supported the anti-Party group against
Comrade Khrushchev and consequently also, as I later realized, the line taken by him on a number of questions of domestic
and foreign policy.

'The anti-Party group was clearly formed long before the
June session of the Central Committee and was waiting for an
opportune moment to act against the leadership of the Central
Committee. My mistaken attitude before the June session to
some extent helped it. Here lies my chief guilt towards the
Party. . . .

'When I realized that they were planning an inadmissible
anti-Party action which might have far-reaching damaging
consequences I reported to the June meeting of the Central
Committee everything that I knew about fractional anti-Party
activities, and about the group. Thus, as is stated in the
resolution of the full session of the Central Committee[1] I realized my mistakes while it was sitting. . . . I have fully confessed

[1] Pervukhin is obviously referring to an internal Party resolution, because
there is no reference to this in the Party resolution published on 4 July 1957—
W. L.

my guilt towards the Party and am anxious to prove myself in the post I have been given'.[1]

The next day, 4 February, Saburov, also criticized himself; this, however, was not published in the Soviet press. According to *Trybuna Ludu* of 5 February Saburov admitted that he had made mistakes in June 1957 and shown political indecision. Although he had not agreed with the attitude of the 'anti-Party group' he had criticized the policy of the Party leadership from the point of view of that group: now he expressed his agreement with Khrushchev's policy. In his new post as director of a factory in Sysrany he would work to make amends for his mistakes towards the people and the Party. In spite of these declarations some speakers at the Party Congress, particularly regional secretaries, made further attacks on the two former economic chiefs, Pervukhin being much more sharply attacked than Saburov. This may be attributable to the fact that from 1953 to 1956, when both men occupied high economic posts, Saburov was in favour of realistic planning and enjoyed great popularity in economic circles, whereas the economic experts regarded Pervukhin with suspicion.[2]

Saburov and Pervukhin were not mentioned in Khrushchev's final speech nor in the resolution of the Party Congress. Evidently Khrushchev and the majority of the Party leaders considered so serious a settlement of accounts as inexpedient or at least premature. The wording of Saburov's self-criticism was not made known until July 1959, when the full stenographic record of the Party Congress was published. It contained one sensational passage: in it Saburov said that he had expressed himself against Khrushchev and his policy shortly before the plenary session of June 1957 but had subsequently broken with the 'anti-Party group' with the help of the 'healthy nucleus' in the Party Praesidium, Khruschev, Mikoyan, and Kirichenko. This means that the 'healthy nucleus' among the leaders consisted of only three out of eleven members of the Praesidium. Two members of Khrushchev's following were missing from Saburov's list, Suslov and Voroshilov, the nominal head of state. It had long been suspected that Voroshilov did not support the Khrushchev group, or that he had at least wavered.

---

[1] Ambassador to East Germany.—W.L.
[2] See Fritz Schenk in the *Observer*, 14 Nov. 1957.

But it was strange that Saburov did not mention Suslov either. It may be that this was because the latter began by supporting the 'anti-Party group' and only later went over to Khrushchev. At any rate, the new textbook on Party history, published in the summer of 1959, says of the session in June 1957 that Suslov, together with Khrushchev, Kirichenko, and Mikoyan, belonged to the 'healthy nucleus'. This was the fourth version. According to the first—current from June 1957 to November 1958—only three members of the Praesidium, Malenkov, Molotov, and Kaganovich, had spoken against Khrushchev's policy and all the others (Mikoyan, Kirichenko, Suslov, Bulganin, Voroshilov, Pervukhin, and Saburov) had supported him. That would have meant a majority of eight to three in favour of Khrushchev. In the middle of November 1958 Khrushchev belatedly added Bulganin to the 'anti-Party group', thus giving himself a majority of only seven to four.

When Pervukhin and Saburov, too, were accused of having supported the 'anti-Party group' it implied that there were only five in favour of Khrushchev (Khrushchev, Mikoyan, Kirichenko, Suslov, and Voroshilov) and six against (Malenkov, Molotov, Kaganovich, Bulganin, Pervukhin, and Saburov). In the Party history of June 1959 Voroshilov was no longer included in the 'healthy nucleus' so that only Kirichenko, Mikoyan, and Suslov supported Khrushchev—the score thus being four to seven. If Saburov's account is to be believed Suslov also drops out and Khrushchev, with Mikoyan and Kirichenko was opposed by all the other members of the Praesidium. Each of these accounts, of course, had a purpose. But they do show how precarious Khrushchev's position was in June 1957.

KHRUSHCHEV'S 'TRANSITION TO COMMUNISM'

The 'Congress of the builders of Communism' was the official description of the Twenty-first Party Congress. Khrushchev deliberately linked the Seven-Year Plan with the final goal of communism. A large part of his speech was intended to give the Seven-Year Plan an ideological basis. He formulated new propositions on the 'transition to communism' because Stalin's directives[1] had been partly overtaken by events.

[1] See *The Economic Problems of Socialism in the USSR*, October 1952.

According to the new definitions socialism and communism have a number of common characteristics—the abolition of the private ownership of the means of production, a planned economy and the end of exploitation and oppression. Under socialism there are still two forms of property (state ownership and collective or co-operative ownership), whereas under communism there is only one, the communist form of property. Under socialism there are still differences between town and country and between intellectual and manual work whereas communism overcomes them all. Under socialism the state still exercises political functions, under communism they gradually disappear, and after the victory of communism on a world-wide scale the state withers away completely. Socialism rewards people according to their achievements, under communism all goods are distributed according to needs.

The Soviet Union had already reached the first phase, that is socialism, by the end of 1936. Since then it has been in a phase of 'gradual transition to communism'. At the Twenty-first Party Congress Khrushchev had said that the Soviet Union had already entered upon the 'period of the comprehensive construction of communism'. But this raises the following questions:

(1) How is the Soviet Union to proceed from the existing two forms of property—collective property in agriculture and public property in industry—to a single form of property? (2) How are the essential differences between town and country and between intellectual and manual work to be overcome? (3) How is the transition to be brought about from payment according to achievement to distribution according to need? And finally: (4) How and to what extent is the state to wither away?

To these questions Khrushchev provided the following answers at the Twenty-first Party Congress.

(1) The frontiers between collective and co-operative ownership and state ownership will gradually disappear. In future the collective farms must co-operate much more closely with one another and with local government organs, and must not only concentrate on agriculture but also build industrial enterprises, power stations, irrigation canals, and roads. This will lead to a 'sort of fusion of collectively and state owned means

of production' and 'general public ownership' will emerge.

(2) Work in the collective farms is being mechanized and is transformed 'gradually into a form of industrial work'. The *kolkhoz* villages are being transformed into attractive places of an urban character, with all the modern communal, cultural, and other amenities. There will arise 'agrotowns' of the kind already proposed by Khrushchev in 1950 and 1951. As production becomes increasingly based on the most modern technical methods, training will become increasingly closely connected with work. In this way 'the main differences between intellectual and manual labour will gradually be eliminated.

(3) This presupposes the 'creation of the material-technical basis of communism', which means:

(a) a highly developed modern industry,
(b) complete electrification of the country,
(c) scientific and technical progress in all branches of industry and agriculture,
(d) complete mechanization and automization of all production processes,
(e) general exploitation of new sources of energy, of the rich resources of nature and of new synthetic materials,
(f) the raising of the cultural and technical level of all workers by hand and by brain,
(g) a further improvement of the organization of production and a rise in labour productivity.

In addition some prerequisites of a moral or political character are necessary, in particular 'a high level of conscientiousness on the part of all citizens'. It is important 'to train the man of the future now'. The 'man of the future' must be distinguished by the following seven characteristics of 'communist morals':

(a) devotion to communism and an implacable hostility towards its enemies,
(b) awareness of social obligation,
(c) active participation in work for the good of the community,
(d) voluntary respect for the basic rules of human society,
(e) comradely help,
(f) integrity,

(g) intolerance towards those who offend against the social order.

Khrushchev, however, made some noteworthy qualifications. Needs did not mean 'whims and demands for luxury goods', but the 'natural requirements of a socially developed person'. Man could not 'use more bread and other foodstuffs than were necessary for his organism'. There were also certain limits for clothing and housing.

(4) 'Many of the functions which are carried out by the state, will progressively be handed over to social organizations'. As a (not very convincing) example Khrushchev mentioned the handing over of the municipal health services to the trade unions and the rural health services to the local soviets (which are, however, state organs). Sport was no longer to be controlled by the State Committee for Physical Culture and Sport, but is to be put into the hands of voluntary sport organizations. These and similar measures did not, of course, 'mean any weakening of the role of the socialist state in the construction of communism'. Now as before, the Soviet armed forces must be strengthened and the organs of state security fortified.

Catching up with the USA in the economic field Khrushchev did not regard as the completion of communism, but only as the 'first phase', an 'intermediate stage'. Communism will only be complete 'when we have created abundance . . . when everyone has learnt to work to the best of their abilities to increase the wealth of society'.

The future communist way of life, Khrushchev said, should not be imagined as a formless, anarchistic mass of people, but would be a 'highly organized, well attuned community of workers'. 'Automatic production has a certain rhythm, which cannot be kept up without regulating man's work accordingly. . . . In order to guide the machines everybody will carry out his social duties at a certain time and according to certain rules.'

THE ECONOMIC INTEGRATION OF
THE COMMUNIST WORLD

Khrushchev's phrase about 'comprehensive communist construction' raised an important problem: should the Soviet Union establish communism alone while the other communist countries remained in the first phase, socialism? Or can these countries join the Soviet Union in the transition to communism in spite of the Soviet lead?

During the conflict between Moscow and Peking in the summer and autumn of 1958 the ideologist, Stepanyan, suggested the following solution: All the East European countries (with the Soviet Union at their head) will achieve communism first, to be followed later by the communist countries of Asia (led by China). At the Twenty-first Party Congress Khrushchev expressed the view 'that the socialist countries can pass more or less simultaneously to the higher phase of communist society through the successful exploitation of the possibilities inherent in the socialist order'. The other countries must speed up their development to catch up with the Soviet Union at an early date. This is no idle theory. The economic integration of the communist world began in 1954 and has progressed particularly fast since the spring of 1956.

The most important instrument of communist integration is the 'Council for Mutual Economic Aid' (COMECON). Until Stalin's death it did not play any very important role: from 1954 onwards, however, it has developed into a powerful instrument for the fusion of the national economies into one unit. The members of the Council are the Soviet Union, with Poland, Rumania, Bulgaria, Hungary, Eastern Germany, Czechoslovakia, and Albania. The communist countries of Asia, China, North Korea, North Vietnam, and Outer Mongolia, attend as 'permanent observers' but also take part in the work of the other organs of the Council. The highest of these is the Assembly which is attended by state delegates from all member countries. It meets once or twice a year. According to the statute the Assembly makes recommendations which acquire legal force in the country concerned after the necessary national laws have been passed. Meetings take place in the capitals of the member states in turn.

The executive organ of the Council consists of one representative of each of the member states, assisted by expert advisers. Sessions of these representatives consider proposals which have been submitted to them, adopt resolutions, and prepare recommendations which are confirmed by the Assembly. They are convened whenever necessary, but not less than twice a month, always in Moscow with the chairmanship rotating among the member states.

The Secretariat of the Council deals with questions of organization and prepares Assemblies. It is headed by a secretary and a deputy, approved by the Council, and has experts and advisers on its staff. The Secretariat also represents the Council in dealings with international economic organizations and at meetings. The seat of the Secretariat too is in Moscow.

Between the Twentieth Party Congress in February 1956 and the Twenty-first Party Congress at the end of January 1959 four meetings of the Assembly of the Council took place which represent important stages on the road towards the integration of the communist world. Fritz Schenk, until his flight in 1957 personal assistant to the East German chief planner, Bruno Leuschner, described these meetings to the writer.

The Assembly of the Council which met in Berlin (18 to 25 May 1956) co-ordinated production programmes for machine building, a number of basic industries, and agriculture. Permanent expert commissions were set up to which all member countries sent representatives. They are responsible for one particular branch of the economy in all the East European countries and independently prepare measures for economic integration under the general direction of the Council. Every commission has its own machinery, with expert representatives from member countries. Twelve expert commissions were set up at the Berlin Assembly, including one for machine building (with headquarters in Prague), for coal (Warsaw), for agriculture (Sophia), and the chemical industry (East Berlin).

The session of the Assembly in Warsaw from 18 to 22 June 1957 decided to co-ordinate the economic plans for 1961–5 of all the member countries in order to create the conditions for overall economic planning. A mutilateral clearing system for the currencies of the East European countries was set up. Standardization of products, exchange of experience, and the joint construction of technical installations were to be encouraged. Member states were to prepare ten- to fifteen-year plans for the most important branches of the economy. The long-term plans were to cover the years 1960–70, or 1960–75. Thousands of engineers, scientists, and economists were employed to do this.

At this stage of integration a number of fundamental considerations at the highest level became important. Therefore the highest Party and state leaders of all the communist countries met in Moscow on 20 and 21 May. Between four and seven of the most important leaders of each country were present. Among the Soviet leaders were Khrushchev, Mikoyan, Kozlov, and the head of the Planning Commission, Kuzmin. The communist countries of Asia were represented by observers, China by the two deputy Prime Ministers, Chen-Yun and Li Fu-chun who, it is interesting to note, played no prominent part in the People's Commune movement, then beginning.

At this 'summit conference' it was decided to develop the Council for Mutual Economic Aid and its subordinate organs. Like the Soviet Union, the whole communist world was now to give precedence to the development of raw material sources, power and chemical production: in addition it was decided to find ways in which to help the less developed countries with their industrialization.

The next Assembly session in Budapest (26 to 30 July 1958) dealt primarily with the raw material shortages which were threatening the fulfilment of all the communist economic plans. Installations for the production of raw materials and power were to be set up particularly in countries with the most favourable conditions. Poland and Eastern Germany for example were to sink lignite mines jointly in Poland, and Rumania and Hungary were to exploit the natural gas of Rumania together, to instal a joint pipeline and chemical factories.

An exact division of labour was also provided for in machine building: it was decided which countries should construct ships, railway rolling stock, diesel engines, electric engines, installations for the mineral oil industry and light industry, lorries, private cars, and motor bicycles. In most cases production was divided between two or three countries, each given an exact quota.

Scientific and technical collaboration was to be pushed ahead. China, North Korea, North Vietnam, were to participate in joint economic research. Three new expert commissions were set up for economic questions (with headquarters in Moscow), building (East Berlin), and transport (Warsaw).

The last Assembly session of the Council before the

Twenty-first Party Congress took place in Prague from 11 to 13 December 1958. Its theme was co-operation and specialization in the chemical and ferrous metal industries. It was decided to raise chemical production in Rumania fourfold, to treble it in the Soviet Union and to double it in Czechoslovakia, Hungary, and Eastern Germany. The manufacture of eleven different synthetic materials, nine forms of synthetic rubber, and six synthetic fibres was divided between the various countries. In addition the Prague conference decided to build long distance oil pipelines from the Soviet Union to Czechoslovakia, Eastern Germany, and Poland to relieve other means of transport. Two more expert commissions for food and light industry were set up.

The progress of the policy of economic integration led the Soviet leaders to modify the thesis of the 'differing roads to Socialism', proclaimed at the Twentieth Party Congress. Although Khrushchev said at the Twenty-first Party Congress that it was necessary to take account of 'the great variety of historic conditions in the various countries', he made it unmistakably clear that the important things were the universally valid laws of development. An essential part of the ideology of the Twentieth Party Congress was thus revoked. The universally valid laws could (and were meant) only to refer to the Soviet example. In practice, however, brutal methods of political suppression and colonial exploitation are no longer applied to the satellites. On the contrary, the Soviet Union tries to link the economic and political interests of the communist countries so closely with one another that a more or less voluntary interdependence is created.

INTERNATIONAL COMMUNISM

The problems of international communism were much more stressed at the Twenty-first Party Congress than at the Twentieth. In 1956 delegations from fifty-five communist parties were present, now there were seventy. In 1956 Khrushchev only referred in passing to questions of international communism, now he dealt with them in detail both in his main speech and his closing address. He stated that there were eighty-three communist parties in 1959 with 33 million members, the majority of whom are, however, members of the parties of the communist countries. This time Khrushchev paid much more attention to the communist parties of Asia, Africa, and South America than to those of Europe. He divided the national liberation struggle into two phases: in the first phase it is a question of driving out the colonial rulers, and in this struggle all national forces are united regardless of their political views: in the second phase social problems have to be solved and in this process the national liberation movement inevitably splits into various class-conditioned sections. During the first phase communists give unreserved and unconditional support to all anti-imperialist national forces. In the phase of social conflict, they are on the side of the progressive elements, the workers and peasants who fight against the capitalists.

With regard to the situation in the European countries Khrushchev said that fascism should not just be linked with the names of Hitler and Mussolini. It was 'not impossible that fascism can re-emerge in other forms'. The 'widest sections of all democratic and truly nationalist forces must be united' against the danger of fascism. This unity of the democratic forces, 'primarily of the working class', was the most reliable barrier against the fascist danger. Unity of the working class must be understood as meaning united action under the leadership of the communist parties. Khrushchev did not suggest discussions between communists and social-democrats; on the contrary, 'the charlatans of anti-communism' had to be removed before one could 'sit down at the same table and adopt a mutually acceptable programme'.

The speeches of all the West European Communist Party leaders were declarations against NATO, against the 'renaissance of German imperialism' and—a new element—against the Common Market.

The speech of Chou En-lai, the head of the Chinese delegation, was a paean of praise for the Soviet Union and its 'leading role in the socialist camp'. Chou En-lai no longer mentioned the fact that China, too, was already in the stage of transition to communism, but described the controversial people's communes as a 'big achievement' and as the best form of socialist development in China.

Khrushchev did not mention the Chinese people's communes at all. But his speech contained some remarks which were unmistakably aimed at the claim that the introduction of the people's communes was beginning the transition to communism in China. For example he said that things that had not had time to mature should not be introduced with undue haste: 'This would lead to distortions of our cause and would compromise it.' He stressed repeatedly that without an abundance of material and cultural goods there could be no communism: 'Communism can only be achieved when we have overtaken the stage of production of the developed capitalist countries and can guarantee a new labour productivity which is considerably higher than under capitalism.'

In spite of these side-thrusts Khrushchev was trying to refute the idea that there were serious differences between the Chinese communists and the Soviet leaders. 'The revisionists search for difference of opinion between our communist parties, but their illusory hopes are doomed to failure,' he said. 'We agree with the brotherly Communist Party of China about everything although its methods of building socialism differ in many respects from our own.'

Khrushchev emphasized that there could be no differences of opinion with the Chinese Communist Party because it 'holds a Marxist-communist position, based on class' and 'maintains the principle of international proletarian solidarity'. On the most important question, the 'preservation and strengthening of class solidarity in the struggle against capitalism' there could not be any difference of opinion among communists: 'This is the most important thing which distinguishes us from the revisionists.'

By revisionists Khrushchev meant the Yugoslav communists who were sharply attacked at the Party Congress. Pospelov, then Ambassador to Peking, the Albanian Party leader, Enver Hoxha, and Mukhitdinov, in particular, held the Yugoslavs responsible for Russia's loss of popularity in the countries of the Near East.

Khrushchev emphatically denied that the national communist parties were dependent on Moscow. At the same time, however, he again claimed that the CPSU was the rightful leader of the international communist movement, a claim incorporated in the declaration of the twelve ruling parties in November 1957 and the cause of the new dispute with Yugoslavia. He advanced three reasons for this claim to leadership: the CPSU had been the first to accomplish the socialist revolution and to take over power, the Soviet Union was the most powerful Communist Party, and thirdly the USSR had been the 'first country to enter upon the period of the comprehensive construction of communism'. The Soviet Union was, therefore, the 'vanguard of the communist world movement, the first to climb the heights of communism'.

THE CULT OF KHRUSHCHEV AND THE NEW GENERATION

Not a single important speaker at the Twenty-first Party Congress—not even Khrushchev himself—mentioned collective leadership. Instead the centre of attention was occupied by Nikita Khrushchev. His speech was no longer described as the 'report of the Central Committee', but as 'Comrade Nikita Sergeyevich Khrushchev's great speech'. Speakers no longer referred to the Party leadership and the Central Committee, but to 'the Central Committee with N. S. Khrushchev at its head', to the 'Party under the leadership of the Central Committee and N. S. Khrushchev personally' or even to 'the Central Committee of the Party under the leadership of N. S. Khrushchev'.

Special praise was showered on Khrushchev's theory of the transition to communism. Nikolai Podgorny, a candidate member of the Praesidium of the Party, spoke of a 'truly titanic task'; Nikolai Belyayev, a member of the Party Praesidium, underlined the 'historic importance' of Khrushchev's thesis, and Semyon Ignatiev, the Tatar Party secretary, described it as 'a Marxist-Leninist analysis of brilliant depth and clarity'.

Many Party speakers thanked Khrushchev personally for solving some question or other. The Head of the State Security Service, Shelepin, said that legality had been restored under the direction of the Party leadership 'and Comrade N. S. Khrushchev personally'. Kuzmin, the Head of the Planning Commission, reported 'that the Seven-Year Plan had owed its existence to the initiative and direct leadership of the Central Committee and Comrade N. S. Khrushchev personally'. Malinovsky, the Minister of Defence, thanked the Party leadership and 'Nikita Sergeyevich personally' for the daily attention which had been devoted to the army. The Party secretary of Omsk, Kolushchinsky thanked Khrushchev for removing 'the despicable and loathsome faction of Malenkov, Kaganovich, Molotov, and Bulganin.'

More technical notes were sounded too. The well-known atomic physicist Kurchatov thanked Khrushchev for installations for the study of thermo-nuclear reactors. The Party secretary of Tadzikistan, Uldzhabaiev, said that the increase in cotton production 'we owe mainly to the untiring activity of the Praesidium of the Central Committee and Comrade N. S. Khrushchev personally'. The deputy Prime Minister Dmitri Ustinov went so far as to attribute successes in building and launching earth satellites and space rockets to Khrushchev 'under whose constant guidance all efforts in this field have taken place'. The prize remark, however, was made by the Party secretary of Omsk, Kolushchinsky, who said: 'Nobody will forget the immense merits and efforts of the indomitable Leninist, the First Party Secretary of the Central Committee Nikita Sergeyevich Khrushchev, in restoring Leninist collective leadership in this country. . . .'

Although paeans of praise for Khrushchev were common to all the speeches certain differences did emerge. The Leningrad Party secretary, Spiridonov, spoke of 'N. S. Khrushchev's outstanding report', whereas Suslov said that the Twenty-first Party Congress had been an extraordinary congress 'and therefore the Central Committee did *not* submit a report'. In general the members of the Praesidium of the Party, particularly Mikoyan, Suslov, Kozlov, Aristov, and Furtseva, as well as some leading economic officials, kept their praise within bounds.

The Twenty-first Party Congress sounded the knell of collective leadership which had been the guiding principle of the Party from 1953 to 1956. Khrushchev was no longer *primus inter pares*. The songs in his praise corresponded to the *de facto* power he had gained in the meantime; they are reminiscent of the early days of Stalin. But as the Soviet Union today is no longer the same as that of the thirties, the analogy should not be carried too far.

Apart from the Khrushchev cult one of the most important

CHANGES AMONG THE COMMUNIST LEADERS SINCE STALIN'S DEATH

(Names are given in alphabetical order)

March 1953 (after Stalin's death)	February 1956 (after the Twentieth Party Congress)	February 1959 (after the Twenty-first Party Congress)	December 1960 (before the Twenty-second Party Congress)
Full members of the Party Praesidium			
Beria	Bulganin	Aristov	Aristov
Bulganin	Khrushchev	Belyayev	Brezhnev
Khrushchev	Kaganovich	Brezhnev	Furtseva
Kaganovich	Kirichenko	Furtseva	Ignatov
Malenkov	Mikoyan	Ignatov	Khrushchev
Mikoyan	Malenkov	Khrushchev	Kozlov
Molotov	Molotov	Kozlov	Kosgin
Pervukhin	Pervukhin	Kuusinen	Mikoyan
Saburov	Saburov	Mikoyan	Mukhitdinov
Voroshilov	Suslov	Mukhitdinov	Podgorny
	Voroshilov	Shvernik	Polyansky
		Suslov	Suslov
		Voroshilov	
Candidate members of the Party Praesidium			
Bagirov	Brezhnev	Kalnbersin	Kalnbersin
Melnikov	Furtseva	Kirilenko	Kirilenko
Ponomarenko	Mukhitdinov	Korochenko	Korochenko
Shvernik	Shepilov	Kosygin	Masurov
	Shvernik	Masurov	Mzhavanadze
	Zhukov	Mzhavanadze	Pervukhin
		Pervukhin	Pospelov
		Podgorny	
		Polyansky	
		Pospelov	
Members of the Central Committee Secretariat			
Khrushchev	Aristov	Aristov	Khrushchev
Ignatiev	Belyayev	Brezhnev	Kozlov
Pospelov	Brezhnev	Khrushchev	Kuusinen
Shatalin	Khrushchev	Furtseva	Mukhitdinov
Suslov	Furtseva	Ignatov	Suslov
	Pospelov	Kirichenko	
	Shepilov	Kuusinen	
	Suslov	Mukhitdinov	
		Pospelov	
		Suslov	
The Praesidium of the Council of Ministers			
Chairman (Prime Minister):			
Malenkov	Bulganin	Khrushchev	Khrushchev
Senior Deputies			
Beria	Kaganovich	Kozlov	Kosygin
Bulganin	Mikoyan	Mikoyan	Mikoyan
Kaganovich	Molotov		
Molotov	Pervukhin		
	Saburov		
Deputies			
Mikoyan	Khrunichev	Kosygin	Ignatov
	Kosygin	Kuzmin	Novikov
	Kucherenko	Ustinov	Ustinov
	Malenkov	Zasyadko	Zasyadko
	Malyshev		
	Savenyagin		
	Tevosyan		

features of this Party Congress was the change of generations in the Party 'apparatus', which Khrushchev announced. He recommended that the young should quickly be promoted to leading positions in the Party, state, and economy. A combination of older and younger officials would greatly help the successful economic and political development of the USSR. 'The young cadres must be promoted more enterprisingly than hitherto', said Khrushchev; other officials, however, who because of their age, 'or for other reasons' were no longer sufficiently energetic and active should 'not be hindered if they expressed the desire to take up another job or to retire'. Alexei Kirichenko, too, demanded that 'young, able, and promising people', who are 'entirely devoted' to the cause of the Party and who 'have organizational ability' should be employed in leading state and Party positions.

The first transfers of officials began soon after the Twenty-first Party Congress. Ivan Kapitonov, the First Secretary of Moscow and a supporter of extremism at the Congress, had to give way to P. N. Demitshev. In Uzbekistan the First Secretary, Sabir Kamalov, was replaced by Sharaff Rashidov, who had become prominent as Chairman of the Uzbekistan Writers' Association and Deputy Chairman of the 'Society for friendship and cultural relations with the countries of the Arab East'. Akhmedov, the Prime Minister, also lost his post. In the White Russian and Moldavian Union Republics, too, important changes were made.

Vladimir Semichastny, who had taken over the leadership of the Soviet Youth League only a year before, became head of the department for Party organs of the Central Committee of the CPSU. At the Thirteenth Congress of Soviet trade unions at the end of March 1959 there was an almost complete change in the leadership. The Chairman of the State Planning Commission, Kuzmin, who had been appointed in May 1957, had to yield his place to the chief expert in consumer goods questions, Kosygin; Khrushchev's supporter Nikolai Ignatov, a member of the Praesidium and Secretariat of the Central Committee, became chairman of the Praesidium of the Supreme Soviet of the RSFSR.

The 'rejuvenation of the Party apparatus' is apparently connected with the reorganization of the four-year schools for

the élite of the Party which took place in June 1956. At that
time, big changes were made in the curriculum—practical
and scientific subjects were specially introduced to train up a
body of up-to-date well qualified Party members. Khrushchev
is apparently hoping to provide himself with a solid foundation
in the state and the Party by means of devoted young officials
who are indebted to him. But nearly all of them have a good
university education, considerable self-confidence, and varied
political experience. In their youth they experienced the Great
Purge, Stalin's reign of terror, and his defeat in 1941. Many of
them had been hoping for freer development after the end of
the war and were disappointed. There followed the Zhdanov
campaign against art and literature, the break with Tito in the
summer of 1948, the struggles for power after Stalin's death,
'October in Poland', and the revolt in Hungary. It is question-
able whether this generation will let itself be made into the tool
of a leader still dominated by Stalin's ideas.

CHAPTER IX

ON THE ROAD TO THE TWENTY-SECOND PARTY CONGRESS

(Developments after February 1959)

SINCE the Twenty-first Party Congress Soviet domestic policy has been characterized by an abundance of efforts to realize the production figures of the Seven-Year Plan which had obviously been put too high. But in 1959 and 1960 domestic and economic problems were frequently overshadowed by questions of foreign policy, particularly by the U2 incident, the conflict with Peking, which broke out again at the beginning of 1960, by the Soviet Union's increasing activity in underdeveloped countries and by the World Communist Conference in November 1960. Khrushchev's journeys abroad, to the United States in September 1959, to China at the beginning of October 1959, to South-East Asia in February 1960, to France in March 1960, his brief visit to Paris on the occasion of the (abortive) summit conference in May 1960, and to Austria in July 1960, led him to be away for prolonged periods and thus repeatedly caused the neglect of domestic problems.

GENERAL POST

The Twenty-first Party Congress which ended on 5 February confronted the Soviet Party with many new tasks. In the second half of February and during March 1959 local Party meetings, plenary meetings of the regional Party committees, and the central committee of the Union Republics took place in the whole Soviet Union. A 'people's competition' was staged in order to mobilize industrial workers in particular for the fulfilment of the Plan.

Within the Party 'apparatus' there began a game of general post, the purpose of which was to spur officials on to greater achievements. In Moscow at the beginning of March, the First Secretary of the Moscow Party organization, Ivan Kapitonov, was relieved of his post in the presence of Aristov and

Kirichenko. Later he was accused of not having behaved as the Party required, demanding too little from his staff: he was succeeded by P. N. Demitshev. In Novisibirsk, the Party secretary had already been dismissed before that for failing to fulfil his duties. In Uzbekistan, the centre of Russian cotton growing, the leader of the Party, Kamalov, and the Prime Minister, Akhmedov, lost their positions and were expelled from all Party bodies. They were accused of neglecting their economic tasks and of appointing their friends to do work for which they were not qualified. Rashidov, who had lately come to the fore as Chairman of the Writers' Association of Uzbekistan and Deputy Chairman of the Soviet League of Friendship with the Arab countries, was made the new Party secretary of Uzbekistan. The first Party secretary of White Russia, Avkhimovich, was also dismissed because he had filled important posts with inefficient people.

These and a number of other changes indicate that Khrushchev and his colleagues hoped to hit the ambitious targets of the Seven-Year Plan by far-reaching changes and the promotion of energetic officials. Even faithful followers of Khrushchev were not spared if their practical work did not show the desired results. On 21 March, for instance, the Chairman of the State Planning Commission, Kuzmin, who until then had always been backed by Khrushchev, was dismissed and replaced by Kosygin. This appointment shows Khrushchev's desire to rely on an experienced economic leader; at the same time, since Kosygin was known as a consumer goods specialist, it indicated that the production of consumer goods was to be expanded.

The changes also extended to the Komsomol leadership and the trade unions. The Komsomol leader, Vladimir Semichastny, who had been appointed only in December 1958, moved up into the central Party machine; he was succeeded by the little known Sergi Pavlov. At the end of March the leadership of the Soviet trade unions changed almost completely. Although Grishin, the chairman appointed in the summer of 1956, continued in office, all but thirty-six of the 197 members of the central council of the Soviet trade unions were replaced by new officials. All these changes directly after the Twenty-first Party Congress indicated the leaders' desire to fill the most important

posts with officials who combined loyalty to the Party and
support of Khrushchev with a capacity for initiative in their
organizational, technical, and economic work.

Khrushchev's birthday occurred in the middle of these
changes. The fact that it was hardly noticed in the Soviet
Union did not mean that the Party leader was being slighted;
the reason was that on 10 May 1956, the Central Committee
had decided to celebrate the anniversaries of leading personalities only on the occasion of their fiftieth birthday and every
ten years after that. As in April 1959 Khrushchev celebrated
his sixty-fifth birthday he was a victim of the decision which he
himself had supported. The other communist countries celebrated his birthday and he also received congratulations from
them, the Chinese communists being very reticent, while the
Hungarians and Bulgarians sent two congratulatory telegrams,
the Czechs four, and the East Germans ten.

THE COMPROMISE WITH THE WRITERS

The preparations for the third Writers' Congress, which met
in the Great Hall of the Kremlin from 18 to 23 May, had begun
in the previous summer. Everything was done, after the
difficulties of past years, to make the Congress a big demonstration of loyalty to the Soviet Union and the Party. Surkov,
who is closely connected with the Party 'apparatus', in his
main speech demanded that the writers should concentrate on
questions of the present, and that Soviet literature should be
enrolled 'to serve the struggle of the day'. The hero of literature
was 'the builder of communism'.

The real problems emerged, at least partially, during the
discussions. The Ukrainian writer, Gonchar, criticized the flat
style of Soviet literature and said many writers were frightened
of being accused of 'false romanticism'. Alexander Tvardovsky
attacked those who always wanted to control, administer, and
direct Soviet literature and appealed to the writers to 'Write in
the way your conscience tells you . . . and don't be frightened
in advance of editors and critics.' During the Congress Ilya
Ehrenburg appealed to the Soviet writers in *Novy Mir* to write
'the truth and nothing but the truth'. Konstantin Paustovsky
went still further in *Literaturnaya Gazeta* on 20 May when he
affirmed the connexion between literature and life, but warned

his audience against trying to achieve this unity by administrative methods. He, too, demanded truthful descriptions, adding, 'Perhaps we are making so much noise about truth in literature because we have not got it.' To direct writers to collective farms or enterprises could do little good. The purposeful optimism which produced a continuation of success stories almost made the impression that, after the Soviet system had been in existence for forty-two years, Soviet writers had their doubts about it. Paustovsky also criticized the primitive presentation of the present, which was suitable at the most for some piece of chronology or journalism.

Many speakers demanded literary equality for the non-Russian peoples. Gonchar protested, carefully but insistently, against discrimination against the literature of the non-Russian peoples: many other speakers made it clear that Soviet literature did not consist only of the literature of the Russian people.

Khrushchev, who also spoke at the Congress, admitted several times that he understood little about literature. He was obviously anxious to come to terms with the writers. He defended Dudintsev who, 'although he made mistakes', had been right 'in many things'. He did not mention Pasternak by name, but some conciliatory phrases in his speech obviously referred to him. 'One does not hit a defenceless person. And when an opponent surrenders in an ideological struggle, admits defeat and declares his readiness to adopt the correct position, then don't reject him, offer him your hand so that he can join the ranks and work together with you.'

Thus Khrushchev tried to uphold the ideological monopoly of the Party without producing new conflicts. Writers should realize, he claimed, that the portrayal of unfortunate characteristics attracted 'our enemies' attention'. Khrushchev rejected administrative censorship and even said that it was stupid to ban works of literature. He was evidently thinking of some kind of control by the writers themselves—though not without the help of the Party—for he said that they should not push the decision of such questions on to the government, but solve them among themselves.

Apart from some extremist speeches by third-rate provincial writers, the tone of the Congress was conciliatory. Khrushchev did not challenge it, but asked for union on the basis of principle. Surkov, the Chairman of the Writers' Union, and Kochetov, the editor of *Literaturnaya Gazeta*, two of the strongest opponents of revisionism who had been sharply attacked at the Congress, were dismissed. Their places were taken by Konstantin Fedin and S. S. Smirnov, who had kept very much in the background in the campaign against the revisionists and who themselves were amongst the critics of official literary policy. Greater attention was also paid to the non-Russian writers. In the elections to the Secretariat ten representatives of Russian literature and sixteen writers from the non-Russian regions of the USSR were elected. But a number of the most prominent writers, including Ilya Ehrenburg, Mikhail Sholokhov, Leonid Leonov, Vera Panova, Margarita Aliger, Nikolai Pogodin, Valentin Ovechkin, and Konstantin Simonov, continued their 'conspiracy of silence'; they did not appear at the Congress, in spite of its relative moderation.

THE PLENARY MEETING ON INDUSTRY

The realization of the Seven-Year Plan depended largely on the introduction of modern technical methods in industry. Early in March a special committee of the Soviet Council of Ministers was created to supervise the transition to automation. Its Chairman was Anatol Kostousov who had first made his name as Minister of Machine-tool Construction (1949–53) and after Stalin's death as Minister of the Machine-tool Industry and finally as Chairman of the Council of the *sovnarkhoz* of the Moscow region. In order to attune the economic and Party functionaries to the modernization of industry the Party leaders called a plenary meeting of the Central Committee for 24 to 29 June which dealt exclusively with this question.

The meeting was attended by the 133 members and 122 candidate members of the Central Committee as well as by *sovnarkhozy* chairmen, members of the State Planning Commission, academic people, technicians, engineers, and Party officials responsible for industry. This time Khrushchev did not make the main speech. He allowed the chairmen of the *sovnarkhozy* of Moscow, Leningrad, Stalinsk, Sverdlovsk, and Dnjepopetrovsk to report on their experiences, in order himself to put forward new proposals in the course of the discussion.

The obstacles to the modernization of Soviet industry emerged clearly during the plenary meeting. There was special criticism of 'technical conservatism', of the reluctance of Soviet directors to modernize their enterprises. Even new equipment, obtained with difficulty from abroad, often lay about unused. The reasons for this 'technical conservatism' were also frankly stated. The Chairman of the State Committee for Chemistry, Fiodorov, said that applications for the installation of new machinery had to be submitted to eleven different authorities. Moreover, workers in enterprises where new machines had been introduced were often worse paid than those working with obsolete equipment because the wage fund of an enterprise depended on the number of workers. Consequently, partially or completely automatized factories received a smaller wage fund, and economic officials and managers were afraid to modernize their enterprises because this brought them into a lower wage category.

Several speakers, including Khrushchev, strongly criticized the system hitherto in force of measuring the plan fulfilment of an enterprise by the weight of the products. Khrushchev said that the mirror industry was making particularly heavy looking-glasses and the furniture industry particularly heavy chairs in order to fulfil their plan more easily.

The relations between science and technology and the training of technical experts were also criticized. Khrushchev said that technical universities should to an increasing extent be transferred to centres of industry. The main emphasis should no longer be on the training of highly qualified engineers, but on technicians with medium qualifications.

The frankness with which defects were described at the plenary meeting stood, however, in noticeable contrast to the decisions taken. Even a layman could see that the difficulties which had found expression at the meeting could only be solved by cutting down interference from the central authorities, by relaxing the regulations and directives of the plan, by giving greater independence to the lower economic authorities, by providing material incentives on a wide scale, and greater freedom and authority for enterprise directors, technicians, and engineers. But none of these measures found expression in the final resolution; the Central Committee restricted itself to giving a mass of instructions to a great variety of authorities, without removing the origin of the difficulties by real reforms. Worse still, the Party organizations' control over economic life was increased.

By a resolution published on 26 June there were set up in all enterprises Party control commissions, whose duty it was to carry out government orders, organize special and export deliveries, and test the quality of the goods produced. The new commissions had also to try to reduce production costs, introduce new technical installations, and automatize production. In trading organizations they were given the right to examine the deliveries of goods, the observation of trading regulations, and the reduction of circulation costs. The 'most highly trained, trusty, and active Party members' were to become members of the Party control commissions, which were to be elected for a year by open vote at Party meetings. The commissions were empowered to report any shortcomings immediately to the Party leadership and the management of the enterprise, and to take the necessary steps in conjunction with the management. If these were not taken, or not quickly enough, the control commission was given the right to go directly to the Central Committee or the Council of Ministers. At the same time, however, the Party control commissions were not to issue their own administrative directives, but only to assist managers and enterprise directors in every way.

Soon after the establishment of these commissions many misunderstandings and difficulties arose. On the one hand the Soviet press lamented the fact that many enterprise directors simply ignored the commissioners' proposals, while complaining on the other that some control commissions exceeded their authority and usurped the functions of enterprise administration.

THE PURGE IN AZERBAIDJAN AND LATVIA

In July and November 1959 an almost complete changeover took place in the Party leadership of the Union Republics of Azerbaidjan and Latvia. This was not a question of the already 'normal' changes, but of resistance to the nationalities policy of the central government. In several Union Republics, even in higher Party circles, doubts had arisen, particularly about the teaching of languages in non-Russian schools as proposed in the school reform law. Until the law had come into force the principle was that three languages were taught in all the schools, of the non-Russian Republics, the local language, Russian, and one foreign language. In the draft of the school reform law, however, it was left to the parents to decide whether to have their children taught in their national language or to send them to a Russian school. As many parents believed— rightly—that attendance at a Russian school would facilitate their children's future career, the practical result was that the non-Russian languages were pushed still further into the background. The law was put into effect in all the Union Republics except Azerbaidjan and Latvia where children continued to learn their native language, Russian, and one foreign language.

The two Union Republics were not to resist for long. On 16 and 17 June there was a plenary meeting of the Central Committee of the Communist Party of Azerbaidjan, attended by Mukhitdinov, a member of the Party Praesidium. Almost all the Party leaders in Azerbaidjan were replaced. The First Party Secretary, I. D. Mustavaiev, was accused of having 'caused bewilderment in the completely clear language question'; another secretary of the Central Committee was accused of 'artificially differentiating between native and non-local officials'. W. Akhundov became the new First Party Secretary and on 12 August the former Komsomol leader, Vladimir Semichastny, took the place of the Second Secretary, Yakovlev. Finally, on 11 December the former Chairman of the Supreme Soviet of Azerbaidjan, N. A. Ibrahimov, was obliged publicly to admit that he had made 'several mistakes over the language question'.

In November there followed a dramatic purge in Latvia as well. The First Party Secretary, Jan Kalnbersin, who had led the Latvian Communist Party since 1940 and who had been a candidate member of the Praesidium of the Party since June 1957, was degraded to the post of Chairman of the Praesidium of the Supreme Soviet of Latvia. He was succeeded by the former Second Secretary, Arvid Pelshe. The Prime Minister, Vilis Lacis, was replaced by Jan Peive. The former minister, J. P. Ostrov, the Latvian Komsomol leader, V. D. Ruskuliv, and the chairman of the trade unions, I. O. Pinxis, were also dismissed. On the 29 November 1958, Lacis had declared himself in *Pravda* in favour of keeping the compulsory study of the Latvian language.

In addition to the language controversy, economic problems probably played a part in the Latvian purge, particularly where relations between Latvia and the interests of the USSR as a whole were concerned. The Deputy Prime Minister of Latvia, Eduard Berklav, had already been dismissed late in the summer. *Pravda* and *Partinaya Zhizn* had accused Latvian Party and state officials of not taking sufficient account of the economic interests of the state as a whole and on 18 August *Pravda* had called upon the Latvian Party organizations 'steadfastly to prevent any symptoms of particularism'.

The purges in Azerbaidjan and Latvia, like the Writers' Congress in May 1959, were another symptom of resistance to russianization. This resistance had its reasons. Even though his successors had moved away from the extremer forms of Stalin's policy of russification, the non-Russian nations remained at a disadvantage. Although in 1958 54·8 per cent. of the Soviet population was Russian and 45·2 per cent. non-Russian, 71 per cent. of all new books published were in Russian and only 26 per cent. in the non-Russian languages. The proportions were still less just among journalistic publications. In the spring of 1959 the press of even the non-Russian Union Republics said that it was 'progressive' that 10·2 million non-Russian Soviet citizens had given Russian as their mother tongue in the census of 15 January 1959. The purges in Azerbaidjan and Latvia indicated, however, that the growing tendency to russianize was meeting with resistance even in some of the higher circles of the Party.

THE NEW CONSUMER GOODS PROGRAMME

In the summer and autumn of 1959 the Soviet leaders were also forced to pay attention to shortages in the supply of consumer goods. Kosygin's appointment as Chairman of the State Planning Commission in March had shown that the Soviet leaders were intending to force the production of consumer goods. From the beginning of the summer news of shortages of consumer goods and in trade were given prominence. The press criticized the fact that the production of consumer goods had fallen in many factories, and that in some it had stopped altogether. Even *Pravda*, on 28 August, described the efforts of a young married couple to find a flat iron, only to discover soon what 'every thinking person knows anyway', that in the last month no iron could be found anywhere. More important was an obviously inspired article by K. Sorokin, an official from Kuibyshev, published by *Izvestia* at the beginning of August; the article sharply criticized the Soviet trade system. It said that the trading organizations had in practice become distributive organs of the factories, selling their goods regardless of whether the consumers were interested in them or not. The quantity of unsold goods was constantly increasing. In Kuibyshev alone there were unsold goods to the value of over 250 roubles. Neither producers nor traders took any interest in considering the wishes of the population.

While these and many other reports were appearing in the Soviet press the decision regarding the increase in the production of consumer goods had no doubt long been taken. In the 'measures to raise production, increase variety, and improve consumer and household goods', published on 16 October, the Central Committee and the Council of Ministers stated that the production of consumer goods had lagged behind the wishes of the population. There were too few television sets, pianos, washing machines, sewing machines, refrigerators; the shortage of mincing machines, crockery, and irons was particularly stressed. In a number of towns and rural districts 'one cannot even get the simplest household goods'. Various Party, state, and economic authorities had failed to pay enough attention to the production of consumer goods and with their consent some *sovnarkhozy* had lately gone so far as to reduce their production.

Under the new plan there was to be a drastic increase in the production of consumer goods—from 45·5 thousand million roubles' worth in 1958 to 57·9 thousand million roubles in 1960 and of 64·6 thousand million in 1961: thus within three years the production of consumer goods was to be raised by 40 per cent. By 1961 the production, among other things, of refrigerators was to be raised from 395,600 to 796,000, of vacuum cleaners from 246,000 to 510,000, and of television sets from 979,000 to 1,928,000. In the same three years the production of sewing machines was to be increased from 2·7 million to 3·5 million, and of motor bicycles from 25,000 to 280,000. This programme was to be started in the last quarter of 1959. Industry received an additional order to make available consumer goods to the value of 647 million roubles. In a commentary in *Pravda* on 18 October 'the well-being of the workers and the improved satisfaction of the population's material and spiritual requirements' were described as the 'most important and constant preoccupation of the Party'.

Not only this phraseology but also the aims of the new resolution were reminiscent of Malenkov's consumer goods programme, announced during the New Course in the autumn of 1953. At that time the Soviet leaders had promised to produce about 500,000 vacuum cleaners by 1956. But in 1958, two years after the deadline, there were only 246,000. At that time it had been decreed that 4·3 million flat irons should be produced, but three years later there were only 2 million. For refrigerators, washing machines, sewing machines, and television sets the quantities promised for the end of 1955 were reached in 1959. The new programme presented an additional liability to the official Seven-Year Plan. If its realization was seriously intended, a shift in emphasis from heavy to light industry and the production of consumer goods would sooner or later have to be announced, as indeed finally occurred.

THE PLENARY MEETING ABOUT AGRICULTURE
(DECEMBER 1959)

The proposed increase in the production of consumer goods was connected with raising agricultural production. But at the plenary meeting of the central committee on agricultural questions on 21 to 25 December it appeared that many agricultural targets of the Seven-Year Plan had not been achieved.

Like the plenary meeting on industry in June the agricultural session in December was intended for the general public. In addition to members and candidate members of the Central Committee it was attended by agricultural functionaries, *sovnarkhozy* chairmen, directors of state farms, chairmen of collective farms, agronomists, editors of agricultural journals, and even specially acclaimed milkmaids, shepherds, and pig breeders. The most important speeches were made by the First Party Secretaries of the seven leading Union Republics,

Polyansky (RSFSR), Podgorny (Ukraine), Belyayev (Kazakhstan), Mazurov (White Russia), Rashidov (Uzbekistan), Uldzhabaiev (Tadzhikistan), and Akhundov (Azerbaidjan). Khrushchev spoke only during the discussion, when he dealt very openly with the faults of Russian farming. In many parts of the Soviet Union, Khrushchev said, the most elementary prerequisites for successful agriculture were ignored—sowing was late, fertilizers were not used properly, weeds were neglected. Bureaucracy continued to rule. Thus Soviet state farms employed an average of twenty-five to thirty bookkeepers and accountants, who answered questionnaires annually and filled in 1·8 million figures in the process. Many agricultural officials knew little about agriculture and some could not distinguish between a nettle and a pigweed. The situation was particularly serious in Kazakhstan and the Altai, the regions of the virgin lands, where the harvest had fallen by 28 and 36 per cent. respectively compared with 1958. Khrushchev severely criticized the First Secretary of Kazakhstan, Nikolai Belyayev.[1] Because of bad organization grain had not been harvested over an area of more than 1·6 million hectares, and 18,000 tractors had not been repaired in time. The Minister of Agriculture, Vladimir Matskevich,[2] was also censured by Khrushchev.

In spite of all this the plenary meeting of the Central Committee adopted a resolution confirming the aim of catching up with the United States in the production of milk, meat, and butter per head of population. The Union Republics and regions were called upon to reach by 1963 the targets set in the Seven-Year Plan for 1965. In some branches of agriculture things were to go even further. While the Seven-Year Plan envisaged an increase in meat production from 8 to 16 million tons by 1965 this goal was now to be reached by 1963 and 20 to 21 million tons of meat to be produced by 1965. Instead of the 50 sugar refineries in the Plan 90 were to be established, instead of 13 million hectares of maize 20 million were to be grown by 1965, the virgin lands campaign was to be continued, and a further 8 to 9 million hectares of land were to be cultivated.

At the same time procurement prices for agricultural products were to be reduced. While they had been raised in

[1] Dismissed Jan. 1960.   [2] Degraded Dec. 1960.

September 1953 to provide bigger incentives for the collective farms, it was now decided to bring the procurement prices for collective farms into line with those for state farms; in many cases this meant a 50 per cent. reduction. It was also announced that the procurement prices of tea, cotton, citrus fruits, and other products were to be reduced.

Finally, the December plenary meeting hinted at the reduction of the peasants' private land. The further development of collective farms, said the resolution, would 'undoubtedly result in a reduction of the role of private holdings'. Collective farms were encouraged to set up more bakeries, restaurants, children's homes, and boarding schools 'to free women from housework and to give them the possibility of working in social production'.

It was noticeable that the December meeting avoided a number of important questions. Among these the chief was the long debated question of the relation of state and collective farms. Nor was any decision reached over the question of the amalgamation of collective farms: the matter was 'handed over to the Praesidium of the Central Committee of the CPSU for examination'.

Like the industrial meeting in June, the December session on agricultural questions was paradoxical. Though on the one hand shortcomings and difficulties were stated in clear terms, on the other no explanation of their causes was given and no attempt made to solve the agricultural problems through serious reforms.

THE FALL OF KIRICHENKO AND BELIAIEV

Shortly afterwards Alexei Kirichenko and Nikolai Belyayev were removed from the Praesidium of the Party. The two dismissals showed that Khrushchev did not hesitate to sacrifice his closest collaborators, whom he himself had promoted to the highest positions, if economic necessities or political conflicts required this.

The fall of Kirichenko was announced in an unexpected fashion. On 13 January *Pravda* reported in a few lines that Kirichenko had been appointed Secretary of the region of Rostov, without referring to his former eminence. Aristov played an active part in his dismissal.

On the occasion of his fiftieth birthday on 25 February 1958, Kirichenko[1] had been praised as an 'outstanding pioneer of the Soviet state'. He had always supported Khrushchev and for a time he came directly after him in the Party hierarchy and was even regarded as the heir presumptive. In the leadership Kirichenko was said to have been responsible for personnel questions in the non-Russian Union Republics, as well as for relations with communist parties in the communist countries and, according to another version, at times also for the security organs of the USSR.

At the Twenty-first Party Congress, while Kirichenko was reporting on the employment of officials in Siberia, he was interrupted by Khrushchev, which usually indicated disapproval of the speaker concerned. Above all it was striking that Kirichenko's speech to officials of the state security service on 18 May 1959 was not published.

No public reason was given for Kirichenko's fall. In Party circles, however, it transpired that Kirichenko had spoken disrespectfully about Khrushchev. He was said to have remarked that the latter largely owed his rise to the Ukrainian Party 'apparatus'. There seem also to have been disputes between Kirichenko and Aristov about their rights over the employment of Party officials. According to one version current in Party circles, Kirichenko, who was only responsible for the employment of Party officials in the non-Russian regions, in fact interfered unduly in the RSFSR, which was Aristov's sphere of authority.

A few days later, on 25 January 1960, Nikolai Belyayev was also dismissed; he was downgraded to the position of Secretary of the region of Stavropol. Stavropol thus became something of a place of banishment for dismissed leaders: one and a half years earlier the former Prime Minister, Bulganin, had also been sent there.

The fall of Belyayev, a member of the Central Committee Secretariat since July 1955 and a full member of the Party Praesidium since June 1957, did not come as a great surprise. Already in December 1957, when he was appointed First Party Secretary of Kazakhstan, Belyayev had been removed from the operative leadership in Moscow. At the plenary meeting in

[1] See above, p. 111, n. 1.

December 1959 he was severely reprimanded by Khrushchev because of his alleged failure in Kazakhstan. 'I asked you, Comrade Belyayev, what do you need to bring in the harvest in time? You said: "We don't need anything, we have been given everything, everything is being done." That, Comrades, is how things really stand. One mustn't work like that, one must keep one's word,' said Khrushchev.

Added to this warning were the words 'friendship is friendship—service is service', a clear announcement that Khrushchev would spare not even Belyayev, his friend and political collaborator. Kunaiev, the former Prime Minister of Kazakhstan, was appointed Belyayev's successor.

With the fall of Kirichenko and Belyayev, who had been promoted by Khrushchev personally, the conflicts after Stalin's death reached a second phase. In place of the struggle between different teams and tendencies which went on from 1953 to 1958, in the course of which Malenkov, Beria, Molotov, Kaganovich, Shepilov, Zhukov, Bulganin, Pervukhin, and Saburov had lost their power and been replaced by the faithful followers of Khrushchev, there now began, with the dismissal of Kirichenko and Belyayev, the process of selection from those officials who had reached the top with or through Khrushchev himself.

THE INTENSIFICATION OF PARTY PROPAGANDA

In another important sphere, ideology and Party propaganda, the turn of the year was of great importance. On 9 January 1960 the Central Committee took the important decision to intensify Party propaganda and to adapt it to the new conditions.

This had become necessary mainly because tendencies were becoming increasingly noticeable in Soviet society which were 'unplanned' and undesired by the leadership. In wide circles of the population discontent was growing about the contrast between technical achievements and the shortage of consumer goods as well as the great social contrasts. In October 1959 inadequate supplies in the virgin land areas led to strikes and tumults among several thousand Komsomol members in Kazakhstan. In the realm of culture there continued to be movements attacking 'Party-mindedness' and 'socialist realism'. On the national plane resistance to the policy of russianization was appearing, while in the economic field there was a tendency towards personal enrichment and in the ideological sphere the Soviet leaders were up against revisionism or the striving after political reform as well as the response which religious sects found even among the young.

In addition to these domestic reasons the Soviet leaders must also have been anxious to increase ideological activities in view of the empirical communism of Belgrade and the dogmatic leftism of Peking.

Hitherto this had been difficult, because a kind of 'ideological interregnum' had existed in Russia since the Twentieth Party Congress. This gap was bridged only at the end of 1959 and the beginning of 1960. New ideological textbooks had appeared by now from which Stalin's antiquated theories had been expunged and replaced by new ones. The new textbook of Party history had appeared at the beginning of July 1959, followed in October by the revised edition of the *Political Economy* and in November 1959 by the second edition of the *Foundations of Marxist Philosophy*. The first attempt of Soviet ideologists to assemble all philosophical, economic, and political teaching in one book finally culminated, at the beginning of 1960, in the publication of the *Foundations of Marxism-Leninism*.

The new textbooks differed from those of the Stalin period in the following respects:

1. Stalin's name is only rarely to be found. Many of his writings, particularly those published after 1934, are not mentioned. Stalin is no longer described as one of the 'classics of Marxism-Leninism', but only as an outstanding leader of Party and state, who had begun by continuing Lenin's work and had fought 'correctly' against 'Trotskyists' and 'rightist deviationists', but who, during the last years of his life, had been guilty of violations of Soviet legality and had made a number of other political mistakes and some economic ones.

2. Stalin's thesis that the class struggle would increase as socialism developed (used by him as ideological justification for his reign of terror) was denounced as being wrong. His earlier theories about 'higher' state property and 'lower' collective, co-operative property, as well as that about 'capitalist encirclement', are no longer to be found in the new textbooks.

3. The philosophical, sociological, economic, and political ideas of the non-Soviet world are given more attention. Their presentation continues to be one-sided and often completely false, in each case having a suitable Party label attached to it.

4. Problems of international communism occupy more space in all the new textbooks. The Comintern, the link of the Bolshevik Party with the communist parties of other countries, is strongly emphasized in the new Party history, while the *Foundations of Marxism-Leninism* contains a detailed account of the character of the Comintern.

5. In place of the customary apodictic theses with appropriate quotations from the 'classics', which are only explained afterwards, the new textbooks try to give the impression of having moved away from Stalin's dogmatism: problems are first put singly and only later brought together into a theory and 'underpinned' by appropriate quotations. But the method usual under Stalin of viewing the past from the point of view of current guiding lines continues to be used. Stalin's long-standing and closest comrades-in-arms, Malenkov, Molotov, Beria, and Kaganovich, are always mentioned pejoratively, while Zhukov is almost ignored.

The completion of the new textbooks provided the conditions for activating Party propaganda. The Central Committee's detailed resolution of 9 January 1960 'concerning the tasks of Party propaganda in present circumstances' contained the directives. For many years (meaning the Stalin era) Party propaganda, it was stated, had been concentrated only on the 'Short Course' in Party history. Although new textbooks had appeared during the last few years and the spread of communist ideology had assumed a livelier character, it continued to be detached from the practical tasks of communism. Thus propaganda lacked actuality and purpose, often taking no account of local conditions, national peculiarities and the differences in age, occupation, and education of the various sections of the population. The ideas of communism were frequently presented in abstract form and the propagandists' explanations were arid and inexpressive. Quite a number of ideologists were obsessed with antiquated and fruitless problems, not those which occupied the mass of the population.

The 'forming of a new type of man with communist characteristics and habits and with a communist morality' was described as the most important aim of Soviet Party propaganda. The Soviet people should be brought up 'in the spirit of unshakeable faith in the cause of Party and people, in the collective spirit and in diligence, in socialist internationalism, and Soviet patriotism'. This included the 'fight against the remnants of capitalism in the consciousness of man, as for example political indifference, nationalism, cosmopolitanism, neglect of work and social obligations, theft of public property, officialism, corruptibility, speculation, sycophancy, drunkenness, and hooliganism.'

Peaceful co-existence did not mean any relaxation of the ideological struggle, and the Party must 'continue to fight implacably for communist ideology—the progressive and truly scientific ideology of the present'. The political vigilance of the Soviet people must be increased 'against a hostile, bourgeois ideology and its right-wing socialist and revisionist preachers'.

The publication of further political and ideological textbooks was announced, including volumes on philosophy, atheism, the management of industrial and agricultural enterprises, the history of the international communist movement and the history of the liberation movements of the peoples of Asia, Africa, and Latin America. In addition selections from every aspect of 'Marxism-Leninism' were to be published as well as books on questions of communist education, 'Marxist-Leninist' ethics, and aesthetics and philosophical problems in the natural sciences. It was further announced that there was to be research on the history of the Communist Party in the Soviet Union, on problems connected with the evolution of communism in the USSR, on the communist world movement, the general crisis of capitalism, and the struggle of national liberation. 'Marxist-Leninist' teaching at the universities was to be intensified, and, beginning in the school year 1961–2 with a new textbook, a course on the foundations of political science was to be started in the upper forms of secondary and vocational schools.

THE BEGINNING OF THE CONFLICT WITH PEKING

The new propaganda campaign was announced by Moscow at a moment when a fresh conflict with Peking was beginning to become visible. Although both communist powers were more or less agreed on their final goal and both, at least officially, professed to believe in co-existence, a divergence in foreign policy had become increasingly clear since the late autumn of 1959. At first the disagreements between Moscow and Peking were the following:

(1) Since the Twentieth Party Congress the Soviet leaders held the view that in our age wars could be avoided, while the Chinese communists continued to cling to the earlier Leninist view of the inevitability of war. (2) The Russian leaders regarded co-existence as long term foreign policy, while Peking was only ready to accept it as a relatively short-term manœuvre. (3) The Soviet leaders believed in differentiation. In the capitalist, i.e. Western, camp policy was influenced by various forces—by aggressive, war-mongering elements as well as by 'soberly thinking representatives' who were moving towards the point of view of co-existence. The Chinese communists, on the other hand, regarded the 'imperialists' as a homogeneous force. (4) Starting from the theory of differentiation the Soviet leaders maintained that it was necessary to try to solve disputed international problems by means of personal contacts between the statesmen of the USSR and the Western powers. Peking, on the other hand, ignored any need for personal contact.

The divergence of views between Moscow and Peking on these questions—others were added in the course of 1960—became more evident after Khrushchev's visit to the United States from 15 to 28 September 1959. Khrushchev was accompanied on this journey by over 100 people, including his wife Nina, his son Sergei, and his daughters Rada (the wife of Adyubei) and Julia. Among the officials who went with him were the Foreign Minister, Gromyko, the leading ideologist of the Party, Leonid Ilyichev, the editor of *Izvestia* and son-in-law of Khrushchev, Alexei Adyubei, and the editor of *Pravda*, Pavel Satyukov. The American visit was celebrated by the Soviet press as the beginning of the end of the cold war. Great publicity was given to Khrushchev's remark in Washington that 'the ice of the cold war has not only cracked, but begun to melt', and to the disarmament proposals which he made before the United Nations. In Peking, on the other hand, the comments on Khrushchev's trip were very cautious.

The differences between the two communist powers became clearer still during Khrushchev's visit to Peking immediately afterwards, that is from 30 September to 5 October 1959. Khrushchev, who was attending the celebrations on the occasion of the tenth anniversary of the Chinese People's Republic, was received with less than the usual enthusiasm. The time of his arrival was not announced beforehand and at first there was only a brief statement about the negotiations between Khrushchev and the Chinese leaders. It was said that a 'cordial discussion' had taken place, but no communiqué was published at the end of the meeting. The big parade in the 'Square of Celestial Peace' at which 700,000 people took part—considerably more than in Moscow on similar occasions—was obviously intended to demonstrate to the Secretary of the Soviet Party China's power and strength.

Khrushchev's speech in Peking on 30 September was more like a lecture than a celebration address. With obvious allusions to Peking's utopian plans he informed the Chinese officials that economic development and improvements in living standards were essential. The future success of the communist world should be assured through peaceful competition, and it was important 'to do everything on our side too, in order to do away with war as the solution of disputed questions'. The communist system 'cannot be imposed on a nation by force'. Finally Khrushchev went so far as to praise President Eisenhower as a statesman who had recognized the need for a lessening of international tension.

Moscow's conciliatory policy was also reflected in the official Party declaration on 7 November 1959. For the first time it called for universal and complete disarmament, as well as for 'friendship and collaboration between the nations of the Soviet Union and the USA in the interest of liquidating the cold war and consolidating peace in the whole world'.

At the same time, however, there were signs of the desire not to let any illusions arise among the Soviet Party functionaries and to warn them against 'conclusions which go too far'. An article by Leonid Ilyichev in the periodical *Problems of Peace and Socialism* (Summer 1959) pointed out that this or that concession might be quite possible and necessary in the political and economic fields, but that there could be no 'peaceful co-existence between socialism and capitalism' in the realm of ideology: 'it can exist no more than a reconciliation between light and darkness.' An 'implacable fight of principle' must be fought 'against all manifestations of bourgeois ideology' together with the 'merciless, consistent unmasking of hostile ideologies in all their forms and varieties'. Ilyichev rejected the free exchange of information and ideas between East and West as 'a clamorous demand' whose sole aim was to 'smuggle into the countries of socialism calumnious inventions and the refuse of the others' civilization'. Co-existence was nothing but a continuation of the class struggle, but with peaceful means. *Voprosy Filosofil* commented in a similar vein and *Kommunist* (November 1959) rejected even a temporary ideological truce: 'only people who do not understand the processes which are taking place in the world at present can think of this.'

Although the Soviet leaders in this way emphasized, more clearly than ever before, the gulf between their diplomatic efforts and the ideological struggle, and for the first time described co-existence as an aspect of the class war, this was apparently not enough for the Chinese. Apart from a tendency towards ideological independence a hardening of Chinese domestic policy was noticeable from the beginning of 1960 onwards—the introduction of people's communes in the towns, which in December 1958 had explicitly been described as 'premature', was now pushed ahead with greater force. The concept of 'Marxism-Leninism' was pushed into the background while 'Mao Tse-tung's ideology' was stressed instead— at a time when nobody in the Soviet Union would have dreamt of speaking of 'Khrushchev's ideology'. On 1 February 1960 *Shan-si Jih-pao* said: 'What theories should we be studying at present? Primarily the thought of Mao Tse-tung. The thought of Mao Tse-tung links the theory of Marxism-Leninism with the practice of the Chinese revolution. It is Chinese communism and Chinese Marxism.' This emphasis upon the independence of Chinese communism was obviously intended as a preparation for an ideological offensive against a number of Soviet theories which did not suit the leaders in Peking.

The controversy found clear expression on the occasion of the ninetieth anniversary of Lenin's birth on 22 April. In Moscow Kuusinen made a speech in which he presented Lenin's saying about 'the end of wars, peace among nations' as Lenin's legacy to all communists, emphasized the Soviet theory that wars can be avoided, described co-existence as the 'only right and viable policy', and praised 'personal contacts with statesmen and public representatives of the bourgeois world'. On the same day at the Lenin celebrations in Peking a different note was heard. With some quite arbitary quotations from Lenin in 1915 and 1916, *Jen-min Jih-pao* said that wars continued to be inevitable. 'To forget this means to become a victim of extreme opportunism.' The recognition of the 'undisputed and ageless truth' of the inevitability of war was 'of particularly great practical importance for the present struggle'.

THE U2 INCIDENT AND THE REORGANIZATION OF THE SOVIET LEADERSHIP

At this stage occurred the U2 incident which resulted in far-reaching changes in the Soviet leadership and led to a dramatic change of policy in Paris. On 1 May 1960, at 5.35 a.m. Moscow time, an American U2 aircraft from the Pakistan base of Peshawar crossed the Soviet frontier at about $12\frac{1}{2}$ miles south-east of Kirovabad in Tadzhikistan. According to the Soviet version the aircraft was kept under observation by the air defence force immediately after crossing the frontier. It had penetrated about 1,250 miles into Soviet territory when it was forced to land near Sverdlovsk—in circumstances which have not yet become clear. Three days later, on 4 May, a surprise one-day meeting of the Central Committee was called. On this occasion Kirichenko and Belyayev were expelled from the Party Praesidium which, at the beginning of May, consisted of fourteen members. This was no surprise since both had already been transferred to insignificant provincial posts. It was interesting, however, that in their place three former candidate members were promoted to full membership of the Party Praesidium: Podgorny, Party Secretary of the Ukraine, Polyansky, Prime Minister of the RSFSR, and Kosygin, who was now able to exert considerable influence as an economic expert at the highest level.

The changes in the Central Committee Secretariat were much more important. This powerful body which until May 1960 had consisted of ten people, nine of whom were simultaneously members of the Party Praesidium, was reduced to six members. Apart from Kirichenko, whose disappearance was to have been expected, four other members were removed, Aristov, Pospelov, Ignatov, and Furtseva. The first two were to concentrate on their work in the Bureau of the Central Committee of the RSFSR, Ignatov was appointed as ordinary Deputy Prime Minister, and Furtseva became Minister of Culture.

The only person brought into the Central Committee Secretariat in their place was Frol Kozlov, a full member of the Praesidium of the Party since June 1957 and First Deputy Prime Minister of the USSR since March 1958. Although he had to give up the latter position, the increase in his power could not be mistaken; he was clearly presented as the second man in the Party hierarchy.

The apex of the state, the Praesidium of the Council of Ministers, was also affected by the changes in the Central Committee Secretariat. In place of Kozlov, Alexei Kosygin, until then an ordinary Deputy Prime Minister and Chairman of the State Planning Commission, became Khrushchev's first deputy in the Soviet government. Kosygin was succeeded in both his former capacities by Vladimir Novikov, who had been deputy minister of the armaments industry during the war, then became Minister of Machine Building, and in recent years had been chairman of the Leningrad *sovnarkhoz* and chairman of the Council of Ministers of the RSFSR.

Two days later Voroshilov resigned from the office of President.[1] His place was taken by the Ukrainian, Leonid Brezhnev, who during the war had been a lieutenant-general and deputy chief of the political administration of the Southern front and who had made a name for himself as First Secretary of the Union Republic of Moldavia (1950–2) and First Party Secretary of Kazakhstan (1954–6); since February 1956 he had been a member of the Secretariat of the Central Committee and since June 1956 a member of the Party Praesidium. Shortly afterwards, however, in the middle of July 1960, Brezhnev had to relinquish his membership of the Central Committee Secretariat.

[1] The official Soviet title is Chairman of the Praesidium of the Supreme Soviet of the USSR.

The extent of the changes emerges from the following table:

Before May 1960	After May 1960
1. Aristov	1. Aristov
2. Belyayev	—
3. Brezhnev	2. Brezhnev
4. Khrushchev	3. Khrushchev
5. Furtseva	4. Furtseva
6. Ignatov	5. Ignatov
7. Kirichenko	—
8. Kozlov	6. Kozlov
9. Kuusinen	7. Kuusinen
10. Mikoyan	8. Mikoyan
11. Mukhitdinov	9. Mukhitdinov
12. Shvernik	10. Shvernik
13. Suslov	11. Suslov
14. Voroshilov	12. Voroshilov
	13. Kosygin
	14. Podgorny
	15. Polyansky

Membership of the Central Committee Secretariat

1. Aristov	—
2. Brezhnev	—
3. Khrushchev	1. Khrushchev
4. Furtseva	—
5. Ignatov	—
6. Kirichenko	—
7. Kuusinen	2. Kuusinen
8. Mukhitdinov	3. Mukhitdinov
9. Pospelov	—
10. Suslov	4. Suslov
	5. Kozlov

Interestingly enough, during this transformation of the leadership the position of Mikoyan, an influential member of the Praesidium of the Party and First Deputy Prime Minister of the USSR, remained untouched, although only a few days before it had appeared to be shaken. In the second half of April

big celebrations had been planned to mark the fortieth anniversary of Soviet rule in Armenia. As might be expected, much
attention was focused on Mikoyan, the only Armenian among
the Soviet leaders and one of the few surviving 'Baku Commissars'; there was, for instance, an article about him in
Kommunist[1] by Akhundov, the First Party Secretary of Azerbaidjan. At the celebration in Baku on 25 April, however,
Mikoyan was absent. Moreover, in Akhundov's speech on this
occasion and in an article of *Partinaya Zhizn*,[2] there were
references to second-rank Armenian Party officials, but not to
Mikoyan.

The 'Mikoyan affair', like the far-reaching changes in the
leadership at the beginning of May 1960, clearly pointed to the
existence of differences among the Soviet leaders. According to
one theory, Khrushchev was personally responsible for the
changes and they led to a strengthening of his authority;
according to others, he was obliged to give way. Serious
political differences had, at any rate, emerged among the
leaders, especially over the question of what line the Soviet
Union should take in foreign policy after the U2 incident and
how the Soviet delegation should behave at the forthcoming
summit conference.

What is sometimes overlooked is that disagreements over
economic policy also weighed, for instance, as to whether the
Soviet Union could already at that time put into effect the
increase in the production of consumer goods over and above
the targets of the Seven-Year Plan and abolish taxation as
Khrushchev wished to do.

Political disputes were probably reflected in the tussles within
the leadership in which the actual issue was not to be for or
against Khrushchev, but to win him over to this or that policy,
probably as an overture to the struggle for his succession.

THE WRECKING OF THE PARIS
SUMMIT CONFERENCE

At the beginning of May 1960 the Soviet leaders were faced
with important decisions about economic and foreign policy.
Khrushchev reported to the Supreme Soviet on both questions

[1] No. 6. This article went to press on 14 April 1960.
[2] This article went to press on 3 May 1960.

on 5 May, only one day after the meeting of the Central Committee. He announced the reduction or complete abolition of income tax and gave details about the shortening of the working day to seven or in certain cases six hours, and at the same time he announced the issue of a new rouble that would be worth 10 old roubles.

Most significant was Khrushchev's statement that an additional 25 to 30 thousand million roubles—over and above the Seven-Year Plan—would be invested in the production of consumer goods and that a considerable improvement in the supply of goods to the population would be undertaken by reforming trade. These changes, on the lines of Malenkov's New Course in 1953, obviously met with resistance from the Party functionaries and even the leaders since Khrushchev found it necessary to attack 'certain comrades' who had described the abolition of income tax and increased capital investment for consumer goods as premature. But he affirmed that these measures had been 'reflected upon' and 'all their aspects taken into consideration'. It was possible to increase the production of consumer goods without detriment to the development of heavy industry. (Several months later, in his speech on 6 January 1961, Khrushchev announced that a part of the investment planned for heavy industry would be devoted to agriculture and light industry.)

Khrushchev did not give an account of the U2 incident until the end of his speech. His statement that the aircraft had been shot down was welcomed with prolonged and violent applause: there were shouts of 'right' and 'shame on the aggressors'. When Khrushchev said that it was an American plane there could clearly be heard in the broadcast relay the interjection 'How does that agree with Eisenhower's unctuous speeches?' Interruptions by members are very rare in the Supreme Soviet; until then Khrushchev had never been interrupted by an ordinary member. This interjection was, however, recorded by the press the next day. It can certainly not be ruled out that it had been pre-arranged, but it is more likely that there were prominent people who opposed Khrushchev's relatively moderate attitude towards Eisenhower. In fact on 5 May Khrushchev was trying to keep President Eisenhower out of the picture: he described the U2 incident as a 'provocative action of the American militarist clique'. His announcement that the Soviet government 'would make serious efforts at the forth-coming summit conference to strengthen world peace' indicated that at that time there was no idea of wrecking the Paris meeting. Although other members of the Supreme Soviet spoke of 'fierce indignation', they expressed no less clearly the hope that the summit meeting in Paris would be successful.

On 7 May, the last day of the session of the Supreme Soviet, Khrushchev showed his hand. 'Comrades,' he said, 'I want to tell you a secret. When I made my speech I purposely did not mention that the airman is alive and that parts of the aircraft are in our hands. . . . The name of the airman is Francis Gary Powers.' Things happened thick and fast after this. On the day that Khrushchev made his revelations twenty-one members of the Soviet air defence force who had helped to shoot down the U2 (or to force it to land) were decorated with medals. Three of them—Lieutenant Sabronov, Captain Shilotko, and Major Voronov—were honoured by having their photographs printed on the front page of *Pravda*. On the same day President Voroshilov was replaced by Brezhnev, of whom it may be assumed that he was the link between the Party and the military leaders.

Khrushchev was obviously still trying to be true to his 'theory of differentiation', to distinguish between the 'provoca-tive militarist clique' responsible for the U2 flight, and Presi-dent Eisenhower; apparently he hoped to induce the American President to apologize publicly for the U2 flight and officially to condemn those responsible. He was probably thinking of the indirect apology of the United States in July 1958 when an American aircraft had flown over Armenia; he may have hoped for a repetition which would have put the Soviet Union in a favourable position for the forthcoming summit conference. Khrushchev's short speech at a reception at the Czechoslovak Embassy in Moscow on 9 May lends support to this theory. There he directly raised for the first time the question of whether and to what extent, the U2 flight had taken place with Eisen-hower's knowledge. He used the opportunity to remind the Soviet military that they were subordinate to the state authorities.

This reminder appeared on 9 May of all days, when the Soviet Union was, as every year, celebrating the 'Day of

Victory', the anniversary of the end of the second world war. This time the celebrations had particular significance, because not for many years had so many promotions been made at the same time, nineteen colonels-general, forty-seven lieutenants-general, and many others. The fact that an important military and political conference took place in the Kremlin from 11 to 14 May immediately before the summit meeting in Paris also supports the view that relations between the army and the Party were of importance during those days. Malinovsky, the Minister of Defence, reported on the 'increase in the readiness to fight', and General Golikov, Head of the Main Political Administration, on Party work in the Soviet armed forces, after which Brezhnev—who had only just been appointed President —made a speech.[1] Two other high ranking leaders, Suslov and Ignatov, took part in the conference.

In the meantime President Eisenhower had officially accepted responsibility for the U2 flight and Khrushchev's theory of differentiation had collapsed. Suddenly an anti-American tone prevailed in Soviet politics and in the press. The first note of protest to the United States on 10 May was followed by others to Turkey, Pakistan, and Norway. On 11 May journalists were invited to inspect the remains of the American aircraft in the Gorki Park in Moscow: Khrushchev joined them and held an improvised press conference there. Although he now expressed himself much more strongly, he still spoke of the hope of a successful summit conference. The Soviet leaders would do everything, he said, 'to bring the international situation into normal channels and to restore good relations with the United States of North America'.

As late as 14 May *Pravda* said in its leading article that the Soviet delegation would go to the summit conference 'with a pure heart and good intentions' and 'would spare no efforts to reach a mutually acceptable agreement'. On his arrival in Paris Khrushchev still expressed himself optimistically.

Whether and to what extent these declarations corresponded to the real intentions of the Soviet leaders, or whether the decision to torpedo the conference had been taken earlier cannot yet be determined. It is probable that Soviet policy was changed between 11 and 15 May, that is to say after the failure

[1] This was not published.

of the attempt to make a distinction between Eisenhower and the 'military clique'. After that, the Kremlin leaders decided to let the conference be wrecked in advance, so that it could be postponed to a date more convenient to them.

Khrushchev's behaviour in Paris, particularly at the press conference on 18 May, made it clear how eager he was that the summit conference should not even start work. On the other hand he did everything to keep the tension within certain bounds. During his subsequent visit to East Berlin he refused the separate armistice with Eastern Germany which the SED officials had expected, and repeated with some insistence that the Soviet Union was interested in a new summit meeting in about six to eight months' time, that is to say, at a moment when, as Khrushchev hoped, the international situation would be more favourable for the USSR.

The collapse of the Paris meeting did not remain without consequences within the Soviet Union. Everywhere meetings took place at which, as might be expected, Khrushchev's behaviour in Paris was welcomed. 'There is no room in international relations for breaches of faith', 'Thus and thus only can one deal with provocation', 'They cannot intimidate us', 'The aggressors will not escape their responsibility', read the headlines of the Soviet press. A few days later there was published a large edition of the pamphlet 'To the pillory with the aggressors—the truth about the provocative penetration of an American aircraft into Soviet air space'. The hardening of policy was not to be mistaken.

Barely two months later, on 10 July, the Committee for State Security and the Public Prosecutor of the USSR announced that the investigations against the U2 pilot, Powers, had been completed. Powers was sentenced under Article 2 of the Soviet law concerning crimes against the state; this article is directed against people who collect or steal state or military secrets on behalf of a foreign power or agency.

THE CONFLICT BETWEEN MOSCOW AND PEKING
INTENSIFIES

Khrushchev's desire not to go too far, in spite of the stiffer approach to foreign policy, showed itself in the Sino-Soviet controversy after his return to Moscow. While Peking had used the ninetieth anniversary of Lenin's birthday on 22 April to mount an attack on Moscow, the Soviet ideologists considered the fortieth anniversary (12 June 1960) of Lenin's pamphlet ' "Left-wing" communism, an infantile disorder' as a suitable occasion to refute the Chinese attacks. *Pravda* published an anniversary article by the Party ideologist, N. Matkovsky, which for the first time referred to 'leftist-sectarian moods and tendencies' in the communist world movement of today. Matkovsky attacked 'some' (which, of course, referred to Peking) who described the policy of co-existence and direct negotiation between the statesmen of East and West as a 'withdrawal from the positions of Marxism-Leninism'. He also objected to 'jumping historical stages', because this 'only provided grist to the enemy's mills'. A few days later *Sovietskaya Rossiya* accused the communist parties of the German Federal Republic, Spain, and Iraq of 'leftist-sectarian deviations'. On 20 June *Pravda* declared in a leading article that there could 'be no two views on the question of peace and war'—thus making it clear that there were.

While these articles were appearing in the press the Soviet leadership had prepared an internal circular of eighty pages aimed at China and pointing out the ghastly consequences of a world war.[1] The circular appealed to all communists to do everything they could to prevent such a thing. A decade of peace would be enough to guarantee the victory of socialism. Even if capitalism continued to exist in some parts of the world, the danger of war could be eliminated. Mao Tse-tung himself had held this view in 1957, the Russians objected, whereas now the Chinese Communist Party questioned the whole doctrine of co-existence.

The Sino-Soviet controversy continued at the Bukarest conference of the twelve communist governments at the end of June 1960. According to Crankshaw's reports, on 26 June Khrushchev attacked Mao Tse-tung bitterly calling him, 'an ultra-leftist, ultra-dogmatist, and left-revisionist', and accusing the Chinese of not knowing anything about modern war. The Chinese speaker, Peng-Tsheng, in his turn accused Khrushchev of only having called the Bukarest meeting in order to attack the Communist Party of China and undermine

[1] See Crankshaw in the *Observer*, 12 and 19 Feb. 1961.

China's prestige. After all, the Chinese had shown in Korea that they knew more about war than other nations. In these circumstances the Bukarest conference ended on 28 June with a very meagre communiqué, which was said to have been signed by the Chinese representative only to avoid a public display of differences.

Beneath the ideological quarrel the Sino-Soviet controversy was becoming increasingly noticeable in practical politics. The Soviet Union continued to refuse to deliver atomic bombs to communist China or to establish a joint Sino-Soviet naval command in the Pacific.[1] The distribution of *Drushba*, a journal expressing Sino-Soviet friendship, was temporarily stopped. The Chinese cancelled their participation in the orientalists' congress in Moscow at short notice. The Soviet Union withdrew most of its technicians from China, on the grounds that the Chinese had not used them as Moscow had intended and had indeed tried to convert them to China's ideology.

The withdrawal of Soviet technicians sparked off a new press controversy. The Chairman of the State Planning Commission of China, Li Fu-chun, said in *Hong-chi* (*Red Flag*)[2] that the policy of the Chinese Communist Party had always been to rely on its own economic resources, and this would 'be still more the case in future'. On 18 August *Sovietskaya Latvia* replied that successful socialist development in China would be impossible if she could not count on aid from all the socialist countries.

According to Crankshaw the Soviet circular of 21 June was answered from China on 10 September. The Chinese communists considered that the differences had begun already at the Twentieth Party Congress, when Khrushchev had criticized Stalin without consulting the 'fraternal parties'. Differences of opinion between Peking and Moscow over the Polish and Hungarian questions in the autumn of 1956 were also mentioned. The Chinese accused the Soviet communists of destroying Chinese prestige, sabotaging the liberation movements in the developing countries and of glorifying negotiations with imperialists.

In spite of the importance of the Sino-Soviet controversy it

---

[1] This, too, emerged from Crankshaw's reports.
[2] No. 16, 1960.

remained a dispute between allies as to how what they claimed to be communism could best be realized throughout the world. The Russian communists are convinced that their own further development will bring them economic domination. This should make it possible to reach their final goal through planned economic expansion and the political exploitation of the conflicts within the West and between the Western powers and the developing countries: military action will be superfluous. The Chinese communists, on the other hand, are trying to introduce their own internal approach into international politics. They hope to accomplish their final aim without delay by exploiting to the full the revolutionary developments of today, and by fomenting civil war on an international scale with all the risks that that entails.

NEGLECTED ECONOMIC PROBLEMS

Meanwhile the Seven-Year Plan, which had started off quite successfully in 1959, was running into difficulties. The rate of growth of industrial production fell from 11 to 10 per cent. and the modernization upon which the plenary meeting of the Central Committee had decided in June 1959 made little progress. A new plenary meeting of the Central Committee was therefore convened for 13 to 16 July 1960. It emerged from the reports of senior economic officials and chairmen of important industrial *sovnarkhozy*, as well as from Khrushchev's speech, that a number of industrial enterprises and whole *sovnarkhozy* had failed to fulfil the plans for the introduction of new methods. The design of new machines was out of date, supplies were held up by the existence of redundant offices, and in some scientific institutions utter confusion still prevailed. The Central Committee called for real improvement.

At this same meeting in July Frol Kozlov reported on the Bukarest conference of communist leaders at the end of June 1960. In addition two changes were announced on 17 July: Leonid Brezhnev was removed from the Secretariat of the Central Committee 'in connexion with his appointment as Chairman of the Praesidium of the Supreme Soviet of the USSR' and the elderly Voroshilov was relieved of his work in the Party Praesidium 'at his own request'.

While the battle for technical progress was made the subject of a big campaign other changes in economic policy took place almost silently. Small news items indicated that Khrushchev's big economic reform of the spring of 1957, which had led to the formation of 104 *sovnarkhozy*, was now being extensively revised. A growth of local spirit in the *sovnarkhozy* led the Soviet leaders to establish new bodies in the Union Republics. On 21 June an All-Russian *sovnarkhoz* was set up under the direction of Ryabikov, to co-ordinate the activities of the 70 *sovnarkhozy* in the RSFSR. Kazakhstan followed suit on 24 June, while similar bodies had already been set up earlier in the Ukraine and Uzbekistan. At the same time the activities of the State Planning Commission, which had been the subject of frequent criticism after the end of 1958, were also curtailed; henceforth it was to restrict itself only to the preparation of economic plans, the execution of which was to be the responsibility of the newly created *sovnarkhozy* of the Union Republics. Through this 'reform of the Khrushchev reform' the centre of gravity of economic activity was now concentrated in the Union Republics—as Malenkov had once advocated.

The most important question of economic policy however, remained the relation between heavy industry and the production of consumer goods. On 9 August 1960 the leaders of Party and state published a resolution concerning changes in the Soviet trading system. Until then the trading organizations had merely distributed the goods produced by industry. Meanwhile the demands of the population had grown considerably. Many old-fashioned or unsatisfactory goods were no longer bought. The new resolution therefore envisaged a radical change in the relation between industry and trade. Industrial enterprises were prohibited from delivering to the wholesale trade goods which had not been expressly ordered beforehand. The relations between wholesale and retail trade were to be changed in similar fashion. Retailers were instructed to order according to demand. The needs of the population were to be more extensively investigated, the trading network to be expanded, and more modern self-service shops to be set up.

These concessions to the Soviet consumer came at a time when the contradiction between the great technical successes and the inadequate supply of consumer goods for the population was becoming ever more striking. A flood of extremely heretical letters on this subject were allowed to appear in the Soviet press. 'We produce the best rockets, we fly round the moon', wrote someone to *Izvestia*. 'We have the first-class Soviet TU aircraft and an atomic ice-breaker. But the cupboards we produce are simply junk. It hurts to look at them. . . . One picks up an article and instinctively grimaces because it is so ugly.'[1] Many letters of this kind showed the discontent of the population over the neglected production of consumer goods. But why were the letters published? Presumably because Khrushchev wanted to justify a change of policy to those who thought him too precipitate.

In addition the Soviet leaders had to come to terms with the 'unplanned' economic forces which exploited the inactivity of the economic authorities for their own purposes. The collective farms were beginning to set up joint centres of production with joint capital. The new economic reform of the 'inter-collective farm organizations', for which no legal provisions existed, received a great impetus in 1960. By the middle of 1960 several thousand inter-collective farm building organizations had been established; they usually built better, more quickly, and more cheaply, than the state building companies. Even scientific planning institutes for building projects were set up on an inter-*kolkhozy* basis. The number of inter-*kolkhozy* power stations rose to over 600 and inter-*kolkhozy* transport organizations shot up like mushrooms. The Soviet leaders, however, failed to provide clear directives for these new efforts towards independence in economic life.

More serious politically was the increase of private enterprise, which assumed such proportions that in the autumn *Kommunist*[2] announced a big offensive against 'tendencies towards private property'. Many 'warning examples' were mentioned. In Riga a private buyer had bought a hectare of land and had made a profit of 230,000 roubles by gardening on his own. An engineer in Georgia had set up a private building firm with two cranes of its own and presented himself to state enterprises as a 'builder and businessman'. Private tailors' workshops were not to be suppressed. Even collective farms increasingly used private firms to build cowsheds or do electrical work. Some collective farms on the Volga simply handed their wood

[1] 24 January 1960. [2] No. 14, September 1960.

procurement over to private enterprises so that they could fulfil their delivery quotas. Quite a few collective farms began to let out land to private individuals. In Uzbekistan this assumed such dimensions that it had to be prohibited by special decree. In the building trade private activities had become so considerable that on 16 October the building of private dwellings and *dachas* was forbidden and all loans for private building were stopped at once.

At the same time a political campaign was announced against 'trends towards private property'. *Kommunist*[1] criticized Party organizations because they were not sufficiently energetic in the fight against private property and individualism. The courts and the militia too were, according to *Kommunist*, too liberal in their attitude towards people 'whose behaviour contradicts the principles of socialism'.

THE FINAL GOAL OF COMMUNISM

In the realm of ideology 1960 was marked by publications about a new, very unusual topic—the question of what life would be like in the communist society of the future. *The Foundations of Marxism-Communism*, in the edition of the autumn of 1959, for the first time devoted a special chapter to this subject under the heading 'scientific prophecies'.

After the beginning of 1960 many other detailed descriptions of the future were published.[2] Questions on particular aspects of the communist future were also dealt with in detail. Dr. Gradov, director of the Institute for Public Buildings, reported on living conditions under communism.[3] G. Zhitariov on the future of the Communist Party,[4] A. Liapin and L. Kogan on the new character of work,[5] N. Kostin on leisure,[6] and A. Kharchev on family life,[7] while E. Strukov wrote a special pamphlet on 'personality under communism'.

These and many other articles first dealt with the way in which technical progress ('the creation of the material and

[1] No. 14, September 1960.
[2] The fullest by Professor Strumilin in *Octyabr*, No. 3, 1960, and *Novy Mir*, No. 7, 1960, and by Dr. Stepanyan in *Octyabr*, No. 7, 1960.
[3] *Izvestia*, 13 Jan. 1960.
[4] *Politicheskoe samoobrazovanie*, No. 7, 1960.
[5] *Voprosy Filosofil*, No. 2, 1960, and *Voprosy Ekonomiki*, No. 8, 1960.
[6] *Voprosy Filosofil*, No. 5, 1960.   [7] *Kommunist*, No. 7, 1960.

technical basis of communism') would change the character of work. Manual labour would increasingly be replaced by machines, the need to practise the same occupation for a lifetime would be overcome. Working hours would be shortened; after 1964 the transition to a 35-hour week would begin and by 1968 the number of free days—excluding holidays—would rise to 110 a year. After the establishment of a communist society people would work only 20 to 25 hours a week, and later even less. Work would no longer be a burden, but become the greatest pleasure, the purest delight. All supervision of work would disappear; money would be abolished. Society would become so wealthy that every citizen would be able to have the wherewithal for a civilized existence. But this did not mean that any odd whim would be satisfied; people in the future communist society would be sufficiently responsible not to demand unreasonable things, like a palace with dozens of rooms or a collection of rare art treasures.

The state would wither away and be replaced by communal autonomy, not to rule over anyone, but merely to direct economic activity. New bodies would be created whose task it would be to establish voluntary collaboration between the various economic organizations, which would make their products available to each other for nothing—since money would no longer exist. Neither force, nor the administration of justice would be necessary.

People would live in 'communal palaces', intended to house between 2,000 and 2,500 people and they would usually eat together. The Communist Party would continue to exist for some time to direct and co-ordinate the work of the communal organizations. It would dissolve only after the victory of communism on a world-wide scale.

Through these changes people's characters would change too. Force, selfishness, dissimulation, egoism, treachery, and vanity would disappear from human relations and would be replaced by new qualities like loyalty, friendship, love of work and of society, honesty, frankness, but intolerance of offenders against the communist order. People would lose interest in private property, and voluntarily give up their *dachas*, preferring to live in communal palaces and holiday homes; instead of having private cars they would rely upon communal garages.

The standard of education would be high so that about half the population would have had a secondary technical education and the other half would have studied at a university. Under communism family relationships would be more steadfast than ever before. Extra-marital contacts would contradict the moral principles of communist society and monogamy would therefore triumph.

With the victory of communism in the whole world, nations would come to understand one another and the slightest discord would become a thing of the past. Cultural and economic matters would gradually be fused, so that in the end a uniform international civilization and later a world language would be created.

Even after the victory of communism, according to *The Foundations of Marxism-Communism*, people will not, however, become passive. For science in particular a mass of new problems will arise, among them how to predict and avoid all natural catastrophes, how to harness all forces of nature to serve man, to make all unsuitable regions fit for life, to increase man's average life to between 150 and 200 years, to conquer old age and fatigue, and 'to learn how to restore human life in cases of premature death'.

This ideal communist society is to come into existence within a remarkably short period of time. *The Foundations of Marxism-Communism* says that 'many of our contemporaries' will 'see what the communist order will be like in its first stage of development'. Professor Strumilin holds out the prospect that by 1975 free midday meals will be provided and that by 1980 there will be free food and free supplies of clothing and footwear, as well as fifteen square metres' space per person gratis. According to Stepanyan the economic conditions will be created in the next fifteen to twenty years (1975-80). During a second, shorter phase, working hours will be reduced step by step to four hours a day and the principle of 'to everyone according to his needs' will be realized. In a third phase communist society will finally be launched. Thus 'a developed communist society will be established during the twentieth century in a considerable part of our planet'.

These articles are not utopian descriptions in literary journals, but serious writings by well-known Russian authorities

published with the approval, probably even at the suggestion, of the Soviet Party leadership. The realization of the final communist goal has thus begun to be transformed from an abstract theory into a practical political question.

The Soviet leaders had apparently decided to devote more attention to propaganda for the final communist goal for three reasons:

1. To distract the Soviet population from current difficulties, which are presented as a necessary stage on the road to the ideal communist society. The Soviet leaders hoped that this would strengthen the will to work and the readiness to accept deprivations for a certain period;

2. To counteract the influence of the managers who were pushing to the fore, neglecting ideology, and concentrating on specialized knowledge and material interest;

3. To be the first Party of the world movement to define and describe the future communist society in order not to be outdone in this important ideological question by the Chinese communists.

THE CONFERENCE OF INTERNATIONAL COMMUNISM

The Party leaders of almost all the communist parties of the world had come to Moscow for the celebrations of the fortieth anniversary of the October Revolution, which were immediately followed by the biggest and longest international communist conference there had ever been. It far surpassed the meeting in November 1957, at which, for the first time since Stalin's death, an international policy had been formulated. Then the consultations had lasted only a few days whereas this time they took three weeks—from 10 November to 1 December. Then the declaration had been signed only by the twelve ruling communist parties and only a peace manifesto, adopted afterwards and signed in the name of sixty-four parties, was published. This time the final declaration was produced in the name of eighty-one communist parties, although there appeared to be only seventy-eight signatories.

According to official Soviet figures,[1] at the time of this conference in Moscow in November 1960 there were eighty-seven communist parties in the world, with a total membership

[1] *Kommunist*, No. 6, 1960.

of 36 million. The lion's share, 30·8 million, fell to the twelve ruling communist parties. The remaining communist parties had a membership of about 5·4 million, of which 2·5 million were in the non-Soviet countries of Europe and 'about 2·5 million' in Asia. Membership figures for the communist parties of North and South America were given as 'over 250,000', of Africa as 50,000, and of Australia and Oceania at 'over 7,500'.

At the meeting there were, inevitably, violent arguments about the Soviet and the Chinese points of view. According to Crankshaw[1] the Soviet and Chinese circular notes formed the basis of the discussion. Suslov submitted a prepared declaration on behalf of the Soviet delegation. Then the representatives of the 'brother parties' reported on local problems. The Sino-Soviet cleavage only re-appeared when Teng Hsiao-ping, the official delegate of the Chinese Communist Party, began to speak. He accused the Soviet Party of being opportunist and revisionist and of having absurd ideas about disarmament; he condemned Russian aid to Nehru and Nasser as only helpful to the imperialists. He believed that peaceful co-existence could at the most be used as a tactical weapon, that the division of labour within the socialist camp as suggested by the Soviet Union was wrong and that China had to go its own way. At first some delegations wavered, but the violence of the Chinese attack and Khrushchev's reply in which he gave a merciless exposition of the dangers of atomic war, to justify the need for disarmament and the policy of co-existence, did not fail to make an impression. Most delegates expressed themselves in favour of Russia. The Chinese were supported only by the leader of the Albanian Communist Party, Enver Hoxha, who attacked the whole of Russia's policy since Stalin's death, including Khrushchev's visit to Belgrade in the summer of 1955, the Twentieth Party Congress, the Soviet disarmament proposals, and the 'peace zone in the Balkans' supported by the Russians.

From communist reports of this conference[2] it emerged later that there had been disagreement over the definition of co-existence, over the direct negotiations favoured by Khrushchev

[1] *Observer*, 19 Feb. 1961.

[2] Khrushchev in *Kommunist*, No. 1, 1961; Walter Ulbricht in *Neues Deutschland*, 18 Dec. 1960, and Suslov in *Pravda*, 23 Jan. 1961.

between statesmen from East and West, over the relations between the communist parties, over the definition of the leading role of the Soviet Party, and over the attitude of the Albanian Party representatives.

The new Moscow manifesto of world communism, published on 5 December 1960, was almost three times as long as the declaration of November 1957. Then it had primarily been a question of restoring the leading role of the Soviet Union and of preparing a joint platform for the communist parties in power; now the main emphasis was on the promotion of communism beyond its own frontiers. Thus the declaration of 1960 presented the communist parties of the world with new tasks in order that the revolutionary aims of the Kremlin should be realized.

The doctrine of co-existence was given a new, less liberal interpretation. In November 1957 the main emphasis had been on the view that the policy of co-existence offered ' reliable basis for peace and friendship between nations'. Ir 1960 declaration, however, co-existence was inseparably ' with the aims of international communism. The policy of co-existence was said to be 'a form of the class struggle between socialism and capitalism'. It spelt 'no reconciliation between the socialist and bourgeois ideologies', but 'on the contrary an increased effort by the working class and all the communist parties for the triumph of socialist ideas'.

The communist attitude towards the Western powers, particularly the United States and the German Federal Republic, was noticeably more intransigent than in 1957. Then the United States was described as the 'centre of world reaction' now they had become 'the biggest international exploiter 'the main bulwark of world reaction, the world gendarme, th enemy of the people of the whole world'. It was now stated th West Berlin had been 'transformed into a centre of internatio provocation', and more specific communist support was pro ised to Eastern Germany. The German People's Republic described as the 'outpost of socialism in Europe' and the 't symbol of the peace-loving efforts of the West German people .

The political directives for communist parties in the developing countries were dealt with in much greater detail than in 1957. The communists were instructed to support the 'national bourgeoisie'—meaning the more educated leaders of the national movements—without forgetting that they are 'fickle' and have a 'split character'. But actions directed against the people must be actively opposed and the 'misuse of socialist slogans' exposed. Communists are asked to work for the formation of 'national-democratic states'—presumably a first step towards people's democracies. These appear to be states which do not allow foreign military bases nor the investment of 'imperialist capital', which guarantee freedom for political organizations and introduce 'social and democratic changes', particularly agricultural reforms.

While the declaration of 1957 exhorted the communist parties to collaborate bilaterally, the declaration of 1960 referred only to international collaboration. The 'continuous consolidation of the unity of the communist world movement' was the 'highest international duty of every Marxist-Leninist party'. The fight against 'revisionism' was described in much stronger terms than in 1957 and the 'further unmasking' of the Yugoslav communists was said to be an 'indispensable duty'.

This time the leading role of the Soviet Union was stressed in different form. In 1957 reference was made only once to the 'socialist states with the Soviet Union at their head'. Now the Soviet *party* (not the Soviet state) was explicitly referred to as the 'recognized vanguard of the communist world movement', and defined as the 'most experienced and hardened column of the international communist movement'. According to a later report on the conference from Khrushchev[1] it was proposed that the Soviet Union should be described as the 'head of the communist world movement'. But this was rejected by the Soviet delegation, which preferred to imply that all communist parties share responsibility for the fate of the communist world movement.

The new declaration was clearly a compromise between the Soviet and the Chinese. The Soviet leaders scored a number of important points. Specific reference was made to the value of a policy of co-existence. In its drastic estimate of the effects of war and the statement that local wars can be suppressed, the declaration goes even further than that of 1957. The paeans of praise for the Soviet Union and the confirmation of Moscow's

[1] *Kommunist*, No. 1, 1961.

leading role in the communist world also demonstrated the success of the Soviet leaders.

On the other hand there was mention neither of Khrushchev himself, nor of his principle of direct negotiation between leading representatives of the socialist and capitalist worlds. Moreover, the Soviet leaders had been anxious to postulate co-existence as essential policy, whereas it was mentioned only rather by the way. The transition to communism and its final goal were not mentioned at all. These omissions or vague compromises suggest that the Soviet leaders were ready to make certain concessions to the Chinese line.

Nevertheless the conflict between Moscow and Peking is not over. The Chinese leaders have signed similar declarations on a number of previous occasions without feeling bound by them, and in any case the new declaration is couched in such flexible terms that it can be interpreted as anyone chooses. More significant is the tendency to fuse the doctrine of co-existence with the aim of world revolution. Thus the character of world communism has become more militant. The communist leaders believe (overestimating perhaps their own strength and the possibilities for revolution in the outside world) that the time has come to state their world revolutionary intentions in unambiguous terms. The emphasis shifts more and more to the developing countries, with which the Moscow declaration deals before the countries of Western Europe and at much greater length.

The days when Stalin described the communist international as a *lavochka*, a market stall, are indeed over, and international revolutionary aims again occupy a dominant position in Soviet policy. The Moscow declaration is evidently intended as a long-term strategic directive. The free world may expect a considerable increase in international communist activity during the coming years.

BIBLIOGRAPHY

Abbas, Khwaja Ahmad, *Face to Face with Khrushchev*, Rajpal, Delhi (1960).

Allen, Robert Loring, *Soviet Economic Warfare*, Public Affairs Press, Washington (1961).

Ayih, Michel, *Ein Afrikaner in Moskau*, Wissenschaft und Politki, Cologne (1961).

Barton, Paul, *L'institution Concentrationnaire en Russie*, Librairie Plon, Paris (1959).

Bauer, R. A., Inkeles, Alec, *The Soviet Citizen: Daily Life in a Totalitarian Society*, Harvard University Press (1959); London: Oxford University Press.

Biographic Directory of the USSR, Institute for the Study of USSR, Munich, New York (1958).

Boettcher, Erik, *Die sowjetische Wirtschaftspolitik am Scheideweg*, J. C. B. Mohr (Paul Siebeck), Tübingen (1959).

Boffa, Giuseppe, *Inside the Khrushchev Era*, Allen & Unwin, London (1959).

Campbell, Robert W., *Soviet Economic Power: Its Organization, Growth and Challenge*, Houghton Mifflin, Boston (1960); Stevens, London.

Conquest, Robert, *Common Sense about Russia*, Victor Gollancz, London (1960); Macmillan, New York.

—— *Power and Politics in the USSR*, Macmillan, London (1961); St. Martin's Press, New York.

Crankshaw, Edward, *Russia without Stalin: The Emerging Pattern*, Michael Joseph, London (1956); Viking Press, New York.

—— *Khrushchev's Russia*, Penguin Books, London (1959).

Deutscher, Isaac, *The Great Contest: Russia and the West*, Oxford University Press, London and New York (1960).

Dinerstein, H. S., *War and the Soviet Union*, Frederick A. Praeger, New York (1959); Stevens, London.

Fischer, Louis, *Russia Revisited: A New Look at Russia and Her Satellites*, Doubleday, New York (1957); Jonathan Cape, London.

Fischer, Ruth, *Die Umformung der Sowjetgesellschaft, Chronik der Reformen 1953–1958*, Eugen Diederichs, Cologne–Düsseldorf.

Granick, David, *The Red Executive*, Doubleday, New York (1960); Macmillan, London.

Gross, D. E., Müller, Kurt, *Die wirtschaftliche Verflechtung der Volksrepublik China mit der Sowjetunion*, Alfred Metzner–Verlag, Frankfurt/M.–Berlin (1959).

Handbook on Communism, edited by Joseph M. Bochenski and Gerhart Niemeyer. Karl Alber, Freiburg–Munich (1958); Frederick A. Praeger, New York.

Harriman, W. Averell, *Peace with Russia?*, Simon & Schuster, New York (1959); Victor Gollancz, London.

Hazard, John N., *The Soviet System of Government*, Chicago University Press (1960).

Hingley, Ronald, *Under Soviet Skins*, Hamish Hamilton, London (1961).

Hofmann, Werner, *Die Arbeitsverfassung der Sowjetunion*, Duncker & Humblot, Berlin–Munich (1956).

Hudson, G. F., Lowenthal, R., McFarquhar, R., *The Sino-Soviet Dispute*, 'The China Quarterly', London (1961); Frederick A. Praeger, New York.

Huebbenet, G. von, *Die rote Wirtschaft wächst*, Econ–Verlag, Düsseldorf (1960).

Hunt, R. N. Carew, *A Guide to Communist Jargon*, Bles, London (1957); Macmillan, New York.

Janko, Klikivac, *Ekonomska Politika Sovjetskog Saveza*, Kultura, Belgrade (1959).

Jasny, Naum, *The Soviet 1956 Statistical Handbook: A Commentary*, The Michigan State University Press (1957); Angus & Robertson, London.

Kalnins, Bruno, *Der sowjetische Propagandastaat*, Tiden Forlag, Stockholm (1956).

Kardelj, Edvard, *Socialism and War*, Methuen, London (1961).

Kindermann, Walter, *Flug nach Moskau: Tagebuch aufzeichnungen*, Ullstein, Vienna (1955).

Knorre, Werner von, *Zehn Jahre Rat für gegenseitige Wirtschaftshilfe (COMECON) des Sowjetblocks*, Holzner–Verlag, Würzburg (1961).

Koch, Hans, *Sowjetbuch*, with the assistance of Dr. Alexander Adamczyk, Dr. Roman Hönlinger, Erika von Kaul, and Dr. Helmut Neubauer. Deutsche Industrieverlags–GmbH, Cologne (1957).

—— *5000 Sowjetköpfe*, with the assistance of Otto Böss and Günter Schäfer. Deutsche Industrieverlags–GmbH, Cologne (1955).

Kolarz, Walter, *Russland und seine asiatischen Völker*, Europäische Verlagsanstalt, Frankfurt/M. (1956).

Kolarz, Walter, *Nationalitätenpolitik der Sowjetunion*, Europäische Verlagsanstalt, Frankfurt/M. (1956).

Lazareff, Hélène and Pierre, *The Soviet Union after Stalin*, Odhams, London (1955); New York Philosophical Library.

Lehmbruch, Gerhard, *Kleiner Wegweiser zum Studium der Sowjetideologie*, Bundesministerium für gesamtdeutsche Fragen, Bonn (1959).

Leneman, Léon, *La Tragédie des Juifs en USSR*, Desclee de Brouwer, Paris (1959).

Mehnert, Klaus, *Soviet Man and His World*, Frederick A. Praeger, New York (1961); Weidenfeld & Nicolson, London.

Meissner, Boris, *Das Ende des Stalin-Mythos: Die Ergebnisse des XX. Parteitages der Kommunistischen Partei der Sowjetunion*. Dokumente und Berichte des Europa–Archivs, Band 13, Institut für europäische Politik und Wirtschaft, Frankfurt/M. (1956).

—— *Russland unter Chruschtschow*, R. Oldenburg, Munich (1960).

Miller, Wright, *Russians as People*, Phoenix House, London (1960); E. P. Dutton, New York.

'Monitor', *The Death of Stalin*, Allan Wingate, London (1958).

Imre Nagy on Communism: In Defence of the New Course, Frederick A. Praeger, New York (1957); Thames & Hudson, London.

Nollau, Günther. *International Communism and World Revolution*, Hollis & Carter, London (1961); Frederick A. Praeger, New York.

Nove, Alec, *The Soviet Seven Year Plan*, Phoenix House, London (1960).

Paloczi-Horvath, Georg, *Khrushchev: The Road to Power*, Secker & Warburg (1960); *Khrushchev: The Making of a Dictator*, Little, Brown of Boston.

Pistrak, Lazar, *The Grand Tactician: Khrushchev's Rise to Power*, Frederick A. Praeger, New York (1961); Thames & Hudson, London.

Poerzgen, Hermann, *So lebt man in Moskau*, Paul List, Munich (1958).

Roeder, Bernhard, *Der Katorgan*, Kiepenheuer & Witsch, Cologne (1956).

Ruge, Gerd, *Gespräche in Moskau*, Kiepenheuer & Witsch, Cologne (1961).

Rühle, Jürgen, *Das gefesselte Theater*, Kiepenheuer & Witsch, Cologne (1957).

Rush, Myron, *The Rise of Khrushchev*, Public Affairs Press, Washington (1958).

Salisbury, Harrison, *An American in Russia*, Harper & Bros., New York (1955); *Stalin's Russia and After*, Macmillan, London.

Schapiro, Leonard, *The Communist Party of the Soviet Union*, Eyre & Spottiswoode, London (1960); Random House, New York.

Schenk, Fritz, *Magie der Planwirtschaft*, Kiepenheuer & Witsch, Cologne (1960).

Schiller, Otto, *Das Agrarsystem der Sowjetunion*, Arbeitsgemeinschaft für Osteuropaforschung, Tübingen. Böhlau–Verlag, Cologne–Graz (1960).

Shabinsky, Wladimir, *Ostlicht: Sowjetische Literatur der 'Tauwetter-periode' 1956/57*, Verlag für internationalen Kulturaustausch, Berlin (1958).

The Soviet-Yugoslav Controversy, 1948 to 1958: A Documentary Record, R. Bass and E. Marbury. Prospect Books, New York (1959).

The Second Soviet-Yugoslav Dispute, L. Benes, R. F. Byrnes, and U. Spulber. Indiana University Press (1959).

Starlinger, Wilhelm, *Grenzen der Sowjetmacht*, Marienburg–Verlag/ Holzner, Würzburg (1955).

—— *Stalin und seine Erben*, Marienburg–Verlag/Holzner, Würzburg (1957).

Sternberg, Fritz, *Wer beherrscht die zweite Hälfte des 20. Jahrhunderts?*, Kiepenheuer & Witsch, Cologne (1961).

Utechin, S. V., *Everyman's Concise Encyclopaedia of Russia*, J. M. Dent, London (1961).

Wetter, Gustav, *Philosophie und Naturwissenschaften in der Sowjetunion*, Rowohlts Deutsche Enzyklopädie Nr. 67.

Wheeler, Geoffrey, *Racial Problems in Soviet Muslim Asia*, Institute of Race Relations: Oxford University Press, London and New York (1960).

Wolfe, Bertram, *Khrushchev and Stalin's Ghost*, Frederick A. Praeger, New York (1956).

INDEX

Abakumov, Viktor, 65, 91–92, 104, 115, 175–9
Abortion, decree on, 116
Academy of Sciences, 148
Administration, persons employed by, 98
Administrative structure, simplification of, 137–42
Adyubei, Alexei, 356
African nationalism, 125–7
Agriculture:
  Collective and state farms: *see* Farms
  Machinery: *see* Machine and tractor stations
  Planning, 98
  Policy, 81–82, 87–89, 92–93, 143–4, 307–9, 348–50
  Private property, 307
  Procurement system reform, 276–9, 349–50
  Production, 313–14, 316
  Stalin's measures, effect of, 34
  Statistics, 274
  Tax arrears, 80–82
Agro-towns, 84, 325
Air Force, 12, 95, 242
Akhmedov, M., 336, 339
Akhundov, W., 345, 349, 362
Albania, 157, 160, 195–7, 204, 257; attacks Soviet policy, 376, 377
Alexandrov, Georgi, 95, 121
Aliger, Margarita, 216, 342
All-Union Soviet, 6, 7, 8
America: *see* United States
Amnesties (1953), 63, 300; (1955), 114
Andreyev, A. A., 42, 175, 182
Andryanov, 83, 164
'Anti-Party Group', 5, 29, 35, 242–5, 248–51, 256, 270–1, 306, 317–23
Antonov-Orseyenko, Vladimir, 131, 132, 166
'Apparachiks', 191–2, 280
'Apparatus': *see under* Central Committee
Appointments, publication of, 24–26

Arab countries, 161, 336, 339
Architecture, resolution on, 115–16, 149
Aristov, Averky, career, 111; appointments, 111, 162, 165, 246, 247, 268, 335, 361; at 20th Congress, 154, 156; speeches, 259, 281; at 21st Congress, 311, 319, 334; and Kirichenko's dismissal, 350, 351; removed from Secretariat, 361; mentioned, 338
Armenia, 84, 141, 265, 362
Army, relations with Party, 9, 12–16, 20, 24, 35, 253–60, 365; new Marshals, 95; demand for revision of history of war, 95–96; leaders rehabilitated, 133; and economic reforms, 241
Art, regimentation of, 33, 76–77, 251
Artemiev, Colonel-General, 74
Arts, Party and the, 286
Arutinov, Grigori, 84, 164
Asia, 125–7, 160, 289, 327, 329, 376
'Association for the Dissemination of Political and Economic Knowledge', 12
Astrakhan, 307
Austria, 229, 260
Authors: *see* Writers
Automation, 312–13, 342–4
Autonomous Regions, 8, 14
Autonomous Republics: *see under* Republics
Avkhimovich, Nikolai, 339
Azerbaidjan, 8, 74, 141, 202, 265, 344–6

Babel, Isaak, 211
Bagdash, Khaled, 161
Bagirov, Mir Dzhafar, 74, 129, 138–40, 164, 335
Bagramian, Marshal, 95, 96
Baibakov, Nikolai, 99–100, 234
Bakinsky, 139
Bakradze, V. M., 66–67
'Baku Commissars', 362
Balkans peace zone, 376